ten·der ténder/ **adj** soft enough for the teeth to go through easily; the point at which something is ready to eat: the leaves of a bunch of spinach, a ripe fig. **Soft or delicate in substance**. Not hard or tough. **Ripe**. Ripe and ready to eat. Yielding readily to pressure. **Fragile**. Of a delicate nature; so soft as to be hurt, crushed or broken easily. Requiring careful handling: a tender subject. **Affectionate**. Benevolent; compassionate; careful. **With gentle feeling**. Showing care, gentleness, sensitivity and feeling.

Botanical. Needing protection from harsh weather, especially frost and cold.
[13th century. Via French *tendre* from Latin *tener* 'delicate, tender' (source also of English tendril).]

Nigel Slater is the author of a collection of bestselling books including the classics *Real Fast Food*, *Appetite* and the critically acclaimed *The Kitchen Diaries*. He has written a much-loved column for *The Observer* for seventeen years. His memoir, *Toast – The Story of a Boy's Hunger*, has won six major awards, including British Biography of the Year.

Also by Nigel Slater

Eating for England
The Kitchen Diaries
Toast – The Story of a Boy's Hunger
Thirst
Appetite
Nigel Slater's Real Food
Real Cooking
The 30-Minute Cook
Real Fast Puddings
Real Fast Food

www.4thestate.co.uk
www.nigelslater.com

Tender | Volume I

A cook and his vegetable patch
Nigel Slater

Photographs by Jonathan Lovekin

FOURTH ESTATE London

First published in Great Britain
by Fourth Estate
a division of HarperCollins*Publishers*
77–85 Fulham Palace Road
London W6 8JB
www.4thestate.co.uk
love this book? www.bookarmy.com

1 3 5 7 9 10 8 6 4 2

A catalogue record for this book is available
from the British Library

ISBN 13 978-0-00-724849-0

Designed by BLOK
www.blokdesign.co.uk
Printed in Italy by L.E.G.O. SpA – Vicenza

Printed on Fedrigoni Freelife Cento
Uncoated recycled paper with 60 per cent
secondary pre-consumer fibre and 40 per cent
de-inked recycled wood-free FSC fibre

FSC

For Allan Jenkins

To Louise Haines, for her tireless encouragement, support and patience. I can never, ever thank you enough. To Jonnie for his pictures and friendship; to Sam Wolfson for her brilliance and to Jiri Merka for all his hard work.

To the wiser and more experienced gardeners whose words I turn to for enlightenment: Beth Chatto; Joy Larkcom; Carol Klein; Jekka McVicar; Sarah Raven; Chris Young; Charles Dowding; Christopher Stocks. To Monty Don and Dan Pearson without whom this garden would still be a back yard. And thank you too to Huw Morgan; Katie Findlay; and to everyone at The Royal Horticultural Society and *The Garden*.

To Jane Scotter, who knows more about growing vegetables than I ever will. Thank you for your beautiful produce, much of which is pictured here in these pages and has become so much a part of my cooking life. Thank you too to everyone at the magical place that is Fern Verrow.

Gratitude is also due to: Jane Middleton; Araminta Whitley; Rosemary Scoular; Victoria Barnsley; John Bond; Julian Humphries; Michelle Kane; Graham Cook; Elizabeth Woabank; Sarah Randell; Mark Adderley; Nadia Sawalha; Tim d'Offay; and to Allan Jenkins, Nicola Jeal, Caroline Boucher and everyone at *The Observer*. To Franco Chung and Rob Watson for their technical expertise and to Dalton Wong and James Duigan for helping me feel better than I have ever done in my life. And an enormous shout to all those kind, generous and communicative readers whose thoughtful words keep me going.

This book is what it is because of you all.

Introduction

I keep lists. Some copied into notebooks in neat italic script in blue-black ink, others scribbled almost illegibly in soft pencil on the back of an old envelope. Most remain in my head. There is the usual inventory of things I need to do, of course, but also less urgent lists, those of books to read or read again, music to find, plants to secure for the garden, and letters to be written (few of which will ever see the light of day). One list that has remained in my head is that of favourite scents, the catalogue of smells I find particularly evocative or uplifting. Snow (yes, I believe it has a smell), dim sum, old books, cardamom, beeswax, moss, warm flapjacks, a freshly snapped runner bean, a roasting chicken, a fleeting whiff of white narcissi on a freezing winter's day.

High on that list comes cress seeds sprouting on wet blotting paper. It is a smell I first encountered in childhood, a classroom project that became a hobby. Cool and watery, fresh yet curiously ancient, as you might expect from a mixture of green shoots and damp parchment, it has notes of both nostalgia and new growth about it. Sometimes, when I have watered my vegetable patch late on a spring evening, I get a fleeting hint of that scent. A ghost-like reminder of how this whole thing started.

I guess I have always grown something to eat: that cress on a blotter when I was still in short trousers; beans in a jam jar; carrots and candytuft in a forlorn strip of my parents' garden. There were the tomato plants precariously balanced on the window ledge of my student digs; orange and lemon pips and other unmentionable plants nurtured under grow lights; salad sprouters; a bucket garden on a balcony. Then there were the herbs in pots that lethally adorned the fire escape of my first flat and its communal garden. That I would one day turn my own lawn into a vegetable patch was, I suppose, inevitable.

Perhaps because I was brought up on frozen peas – they were virtually the only vegetable that passed my lips till I was in double figures – I now have a curiosity and an appetite for vegetables that extends far beyond any other ingredient. Shopping at the market on a Saturday morning, I will spend four or five times as long choosing my beans, tomatoes or lettuces than I will buying anything else. Vegetables beckon and intrigue in a way no fish or piece of meat ever could.

The beauty of a single lettuce, its inner leaves tight and crisp, the outer ones opened up like those of a cottage garden rose; the glowing saffron flesh of a cracked pumpkin; the curling tendrils of a pea plant; a bunch of long, white-tipped radishes; a bag of assorted tomatoes in shades of scarlet, green and orange is something I like to take time over. And not only is it the look of them that is beguiling. The rough feel of a runner bean between the fingers, the childish pop of a peapod, the inside of a fur-lined broad bean case, the cool vellum-like skin of a freshly dug potato, are all reason to linger. And all this even before we have turned the oven on.

Their beauty and tactile qualities aside, what you do with them is loaded with even greater sensual pleasure. Just listen to this: a supper of golden pumpkin with a crisp crumb-crust flecked with parsley and garlic; a dish of emerald cabbage leaves with shards of sizzling ginger; a crumbling soft-pastried tart of leeks, cream and cheese; a bright carrot chutney on a mound of ivory-coloured rice to make your lips prickle. Soporific risottos of asparagus; gratins of potato, garlic and cream; yellow tomatoes with a sauce the colour of terracotta that makes your mouth tingle with chilli, lemongrass and fresh mint. None of this is difficult, time consuming or expensive. It is straightforward, approachable cooking, for eating either for its own sake or on the same plate as a piece of meat or fish.

While still enjoying my crackling pork roasts and chargrilled lamb, my baked mackerel and crab salad, I have become more interested than ever in the effect of a diet higher in 'greens' than it is in meat – both in terms of my own wellbeing and, more recently, those implications that go beyond me and those for whom I cook. As Michael Pollan, author of *In Defence of Food* (Allen Lane, 2008), says: 'In all my interviews with nutrition experts, the benefits of a plant-based diet provided the only point of universal consensus.' On a personal note, I would simply say that I feel much better for a diet that is predominantly vegetable based.

Every little helps

We have damaged this planet. We have plundered its natural resources, emptied its seas, scorched its earth, turned its beating heart into a toxic rubbish tip. There have been decades, if not centuries, of take rather than give. I do not wish to relinquish entirely the deep sense of fulfilment I get from eating meat and fish, but I now place less importance on them in my diet than I did. It is the meat and the crackling rather than the vegetables

that are now on the side. When you lift the lid of my casseroles, peer into my pots or read my plate, it is the veggies that play the starring role.

And yes, it is worth 'reading' our plate before we tuck in. Where did that food come from? Does it sit comfortably with our conscience and what we believe good food to be? What, other than our immediate appetite, does it benefit, and crucially, what damage is that plate of food doing?

If digging up our gardens, getting an allotment, shopping at farmers' markets, growing organically and eating sustainably is seen as a sign of our collective guilt for what we have done to the planet, then so be it. We can never totally undo what has been done. But there are some of us, hopeful, deluded, possibly a wee bit mad, who are happy to try to put in more than we take out. One of the ways we can do that is to eat a greener diet.

Swapping my lawn for leeks and lettuces has a lot to do with wanting to know as much as possible about what I am eating. It is, I suppose, my way of making a deeper connection with my food, a desire to know the whole story rather than just what it says on the label. More than anything, the move is about a desire for simplicity. Our food production has become so complicated, with its air miles, pesticides, extended shelf life, marketing and packaging. I hanker after something simpler, more honest and direct. More holistic, if you like. The idea of planting a seed, watching it grow, then eating the result instantly does away with much of the baggage that goes hand in hand with our modern food supply.

I don't have to grow or cook. There is enough good food out there for a life free of both garden and stove. But in much the same way as I cook partly for the gratification of watching a potato turn from ivory to gold in the pan, for a taste of the sticky stuff on the surface of meat as you turn it in the roasting tin, for the feel of a ripe peach and its blessed juice trickling down my stubbly chin, I grow for the joy it brings. I like getting my hands in the soil as much as I like rubbing butter into flour to make pastry. Sometimes there's bread dough under my fingernails, sometimes manure. Sometimes, truth be told, there's a bit of both.

I plant seeds because I get a buzz from watching green shoots poke through the soil, from looking after them as something precious and vital, protecting them from the pigeons and foxes and clumsy feet that roam the modern city garden, from feeding them and watching them bloom. Cooking with vegetables you have grown gives not only an extraordinary sense of completeness and a simplifying of the food chain, but also the chance to experience a profound respect for an ingredient – something we are unlikely to feel for an item picked up in a 'two for the price of one' promotion in a supermarket. It helps us to understand our food and to appreciate its value, I might even suggest to develop a certain reverence.

I don't own acres of land and probably never will. The bulk of my fruit and vegetables still come from market stalls, shops and a weekly organic box delivery. I still go to the greengrocer's and the supermarket for much of my fruit. What I grow is simply the icing on the cake. If it seems as if I'm playing at it, then fine, I will wear whatever label you want to hang round my neck, but all I know is that I am having fun with the space I have and eating some great food.

Right now, as I write, my little urban garden is home to three varieties of courgettes, two of broad beans, climbing beans, runner beans, borlotti, ruby, white and yellow chard, peas – both mangetout and purple-podded – spinach, five varieties of tomatoes, three of potatoes, summer squash, pumpkin and beetroot. I have seven varieties of lettuce, plus rocket, cabbage, cavolo nero, Brussels sprouts, globe and Jerusalem artichokes, carrots, leeks, red cabbage and more herbs than you can shake a mezzaluna at. I'm not sure the cauliflower will survive, though – you need to know what you are doing with that one.

And to think I could have had a piece of grass on which to kick a ball around instead.

Moving in

I moved into this house on a scruffy London terrace on the eve of the new millennium – the date chosen not for the possibility of harnessing any beneficial cosmic energy abroad on that auspicious point in the calendar but simply because I knew it would be the only day of the year the 'Aussie humpers' could block the exceptionally narrow lane with a removal van and get away with it. As revellers' fireworks lit up the night sky and the whole world partied, I released three elderly and somewhat bewildered cats into their new and laughably empty home, upended a bottle of not very cold champagne into the only glass I could find and toasted the echoey old house and its long, thin and abandoned garden.

The house had previously been home to a celebrated collection of Italian art, a Victorian slum so grim it had a closing order slapped on it, and a hospice run by Catholic nuns (one of whom appears not to have quite departed). It had also had one of its front windows blown out during the War. It holds mysteries, too. Why is there a false wall in the scullery and what does it hide? The attached garden has the elongated, rectangular proportions typical of many terraces all over the country but has the advantage of being west facing and a good bit longer than usual. Curiously, it looks much (much) larger in photographs, particularly those taken from the chimneystacks, than it really is. At only 12 metres long, we are hardly talking about much more space than the average allotment.

The land on which the house sits had, until the early 1800s, been pasture for the local dairy farms. The remains of dairies are scattered all over this part of London. There has been a cheesemonger, in various guises, further along the terrace since Victorian times. Mostly laid to lawn that had

gone to seed, the garden had but a single fig tree, its grey branches stretched out like spindly, adolescent arms across the brown grass, and an old and graceful golden robinia. The space was basically a clean slate.

At the stroke of midnight, I sat down on the back steps and vowed to dig up my lawn and grow at least some of my own vegetables and fruit.

In a city garden as small as this, I could only dream of any idea of self sufficiency (this is hardly the lost gardens of Heligan), but over the next few years I would go on to grow dark, smoky-leaved cabbages, violet carrots, Turkish orange aubergines, eight varieties of potato, speckled climbing beans and gnarled and exquisitely flavoured heritage tomatoes. I would experience the pleasure of growing food from seed, to complement the food I trudged home with from the shops; vegetables and fruit that have become the new backbone of my daily cooking and eating and have signalled an important, life-enhancing new order in my kitchen.

The site

A friend, perhaps after one glass of rosé too many, once referred to the space as having a cloister-like quality to it. True, its high hedges and tall gates make for a feeling of solitude. You do indeed feel hidden. And yes, there is shade and a corridor around the perimeter, and the vegetable patch is laid out in a series of six small beds similar to those of early monastery gardens. At night you can hear your footsteps on the deep gravel paths and the stone terrace. In winter you can see fox prints in the snow. At dusk in midsummer the garden is heavy with the scent of white jasmine and crimson sweet peas. There are bees, butterflies, squirrels, foxes and, two gardens away, a resident woodpecker. But in reality, it is nothing more than just the back garden to a London terraced house. And a shabby one at that.

The garden's feeling of enclosure and protection – of a secret space – exists partly because of the trellis mounted on top of the old brick walls and the thick growth of ivy that has formed a solid, tangled mass around it. In places, I need to climb a ladder to trim the top and use a machete to beat it into submission. At the far end is a row of tall hornbeams, chosen for the piercing green of their young leaves in spring and the fact that their bright leaves offer reflected light to the neighbouring houses, rather than blocking it as would leylandii.

Small though it is, the garden is split into three distinct enclosures: an old York stone terrace that is home to the rickety, recycled dining table; the diminutive vegetable patch of which I now write, and a tiny, gated section of tranquil, fragrant green and white shrubs. My sanctuary. I should also include the wide garden steps that are currently home to pots of everything from Tradescant roses and lemon thyme to purple sage, runner beans and wild strawberries. Getting much afternoon sunshine, this space is useful

for ripening tomatoes and even, in a good year, aubergines. It is an absurd amount to cram into a tiny city garden, but I like the fact that every centimetre is put to good use.

There is also a large, deep lightwell, to which I have never really given a name. 'Terrace' would imply endless sunshine, 'patio' makes me cringe and 'basement' just sounds plain depressing. Whatever you call it, the space is sheltered, warm, and enjoys the afternoon sun. Lined with tiny, French wire-cut bricks rescued from the restoration of St Pancras station, it is home to a large and much used cold frame (the best money I have ever spent), terracotta pots of tomatoes and courgettes and, in deepest summer, an eight-foot tepee of green beans. It is where I plant all my seeds, pot up seedlings and over-winter the pelargoniums and the more fragile of the potted herbs. A Petite Negra fig tree has made its home here too, its branches dripping with almost black fruit in late summer. A billowing rose – Souvenir de Madame Léonie Viennot – clambers up the sunny side, hiding a dodgy wall that desperately needs attending to. It is dark and a little damp in the way that basements often are, and is very much a silk purse made from a sow's ear, but an invaluable little space nevertheless. It often makes me feel I could have made more of 'basements gone by'.

Every wall is used: an espaliered Doyenne du Comice pear on the south-facing wall, a fig in the basement, a Fragola grapevine framing the kitchen doors. I would put something up the kitchen walls if it didn't mean removing the headily fragrant Chinese jasmine that frames the scullery window.

I realise I have created what is effectively an allotment to which I don't have to travel. But then, the waiting list for an allotment in my part of the world runs into years. When I look at the garden now, with its ivy-clad walls, its rows of radishes, its quinces and espaliered pears, not to mention the bed of Arran Victory potatoes and 'dinner-plate' dahlias, it is hard to picture it nine years previously, when it was just a patch of ill-mown grass.

By default, the space has become a haven to butterflies, bees and ladybirds, and amidst its low box hedges, rambling nasturtiums and small fruit bushes lives a family of cute but not totally welcome urban foxes.

Self-sufficiency – dream on

There is no possible way I could be self-sufficient in vegetables and fruit with a garden of this size. Most friends with allotments treat what they pick as a bonus rather than expecting it to meet all their vegetable needs. That is not the point. I grow simply for the pleasure of growing; for the joy of watching seeds turn into plants and seeing them – sometimes – come to fruition. Failures? Listen, there's been more than a few. But the surprising successes, such as the eighty bunches of Fragola grapes that hung like fairy lights from the two tiny vines in the (appallingly wet) summer of 2008, the endless tomatoes or the glowing yellow courgette flowers that greet me each autumn morning, are worth the occasional row of lettuce seedlings disappearing overnight or the Florence strawberries that were eaten by everything in the garden except me.

I have sown somewhat more than I have reaped. But as somewhere to watch things grow, a place to tend and nurture, to sit and eat, to drink and think, to taste and smell, and most importantly to understand the unity of growing, cooking and eating, it is a monumental success. At least it is to me.

The soil

I garden on clay and I cannot tell you how much hard work has gone into getting the soil right. A few weeks after I moved in, Montague Don, friend and at that time stablemate at *The Observer*, stuck his spade into the parched soil and declared it 'typical London clay. It's going to need a lot, and I mean a lot, of organic matter'.

And organic matter it has had. Bucketfuls of compost made from my own vegetable peelings, bag after bag of well-rotted horse manure, bracken and sheep's wool from a traditional hill farm in the Lake District, and much from my local council's green waste system (it collects our garden trimmings, even our old Christmas trees, turns them into compost, then offers the sweet, tobacco-textured results back to the community). The garden's soil is now as rich and sweet as sachertorte.

The ground has seen no chemicals and no peat since the day I picked up my spade. Every cell in my body believes in organic gardening, even if it does mean the odd heartache when a row of broad beans is munched by slugs overnight because (whisper it) the organic slug pellets don't work as well as the non organic ones.

Once the lawn was dug up and recycled, the ground dug first mechanically, then by hand, the real work of getting the soil 'right' started. Many are the days I could barely straighten my back from carrying bags of manure from the pavement through to the garden. Like many typical terraced homes, we have no back entrance, so there is no alternative but to carry eighty bags of steaming horseshit through the house. I have learned to pick a dry day.

My soil is now what I hope Monty might call 'in good heart'. If I have one piece of advice for anyone 'growing their own', it is to get this right before you plant a single seed. Even if it means missing a season whilst you plant green manure such as red clover or trefoil. The soil is like a bank account. We should put in more than we take out.

The seeds

I get my seeds from friends, seedsmen's catalogues and specialist nurseries. I have always preferred the artisan and the cottage industry to big business, and tend to take that approach with seeds too. It's not that there is anything wrong with the big seed companies, far from it, it is just the way I like to do things. The choice of organically grown seeds is getting wider by the year. It is a mistake to turn our noses up at the more pricey seeds, which can often turn out to be better value. I have found that you generally get what you pay for, and bargain-basement seeds often mean a poor germination rate.

Wherever your seeds come from, they need some form of organisation. An old shoebox, constantly in a state of suppressed chaos, sufficed for several years. When it finally fell to pieces, I found opened packets five years past their best-before date. Then someone gave me an old church collection box, much polished, with spookily creaking hinges and two compartments just the right size for seed packets. What used to hold the harvest festival coppers now holds a harvest festival of its own. The important thing is that your seeds have somewhere dark, dry and cool to wait. Heat, moisture and light will render them impotent in no time.

The seed catalogues have become an annual source of inspiration, information and temptation. Winter afternoons are often spent thumbing through seedsmen's pamphlets and trawling internet sites before putting in my order for violet-coloured beans and firecracker-red chillies. It is almost impossible not to get carried away. You could do worse than follow my habit of writing out your wants list in the late afternoon, then taking a red pencil to it the next day. A night's sleep can often induce a reality check.

I struggle for outdoor space to grow, but more crucially for space indoors to germinate. This old house has just two tiny windowsills. Both are filled to bursting with little coir pots, loo roll middles and seed trays, all filled with seed compost by the first week in March. Sprouting seed by the window is fine for the initial germination but can produce spindly plants unless the room is cool. As luck will have it, this house is almost permanently cool, even in deepest summer. Friends have been known to wear a fleece to dinner.

It was with great relief that I discovered the joy of the garden-ready plug plant – a bag of plump little seedlings delivered to your door all ready to pot up. What seems expensive at first glance turns out to be a saving, in that I treasure each little plant even more. I use this system for things I find tricky to germinate, which includes the brassica family and tomatoes. Everything else I grow from seed.

Into the garden

The decision to surround each of the six beds with box hedging is an attractive one, but to be honest I wouldn't do it again. Raised beds would be my recommendation to anyone setting up a vegetable garden from scratch. Hedges, however neatly they frame your peas, beans and swaying sunflowers, are also snail hotels, providing a home for hundreds of gastropods who come out at night, drink from your beer traps, then go on a drunken rampage. So, unlike the average allotment holder, I cannot plant directly into the soil. I have to germinate my seeds in pots, then transfer them when they are big enough to put up with losing the odd leaf or two to munching snails. Too many have partied on my carefully nurtured seedlings. I sometimes think the hedges would have gone long ago if it wasn't for the achingly beautiful sight of them covered in snow.

Compost

At the very back of the garden, hidden in the last of the small enclosures and shaded by the branches of a damson tree, is the compost heap. A mixture of prunings, annual weeds, vegetable peelings and the odd bit of cardboard, this source of horticultural treasure has at last done well. After a tricky start, I now have a deep store of black, moist, homemade compost.

Despite being properly constructed of heavy, untreated wooden slats with air holes and a strong lid of old carpet, the compost heap at first refused to work. Nothing seemed to rot down, the prunings and peelings remained in much the same state for months on end. Visiting the Fern Verrow biodynamic farm in Herefordshire and admiring their several heaps at various stages of production, I could see straight away that mine was too dry. The pile had too many twigs and not enough moist green stuff. It needed a drink. Watered regularly, topped up with every bit of soft, green leaf or vegetable peeling I could muster, the decomposition process soon started and the heat built up.

Turning the compost is something that serious gardeners tend to get almost emotional about. Not me. I often fail to remember to turn the contents over for weeks on end, forget to cover it in winter and allow two-metre-high potato plants to take root in it. Yet now it has got going, it seems to cope with my neglect just fine. Ideally, I should go in there with the pitchfork once a fortnight and lift the bottom to the top. At the very least I should push the hosepipe down into its depths in dry weather. But invariably I just leave it to sort itself out. Which it now does. Just remember to keep your heap moist and give it more green stuff than brown.

Slugs, snails and other buggerances

I am troubled by slimy creatures more than most because of the box hedging around the veg beds and the ivy covering the walls. I use a twice-annual application of nematodes to fight off the slugs. The snails meet a quicker end.

Having been through the lexicon of slug and snail protection methods, I have settled on the following: young plants get a deep copper ring placed around them that gives any approaching snails a mild electric shock. Tender plants are also protected by wicker cloches, which, though not entirely slug-proof, do help a bit. I sometimes resort to environmentally friendly slug pellets. The most successful deterrent of all is 'the gardener's shadow'. One trip into the garden after a rainfall and I can collect a hundred of them in just a few minutes. Another good way is to upturn stones, bricks and old pots in winter. You will find them clustered together, spending the winter in little communes.

The urban fox is a problem, and none more than the ones who live under next door's robinia tree. They look cute enough sunbathing on their lawn in the afternoon, sometimes six at a time, and they spend time in my garden, curled up in a flowerbed three feet from where I am digging, but they also cause untold damage. They dig up plants, excavate vast holes under the compost and loosen the boards. I have found nothing that will deter them (infuriatingly, the cubs sleep next to the expensive electronic fox-scarers). Worst of all is when they go shopping, bringing other people's carelessly stored rubbish bags into my garden. Yes, there are times when I could happily shoot them myself, but they remain part of this garden, and I feel it is as much their space as mine. Probably more so.

I resort to organic sprays for serious attacks of white, green and black fly, but also plant chives, garlic and masses of marigolds to deter them. And even if the pyrethrum they contain doesn't do the trick, nothing looks prettier than a marigold in a vegetable patch.

Kit, and why it matters

My gardening tools mean as much to me as my kitchen equipment. Yes, every trowel, plant label and piece of string is beautiful and with good reason. Just as a carpenter takes care of his chisels, just as an architect cares about what pen they use for their drawings (believe me, they do), then I care about my kitchen and gardening kit. It matters to me that something feels good in the hand, that it has a certain patina and that it does the job well. Most of my stuff is second hand and much loved. Yes, my copper spade and Japanese pruning sheers cost a bob or two but, like a decent kitchen knife, they make each job all the more pleasurable.

The pay-off

There are two ways to put up a set of shelves. There are those who buy them flat-packed and put them up as quickly as they can. Job done. Something to hold the books and DVDs while they watch television. Then there is the sort of person who makes them from scratch, choosing their wood, feeling the grain, taking their time over every detail and enjoying the process. The shelves become more than just something to hold books.

It's the same with cooks. There is the 'do-it-and-dust-it' cook, who does it purely to get something on the table with which to fill their belly, and then there is the one who takes delight in unfolding a cabbage leaf by leaf, rubbing their hands over the rough skin of a Russet apple, or sniffing a freshly cut lemon. The person who finds satisfaction in choosing the right knife and picking the right pot, who enjoys the scent of ingredients and the feel of food in their hands. Chopping, slicing, stirring, tasting, seasoning all become acts of contentment rather than chores to be hurried through. Although there is something in this book for both sorts of cook, it is this second person who I suspect and hope will get the most out of it.

Watching someone you love eat a tomato you have grown yourself makes it more than just a tomato. It becomes a source of glorious, yet strangely humbling, pleasure.

In the kitchen

I am a gentle cook, and one who believes that there is delight in food far beyond what is on the plate. Choosing a seed from a catalogue (who could resist a squash named Amish Pie or an apple called Cornish Gillyflower?), planting it, nurturing it to harvest, then picking it and taking it into the kitchen adds more to the satisfaction of a supper than any amount of flashy presentation. Even a vegetable or fruit chosen with care at the market, brought home in its paper bag and treated with respect can bring a certain fulfilment.

There is little point in taking the trouble to grow our own vegetables unless we can find an adequate technique to get to the heart of the ingredient. With a sweet potato, that technique would involve using dry heat such as baking or roasting to unleash its melting sweetness. An onion is cooked slowly in olive oil, duck fat or butter to tease out its hidden sugars. A head of fennel is sliced as thin as parchment to temper its unrelenting aniseed notes. A pumpkin is left to mellow, a Brussels sprout to freeze. That is why it is often fascinating and sometimes difficult to cook something you don't know very well, working out the best way to get it to show you its reason for being.

Sometimes, capturing the energy that emanates from that vegetable or fruit is straightforward. A bright, vivid green spinach leaf might need nothing other than a little steam and lemon juice to do it justice; a fat, starchy parsnip might ask for little more than a good roasting to prove to us its worth. Other vegetables are more complex and difficult to get to know (I am still trying to discover what makes kohlrabi tick).

I would like to think I know more now than I did before I picked up my trowel and dug that first furrow for red and white radishes. How to get the best out of a vegetable, yes, but also the different ways to treat it in the kitchen, which seasonings will make it sing, what other ingredients it is most comfortable or most exciting with. What are the classic recipes not to be missed by a newcomer and what new ways are there which might be of interest to an old hand.

Right now, I have come in from the vegetable patch – a romantic mingling of vegetables, fruit, herbs and flowers – and feel elated. There is an unusual abundance, even for midsummer, and a sense of energy in the garden. I have just picked the first tomatoes of the year. Tiny, green-shouldered Sungold, no bigger than a Malteser. They are sweet-sharp and burst refreshingly in my mouth. Almost best of all is the deep, herbal scent of tomato leaves on my fingers. Another one for my list.

Asparagus

There is a moment in late April, somewhere between the end of the plum blossom and the height of the apple, just as the Holly Blue butterflies start to appear in the garden, that the early asparagus turns up at the farmers' market. Tied in bunches of just six or ten, these first green and mauve spears of *Asparagus officinalis* are sometimes presented in a sacking-lined wicker basket, as if to endorse their fragility and their expense. Their points tightly closed, a faint, grey bloom of youth still apparent on their stems, it would take a will stronger than mine not to buy.

The older I get, the more interested I become in the shoots that the Persians called *asparag*, and in Pershore, the heart of the old British asparagus trade, they still call 'sparrow-grass'. The farms around Kent and Suffolk sell it from open sheds an egg's throw from the field in which it has been grown, and where I have been known to bring it back by the armful when it's cheap enough. You see the occasional row on an allotment, but the plants take up the most space of any vegetable and require vigilant picking and careful carriage home. 'Grass', as it is so often known by greengrocers and farmers alike, remains expensive for a reason.

Life is full of small rituals, and never more so than in my kitchen. The first asparagus of the year is boiled within minutes of my walking through the door with it, butter is carefully melted so that it is soft and formless but not yet liquid, then I eat it with the sort of reverence I usually reserve for mulberries or a piece of exquisite sashimi. It is almost impossible not to respect those first spears of the year.

The short, six-week season starts in late April, and once it is up and running, the price drops and the bundles get fatter. I could have it every day – in a salad with cold salmon; stirred into a frugal rice pilaf; chopped and stirred into the custard filling of a tart; or grilled and served with lemon juice and grated pecorino. I might get tired of its side effects – it contains methyl mercaptan, which makes most people's pee stink – but its flavour is the strongest sign yet that summer has started.

By mid June all but a few stragglers have gone, and the farmers rest their ancient plants till next spring.

Asparagus in the garden

There are days when I covet my neighbours' untended, overgrown garden. It's a haven for the foxes whose earth stretches far under the 'lawn', on which they lie sprawled in the sun, six at a time. The land would make a much-needed overflow for my own vegetable patch.

In celebration of the luxury of more space, my first planting would be asparagus, one of the few vegetables I have yet to grow for myself. The crowns, as the root balls are known, take up a considerable amount of room, far more than I can afford to offer them in my own tiny garden. You can raise plants from seed, if you are capable of waiting three years for them to gather strength before your first pick. Most people buy two- or even three-year-old crowns instead. They are usually delivered in late spring, wrapped in newspaper, a mass of dangling, spider-like roots sporting a short stalk or two. You dig them in – they thrive on sandy soil and sunshine – planting them in deep, manure-lined trenches under a generous 10cm of soil, and then you must pamper them with seaweed and more manure and ply them generously with drink.

As a thank you, they will send up occasional spears from late April to midsummer. Picking stimulates growth, but it is unwise to pick for too long. The farmers around my childhood home in Worcestershire would never harvest for more than six weeks for fear of exhausting the plants. Leaving a few late arrivals to develop into feathery fronds – the sort a bridegroom attaches to a buttonhole carnation – will help to restore the crown. Resting fields in growing areas can be spotted in late summer by tall fronds dotted with carmine berries, waving in the breeze.

Asparagus needs to be cut, never pulled, and you should slice as near to the crown as possible. The temptation to pick every last spear should be avoided. I have seen growers lowering their bundles into buckets of water after cutting to keep the ends moist. Dried up, they will find few takers.

Asparagus in the kitchen

There are two types of asparagus of interest, three if you count the fat 'jumbo' spears, whose flavour is rarely as impressive as their size: the thin 'sprue', finer than a pencil, and the thicker spears for picking up with our fingers. Sprue is my favourite size for working into a salad with samphire, melted butter and grated lemon. Being supple, it tangles elegantly round your fork.

The thicker spears are most tender at their flowering point, less so at the thick end where the stalk has been cut from the plant. You can often eat the entire spear, and a tough end is no real hardship – it acts as something to hold whilst we suck butter off the tastiest bits. Some people prefer to trim their 'grass', whittling the white end to a point with a paring knife or peeler.

Get the spears to the pot as quickly as you can. They lose their moisture and sweetness by the hour. If you have to keep them (I often buy three bunches at once at the Sunday farmers' market), stand them in a bowl of water like a bunch of flowers.

We can safely ignore the more far-fetched ways to boil asparagus, which range, in case you have a fancy to try, from standing them upright in a pan with their feet supported by new potatoes to cradling them over the water in a tea towel like a baby in swaddling clothes. Well intentioned, but unnecessary. Just lower the bundle of stalks tenderly into a shallow pan of merrily boiling water. If they are too long, let the points rest on the edge of the pan, where they will steam whilst the thicker ends tenderise in the water. They are good grilled over charcoal too, where the smokiness they take on makes up for the very slight lessening in juiciness. And they can be baked in foil or baking parchment with butter, a few sprigs of tarragon or chervil and some moisture in the form of white wine or water so that they effectively steam in the sealed parcel.

Once we have tired of boiled asparagus and melted butter, the spears make a deeply herbaceous soup or a mild, rather soporific tart and marry well with pancetta or soft-boiled eggs. A few in a salad will make it feel extravagant, even if the only other ingredients are new potatoes, oil, lemon juice and parsley. My all-time favourite asparagus lunch is one where a small, parchment-coloured soft cheese is allowed to melt lazily over freshly boiled spears. The warm cheese oozing from its bloomy crust makes an impromptu sauce.

Seasoning your asparagus

Butter Melted, for dressing lightly cooked spears.

Lemon juice An underused seasoning for buttered asparagus. Particularly good where Parmesan is involved.

Tomato A fresh tomato sauce, made by roasting small tomatoes, crushing them with a fork, then stirring in olive oil, crushed garlic and a splash of red wine vinegar.

Parmesan Finely grated over buttered spears or used to form a crust on a gratin of asparagus and cream.

Bacon Toss a pan of bacon or pancetta snippets and its hot fat over freshly cooked spears.

Cheese Soft, grassy cheeses, especially the richer cow's milk varieties.

Eggs As a filling for a tart, or simply soft boiled, as a natural cup of golden sauce in which to dip lightly cooked spears.

And...

* Weed your asparagus bed by hand. A hoe may damage emerging shoots.
* Despite not providing a harvest for the first three years, a crown can remain prolific for twenty years or more. I have heard of them even older.
* I was taught how to pick asparagus by a grower in Evesham. He showed me how to push the soil gently away from the lower part of the stalk with your fingers to reveal the end, which you then cut as close as possible to the crown, taking care not to cut into it.
* This vegetable loses its sweetness by the hour. Anything that has travelled from overseas is likely to disappoint.
* Avoid cooking asparagus in aluminium pans. It can taint the spears.
* Roll lightly cooked spears in thinly sliced ham, lay them in a shallow dish, cover with a cheese sauce and a heavy dusting of Parmesan and bake till bubbling.

A pilaf of asparagus, broad beans and mint

Asparagus is something you feel the need to gorge on, rather than finding the odd bit lurking almost apologetically in a salad or main course. The exceptions are a risotto – for which you will find a recipe in *Appetite* – and a simple rice pilaf. The gentle flavour of asparagus doesn't take well to spices, but a little cinnamon or cardamom used in a buttery pilaf offers a mild, though warmly seasoned base for when we have only a small number of spears at our disposal.

enough for 2
broad beans, podded – a couple of handfuls
thin asparagus spears – 12
white basmati rice – 120g
butter – 50g
bay leaves – 3
green cardamom pods – 6, very lightly crushed
black peppercorns – 6
a cinnamon stick
cloves – 2 or 3, but no more
cumin seeds – a small pinch
thyme – a couple of sprigs
spring onions – 4 thin ones
parsley – 3 or 4 sprigs

to accompany the pilaf
chopped mint – 2 tablespoons
olive oil – 2 tablespoons
yoghurt – 200g

Cook the broad beans in deep, lightly salted boiling water for four minutes, till almost tender, then drain. Trim the asparagus and cut it into short lengths. Boil or steam for three minutes, then drain. Wash the rice three times in cold water, moving the grains around with your fingers. Cover with warm water, add a teaspoon of salt and set aside for a good hour.

Melt the butter in a saucepan, then add the bay leaves, cardamom pods, peppercorns, cinnamon stick, cloves, cumin seeds and sprigs of thyme. Stir them round in the butter for a minute or two, until the fragrance wafts up. Drain the rice and tip it into the warmed spices. Cover with a centimetre's depth of water and bring to the boil. Season with salt, cover and turn the heat down to a simmer. Finely slice the spring onions. Chop the parsley.

After five minutes, remove the lid and gently fold in the asparagus, broad beans, spring onions and parsley. Replace the lid and continue cooking for five or six minutes, until the rice is tender but has some bite

to it. All the water should have been absorbed. Leave, with the lid on but the heat off, for two or three minutes. Remove the lid, add a knob of butter if you wish, check the seasoning and fluff gently with a fork. Serve with the yoghurt sauce below.

To accompany the pilaf
Stir 2 tablespoons of chopped mint, a little salt and 2 tablespoons of olive oil into 200g thick, but not strained, yoghurt. You could add a small clove of crushed garlic too. Spoon over the pilaf at the table.

Warm asparagus, melted cheese

I have used Taleggio, Camembert and our own Tunworth from Hampshire as an impromptu 'sauce' for warm asparagus with great success. A very soft blue would work as well.

> *enough for 2*
> thick, juicy asparagus spears – 24
> a little olive oil or melted butter
> soft, ripe cheeses such as St Marcellin or any of the above – 2

Put a deep pan of lightly salted water on to boil. Trim any woody ends from the asparagus and lower the spears gently into the water as soon as it is boiling. Cook for four or five minutes, until tender enough to bend. Lift the spears out with a draining spoon and lower them into a shallow baking dish. Brush them lightly with olive oil or melted butter.

Get an overhead grill hot. Slice the cheese thickly – smaller whole cheeses can simply be sliced in half horizontally – and lay them over the top of the spears. Place under a hot grill for four or five minutes till the cheese melts. Eat immediately, whilst the cheese is still runny.

A tart of asparagus and tarragon

I retain a soft spot for tinned asparagus. Not as something to eat with my fingers (it is considerably softer than fresh asparagus, and rather too giving), but as something with which to flavour a quiche. The canned stuff seems to permeate the custard more effectively than the fresh. This may belong to the law that makes canned apricots better in a frangipane tart than fresh ones, or simply be misplaced nostalgia. I once made a living from making asparagus quiche, it's something very dear to my heart. Still, fresh is good too.

enough for 6

for the pastry
butter – 90g
plain flour – 150g
an egg yolk

for the filling
medium-thick asparagus spears – 12
double cream – a medium carton (284ml)
eggs – 2
tarragon – the leaves of 4 or 5 bushy sprigs
grated pecorino or Parmesan – 3 tablespoons

Cut the butter into small chunks and rub it into the flour with your
fingertips until it resembles coarse breadcrumbs. Mix in the egg yolk
and enough water to make a firm dough. You will find you need about
a tablespoon or even less.

Roll the dough out to fit a 22cm tart tin (life will be easier when you
come to cut the tart if you have a loose-bottomed tin), pressing the pastry
right into the corners. Prick the pastry base with a fork, then refrigerate it for
a good twenty minutes. Don't be tempted to miss out this step; the chilling
will stop the pastry shrinking in the oven. Bake blind at 200°C/Gas 6 for
twelve to fifteen minutes, until the pastry is pale biscuit coloured and dry
to the touch.

Bring a large pan of water to the boil, drop in the asparagus and let
it simmer for seven or eight minutes or so, until it is quite tender. It will
receive more cooking later but you want it to be thoroughly soft after its
time in the oven, as its texture will barely change later under the custard.

Put the cream in a jug or bowl and beat in the eggs gently with a fork.
Roughly chop the tarragon and add that to the cream with a seasoning of
salt and black pepper. Slice the asparagus into short lengths, removing any
tough ends. Scatter it over the partly baked pastry case, then pour in the
cream and egg mixture and scatter the cheese over the surface. Bake, the
oven temperature lowered to 180°C/Gas 4, for about forty minutes, until
the filling is golden and set. Serve warm.

Roast asparagus

There is no joy in undercooked asparagus. Neither, curiously, is there much flavour. It must be soft and juicy, otherwise it loses much of its magic. Baking the spears in a foil parcel in the oven will suit those who don't like messing around with boiling water and steam, and keeps the asparagus surprisingly succulent.

enough for 2
thin asparagus – 450g
light, mild olive oil – 2 tablespoons
the juice of a lemon

Place the spears on a large sheet of kitchen foil. Drizzle over the oil and lemon juice and then scatter over a seasoning of salt. Bring the edges of the foil up and seal them tightly (you want the asparagus to cook in its own steam). Bake at 180°C/Gas 4 for fifteen to twenty minutes, until the spears are tender.

Asparagus with pancetta

Cured pork products get on well with our beloved spears, bacon and pancetta especially. Although it is not especially easy to eat, requiring fingers and forks, a rubble of cooked, chopped pancetta, and especially its melted fat, makes a gorgeous seasoning for a fat bunch of spears.

Boil a bundle of asparagus until it is just tender. Drain it carefully, then lay the spears in a shallow baking dish. Heat the oven to 200°C/Gas 6.

Melt a generous slice of butter in a shallow pan and fry a handful of diced pancetta, or mildly smoked bacon if that is what you have, until its fat is golden. Tip it, and the butter, over the asparagus, then sprinkle with a little grated Parmesan. Bake for ten minutes, till the cheese has melted.

Aubergines

The aubergine seduces. No other vegetable can offer flesh so soft, silken and tender. You don't so much chew an aubergine as let it dissolve on your tongue.

I fell in love at first taste: baked till its flesh had almost melted, heavy with olive oil, musky with cinnamon and allspice, cumin and ginger, sweet with golden sultanas. A dish in shades of chocolate, tobacco and amber, heady with garlic and with a fragrance at once both ancient and mysterious.

The big purple shlong we know so well is just one of the many varieties of what Americans and Australians call the eggplant. Its beauty is nothing compared to the ivory varieties, their pale skins blushed with lilac or rose as if someone had taken an artist's brush to them. Finger aubergines, slender, cute in shades of lavender or black, are as elegant as any vegetable – or berry to the botanically pedantic. Some curl up at the end like Turkish slippers, others are ridged and bulbous, whilst some are as perfectly oval and unblemished as a duck's egg. I have always thought it a shame that commerce has chosen the glossy, long-keeping varieties over the softly hued ones with their sugared-almond colours.

The aubergine, *Solanum melongena*, is not of our world. A native of India and Sri Lanka, it thrives in long, hot summers, which we can only really replicate under glass. They have survived three summers out of four on my kitchen steps but truly thrived only once. China has long honoured the aubergine in its cooking (stuffed with pork, battered and fried; steamed and tossed with chilli sauce) and was the first to mention its existence, in *Qí Mín Yào Shù*, the ancient Chinese agricultural study.

More recipes for aubergines exist in Arabic cultures than in that of the Mediterranean, and most of what I do with them has a Middle Eastern or Indian feel. They are a member of the nightshade family, like tomatoes and potatoes, and initially aroused suspicion. They are still indigestible to a few and generally avoided, like peppers and tomatoes, by arthritis sufferers.

Those puzzled by its American name are less so once they have seen the exquisite Casper and Easter Egg varieties. In the markets of Delhi and India I have seen this fruit the size and colour of an ostrich egg, and in Bangkok as small and round as a Malteser. None relies on flavour to sell itself, but maybe we would use them more if we had a choice that included the exquisite Rosa Bianca or Turkish Orange.

The aubergine is at its most sensuous in a haze of olive oil and garlic, onions and sultanas, pine kernels, yoghurt and fresh mint. The fragrance is beguiling, sumptuous, heady. The flesh of *Solanum melongena* loves the muskier spices such as cumin and saffron, the piercing sharpness of pomegranate seeds, the faintest breath of rosewater. But nothing does quite so much for it as being grilled over charcoal. Smoke seeps into the spongy flesh, lending a note of intrigue and exposing an altogether darker undertone.

The thick stems, with their light, fine hairs, the mauve flowers drooping down as if in shame, the first hint of ivory or purple fruits and the soft, jade-green leaves make this one of the most covetable plants to own. And if it gives us only two or three ripe fruits at the end of an infrequent hot summer, we should just be thankful. Rarely is the cook given anything quite so beautiful to work with.

An aubergine in the garden

With luck and a good summer, we can grow aubergines as successfully as anyone in the Med. I grow them in deep clay pots, against my warmest wall. The slimmer varieties do best here, but given a long, hot ripening season, even the fat, mauve-blushed versions will come good.

We must replicate the conditions of their natural home, so growing them under glass is the most reliable way of ensuring your plants will fruit. They thrive in fine, well-drained soil and prefer masses of heat. I have no greenhouse, so they have to live in the biggest suntrap I can offer them – on the steps by the back door, their backs to a white wall. Neither are they fond of wind, so a sheltered place is essential.

The seeds need gentle heat to germinate, about 20°C. They will grow on a windowsill, but you need to start them early, sowing in late winter. The heat must be constant. Even given the right conditions, the seeds can refuse to germinate, so I plant two to a pot. Pot them on when they are about 4cm high. Although you won't get much in the way of choice, you can also pick up small plants at farmers' markets, nurseries and by mail order from specialist suppliers – the easy option for anyone without the space and heat to grow from seed.

It is a good idea to pinch out the tips of the growing plant when it reaches about 20cm. You will get a less fragile, more bushy plant. As soon as the first flowers appear, mist them with a fine water sprayer to encourage the fruit to set, and feed the plants once a fortnight or so with tomato food. Keep an eye out for whitefly. They are rather partial to a young aubergine.

You will get about half a dozen fruits per plant, so we are not talking about vast crops here. But what a plant lacks in quantity it makes up for in the sheer pleasure of seeing the young fruits form on their furry stems. The mauve flowers are beautiful. Expect your first pick in early autumn, a little earlier if you are growing under glass.

Varieties

Violetta di Firenze White fruit, flushed with violet.
Rosa Bianca Creamy-white skin with a pink blush.
Applegreen An heirloom variety, with pale green, egg-shaped fruits.
Thai Green Small, ancient variety the size of a large pea. Often used in Southeast Asian soups.
Baby Rosanna Golf-ball-sized on dwarf plants (60cm).
Prosperosa Large, somewhat flat-sided fruits that you could slice and fry as a steak.
Early Long Purple Lives up to its name, often with a slight bend at the end.
Black Beauty Lustrous, handsome, extraordinary girth.

An aubergine in the kitchen

The heart and soul of the aubergine is not its flavour but its unique texture. It has the ability to turn an outwardly spongy blandness into a mass of silky, melting flesh that is effortless to eat. But no amount of heat alone will work this magic. The aubergine relies on the cook's generosity with the olive oil bottle. It is the fruit's ability to soak it up that makes it interesting in the kitchen.

The skin is rarely eaten, but it can be. Much depends on the way it is prepared. Peel an aubergine to be sliced and stewed (say, with tomatoes, onions, cinnamon and dried fruits) and it will collapse during cooking. Halved and baked, the skin can sometimes be tough and occasionally bitter. I usually serve it intact, then cut a piece off to try. If it is on the stringy side, I just scrape off all the flesh and leave the skin.

An aubergine has little going for it without other ingredients to add interest to its mild flesh (it is one of the few vegetables that is completely inedible raw). The simplest way to prepare it is probably to slice and grill it, but even that will need some form of dressing or sauce. No other vegetable needs quite so much help from its close friends as this one – by which I mean onions, tomatoes, garlic and herbs.

You can fry an aubergine in shallow oil, most of which it will soak up, until its edges are crisp. You can bake it whole or cut in half, its skin scored to soak up more oil, or you can grill or stew it. Boiling and steaming do nothing for this one.

It is the blackening of its skin that gives many of the most famous aubergine dishes their character. Moutabal, or baba ganoush, the soft purée of the roasted or grilled fruit beaten with olive oil and garlic, relies on the smoky notes of the charred skin for its essential flavour. Grilled aubergine with yoghurt sauce again needs the smoky notes from having been cooked on the grill as much as it needs salt and pepper.

Classic aubergine recipes tend to involve spices rather than herbs. Whilst fresh coriander and basil appear at the end of many recipes, it is the spices – cinnamon, cumin and coriander seed in particular – that are considered essential.

Salting – the process of leaving the sliced or cubed fruit in a colander, its cut surfaces encrusted with salt – is thought to remove the bitterness present in some varieties. Most of this attribute has been bred out, but I have experienced it occasionally in my home-grown fruits. Salting is still worthwhile, even for thirty minutes or so, simply to relax the cells of the flesh, preventing it from soaking up all your precious olive oil.

Seasoning your aubergine

Olive oil It is the fruit's ability to soak up copious quantities of liquid that makes our choice of oil all the more important. The aubergine's flesh is nothing without oil, and in particular a green and deeply fruity olive oil. Some of the light olive oils on the market are good for cooking, but ones such as groundnut and vegetable add a fatty quality while offering nothing in terms of flavour. Walnut and other nut oils are too strong and burn too quickly for this use. Olive oil is what makes an aubergine worth eating.
Garlic You can throw any amount of garlic at an aubergine. They are in total harmony with one another.
Salt The addition of salt after chopping will draw out the aubergine's juices and relax the flesh. This means your aubergine will soak up less oil during cooking. If there is any bitterness present – the heritage varieties occasionally carry a little – it should disperse that too. Use sparingly at the end of the dish.
Tomato A perfect pairing, especially when olive oil and garlic are involved.
Mint Whilst basil and thyme also get on well with this particular ingredient, it is mint that is heavily involved in its history. Many Middle Eastern dishes include the clean taste of mint, which cuts the oiliness.
Onion Use as a base for any slow-cooked dish or include in a stuffing.

Onions feature in the famous imam bayildi, the Turkish stuffed aubergine recipe.

Yoghurt Spices, mint and yoghurt form a romantic seasoning for the aubergine. You can also stir it into a stew or curry, or trickle it over grilled aubergine as a dressing.

Pine kernels Toast and scatter.

Walnuts Lightly crushed, sprinkled over grilled aubergine slices.

Spices Add depth and mystery. Cumin, cinnamon, paprika and cardamom are the most comfortable here, but ground coriander and turmeric are very good in vegetable stews.

Parmesan Grated. Its fruity notes bring out the fruit's subtle flavour.

Pomegranate seeds Either fresh or dried. Scatter the little jewels over grilled aubergine, along with sultanas and pine kernels. Add dried ones to stews.

And...

* Aubergine flowers droop, almost hiding themselves from the bees. Plant brightly coloured flowers such as marigolds close by to attract the interest of passing insect life.

* Beware the pale green calyx at the stem end. It packs a number of small, sharp thorns.

* Certain varieties have seeds inside, and they can be quite pronounced in older specimens too. It is not necessary to remove them. They are perfectly edible when cooked.

* Indian cooks often refer to the aubergine as *brinjal*, a name that is sometimes used to label them in Indian shops. Generally, it refers to the slim, elegant fruits grown there rather than the fat, black whoppers we get here.

* Aubergines dislike the fridge. Keep them at cool room temperature.

Baked finger aubergines, yoghurt and cucumber

The slim aubergine varieties, often with a lavender blush, that are to be found in Middle Eastern and Indian shops are especially suitable for grilling, since they cook quickly and evenly. I rarely salt these little chaps.

enough for 4
finger aubergines – about 8
olive oil

for the yoghurt
half a cucumber
thick natural yoghurt – 200g
a clove of garlic
mint leaves – about 12
black onion seeds – a teaspoon (optional)
warm flat bread such as pitta, to serve

Set the oven at 200°C/Gas 6. Wipe the aubergines and cut them in half lengthways. Pour a thin layer of olive oil into a baking tin and place the aubergines cut-side down in the oil. Bake till soft and squishy, about forty minutes.

To make the cucumber yoghurt, wipe the cucumber half and grate coarsely. Sprinkle lightly with salt and set aside in a colander for half an hour. Squeeze the cucumber dry in the palm of your hand, then stir it into the yoghurt. Peel and finely crush the garlic, chop the mint leaves and stir both into the cucumber and yoghurt. Toast the black onion seeds lightly in a non-stick pan. Transfer the yoghurt to a serving bowl and sprinkle with the onion seeds.

Serve the aubergines on plates with the cucumber yoghurt. Spread some of the baked aubergine on to a piece of the bread, spoon over a little of the yoghurt and eat.

Grilled aubergine, creamed feta

This is one of those recipes I find come in handy on several levels. I use it as both starter and main dish – often with parsley-flecked couscous on the side – but it is also a fine dish to bring out as one of the constituents of a laidback summer meal in the garden. The sort where you just put a few simple dishes on the table and let everyone help themselves.

enough for 2
medium-sized aubergines – 2
feta cheese – 200g
natural yoghurt (preferably sheep's) – 200g
chopped basil, parsley and mint – a tablespoon of each
olive oil
warm flatbreads, to serve

Slice each aubergine lengthways into five or six long steaks. Sprinkle with sea salt and allow to stand for up to an hour or so whilst you make the creamed feta. This salting will ensure the aubergines soak up as little oil as possible.

Crumble the feta into a bowl and mash it with a fork. Stir in the yoghurt, 3 tablespoons of water and then the chopped herbs. Season with black pepper, but not salt unless your feta was extraordinarily mild.

Rinse the aubergines gently and pat them dry. Brush with olive oil and place on a barbecue or a hot grill pan, the ridged sort that sits over the hob. When they are tender – a matter of five or six minutes on each side – and appetisingly charred in patches, lift them off the grill and place on a serving dish. Trickle immediately with olive oil. How much they absorb will depend on the aubergines but make certain they are all thoroughly soaked. Leave them to cool a little, then serve with the creamed feta and flatbreads.

Smoky aubergines and a punchy, bright-tasting dressing

I am always on the lookout for simple but interesting side dishes to eat with cold roast meats. A little pile of grilled aubergines, their smoked edges moist with a vibrant green dressing, wakes up yesterday's cold roast chicken or beef.

enough for 2
a large aubergine
olive oil
parsley leaves – a generous handful
mint – 6 bushy sprigs
basil leaves – a handful
garlic – 2 cloves, crushed
Dijon mustard – a tablespoon
capers – 2 tablespoons, rinsed
extra virgin olive oil – 6 tablespoons
lemon juice – 2 tablespoons

Slice the aubergine lengthways into five or six pieces. Brush lightly with oil and sprinkle with sea salt, then set aside for thirty minutes or so. Grill them over a low to moderate heat on both sides till they are soft and tender.

To make the sauce, chop the herbs quite finely, but not so small they look like tealeaves, then stir in the garlic, mustard and capers. Slowly pour in the extra virgin olive oil, beating with a fork. Stir in the lemon juice and season with sea salt and black pepper. Be generous with the seasoning, tasting as you go. The sauce should be lively and piquant.

Remove the aubergine from the grill, toss gently in the sauce and serve.

A quick supper of aubergines and pesto

Cut the aubergines in half and score deeply almost down to the skin. Roast them in a hot oven with a good dousing of olive oil. When they are squishy and meltingly tender, spread them with pesto sauce and return to the oven for a few minutes. Serve hot.

Roast aubergines, chillies and thyme

A sort of lazy-guy's ratatouille this, but better, I think, for its freshness and clean taste. I keep the chillies large here, which is partly why I have suggested using the milder varieties but, as always, it's up to you.

This works hot as an accompaniment to so many main dishes – roast lamb comes to mind – but as a warm salad too, and indeed, piled on hot toasted ciabatta as a weekday supper.

enough for 4
medium-sized aubergines – 2
cherry tomatoes – 2 large handfuls
garlic – 3 cloves
peppers (red or orange) – 2
large, mild chillies – 2 or more
thyme – 6–8 sprigs
olive oil – 150ml
toasted ciabatta, to serve

Set the oven at 200°C/Gas 6. Wipe the aubergines and cut them into thick slices or segments (salting them if you wish). Put them into a roasting tin or baking dish with the tomatoes, halved if on the large size.

Peel and crush the garlic and add it to the aubergines. Cut the peppers in half, scrape out and discard the seeds and central core, then cut the flesh into thick pieces. Cut the chillies in half, remove the seeds and slice the flesh thickly (cut it too thinly and it will burn). Add to the aubergines with the sprigs of thyme, olive oil and a generous seasoning of salt and black pepper, then toss gently until everything is glistening with oil.

Bake for forty to fifty minutes, turning once or twice, till everything is sweet and tender. A little black here and there will only add to the deliciousness. Serve piled up on the toasted ciabatta, drizzling over any remaining sweet, garlicky roasting juices.

An aubergine bruschetta

I can live without 'bits' with drinks (you might get an olive if you're lucky), but from time to time the genre gets an outing. They tend to be more substantial than most, as I have a fear of anything that might fit the name canapé. Little rounds of toast piled with grilled aubergine in a lemon and herb dressing is a tantalising mixture of crisp and soft.

> *makes 4–6 small rounds of toast, maybe more*
> large aubergines – 2
> extra virgin olive oil – 6 tablespoons
> the grated zest and juice of a lemon
> basil leaves – a small bunch
> mint – a small bunch
> country bread – 4–6 thick slices, toasted, then drizzled
> with olive oil just before you add the aubergines

Cut the aubergines into slices about the thickness of two one-pound coins, put them in a colander, sprinkle with sea salt and leave for half an hour. Get a grill or griddle pan hot. Rinse and dry the aubergines, then place them on the grill. Whilst they are cooking, pour the oil into a bowl, then add the lemon zest and juice and a mild grinding of salt and coarse black pepper. Tear the basil leaves into large pieces, remove the mint leaves from their stalks and toss them into the dressing with the basil leaves.

When the aubergines are tender and nicely charred on both sides, add them to the herbed oil. Toss gently and leave to marinate for a good fifteen minutes or so (longer will not hurt), then pile on to the hot toast. Drizzle over any remaining dressing.

Hot aubergine, melting cheese

It is essential to get an aubergine truly tender. The knife should barely have to cut it. This is easier to achieve when baking or frying than when an aubergine meets the grill. It is, I think, essential that the heat is lowered during cooking so that the inside of the slice has a chance to soften whilst the crust lightly browns.

> *enough for 2 as a light lunch*
> a large aubergine
> basil leaves – a small handful
> olive oil
> bocconcini (baby mozzarella) – 12

Cut the aubergine into long, thin slices. You should get about six from a large fruit. Salt them, leave for half an hour then, when they have relaxed, wipe off the salt. Get a grill or griddle pan hot. Grill the aubergine slices till soft and lightly coloured (four or five minutes on each side), then place on a baking sheet.

Tear the basil leaves, mix them with a couple of tablespoons of olive oil, then season with salt and pepper. Brush the slices of cooked aubergine with the seasoned oil. Slice each mozzarella in half and place the halves on the aubergine slices. Let the cheese melt under a hot grill and serve immediately, before the cheese has a chance to colour.

Moutabal – a heavenly purée

The smoky, parchment-hued cream, moutabal, is one of my desert-island dishes. Few recipes can produce anything as soft and sensuous as grilled aubergine, mashed to a pulp and seasoned with lemon and sesame paste. The lemon is essential, working an ancient magic when involved with anything charred and smoky.

Many lightly bake their aubergines for this, but without a good charring they lack the mysterious, smoky back notes that I consider as much a part of the ingredients as the aubergine itself.

enough for 2
large aubergines – 2
juice of a lemon
garlic – 2 cloves, crushed
tahini paste – 2 tablespoons
olive oil – 3 tablespoons

Slit the aubergines here and there with a sharp knife and bake them at 200°C/Gas 6 until their skin is black and charred and they are melting and tender inside – about forty minutes. When they are cool enough to handle, scrape out the flesh with a teaspoon. This is a messy business, but try not to get any of the skin in with the flesh. Mash the flesh with a fork, beating in the lemon juice, crushed garlic, tahini paste, olive oil and a good seasoning of salt. It may look a little curdled but it will taste wonderful.

A classic caponata

Sicily's cooks make much of the aubergine. They fry it in crisp discs with mint and vinegar, bake it with tomato sauce and salty caciocavallo cheese, stuff it with anchovies, parsley and capers, or grill it over charcoal before seasoning with garlic and oregano. Occasionally, they will roll up a thick jam of aubergine in soft discs of dough like a savoury strudel, called *scaccie*, whilst all the time matching it to the Arab-influenced exotica of their cupboards: anchovies, olives, fennel, mint, pomegranates, currants and pine kernels. The thin, Turkish aubergine with the bulbous end is the one they prefer, though you could use any shape for their famous caponata, the rich sweet-sour stew braised with celery, sultanas, vinegar and peppers. I can eat this fragrant, amber slop at any time of year, but somehow I always end up making it when the sun is shining, eating it outside with flat, chewy bread and maybe some grilled sardines flecked with torn mint leaves and lemon. If you make it the day before, its character — salty, sweet and sour — will have time to settle itself.

> *enough for 4*
> very large aubergines – 2
> a large onion
> olive oil
> garlic – 2 cloves, sliced
> celery – 2 large sticks, thinly sliced
> a large red pepper, cored and sliced
> tomato purée – a scant tablespoon
> tomato passata – 200ml
> golden sultanas or raisins – 2 tablespoons
> red wine vinegar – 4 tablespoons
> sugar – a tablespoon
> capers – a tablespoon
> green olives – a handful

Peel the aubergines and remove their stalks. Cut them into large chunks, place in a colander and sprinkle with salt. Set aside for an hour.

Peel the onion and slice it thinly, then let it soften – but not colour – in a shallow layer of oil. Add the garlic towards the end of cooking. Remove the onion and garlic from the pan, then fry the celery and pepper in it till soft. Remove and add to the onion.

Rinse the salt from the aubergines, pat dry with kitchen paper, then soften in the same pan. As they approach tenderness, return the onion, garlic, celery and pepper to the pan, stir and continue cooking over a gentle heat until the aubergines are truly tender.

Stir in the tomato purée, passata, sultanas, red wine vinegar, sugar, capers and 150ml water. Season and leave to simmer gently for about twenty-five minutes, keeping a careful eye on it to ensure you end up with a soft tangle of sweet-sour vegetables. Chill overnight, then serve with bread.

Aubergines baked with tomato and Parmesan

Aubergine and tomato are excellent bedfellows; the sweet sharpness of the tomato adding much in the way of succulence to the bland flesh of the aubergine. Garlic and olive oil are almost certain to come along for the ride. What follows is a recipe I use over and again as a relatively quick supper, occasionally introducing mozzarella instead of Parmesan, and sometimes adding basil with the tomatoes.

> *enough for 4*
> aubergines – 2
> olive oil
> tomatoes of assorted colour – 350g
> a ripe chilli
> a clove of garlic
> grated Parmesan – 6 tablespoons

Set the oven at 220°C/Gas 7. Slice the aubergines into thick rounds, place them on a baking tray, brush generously with olive oil and season with salt and black pepper. Bake for twenty to twenty-five minutes, until soft and tender.

Chop the tomatoes, chilli and garlic and cook them in a shallow pan with a little olive oil and plenty of salt and black pepper for twenty minutes or so, till cooked down to a mush.

Pile the tomatoes in the middle of each slice of aubergine, scatter over the grated cheese and bake for fifteen to twenty minutes, till sizzling. If there is any tomato mixture left over, serve it at the side.

Baked vegetables with an aubergine sauce

enough for 4
tomatoes – 4 large or several smaller ones
courgettes – 3, cut into quarters lengthwise
peppers – 2, cored and thickly sliced
an onion, peeled and cut into wedges
olive oil
ground cumin – a teaspoon
harissa paste (or other hot sauce) – 2 teaspoons
pine kernels – a handful
raisins – a handful

for the aubergine cream
large aubergines – 2
olive oil
creamy yoghurt – 100g
mint leaves – a handful, chopped

Set the oven at 200°C/Gas 6. Make the aubergine cream: cut the aubergines in half lengthways, score the flesh with several deep etches, then sprinkle generously with salt and set aside for half an hour. Wipe off the salt, place in a baking dish, pour over a few glugs of oil, then bake until thoroughly soft. You should be able to crush the flesh with a fork.

Scrape the aubergine flesh from the skin and mash with the yoghurt and enough olive oil to make a paste that is thick enough to trickle. Season with salt, black pepper and the chopped mint.

Meanwhile, put the vegetables in a roasting tin or baking dish, toss with olive oil and a little salt and roast at 200°C/Gas 6. They will take a good forty-five minutes to an hour to become tender. Towards the end of cooking, gently stir in the cumin, harissa paste, pine kernels and raisins. Remove from the oven and serve with a trickle of the aubergine sauce.

Baked aubergine, miso dressing

You could probably use any finely ground chilli for this, but I like the
assorted ground chilli pepper known as nanami togarashi. Togarashi is
simply the Japanese term for red chilli pepper but this one is blended with
orange peel, sesame seed and ginger. It has a slight grittiness which works
well with the silky softness of the aubergine. You can find it in any Japanese
food shop. Get the yellow miso, by the way, not the darker and substantially
saltier one. Small aubergines are best for this, available from Chinese and
Asian grocers.

serves 4 as a side dish

for the aubergines
small, long aubergines, about the size of a courgette   6
mirin – 2 tablespoons
groundnut oil – 2 tablespoons

for the miso dressing
mirin – 120ml
yellow miso paste – 2 level tablespoons
sugar – 1 tablespoon
togarashi – a half to one teaspoon

Set the oven at 180°C/Gas 4. Cut the aubergines in half lengthways, or,
if they are on the large side, into thick slices.

Score each one across the cut side, cutting almost down to the skin.
Lay them in a baking dish.

Mix a couple of tablespoons of mirin with the oil and brush it over the
aubergines. Cover the top with foil and bake for forty minutes to an hour
until they are truly soft and melting. You can brush them with a little more
of the mixture if you think they need it.

To make the miso dressing, pour the 120ml of mirin into a saucepan and
warm gently. Stir in the miso paste and the sugar. When they have dissolved,
remove from the heat and stir in the togarashi.

Remove the aubergines from the oven, toss them in the dressing and
return them to the dish. Bake for five minutes or so, till the dressing starts
to lightly caramelise.

Aubergines with mint and feta

Slice a large aubergine thickly, salt it if you wish, then brush it with a little oil and grill on both sides till completely tender. Make a dressing with four parts olive oil, one of red wine vinegar, a little salt and plenty of chopped fresh mint.

Whilst the aubergine slices are hot from the grill, toss them gently with the mint dressing, then serve with thick slices of feta cheese and warm flatbread such as pitta.

Spiced aubergine stew

A lovely, deeply flavoured vegetable stew. This is one of those dishes that is all the better for a day in the fridge, during which time the flavours seem to mellow. I have kept it quite spicy but the final seasoning will depend on how hot your chillies are, and you will need to adjust it accordingly. Something to take your time over. I eat it with steamed basmati rice.

enough for 6
aubergines – 1kg (2 very large ones)
medium onions – 3
groundnut oil – 2 tablespoons
green cardamom pods – 8
coriander seeds – 2 tablespoons
black peppercorns – 2 level teaspoons
garlic – 4 plump cloves
ginger – a thumb-sized piece
ground turmeric – 2 rounded teaspoons
medium-sized tomatoes – 10
vegetable stock – 500ml
coconut milk – two 400ml tins
small, hot red chillies – 4, finely chopped
mint – a small bunch
fresh coriander – 2 small bunches

Wipe the aubergines, cut the stalks from them and cut them into fat chunks. The dish will be more interesting to eat if you don't cut them too small. Tip them into a colander, put it in the sink and sprinkle sea salt over them. Leave them for a good half hour, longer if you can.

Peel and roughly chop the onions, then cook them with the oil in a large pan over a moderate heat until they are soft, translucent and sweet.

While the onions are cooking, crush the cardamom pods with the flat blade of a knife or a rolling pin and shake out the little black seeds into a mortar or spice grinder (or a clean coffee grinder). Add the coriander seeds and the peppercorns and grind them to a coarse powder. The smell as you grind will convince you that there is much to be missed in buying ready-ground spices.

Thinly slice the garlic. Peel the ginger and cut it into thin, matchstick-like shards. Stir the garlic and ginger into the onions along with the turmeric and ground spices. Peel and seed the tomatoes and add them to the pan.

Rinse the aubergines of their salt and pat dry. Without oiling them, grill them on a ridged cast-iron grill pan till they are starting to soften and have dark grill lines across them. Turn them as you go, so that they are cooked on both sides, removing them as they are ready and replacing them with another batch. Add them to the onions, then pour in the stock and bring to the boil. Add the coconut milk, chillies and a little salt and continue cooking at a simmer for about forty-five minutes. The aubergines should be very soft and silky but not actually falling apart.

Lift out the aubergines, tomatoes and some of the onion with a draining spoon. Reduce the rest of the sauce by boiling hard for five minutes or so. Now ladle most, but not all, of the sauce into a blender and blitz till smooth and thick (take care to cover the top with a cloth before you turn it on, the sauce is very hot). Return the vegetables and the sauce to the pot, then chop the mint and coriander leaves and stir them in, together with a final seasoning of salt and black pepper. Serve with rice.

Grilled lamb with aubergines and za'atar

Za'atar is a mild spice mixture available in Middle Eastern stores and some supermarkets. Fragrant and green, it is usually prepared using dried thyme, oregano, marjoram, toasted sesame seeds and salt. Some varieties may add savory, cumin, coriander or fennel seeds.

enough for 2
aubergine – 350g
olive oil – 100ml
za'atar – 2 teaspoons
a lemon

for the lamb
lamb cutlets – 6 nice little ones
olive oil
home-made or good-quality bought hummus – 150g

Set the oven at 200°C/Gas 6. Cut the aubergine into quarters lengthways, then into fat chunks. Put them into a bowl and pour over half the olive oil, then season with sea salt and black pepper. Tip the aubergine on to a baking sheet and bake for twenty minutes, till the flesh is truly tender.

Rub the lamb cutlets with olive oil, salt and black pepper and grill them until they are sizzling outside and still pleasingly pink in the middle. Whilst they are cooking, turn the hummus into a bowl and drizzle it with a little olive oil.

Warm the remaining 50ml olive oil in a shallow, non-stick pan over a moderate heat, then add the za'atar. Transfer the aubergine to the pan and let it cook, turning the pieces occasionally, for three or four minutes. Squeeze over the lemon juice and serve with the lamb cutlets and hummus.

A hot stew with tomatoes and coriander

Hot, clean and vibrant, a mouth-popping stew for scooping up with soft, warm naan or, if you prefer, rice. Should you want something richer and less spicy, then stir in a tub of yoghurt, about 250g, at the end and simmer for a further seven or eight minutes.

> *enough for 4*
> medium-large aubergines – 2
> ginger – a piece about the size of your thumb
> garlic – 4 cloves
> the juice of a large lemon
> medium-sized tomatoes – 4
> small, hot red chillies – 2
> coriander – a large bunch (about 40g)
> groundnut oil – 4 tablespoons

Cut the stalks from the aubergines and discard. Slice each fruit in half lengthways, then again, then cut the long strips into short, fat chunks. Put these in a colander and sprinkle generously with sea salt. Leave them for a good thirty minutes.

Peel the ginger and chop it finely, then do the same with the garlic. Put them into a blender (or a food processor) along with the lemon juice. Whiz till you have a smoothish purée. This may take a bit of doing.

Roughly chop the tomatoes. Slice the chillies thinly, without removing the seeds; you want the dish to be really quite spicy. Roughly chop the coriander.

Once the aubergines have relaxed, rinse them of their salt and pat them dry. Heat the oil in a large pan, then, when it starts to sizzle, add the aubergines, letting them colour on their cut edges, turning them so that they are golden all over.

Tip in the garlic and ginger paste and stir to coat. Mix in the tomatoes and chillies, shortly followed by the coriander and 4 tablespoons of water. Season with salt and leave to simmer gently for four or five minutes, till the aubergines have softened further. Taste for seasoning, check the aubergines for tenderness – they should be soft to the point of collapse – and serve with warm naan to mop it up.

A fragrant supper for one

I make the most of cooking just for myself, with a supper of intense frugality that might not appeal to others. A favourite is a bowl of white rice seasoned with Vietnamese fish sauce and masses of mint and coriander, eaten from my most fragile and precious bowl. A humble meal of consummate purity.

A baked aubergine may not sound like an indulgence, but its luxury and richness lie in its texture rather than its price. A simple supper that feels more expensive than it actually is. Some soft Middle Eastern bread would be good here.

> *enough for 1*
> a large, firm aubergine
> olive oil, a good everyday one
> garlic – 2 cloves
> yoghurt, sheep's if you can – 3 or 4 tablespoons
> ground paprika – a pinch or two
> mint leaves – a small palmful

Wipe the aubergine, removing its leaves, and slice it lengthwise down the middle. Score across the cut sides, going deep down into the flesh, in a lattice pattern. This will help the heat and olive oil penetrate the aubergine.

Place the halves cut-side up in a small baking dish or roasting tin, then drizzle generously with olive oil. Grind over a little salt, then flip the aubergines over, so that their cut sides sit flat on the dish. Put the garlic cloves, whole and unpeeled, into the dish too. Bake at 200°C/Gas 6 until the aubergine is tender and melting, the flesh translucent with oil. This will take a good forty-five minutes, but much will depend on the size of your aubergine, so keep an eye out.

When the aubergine is totally soft and juicy, lift it on to a plate, squeeze the soft garlic flesh from its skin and smooth it into the aubergine. No need to make a big deal of this, just wipe it over the flesh. Spoon over the yoghurt, dust very lightly with paprika and scatter the mint leaves on top. Scoop the flesh from the skin as you eat it, mashing it with the yoghurt and mint.

Baked aubergines with thyme and cream

This is a gorgeous dish, sumptuous and rich, a perfect accompaniment to grilled lamb or to steak. I have served it as a vegetable main dish with brown basmati rice too. By rights, cream and aubergines should never meet, but here they seem to work splendidly.

enough for 2 as a main dish with rice, 4 as a side dish
aubergines – 1 very large or 2 smaller
a medium onion
olive oil
garlic – 2 juicy cloves
thyme – a few bushy sprigs
whipping or double cream – 400ml
Parmesan for grating

Wipe the aubergines and cut them into long slices, about the thickness of two one-pound coins. Put the slices in a colander and sprinkle with salt. Leave for a good half hour, until they have relaxed (each piece will go a bit floppy), then rinse and dry.

Peel and thinly slice the onion. Cook it in a little olive oil till it has softened, but stop before it colours. Peel and slice the garlic and add it to the onion as it cooks. Lift out the onion and garlic and place in a shallow baking dish. Put more olive oil into the pan and add the rinsed and dried aubergine. As each slice starts to colour, turn it over, then, when all are golden – though far from brown – drain them thoroughly on kitchen paper. This is essential if there is not to be too much oil in the finished dish.

Lay the aubergine slices in the baking dish on top of the onion, scattering with salt, pepper and thyme leaves as you go. Pour the cream over the aubergine and onion, scatter over a couple of spoonfuls of grated Parmesan and bake at 180°C/Gas 4 for thirty-five to forty-five minutes, until bubbling and lightly browned here and there.

Oh, and can I remind you of the Green Curry of Prawns and Thai Aubergines in *The Kitchen Diaries*.

Beetroot

I have a weakness for beetroot in all its guises: sliced in a sweet-sharp salad; slowly baked with cream; grated in a mustardy remoulade; pickled in a lip-smarting vinegar; and as an ingredient in contemporary meat patties. Newly harvested and pushed through the mill of a juicing machine, fresh beetroot can sometimes taste as if you are biting into clean, sweet earth.

The earthiness is not to everyone's taste. Neither is the sugar quotient that can make the beetroot difficult to marry with other ingredients. The intensely savoury qualities of beef and its roasted fat contrast well, as do the knife-edge notes of soused herring or mackerel. Anything exceptionally acidic or high in umami – an aged Parmesan, perhaps, or some thin slices of dark, treacly rye bread – is worth a try. Soy sauce can be a strangely good partner too, but the two are difficult to bring together in a recipe without upsetting purists.

Beet's concentrated jewel-like colour is both its joy and its downfall. It is sod's law that it should marry so happily with the virginal white of goat's cheeses, mascarpone and thick puddles of crème fraîche, none of whose looks are improved by a pink stain curdling the outer edge. Unable to take baby-pink food to heart, I make a habit of mixing the scarlet roots with dairy ingredients or mayonnaise only at the last minute, often passing a bowl of soured cream and chopped dill around for everyone to anoint their own salad at the table. The exception being beetroot 'dauphinoise', an extraordinarily successful, if luridly coloured, accompaniment to a roast rib of beef or a bowl of brown basmati.

The organic vegetable box has introduced many of us to the opportunity that is a bunch of beets. It was initially the inclusion of beetroot in my weekly delivery that caused the most angst in my house. To waste an old swede for want of inspiration was one thing; to fail to cook a bunch of garnet bulbs and their blood-veined plumes of green leaves quite another.

At first, I returned the tops to the fridge with a promise to use them tomorrow (then forgetting). It took a while to learn that I needed to pounce upon them the moment the box arrives. Once they have even slightly wilted, they are as good as compost.

In deepest summer I have taken to buying a bunch of golden beetroot – much used in Victorian kitchens but all too rare now – whenever I see them, if only for the interest they arouse. Steamed, sliced and tossed with walnut oil, white wine vinegar and a pinch of grated orange zest, they glow on the plate. They bleed less dramatically than their bloody soulmates, yet possess the same earthy qualities. Elegant and cheering on a grey summer's day with rounds of chalky sheep's cheese and slices of tobacco-brown bread.

The red-black globes we know so well are the domesticated form of wild sea beet, which grew around the coastlines of the Mediterranean. Cultivated by the Greeks and the Romans, their leaves were used as pot-herbs, whilst the swollen roots were used medicinally rather than in the kitchen. Stephen Nottingham, whose worship of all things beetroot has provided a fascinating and exhaustive internet study, points out that the Romans used the roots to produce a curative broth. To this day, beetroot juice is drunk to 'stimulate and cleanse the kidneys'. But we can thank the Victorians for giving it the prominence it has in our kitchens today.

A beetroot in the garden

I grow beetroot two ways: firstly a single row planted in the same sunny bed as the summer squash, and secondly as salad leaves in seed trays, to be picked long before they get the chance to form a bulbous root. The large beetroot leaves I cook instead of spinach tend to come as a gift with those bunches of deep-red roots I buy at the market, the large leaves from my garden-grown roots being too tatty to serve as a vegetable.

Bolthardy is the variety I have grown most successfully. It is reliable and has no inclination to bolt (though its leaves could be more prolific). The golden beets in my patch have so far stayed on the small side, but were nevertheless worth the space.

Most people sow in April and I usually follow suit, but it is a mistake to plant too early. If spring is cold, then wait a while, otherwise things tend to sulk. Those wanting to keep themselves in beetroot through to the autumn might like to sow in June, too. Sow the seeds in clusters, then thin to 7cm apart, chucking the thinnings into the salad bowl. Seeds take approximately twelve weeks to mature, though some of mine have taken considerably longer. April sowings should be just about large enough in August. June plantings will keep you going through to early winter. Keeping the snails away from their tuft of leaves is a problem. I resort to eco-friendly slug pellets.

Varieties

Bolthardy Self-explanatory really. It's hardy and bolt resistant.
Bull's Blood An eighteenth-century variety with exceptionally dark red leaves.
Chioggia Barbietola A sweet variety with red and white rings inside. Cooks to a slightly disappointing pink.
Cheltenham Green Top Elongated, tapering root, dull green leaves.
Burpees Golden A round root of saffron gold and green leaves with yellow veins. Turns a deep orange-yellow when cooked.
Egyptian Turnip-rooted A slightly flattened, deep-red root, much of which grows out of the ground. Good for those with shallow soils.
Blankoma A large, white variety I can get less than excited about.

A beetroot in the kitchen

If you boil a bunch of small summer beets they will be ready in twenty minutes. Their skins should come off with a brush of the thumb – a soothing job if you don't mind carmine fingers. The wiry tuft of stem can be pushed out easily enough too. Cut the warm beets into quarters and toss with a fruit vinegar such as raspberry, a splash from the walnut or hazelnut oil bottle and perhaps some fresh dill. A sweet salad such as this is particularly good with oily fish fillets grilled till their skin crisps.

Older specimens whose circumference is approaching that of an orange can take up to forty-five minutes to reach tenderness but are still rarely less than delicious. There is likely to be a more obvious earthiness in older roots, but the inherent sweetness will still be there. Dressing them with something sharp while they are still warm will balance the sugar level. Try a shake-up of cider vinegar, walnut oil, and a pinch of warm, musky caraway seeds that you have briefly toasted in a shallow pan.

If the oven is on anyway, I sometimes bake my beets, each one wrapped in loosely crumpled foil so they partially steam as they bake. It's a good use for those bits of used-but-clean foil you keep for recyling yet rarely do anything with. A little water in each will stop them scorching. The flavour and indeed the sweetness seem particularly intense. They take longer to cook this way – much longer, a good hour for a small one – but the cost is negligible if there's a slow roast in the oven anyway. They are ready when you can pierce them through the heart with a skewer. As you might a vampire.

The all-staining juice that seeps from a cut beetroot will leave its print on anything it touches, and you will be lucky not to colour at least your fingers, if not your shirt. Much of the leakage can be avoided by keeping the beetroot's skin intact and the plug of stem in place throughout the cooking process. Cut either one beforehand and the juice will seep into the cooking water, leaving you with Barbie-pink beets and a pan of blood-red water. The only time I peel at the outset is when I'm using one raw.

A raw beetroot has much going for it. I toss the coarsely grated roots into a carrot salad (dressed with lemon and mint leaves); fold them into yoghurt with a hint of crushed garlic to make a beetroot tzatsiki to accompany falafel; introduce them into a celeriac remoulade; and occasionally toss them through a salad of winter leaves. The trick is not to over-mix or prepare too early. A light, last-minute stirring of grated roots through the yoghurt or mayonnaise is all that is needed. Any earlier or more thoroughly and you have got a marshmallow-pink lunch.

Oily fish love a beetroot at their side. I often include them, boiled and thinly sliced, in a herring salad (both ingredients enjoy being partnered with dill) and have served a salad of yellow beetroot with grilled sardines before now. I also like a pile of it, grated raw, on the same plate as gravadlax. It is a sensation with the traditional accompanying mustard sauce.

Perhaps unsurprisingly, this vegetable is good in sweet things. I use it in a cake whose crumb is also freckled with blue-grey poppy seeds, where its inclusion keeps the cake moist. I rarely mention the addition of the vegetable till everyone reaches for a second slice.

And then there are the leaves. Many greengrocers, farmers' markets and vegetable boxes supply their *Betula vulgaris* with its plume of leaves intact. It is a reliable sign of freshness, as they wilt after only a day or two. They are good to eat, but are less tender and more robustly flavoured than those members of the beet family grown for their leaves alone, such as chard.

My own beet leaves have never been particularly plentiful, possibly because I grow a relatively new variety that was developed for its bulbous root rather than its leaves. Heritage seeds may give a more plentiful crop.

The early leaves that appear three or four weeks after planting are fine in a salad. To prevent them softening too much, dress them only minutes before eating. The older leaves can be steamed in a shallow pan containing a finger's depth of water. Cover with the lid and they will steam themselves to tenderness in a minute or two. Stir-frying with garlic and spring onion is an instant vegetable dish, though they do tend to disappear in the pan the way spinach does.

Seasoning your beetroot

Dill Scatter chopped fronds over a beetroot salad.
Rye bread Dark, treacly bread, cream cheese, sliced beetroot.
A sandwich of great sophistication.
Gherkins The sour note is a balance for the sweetness.
Onion A savoury base for any warm beetroot dish.
Soured cream, fromage frais, crème fraîche Piquant dairy produce,

including buttermilk and yoghurt, provides an uplifting note that is exciting with the sweet earthiness.

Vinegar Almost any vinegar works well, including the more mellow versions such as balsamic and those made with soft fruit. Possibly the only use for malt vinegar outside pickling and the chippie.

Cumin The dusty, almost fetid notes of toasted cumin seeds can be included in any beetroot dish, but particularly when it is served as a soup.

Apple juice Apples can always be worked into a beetroot salad, but the juice can be included in a refreshing dressing too.

Horseradish Freshly grated in a salad; stirred into crème fraîche as an accompaniment; scattered over a beetroot mash.

Walnut oil The most appropriate oil for dressing the warm roots.

Mustard A sound choice for seasoning a salad.

Capers A sharp shock to make the sugary roots sing.

Chocolate File under strange but true. Better still, make the moist beetroot cake (page 078).

And...

* Whilst walnut oil is probably the most appropriate dressing for a beetroot salad, the most suitable cooking medium is a flavourless oil such as groundnut or vegetable.

* The pink and white striped Chioggia variety doesn't bleed as dramatically as the red varieties. The yellow ones don't seem to bleed at all.

* Oily fish, sardines, mackerel and herring are a safe bet for a beet-type accompaniment. Grilled or marinated (soused) fish are particularly fine.

* Beetroot risotto is often cited as worth eating. Use a strongly flavoured stock and be generous with the Parmesan.

* Try adding grated raw roots with chopped dill to an omelette.

* Roast, peel, cube and dress with walnut oil and lemon juice as a side dish to cold roast pork.

* Shred raw and mix with mustard mayonnaise to make a pink-freckled remoulade, as an accompaniment to thinly carved air-dried ham.

* Steam and mash to eat alongside boiled gammon and parsley sauce. A pretty plateful.

* Use as a substitute for carrots in a traditional carrot cake.

* Partner with pickled fish such as rollmops in a salad with spinach leaves.

* Thinly slice roasted or steamed golden beetroot, then dress with a vinaigrette of olive oil, balsamic vinegar, a dab of Dijon mustard and the zest and juice of an orange. A few rings of paper-thin onion, raw and sweet, wouldn't go amiss. Call it a carpaccio if you must.

* I once made a beetroot quiche. As it came from the oven, it looked like a huge round bruise.

A light touch for meatballs

Late spring, 2007. Six small beetroots, round as golf balls and not much bigger, arrive in a thick brown paper bag, its edges sewn together with string. The air of moist Riverford soil and sweet roots wafts up as the bag is torn open, but the day is leaden with damp and cold and I have rarely felt less like eating a beetroot salad.

Supper is going to be meatballs: fat, crumbly patties of minced lamb with garlic, dill and parsley. It crosses my mind that a handful of grated beets might sweeten the mince and lighten their texture.

What we end up eating on the coldest spring day for years is plump rounds of sweet and spicy meat, crunchy with cracked wheat and crimson with the vivid flesh of finely grated beetroot. The inclusion of the roots has broken up the solid lump of minced meat and married well with the garlic and clean-tasting herbs. We dip the sizzling patties into a slush of shredded cucumber, yoghurt and mint, given a snap of piquancy (to balance the beetroot) with a spoonful of capers.

makes 12–16, enough for 4 or more
fine or medium cracked wheat – 75g
raw beetroot – 250g
a small to medium onion
minced lamb – 400g
garlic – 2 large cloves, or even 3, crushed
chopped dill – 2 heaped tablespoons
parsley – a small handful, chopped
a little groundnut oil

for the dressing
cucumber – about a third of a medium one
mint – the leaves from 4 or 5 sprigs, chopped
capers – a tablespoon
yoghurt – 200g

Put the cracked wheat in a bowl, pour over enough boiling water to cover, then set aside to swell.

Peel the beetroot and onion and grate them coarsely into a large bowl. Add the minced lamb, garlic, dill, parsley and a generous grinding of salt and black pepper.

Squeeze any water from the cracked wheat with your hands and add to the meat. Mix everything together thoroughly, then squish the mince into little patties about the size of a flattened golf ball. Cover with cling film (I do this tightly because the chopped garlic will taint everything in the fridge), then chill for at least an hour.

Set the oven at 180°C/Gas 4. Make the dressing by grating the cucumber coarsely and leaving it in a colander, lightly sprinkled with salt, for half an hour. Squeeze it dry, then mix it with the chopped mint, capers and yoghurt. Season with salt and black pepper.

Heat a non-stick pan, brush the patties with a little groundnut oil and fry till golden on both sides. Try not to move the meatballs very much when they are cooking, you risk them falling apart. Once they are lightly browned on both sides, carefully lift them into a baking dish and finish in a hot oven for fifteen to twenty minutes (incidentally, you can only tell if they are done by tasting one, as the beetroot gives them a rich red colour, making it impossible to gauge by sight whether they are cooked).

Drizzle with the cucumber dressing and eat.

Chickpea patties, beetroot tzatsiki

The chickpea possesses a dry, earthy quality and a knobbly texture that I find endlessly useful and pleasing to eat. No other member of the legume family has quite the same mealy, warm nuttiness.

This is the bean I want bubbling on the stove when there is pouring rain outside, filling the kitchen with its curiously homely steam as it slowly simmers its way to tenderness. Unlike its more svelte cousins, the flageolet and the cannellini, the chickpea is almost impossible to overcook. The length of time it takes to soften rules it out of weekday cooking for me, so I sometimes resort to opening a can. Chickpeas, often labelled *ceci* or *garbanzo*, leave their can relatively unharmed, which is more than you can say for a flageolet. They make good patties that you can season with cumin, chilli, garlic, sesame or coriander and fry till lightly crisp on the outside.

Chickpea patties need a little texture if they are to be of interest. I process them only so far, leaving them with a texture that is partly as smooth as hummus with, here and there, a little crunchiness.

The patty mixture needs a good ten minutes to rest before cooking. To calm the garlic notes, I spoon over a sauce of yoghurt, grated cucumber and mint or a similar one of shredded beetroot, taking care not to overmix it to a lurid pink.

makes 6 small patties, enough for 2
chickpeas – a 400g can
garlic – 2 cloves
ground cumin – a teaspoon
ground coriander – a heaped teaspoon
hot paprika – a scant half teaspoon
an egg
flat-leaf parsley – a small bunch
mint – a small bunch
olive oil
lemon wedges, to serve

for the tzatsiki
beetroot – a large raw one
natural yoghurt – 200g
garlic – a single juicy clove, well crushed
mint leaves – a few

Drain and rinse the chickpeas. Put them in a food processor with the garlic, ground cumin and coriander, paprika, egg and a generous grinding of salt and black pepper. Chop the parsley and mint leaves roughly (I use a couple of tablespoons of each), add to the processor, then blitz till smooth, but still with some small pieces of chickpea detectable. It is much more interesting with a slightly lumpy texture than a totally smooth one. Leave to firm up for a few minutes while you make the tzatsiki (your first thought may be that the mixture is too soft to make patties).

Grate the beetroot finely. Stir in the yoghurt, a little salt and black pepper, the garlic and a few chopped mint leaves.

Warm a very shallow layer of olive oil in a non-stick frying pan. Take heaped tablespoons of the mixture out of the bowl and place them in the hot oil, pressing down lightly to smooth the top. Leave them be till the underside is golden. I avoid any temptation to prod and poke; they must be allowed to form a thin crust. Flip over confidently but tenderly with a palette knife to cook the other side. They are done in three or four minutes, when the outside is faintly crisp and biscuit coloured and the inside is soft and creamy. Serve with the beetroot tzatsiki and the lemon wedges.

Goat's cheese and beetroot salad with toasted hemp and poppy seeds

A good contrast here between the sweetly warm beets, nutty hemp and tangy goat's cheese. Any crisp, slightly bitter salad leaf will work. The English-grown ivory and crimson chicory, crunchy, juicy and appealing to the eye, works well but the classic white would be just as welcome.

enough for 4

for the salad
small to medium beetroot – 8
hemp seeds – 2 teaspoons
chicory – 200g
goat's cheese – 12–16 slices
a small punnet of mustard and cress
poppy seeds – 2 teaspoons

for the dressing
red wine vinegar – a tablespoon
Dijon mustard – a tablespoon
hemp seed oil – a tablespoon
olive oil – 3 tablespoons
roughly chopped parsley – 2 tablespoons

Bring a deep pan of water to the boil. Make the dressing by mixing the vinegar and mustard together and then adding the oils. Stir the parsley into the dressing with a grinding of salt and black pepper.

Trim the leaves from the beetroot (save them for cooking like spinach), taking care not to cut the skin. Wipe the beetroot clean of any mud or sand. Put them into the boiling water and turn down to an energetic simmer. Test the beetroot occasionally for tenderness, either by lifting them from the water and rubbing the skin – it will peel off easily if the beetroot is ready – or by testing with a skewer. They should be ready in about thirty minutes, depending on their size and age.

Drain the beets and, when they are cool enough to handle, remove their skins. Cut each one into six wedges from stalk to root. Toss gently in some of the dressing and set aside.

Toast the hemp seeds in a non-stick pan for a minute or two, till they smell warm and nutty. Separate the chicory leaves and toss gently with some of the dressing. Divide them between four plates. Add the goat's cheese and mustard and cress and tuck in the beetroot. Scatter the poppy seeds and toasted hemp over the salad.

Marinated mackerel with dill and beetroot

Clean favours here, a delightful main-course salad for a summer's day. You could use other fish, such as red mullet, if you prefer but mackerel suits this treatment well, and the richness of its flesh goes well with the sweet beetroot and tart marinade. Some watercress, lush and deep green, would be good with this, and maybe a few slices of dark bread and butter.

enough for 4
medium beetroot (golden or otherwise) – 4
a little olive oil
mackerel – 4, filleted

for the marinade
cider vinegar – 50ml
lemon juice – 120ml
bay leaves – 2
a small carrot
an onion
garlic – a small clove
sugar – a teaspoon
coriander seeds – a teaspoon
juniper berries – about 12
white peppercorns – 5
black peppercorns – 5
olive oil – 80ml
a little fresh dill – finely chopped

Wash the beetroot and wrap them in foil, then bake at 200°C/Gas 6 for fifty minutes or so, till tender – or, if you prefer, boil them in deep, unsalted water for about thirty minutes, until knifepoint tender. Remove and discard their skins. Slice into thick rounds and set aside.

For the marinade, pour the vinegar and lemon juice into a stainless steel saucepan with 150ml water. Add the bay leaves. Scrub the carrot and slice it finely. Peel the onion and slice that similarly. Peel and squash the garlic and add it to the pan, together with the carrot and onion, sugar, coriander seeds and juniper berries. Bring the lot to the boil, then add a teaspoon of salt and the peppercorns. Pour in the olive oil and let the mixture simmer for a minute or two, until the onion has softened slightly. Turn off the heat.

Warm a little olive oil in a non-stick frying pan. Season the fish fillets and lay them skin-side down in the oil. Let them colour, then turn them over. Lift them from the pan and place in a shallow dish.

Add the dill and beetroot to the marinade. Pour over the fish and leave to cool. Lift the fish on to plates and spoon over the vegetables and liquor.

A chilled soup of goat's cheese and beetroot

In the 1980s blitzed beetroot, snipped chives and swirls of soured cream made a startling chilled soup that became an almost permanent fixture at the café in which I cooked for much of the decade. The most outrageous Schiaparelli pink, it was a picture in its deep-white porcelain tureen. I wish now I had had the nous to include the finely chopped gherkins whose sweet-sour pickle notes could have lifted the soup from its candy-cane sweetness. One glance at a Russian or Swedish cookery book would have been enough.

enough for 4
raw beetroot – 500g
groundnut or vegetable oil – 2 tablespoons
spring onions – 4–6
vegetable or light chicken stock – 750ml

for the goat's cheese cream
softish goat's cheese – 100g
thick yoghurt – 3 tablespoons
mixed chopped chives and mint – 2 tablespoons

Set the oven at 200°C/Gas 6. Cut the leaves from the beetroot (cook them later, treating them as you might spinach) and scrub the beets well. Put them in a roasting tin with a tablespoon of oil and three of water and cover tightly with foil. Roast for forty-five minutes to an hour, till dark and almost tender.

Warm the second tablespoon of oil in a shallow pan. Chop the spring onions and let them soften for five minutes or so in the oil. Set aside.

Peel the beets and chop the flesh roughly. Put them in the pan with the onions, pour over the stock and bring to the boil. Simmer for seven or eight minutes, cool slightly, then put through a blender till smooth. Check the seasoning. It will need salt and black pepper. Pour into a jug and chill in the refrigerator.

To make the cream, remove the skin from the goat's cheese and mash the flesh with a fork. Stir in the yoghurt and chopped herbs. Serve the soup when it is thoroughly chilled, adding spoonfuls of the herb cream at the table.

Beetroot seed cake

This tastes no more of beetroot than a carrot cake tastes of carrots, yet it
has a similar warm earthiness to it. It is less sugary than most cakes, and the
scented icing I drizzle over it is purely optional. The first time I made it, I
used half sunflower and half Fairtrade Brazil nut oil, but only because the
Brazil nut oil was new and I wanted to try it. Very successful it was too, not
to mention boosting everyone's zinc levels. (See photograph overleaf.)

enough for 8–10
self-raising flour – 225g
bicarbonate of soda – half a teaspoon
baking powder – a scant teaspoon
ground cinnamon – half a teaspoon
sunflower or Brazil nut oil – 180ml
light muscovado sugar – 225g
eggs – 3, separated
raw beetroot – 150g
juice of half a lemon
sultanas or raisins – 75g
mixed seeds (sunflower, pumpkin, linseed) – 75g

for the icing
icing sugar – 8 tablespoons
lemon juice or orange blossom water
poppy seeds

Set the oven at 180°C/Gas 4. Lightly butter a rectangular loaf tin (20 x 9cm,
measured across the bottom, and 7cm deep), then line the base with
baking parchment.

Sift together the flour, bicarbonate of soda, baking powder and
cinnamon. Beat the oil and sugar in a food mixer until well creamed, then
introduce the egg yolks one by one. Grate the beetroot coarsely and fold
it into the mixture, then add the lemon juice, sultanas or raisins and the
assorted seeds.

Fold the flour and raising agents into the mixture while the machine
is on slow.

Beat the egg whites till light and almost stiff. Fold gently but thoroughly
into the mixture, using a large metal spoon (a wooden one will knock the
air out). Pour the mixture into the loaf tin and bake for fifty to fifty-five
minutes, covering the top with a piece of foil after thirty minutes. Test with
a skewer for doneness. The cake should be moist inside but not sticky. Leave
the cake to settle for a good twenty minutes before turning it out of its tin
on to a wire cooling rack.

Make the icing. Sift the icing sugar into a bowl and add enough lemon juice or orange blossom water to achieve a consistency where the icing will run over the top of the cake and drizzle slowly down the sides (about three teaspoonfuls), stirring to remove any lumps. Drizzle it over the cake and scatter with poppy seeds. Leave to set before eating.

An extremely moist chocolate beetroot cake with crème fraîche and poppy seeds

I have lost count of the number of appreciative emails and blog mentions about the brownies and the chocolate almond cake in *The Kitchen Diaries*. They are received gratefully. It is true that I am rarely happier than when making chocolate cake. I especially like baking those that manage to be cakelike on the outside and almost molten within. Keeping a cake's heart on the verge of oozing is down partly to timing and partly to the ingredients – ground almonds and very good-quality chocolate will help enormously. But there are other ways to moisten a cake, such as introducing grated carrots or, in this case, crushed beetroot.

The beetroot is subtle here, but it is a lot cheaper than ground almonds and blends perfectly with dark chocolate. This is a seductive cake, deeply moist and tempting. The serving suggestion of crème fraîche is not just a nod to the soured cream so close to beetroot's Eastern European heart, it is an important part of the cake. (See photograph overleaf.)

enough for 8 as a dessert
beetroot – 250g
fine dark chocolate (70 per cent cocoa solids) – 200g
hot espresso – 4 tablespoons
butter – 200g
plain flour – 135g
baking powder – a heaped teaspoon
good-quality cocoa powder – 3 tablespoons
eggs – 5
golden caster sugar – 190g
crème fraîche and poppy seeds, to serve

Lightly butter a 20cm loose-bottomed cake tin and line the base with a disc of baking parchment. Set the oven at 180°C/Gas 4.

Cook the beetroot, whole and unpeeled, in boiling unsalted water. Depending on their size, they will be knifepoint tender within thirty to forty minutes. Young ones may take slightly less. Drain them, let them cool under running water, then peel them, slice off their stem and root, and blitz to a rough purée.

Melt the chocolate, snapped into small pieces, in a small bowl resting over a pot of simmering water. Don't stir.

When the chocolate looks almost melted, pour the hot coffee over it and stir once. Cut the butter into small pieces – the smaller the better – and add to the melted chocolate. Dip the butter down under the surface of the chocolate with a spoon (as best you can) and leave to soften.

Sift together the flour, baking powder and cocoa. Separate the eggs, putting the whites in a large mixing bowl. Stir the yolks together.

Now, working quickly but gently, remove the bowl of chocolate from the heat and stir until the butter has melted into the chocolate. Leave for a few minutes, then stir in the egg yolks. Do this quickly, mixing firmly and evenly so the eggs blend into the mixture. Fold in the beetroot. Whisk the egg whites till stiff, then fold in the sugar. Firmly but tenderly fold the beaten egg whites and sugar into the chocolate mixture. A large metal spoon is what you want here; work in a deep, figure-of-eight movement but take care not to over-mix. Lastly fold in the flour and cocoa.

Transfer quickly to the prepared cake tin and put in the oven, turning the heat down immediately to 160°C/Gas 3. Bake for forty minutes. The rim of the cake will feel spongy, the inner part should still wobble a little when gently shaken.

Leave to cool (it will sink a tad in the centre), loosening it around the edges with a palette knife after half an hour or so. It is not a good idea to remove the cake from its tin until it is completely cold. Serve in thick slices, with crème fraîche and poppy seeds.

Broad beans

I only truly appreciated broad beans once I had seen them growing. The flowers, pure white, black and white, or the deep crimson-pink of an archbishop's robe, have a scent that wafts lightly on the air. The smell takes you by surprise on a cold spring day, like a sudden blast of winter jasmine, hitting you when you least expect it. As a child, I wouldn't eat the bean American cooks call the fava, and yet for all its faults – mealy texture, musty smell, papery skins – I knew that the broad bean was essentially a beneficial thing. I wanted to like them. It wasn't until my teens, finding my stepmother's tiny home-grown offerings under a white sauce speckled with parsley (and alongside a slice of steaming, fat-framed pink gammon), that I found them acceptable. The sight of them in our new country garden, festooned with smart black and white flowers and held up by sticks and brown string, amused a displaced and lonely city boy. Their ability to stay green even in the coldest weather, their gentle scent and the fact that the seed germinated so reliably made me think differently about the bean I had previously refused to eat.

The first pink-flowered variety I saw was at the Chelsea Physic Garden in a bed behind the pelargonium house, three feet high, its deep magenta blossoms singing out against soil the colour of wet tobacco. I guess that is when I truly fell in love with them. I could have been persuaded to relish them sooner had they been served without their grey, parchment-like skins. But it was the sight of their flowers, like butterflies clinging to a stick, that finally seduced me.

Now I respect them and their fur-lined pods in much the same way that others revere asparagus or artichokes. In a salad with crumbly white cheese, baked with cream and parsley, tossed with chopped dill and fat bacon, they take on a must-have quality. I grow them in my own garden now, the ancient Aquadulce, Grando Violetto and the crimson-flowered variety, too.

A broad bean in the garden

We have cultivated this flat, wide bean since the Bronze Age. I have grown it for the last seven years. The only truly frost-hardy bean, it will usually survive throughout the coldest winter. Autumn planting is popular, to get a head start, picking them in early summer before many other crops have crossed the starting line. But you can, and I often do, sow as late as April.

I have found this bean to be the least fussy vegetable of all. Wherever I plant it, in my clay soil or cosseted in warm pots of compost, the seeds germinate without fail. If only everything was as good-natured and tolerant. Generally it is accepted that broad beans do well on a deep, heavy soil. They have long roots and do like the ground to have had a digging over before they go in.

There are two distinct cultivars: those with a long pod such as the Aquadulce I grow each year, and the shorter 'Windsor' pods with three or four plump beans, such as Jubilee Hysor or Crimson Flowered. I get on well with the long-podded types, apart from the odd bit of blackfly here and there.

Sheltered gardens allow seeds to be sown directly in October, but most survive more reliably if sown indoors, then planted out in early spring. As a rule, spring sowing can be done under cover in February or March (plant out in late April or early May and water in well) or in April where they are to crop. They need 20cm between each plant and 45cm between the rows, although I have often allowed less.

I keep blackfly to a minimum by picking out the top shoots two weeks or so before the pods are ready to pick. You can stir-fry the young leafy tops with garlic.

A broad bean diary

The catalogues are offering Aquadulce Claudia for autumn sowing (and for which I am too late), Giant Exhibition, which sounds like a tough old man fit only for winning awards at country shows, and the Sutton Dwarf, a bush variety and apparently prolific. One or two mention the magenta-flowered bean that stole my heart.

I order Aquadulce, a nineteenth-century Spanish variety. The Catalans have wonderful bean recipes, including one where the beans are cooked in earthenware with pork fat, onion, parsley, oregano, rosemary and olive oil and served with blood sausage. You don't need a recipe – just pile the ingredients in, cover with a little stock and a lid and leave to cook in a low oven for a couple of hours.

March 11 I plant the seeds, pale grey-brown and the size of my thumbnail, in peat-free potting compost in tall, root-trainer pots, two to a pot. Not too deep, just a couple of centimetres below the surface. I put wet newspaper in first, which they seem to like, then compost. The surface smoothed off, the pots go into the cold frame. Others are dibbed straight into the soil, each one marked by a copper ring to ward off slugs and to remind me of life below the surface. More organised gardeners will have planted theirs in January to grow more slowly and to give a late-May or early-June harvest. Unable to resist, I also plant the ancient Grando Violetto and once again the red-flowered beans I picked up from the Chelsea Physic Garden whose seeds are the most beautiful of all, a sultry jade-green colour and slightly smaller than Aquadulce.

March 24 A pool of water has frozen solid on the buckled top of the garden table. Before the cold, grey light fades, I spot the first beans poking through the compost, a single stem, pointed like a bird's beak, poised, ready to unfurl.

May 4 The Grando Violetto, red flowered and Aquadulce Claudia have germinated with just a single failure. Those sown outside are shorter by half, but seem stronger and stiffer than those wallowing in the luxury of the cold frame, whose swollen stems are already in need of a stick. Once they are 10cm high, I plant the indoor-grown ones out on the cool, moist side of the garden, about 20–25cm apart and with sticks for each to climb.

May 24 The stems are full of carmine and white flowers and the first plump bean pods are the length of my little finger. I tie the stems to stiff canes.

June 6 A few straggling flowers still grace the plants but it is the beans that are the stars now, their pods quickly thickening up with the heavy rain. I pick almost constantly for a full month.

July 20 I rip up the bare stems that are now crisping in the sun to make way for cabbage plants. Any legume leaves behind a quantity of nitrogen in the soil that is heartily welcomed by members of the brassica family.

Varieties

Aquadulce Claudia A long bean of good flavour and disease resistance. Comes up trumps for me every time.

The Sutton Dwarf A short bushy bean, barely 35cm in height, so useful for small gardens like mine or on windy sites where a taller bean would come to grief. The beans are small, like the plant, the flowers black and white.

Green Windsor One of the deepest-flavoured varieties, but inclined to be tender, so best for spring sowing. A short bean, it has been with us since the 1750s. The original 'unimproved' variety, with short, plump pods and beans of incomparable flavour, can be found in specialist seedsman's lists like those of Thomas Etty or the Organic Gardening Catalogue.

Crimson Flowered An enchanting sight in the spring garden, alongside pale green pea shoots and young mint. The jury is out on the flavour, but I find it delicate and appealing; others feel it is more of an ornamental addition to the allotment.

Bunyard's Exhibition A long pod and a prolific cropper. Yet another long-lived vegetable from Bunyard, the eighteenth-century nursery. Good flavour. Will need some support in the form of sticks and string.

Grando Violetto Old variety with purple beans in green pods.

A broad bean in the kitchen

Vicia faba, incidentally the only bean native to Europe, has three stages when it is of interest to the cook. The first is when the pods are the size of an index finger, the immature beans barely the length of a large vitamin pill. It is at this point that I have cooked them whole, pod and all, with cubes of bacon, olive oil, mint and a little water. Stewed for twenty minutes, the pods become tender enough to eat as they are, with hunks of bread to dip in the oily juices.

The second stage is when the pods are plump, the shadowy undulations of the beans visible through them, the skins bright and shiny. They are at their most useful point and work as well in a salad as they do in a risotto.

At the end of their lives, the beans start to get mealy, losing their nutty sweetness. Even now there is no reason to despise them. I often make a purée of these older specimens, thinning it to the consistency of hummus with olive oil and chopped dill or mint – a treat with roast lamb.

Had my first experience been of a sweet, young specimen, or of a larger one that had been skinned, then I might have taken to them earlier. Grey food tends not to win a child over.

I don't bother to skin young beans. Their skins are thin, pale green and dissolve sweetly in the mouth. Anything larger than a thumbnail and I skin them. Popping them out of their parchment-like skins after cooking takes but a minute, and is actually a rather agreeable kitchen task. Unless, of course, you are in a hurry.

Seasoning your beans

Pork Of any persuasion, but especially in the form of black pudding, prosciutto and bacon.
Onions Particularly spring onions and even onion tops.
Mint Perhaps in a sauté of beans, spring onions and olive oil.
Dill In a salad or for a purée of the beans with oil and hot sesame bread.
Salty cheeses Such as ricotta, goat or sheep's cheese, especially feta, where it works well in a salad with coriander and radishes. Blue cheeses, used in a salad or risotto, can intensify the sweetness of young, mild beans.

And...

* Although I have included a recipe for beans with cream, mint and parsley, I also make a side dish for fish by stirring boiled and skinned broad beans into a classic parsley sauce. Sublime with any white fish or, indeed, a lump of gelatinous boiled gammon.
* Planting summer savory between the rows will deter aphids. Blackfly hate the smell (or so they tell me). The savory can always be chucked on your pizza.
* I scatter a layer of grit around the stems of my newly transplanted young plants to stop the slugs getting too close.
* The beans keep better in the pod than out of it. I store mine in a thick brown paper bag in the fridge. Their sugar turns to starch quickly, so the less time they spend in storage the better. They freeze exceptionally well, possibly better than any other vegetable, but should be removed from their pods first.
* Cooked beans don't store very well. If I have cooked a glut and find them having to 'overnight' in the fridge (say, for a salad with bacon and mint tomorrow), I pour in a glug of olive oil, toss well and cover the dish with clingfilm to prevent them drying out.
* Broad beans like a bit of acidity. I find them at their best with goat's cheese; tossed with a little thick yoghurt and olive oil; served with a shaving of lemon zest; or dressed with a vinegar-heavy vinaigrette. The sharpness is an effective contrast to their slightly mealy quality.

'Mangetout beans' for eating with ham or roast lamb

I was wary of the idea of eating the pods until I grew my own beans; young vegetables tempt in a way that full-sized specimens often don't. The recipe is only worth doing when you can get your hands on unblemished beans without the cotton-wool lining to their pods and no longer than a middle finger. If you can catch them at this point in their lives, then you can eat them whole, like mangetout. Serve warm, with thick pieces of bread or as a side dish for roast lamb or cold ham.

> *enough for 4*
> olive oil – 150ml
> a medium onion
> smoked bacon – 100g
> very young broad beans in their pods – 500g
> water – 400ml
> a bunch of fresh mint
> a lemon

Warm the olive oil in a large pan. Peel and finely chop the onion and add it to the oil. Cut the bacon into bite-sized chunks and stir it into the softening onion. The bacon fat should turn pale gold; the onion should soften without colour.

Put the broad bean pods into the pan and pour in the water. Bring to the boil, then turn down to a light simmer and leave for fifteen to twenty minutes, until the pods have lost their bright colour and are meltingly tender.

Roughly chop the fresh mint and stir it into the beans. Serve with a thick wedge of lemon to squeeze over, and torn hunks of flour-crusted bread to mop up some of the golden olive oil dressing.

A risotto of young beans and blue cheese

Green stuff – asparagus, nettles, peas, spinach and broad beans – adds life and vigour to the seemingly endless calm of a shallow plate of risotto. My first attempt found me convinced that I didn't need to skin the beans. In theory it works, but the skins interfere with the harmony of stock, rice and cheese and add an unwelcome chewiness. I am not sure you should ever need to chew a risotto.

enough for 4
shelled broad beans – 300g
butter – 50g
a small onion
arborio rice – 300g
a glass of white wine
hot stock – 1.5 litres
soft blue cheese, such as Gorgonzola or Cashel – 200g

Cook the broad beans in deep, lightly salted boiling water for four or five minutes, then drain and set aside. Unless the beans are very small, you may want to pop them from their skins. The choice is yours. Melt the butter in a heavy-based pan. Peel and finely chop the onion, then leave it to cook in the butter until it is soft but shows no sign of browning. Tip in the rice, stir briefly to coat in the butter, then pour in the wine.

Little by little add the hot stock, stirring pretty much continuously, adding more only when each ladleful of stock has been absorbed by the rice. Check the rice for tenderness as you go; it should be ready about twenty minutes after adding it to the onion, and should still have a bit of bite. Stir in the cooked beans and the cheese in pieces, check the seasoning and serve.

Green beans, cool white cheese and hot radishes

The tiniest of broad beans have an affinity with young, snow-white goat's cheeses. I like to use them in an early summer salad with Ticklemore, the cheese that Robin Congdon makes at his farm in Devon with milk from Sharpham Farm, the Buddhist retreat. Otherwise, I'll use whatever is suitably crumbly, milky and mild. It is a salad that seems to gain much from being eaten outside, under the shade of an umbrella, when there is much new, pale green growth in the garden.

For two of us I use 125g podded beans, an equal weight of cheese, ten radishes and three or four sprigs of parsley. I use the parsley leaves whole, adding them to the boiled and skinned beans, the cut radishes and the thinly sliced cheese with just a splash of olive oil, the mildest I have. The coolness of the cheese, the heat of the radishes and the buttery taste of the beans make a fresh, clean-tasting salad of utmost purity.

The Italians, and especially the Florentines, who were known as 'the bean eaters', have some noteworthy recipes for this mild bean. In the late 1980s I ate them lightly cooked and skinned in a rocket salad, then on the same trip, in a risotto with Gorgonzola. At home, I have also used the beans in risotto with goat's cheeses the texture of fudge and with the saltier blues such as Beenleigh and the majestic Stichelton.

Broad beans and the pig

Broad beans have a kinship with ham in all its forms. At its most basic, raw broad beans can be slit down the middle with a thumbnail and eaten in the same bite as a piece of thinly cut ham. The most interesting version of this I have eaten involved newly picked beans from a friend's garden, each the size of a jellybean, tucked inside slivers of dark, moist Joselito Gran Reserva ham from acorn-fed pigs. At a less rarefied level, streaky bacon and boiled broad beans tossed in the bacon fat is a supper to which I return time and again.

A lump of smoked ham, served hot with some of its thin cooking juices and a thick mash of the beans, is warming on a chilly summer evening. (It works even better in winter if you remembered to freeze a few beans in the summer.) Ends of fatty bacon, which you can often buy for a song from a deli, make a quick weekday meal when chopped and sautéed with lightly boiled broad beans and lots of flat parsley, its leaves thrown almost whole into the pan. The merest splash of dry sherry will turn it into something altogether more soulful.

Broad beans, herbs, bacon and its fat

enough for 2
shelled broad beans – 250g
spring onions – 6
a small bunch of dill
a small bunch of mint
white wine vinegar – 2 tablespoons
olive oil
smoked back bacon – 4 rashers

Cook the broad beans in a deep pan of lightly salted boiling water. They should be tender in four or five minutes. Cool them under running water, popping the bright green beans from their pale skins with your finger and thumb and dropping them into a bowl as you go. If the beans are really small and young, I sometimes leave the skins on.

Finely slice the spring onions and drop them into a mixing bowl. Chop enough dill to give you a couple of heaped tablespoons. Pull a loose handful of mint leaves from their stalks and add them to the onions with the dill and white wine vinegar. Crumble in a little salt and some coarse black pepper, then stir in enough olive oil to make a slushy dressing. I find 80–90ml is enough.

Lay the bacon in a non-stick frying pan with the merest drop of olive oil and let it fry till the fat is golden and verging on the crisp. Fold the skinned beans into the herb dressing and divide between two plates. Put a couple of rashers of bacon on each, tipping any hot fat in the pan over the beans.

The simplicity of broad beans and Spanish ham

There is a Spanish stall at the market. Each Saturday in midsummer I
wait patiently at the counter while the *jamon* is carved. I am unsure which
is more beautiful: the long, elegant leg on its steel stand or the fluid,
methodical way in which the carver slices the gossamer-thin morsels of meat
from the bone. I never take much, its price is breathtaking, but once home
I savour every mouthful, as much out of respect for my wallet as for the pig.
If I find young broad beans, or the ones in the garden are ready to pick, I
marry the two – a simple plate of densely flavoured, fat-besplodged ham the
colour of dried blood and fresh, bright-green beans. There is usually soup
on the table too, watercress or spinach or fresh pea, and some scraps of dry,
mild-tasting Manchego.

enough for 4 as a starter or as part of a light lunch
broad beans in their pods – 1kg
air-dried ham – 100g, very thinly sliced

for the dressing
sherry vinegar – a tablespoon
smooth Dijon mustard – half a teaspoon
olive oil (a fairly light one is best here) – 3 tablespoons
a handful of parsley leaves

Bring a pan of water to the boil. Pod the beans. Very lightly salt the water
and tip in the beans. Bring the water back to the boil, then turn down the
heat so that they boil merrily for three or four minutes or until they are
tender. The exact cooking time will depend on the size and age of your
beans but generally they take less time than you might expect. Drain them
and cool under running water.

Pop the beans from their skins, unless they are very young and the size
of a fingernail. This is a very pleasant way to spend ten minutes on a lazy
afternoon. Place the pieces of ham, which should be in snippets about twice
the size of a large postage stamp, on a serving plate.

Make the dressing by adding a small pinch of salt to the sherry vinegar
and letting it dissolve. Add half a teaspoon of mustard – no more – then
whisk in the olive oil with a fork. Chop the parsley leaves quite finely and
add them to the dressing. Lastly, a few grinds of pepper. Toss the beans
gently in the dressing and set aside for twenty minutes or so (they are fine
for several hours if it makes life easier).

Scatter the beans over the ham and eat.

Creamed beans with mint

Broad beans are gentle, soothing, calm (particularly so when they have been skinned), a vegetable without the vibrancy of spinach or even peas. Surely we don't always want vegetables to be full of fireworks? Rather than fight this mild character with an addition of spice or bright tastes, I go along with it, and often serve the beans as a side dish with cream and perhaps a stirring of parsley. A dish as soporific as it is beautiful. Some poached gammon would be nice here, as might a piece of lightly cooked white fish. Though I would be more than satisfied with some triangles of hot brown toast.

Should you happen to have any summer savory in the herb bed, this is your chance to use it.

enough for 4
shelled broad beans – 400g
double cream – 250ml
a knifepoint of ground nutmeg
a handful of parsley leaves, chopped
mint – the leaves from 3 or 4 sprigs, chopped

Boil the beans in deep, very lightly salted water. When they are tender, drain them and put them back into the pan. Pop them out of their skins, if you like. Pour in the cream, add a little salt, some black pepper and the nutmeg, perhaps, then fold in the chopped parsley and mint. I tend to keep it quite fine for this dish. If you are using savory, introduce it now. Bring the mixture to a quiet simmer, then spoon it alongside your ham, halibut or whatever.

A green hummus

Elderly broad beans are possibly not on everyone's shopping list but in late July, when their sugar has turned to starch and their skins are as thick as writing paper, I have still made a good meal of them. They make a fresh-tasting hummus that always surprises people with its green notes. A silk purse out of a sow's ear if ever there was one. There is another recipe for this in *The Kitchen Diaries*, but with dill. Good with bread, roast lamb, even alongside a piece of grilled fish. Like the popular chickpea recipe, somewhat addictive.

> *enough for 4*
> broad beans in their pods – 1.5kg
> olive oil – about 4 tablespoons
> the juice of a small lemon
> mint – the leaves from about 8 stems

Pod the broad beans and check for blemishes. Boil them in lightly salted water for six to nine minutes, depending on their size. The longer cooking time is because of the beans' age. Big brutes may take up to ten minutes. Drain and blitz in a food processor with the olive oil, lemon juice and mint leaves. I carry on blending, adding more oil if necessary, till I have a smooth pulp the consistency of raw cake mixture.

A broad bean frittata

This little pancake has a spring-like freshness with its filling of young, peeled broad beans and freckling of feathery dill. Curiously, it is not at all 'eggy'. In fact, a devout non-eater of eggs, I have been known to finish a whole one by myself. A trickle of yoghurt over its crust or a few slices of smoked salmon at its side are possibilities too.

I really think this is only worth making with the smallest of broad beans, and they really must be peeled.

enough for 2 as a light main course
young broad beans – shelled weight 200g
Parmesan – 50g
eggs – 3
dill – about 2 tablespoons
butter – a large knob

Bring a deep pan of water to the boil, drop in the broad beans and boil till tender. They should be ready after four or five minutes, depending on their size. Drain, cool slightly under running water then pop the beans out of their little skins. Chop them roughly and set aside.

Finely grate the Parmesan. Break the eggs into a small bowl and mix them lightly with a fork. Stir in the Parmesan and the chopped dill. Heat an overhead grill.

Melt the butter in a shallow pan, about 20cm in diameter. When it starts to froth, pour in the egg and cheese mixture. Add the peeled broad beans and let the frittata cook over a relatively low heat till the bottom has formed a golden crust. Lift the pan from the heat and slip it under the grill till the eggs have set and the top is lightly coloured.

Cut into wedges, like a cake.

Broccoli and the sprouting greens

And then, just as I feel the days of darkness and parsnips will never end, I spot the first spears of sprouting broccoli at the market. Early-season sightings are not something that usually excites me unless they are in my own garden. The blurring of the seasons put paid to that sentiment long ago. The first rhubarb, asparagus, even redcurrants barely get me to raise an eyebrow now (though catch-us-if-you-can gooseberries and damsons still set my heart pumping), but spotting the first home-grown sprouting at the end of a long winter feels as if someone is throwing you a life raft.

Broccoli, both the fat, cloud-like bunches we get all year (officially 'calabrese') and the longer, slimmer stems of 'sprouting' around in the earliest days of spring, are made up of masses of tight flower buds. Buds that, left unharvested, will open into simple, nectar-heavy, yellow flowers that are adored by bees. We pick them long before the buds burst, in order to catch the shoots at the most sweet and tender.

The members of the brassica family that form a head kindle greater respect than the leafier varieties such as kale and cabbage. The long-stemmed heads are so fine, so elegant, so beautiful on the plate that you wonder, briefly, why they aren't considered the most precious vegetables in the world. In our house, they are.

Tough in the garden or the field, where they will shrug off the hardest frosts, 'heading' greens need a tender touch in the kitchen. Although I should, as a nod to some sort of botanical correctness, include cauliflower here, it behaves very differently in the kitchen and so gets its own chapter.

Green, white or purple sprouting, with its long stems and shadowy heads, marks a turning point in the year in much the same way as spying the first pumpkin, only with a lighter heart. You know that spring and its pulse-quickening air is not far behind. You have crossed a line – a line that you can often smell and feel even before you can see it. Sprouting is the proof.

The first British-grown shoots of sprouting broccoli usually appear in the shops in late February and early March, though I have seen them earlier. They will be with us till May, by which time I will have had my fill and be keen to get to the asparagus and the first peas.

The broccoli family in the garden

You can grow both the plump everyday calabrese and the slimmer-stemmed sprouting broccoli from seed, sowing the latter in mid to late spring in drills 1cm deep and 30cm apart. Most find it easier to sow in pots or seed trays and then transplant when the plantlets are a finger or so high. Harvest in late winter and early spring by snapping off the shoots, leaving the large leaves in place, as these will protect the next batch of shoots.

I have yet to grow either from seed, preferring to buy them as young plants ready for the garden. Sometimes I pick up a tray at the farmers' market, other times I order them online.

A broccoli diary

January Order seeds.
April Realise I am never going to get round to sowing it, so order 'plug plants' online instead.
June I am concerned when a newspaper parcel of Red Spear sprouting broccoli and large, domed Marathon arrives with what I consider a worrying amount of yellowing leaves. 'Stress,' I mutter, and give them an hour or two's soak in a bucket of rainwater while I give the bed a final going over with the rake to remove any leaves and break up large clods.

The plants, with their neat plug of sticky soil around the roots, go into holes deep enough to reach just below the lowest of their leaves. I firm them in with a carefully placed foot – they hate to wobble around – spray them with liquid soap and place an organic 'brassica collar' around each stem to ward off the cabbage root fly that is so fond of laying its eggs where stem meets soil. They come in packets of thirty from gardening suppliers.

All this is done on a Saturday morning in pouring rain. I like the refreshing prickle of drizzle on my skin but there comes a point when your clothes becomes heavy with water, rain drips down your neck and the soil becomes too damp to step on without risk of compacting it. I stop when my socks feel wet. The plants look happier now they are trimmed of their weaker leaves and have their feet in good-hearted soil.
August After a few weeks of sulking, the sprouting has got a spurt on, the stems have straightened and the plants appear in a good state of health. Over the next few weeks I pay very little attention to them.

January A warm Christmas, followed by a freezing New Year. The garden is dark almost as soon as lunchtime soup is finished and the bread and cheese packed away. Creep out with a shining torch and the leaves and heads glisten in the frosty air, standing happily till we are ready to bring them in. Few vegetables, or plants of any sort, thrive so positively in minus temperatures. I can hardly wait to tuck them under a blanket of blisteringly hot cheese sauce.

Varieties

Calabrese
The ubiquitous, cloud-like heads of blueish green that are as easy to find as frozen peas. No supermarket, however small, is without its box of cling-wrapped, usually Spanish, supply of what we have come to know as 'broccoli'. The British crop, like plump, green clouds, is generally sown in spring and can be harvested from June to November.

Fiesta Horrid name for heavy heads of a reliable and vigorous variety.
Trixie Even worse name, like something you might call a toy poodle, for what is one of the only varieties to be resistant to the dreaded club root.
Belstar Handsome, blue-green domes with tight, small beads. Does well for organic growers and has an exceptionally fine flavour.

Purple sprouting
Bordeaux Summer and autumn cropping variety. Won't survive the cold. Sow in April.
Red Spear Cold, hardy, small, deep-purple spears of great tenderness and flavour. Will stand happily through the coldest nights. Sow in late summer for February-to-March picking.
Rudolph Pick early, from mid winter.

White sprouting
The white varieties are finer and (I find) more fragile in both garden and kitchen. They are less happy with serious cold than the purple forms and they tend to break up more easily in the pot. Their flavour is more delicate too. White Eye and White Star are currently the two that are easiest to find. Sow indoors during April and May.

Calabrese and purple sprouting in the kitchen

My early attempts to understand this family of top-notch vegetables failed on two counts. First I overcooked it, massively, and then, wastefully, failed to realise the delicious potential of its stalks. The overcooking was almost certainly due to not having seen the vegetable anywhere but in the supermarket. Once you see the stems and their tight heads growing, as they are in my vegetable patch as I write, it is easier to understand what you are dealing with: in this case exceptionally young, tender shoots, their leaves barely unfurled, that will require little cooking time.

Then, I cut them too short, as if it was all about the heads, discarding far too much of the toothsome stalk. Picked young enough, the stalks are the best bit – a mouthful of lightly crunchy, vivid-green vegetable that is immediately sweet and juicy. Anyone who eats at a good Chinese or Vietnamese restaurant soon understands the pleasure of the stalks, especially once they meet the holy trinity of ginger, garlic and soy.

Some shoots are deepest purple. We can cheerfully take no notice of the seed catalogues and cookery books that tell you purple sprouting broccoli always turns green when cooked. Many varieties will stay darkly purple unless you insist on cooking it to death.

My organic box company sends a plastic bag of purple sprouting, its flower heads tightly closed, its stems still moist from being recently cut. They once delivered exceptionally late in the day (I thought I had been forgotten), by which time the pork chops were almost on the plate. It turned out to be the point at which I finally understood the treasure I had before me. By leaving myself no time in which to cook them, I used just a shallow depth of water and, with the chops rapidly cooling on their plates, whipped the spears out before they were fully cooked. Brilliant purple and green, the stems *al dente* and still with some crunch, it turned out to be the best thing that could have happened.

That said, you can successfully slow-cook the sprouting version. Rather than steam, you bring it to tenderness (and beyond) with olive oil, lemon, a scattering of dried chillies, garlic and water, then dress it with more olive oil and chopped anchovies. Dust it with heroic quantities of Parmesan. Yes, it ends up the colour of a frog, but the flavour is extraordinary. The stems are sweeter and milder, the texture almost buttery. A relaxing change from the usual uptight *al dente* treatment.

The large, clustered heads of calabrese need breaking up into more manageable florets, where they will cook more quickly and evenly. Otherwise the outer florets will be overcooked by the time the heat has penetrated those hiding near the stalk. The stalks, though short and thick, are surprisingly tender and shouldn't be discarded.

Sprouting needs no such preparation. The whole, lightly trimmed stems can be dropped into boiling water, steamed, or pampered like asparagus with the tips slightly out of the water, so that the buds steam whilst the stems boil. Whichever way you go, the stems are ready when a knifepoint inserted into their thickest part goes in without pressure.

I must put in a word for the leaves. I never discard them. Slender, quietly flavoured, elegantly fringed, they cook in seconds. It would break my heart to see them sent to the compost.

Only the very thickest stalks will prove unpleasantly tough. The ideal seems to be roughly the thickness of an asparagus spear. I leave the gently curling leaves on. The fragile bracts can occasionally hold caterpillars that you really won't want to eat. Wash them tenderly in a bowl of cool water, as if you were rinsing dirt from a child's hand. Try not to break them up. Once a floret has broken away from its stem, it tends to get lost in the cooking water.

I rarely boil the stems now, preferring to let them steam in a large shallow pan in a finger's depth of water. Get the water boiling first. Lay the stems in a single layer, with most of the stalks and heads lying proud of the water; covered with a lid they will steam rather than boil. Rolling around in deep boiling water like washing in the machine, the florets are easily damaged. The difference between a serving of sprouting that has been treated with respect and one that arrives on the plate in a broken heap is astonishing.

For the tubbier calabrese, I have had much success with one of those flat 'waterlily'-style steamers that sit in a shallow pan. Wooden Chinese steamers are efficient too.

If I am cooking them for lunch, a matter of just three or four minutes in the steamer, I lower the heads into a bowl and scatter them with a mixture of toasted pine kernels, dark, smoky raisins and a trickle of olive oil. On this occasion, trickle means exactly what it says.

Broccoli seems to go cold quicker than any other vegetable (this could, of course, be my imagination, but it explains why cauliflower is usually served under a duvet of blistering cheese sauce). A hot plate is more important than usual, and will keep your calabrese warm for a little longer.

Seasoning the broccoli family

Butter A simple way to start and where, I guess, many would be tempted to leave it.

Hollandaise There is no other sauce that can do for this vegetable what a jug of hollandaise can.

Anchovies Chop them finely, let them soften in a little butter over a moderate heat, then pour them over freshly steamed spears. A squeeze of lemon will add much excitement.

Mustard Either in a dressing with olive oil and lemon juice, stirred into a runny hollandaise-type sauce or as a seasoning for cheese sauce to cover your lightly cooked heads.

Ginger Shredded and frizzled and tipped over the top with browned garlic.

Soy The salty notes of soy work particularly well with calabrese. Even a few drops of dark soy added at the table will make it sing.

And...

* There is much confusion over the term broccoli. Many – including most supermarkets – use it to refer to the plump, short-stemmed heads of green calabrese. Others use it purely for purple sprouting. Officially, it is used as a catch-all term for members of the family that includes stubby calabrese and the longer shoots of purple and white sprouting.

* Calabrese can mean different things in different parts of the country. When I lived in Cornwall, we used it to refer to cauliflower.

* Raw-food lovers often find this family hard-going, but the smaller shoots eat well enough if you leave them in a dressing of oil, lemon and balsamic vinegar for twenty minutes before adding them to your bowl of leaves.

* Served as an accompaniment, broccoli introduces a flash of brilliant green to our supper, and isn't fussy about what it shares a plate with. That said, it seems particularly suited to any form of cured pork. It is in hog heaven with boiled gammon, speck or those plate-sized bacon steaks. Bring meat and vegetable together with some parsley sauce and you have one of the great culinary threesomes of all time.

* The rather old-fashioned habit of surrounding cauliflower cheese with triangles of toast, very *à la mode* in 1950, is an idea worth updating with broccoli and cheese sauce. I use a seedy loaf, one of those whose crust is speckled with pumpkin and sesame seeds, toasted and tucked on the side. It makes a perfectly honourable main course.

* Slow-cooked sprouting, baked with garlic, lemon juice and Parmesan, is something to serve with a pork chop, but it is also excellent as a dinner in its own right. I spoon the deliciously disintegrating heads and their cooking juices over brown rice or cracked wheat for a cheap and homely supper.

Sprouting and blood oranges on a frosty March day

The market: stumpy carrots, the prickle of frost, dark greens, the scent of wet soil. Here and there amongst the trestle tables are shallow baskets: Russian kale, tips of cavolo nero with their infant leaves, broccoli heads the size of a mushroom and sprigs of purple and white sprouting so small you can hold ten in the palm of your hand.

Each sprig of vegetable is so precious, so diminutive, as timid as a chanterelle. I pick them up with finger and thumb, which seems the way they must have been picked from their stalks. These are shoots plucked from the stem after the growing heart of the plant has been removed. No smothering of cheese sauce, just a three-minute trip in the steamer and a classic hollandaise to dip them in, let down with a dash of cream and a grating of zest from a blood orange.

> *enough for 3*
> purple sprouting – 4 large handfuls, steamed
> egg yolks – 3
> melted butter – 200g
> lemon juice
> the finely grated zest of a blood orange
> double cream or crème fraîche – 3 tablespoons

Put a pan of water on to boil and find a glass or heatproof china bowl that will fit neatly into it without actually touching the water. Drop the yolks, large, deep orange ones if you have them, into the bowl and then a splash of water. Whisk, pouring in almost all the melted butter, slowly at first as if you were making mayonnaise, then as the sauce thickens up, a little faster. The water in the pan should be simmering rather than boiling and if you stop whisking your sauce will fail (though I have occasionally brought it back to life with a splash of simmering water from the pan).

Once it is thick and creamy, squeeze in a little lemon juice and stir in a good pinch of salt. No pepper. The sauce can be used as it is.

One late-spring day last year, I got this far, then decided to add the finely grated zest of a blood orange and three tablespoons of thick double cream, whisked in at the end. The idea of bright green vegetables and vivid blood oranges seemed right for a day that saw the garden freckled white with frost and the sky clear and pale grey. I spooned thick lines of the orange hollandaise over the tiny stems of steamed sprouting and ate it with rounds of grilled ciabatta.

A soup of broccoli and bacon

A good use for the older, tougher specimens. I have made this with those plastic-entombed bunches from the late-night corner shop and you would never have known it.

> *enough for 6*
> a medium onion
> butter – 30g
> smoked streaky bacon – 200g
> potatoes – 3 smallish
> chicken or ham stock – 1.5 litres
> broccoli, purple sprouting or other dark calabrese – 300g
> milk – 150ml

Peel the onion, chop it roughly and soften it in the butter in a deep pan. I never let it colour, preferring to keep it pale and translucent. Stir in half the bacon, snipped into short lengths (keep six short pieces for later), then the potatoes, scrubbed and cut into small pieces. Let the ingredients marry with as little colour as possible, then pour in the stock and bring to the boil, adding salt and pepper as you go. Turn the heat down so that the mixture simmers gently for fifteen to twenty minutes or so, till the potatoes will collapse against slight pressure from the back of a spoon.

Introduce the greens, trimmed of any exceptionally rough stalks, and simmer for ten minutes. The greens should still live up to their name. Pour in the milk, simmer briefly, then process the mixture in a blender till smooth, checking the seasoning as you do so. Grill the remaining bacon till crisp, then serve the soup in warm bowls, each with a piece of crisp bacon on its surface.

Pasta with sprouting and cream

Pasta sends me to sleep. Actually, it always has done, it's just that for years I failed to make the connection between my post-prandial tiredness and what had been on my plate. I now take my dough of flour, eggs and water in much smaller quantities, using it as the supporting actor rather than the lead. The result is a fresher, less heavy plate, yet somehow just as comforting. In many cases the pasta is padded out with vegetables: spinach, mushrooms, tomatoes, aubergines, peas, black cabbage or broccoli.

Members of the broccoli family work rather well with pasta, the folds and hollows of the cooked dough neatly holding on to crumbs of green vegetable. In what follows, we get a lot of pleasure for very little work: a plateful of soothing carbs with a creamy, cheesy sauce and masses of lightly cooked green vegetables. In short, a cheap, quick weekday supper.

enough for 2
purple sprouting broccoli or other young greens – 250g
orecchiette – 250g
butter – 30g
garlic – 2 cloves, thinly sliced
anchovy fillets – 4, rinsed and chopped
crème fraîche – 250g
Gorgonzola cheese – 170g, crumbled

Put two deep pans of water on to boil. Trim the purple sprouting, keeping the leaves intact and discarding any dry ends or tough stalks. Generously salt the water in one of the pans and drop in the pasta.

Lightly salt the water in the other pan and add the purple sprouting. As soon as it is tender, a matter of three or four minutes, drain it and wipe out the pan, returning the pan to the heat with the butter, garlic and anchovies. Let the garlic and anchovies cook slowly for a minute or two – the anchovies will almost dissolve – then spoon in the crème fraîche and crumbled cheese and bring to the boil, stirring and immediately turning it down to a slow bubble. Chop the purple sprouting roughly, then add it to the sauce and season with black pepper.

Drain the pasta lightly (a few tablespoons of the cooking water will help thin the sauce to the right consistency) and tip it into the broccoli sauce.

A stir-fry of broccoli and lamb

Broccoli doesn't stir-fry well from raw. The beaded crown – the tight flower buds – tends to burn before the stem even approaches tenderness. Heads that have been briefly blanched in boiling water will, however, stir-fry deliciously, soaking up the ginger and soy or whatever other seasoning you might throw at them. In the last year or two I have taken to adding them to stir-fries of minced lamb or pork, letting the meat thoroughly caramelise in the thin pan before adding the greens.

It's a very quick, bright-tasting supper, invigorating and toothsome. But you do need to be brave with the meat, letting it glisten and almost crisp before you add the rest of the ingredients.

enough for 2
broccoli – a large handful of florets
spring onions – 3
garlic – 3 plump cloves
hot red chillies – 2
groundnut oil – 3 tablespoons
minced lamb – 300g
a lime
nam pla (Thai fish sauce) – 1 tablespoon
sugar – a teaspoon
coriander leaves – a small handful

Blanch the florets of broccoli in boiling water for one minute. Drain and set aside. Chop the spring onions, removing the darkest green leaves as you go. Peel the garlic and chop it finely, then seed and chop the chillies. Get the oil really hot in a shallow pan or wok, then cook the onions, garlic and chillies till soft but not coloured, moving them quickly round the pan as you go. It will appear there is too much oil, but bear with me.

Add the minced lamb and let it colour appetisingly. It should go a rich golden colour. Add the drained broccoli. In a small bowl, mix the juice of the lime with the nam pla and sugar. Tip into the hot pan and leave to sizzle briefly, scraping at the gooey stickings on the bottom of the pan and stirring them in as you go. Check the seasoning – you may need a little salt – and stir in the coriander.

Brussels sprouts

This garden is at its most magical when deep in snow. The branches of the fig tree stretch out across the vegetable patch like witches' fingers. A Winter Nellis pear hangs from the little tree by the kitchen door, frozen on its stem. The purple sprouting, red cabbage, artichokes and kale lie under a thick snowflake mantle.

February 2 2009. I wake to a deep, eerie silence, the vegetables sleeping under layers of heavy snowfall, my yew hedges and climbing roses turned into a scene from Narnia. It's the rosehips that make my heart melt, plump amber and scarlet baubles still visible beneath the powdery snow. That and the fox tracks leading from the compost heap, whose carpet covering he often curls up on, to the kitchen door. A walk of hope if ever there was one.

Brussels sprouts are the only vegetable I cannot eat unless the weather is cold. No frost, no sprouts. I am not alone. The Brussels sprout, a cabbage leaf in bud, has never been part of the cooking of the Mediterranean or Asia, and barely left Belgium and northern France before the late nineteenth century. Frost makes the sprout. It takes the bitterness out and gives us an appetite for strong flavours. Lightly cooked, so its colour is bright and there is still crispness at its heart, the Brussels has much going for it. Eaten at the wrong time of year, cooked too long or served with too much else on the plate, the sprout is hard going. At least it was for me, and for many years, too.

A sprout in the garden

The joy of growing from seed is that you can nurture old varieties of Brussels sprout, such as Bedford Fillbasket or Evesham Special from the 1920s. Both conjure up the thought of sepia photographs of farm labourers and wicker hampers laden ready for market. The pleasure of picking up a net bag of ready-prepared sprouts from the supermarket is that you don't have to grow them, let alone consider the variety.

Somewhere in between these two extremes of getting vegetables into your kitchen lies the plug plant. These ready-grown young plantlets, usually 8–10cm high, provide the possibility of growing your own for those disinclined or unable to plant seed or who think of the supermarket as the devil's own child.

Brussels sprouts are easy to grow from seed. You need light potting compost and module trays. Sow in April. They benefit from a rich soil, but too much nitrogen will make them bushy rather than productive. Transfer the plants to prepared beds when they have four true leaves above their seedling leaves. You will need a good 50cm between them and they will take up a lot of your growing space all summer and autumn. A stick up each one is essential. It will support the stems so the plant can concentrate on being productive.

A Brussels diary

Mid August A bundle of small plants the length of a pencil arrives in the post. Previously I have bought them from the farmers' market, where they often have boxes of young plants in June and July, but I wanted to be specific about the variety, so mail order works better for me. So no Bedford Fillbasket, but a modern variety called Maximus, described by the National Vegetable Society as 'superbly flavoured, smooth, tight buttons that hold well on the plant for picking from late September to Christmas'. I plant them early in the evening when the day has cooled and water them in well.
August 25 I put in cane sticks to support the stems, tying them loosely with string. Even in a wet summer, they appear to need a good soaking at least twice a week. Keeping the pigeons away is an endless task. Tired of running up the garden waving a tea towel at them, I place a sheet of plastic net over the plants (and spend the remainder of the summer detaching snails and leaves from its clutches).
October 1 The plants are now a good eighteen inches high, jade green and dusky mauve. As beautiful a vegetable as you could ever imagine. I worry that their stems are not as thick as I would wish.
December I have rather ignored all the brassicas for the last few weeks. They are at the stage where they must get on with things unattended.

A slightly disappointing number of actual sprouts this year, but the 'tops' are glorious, especially those that I pick from the snow after Christmas. For all the space they take up, a row of Brussels is a beautiful sight in a garden or allotment. Standing blue and green against the winter's sky, like something from a fairy story, they are worth every inch of space they consume.

Varieties

As vegetables go, I feel that sprouts show less of a difference between varieties than most. We don't exactly get a choice at the greengrocer's or the supermarket, but my own pick for the garden was Maximus. I was guided purely by what I had been told about their flavour, but yield is a consideration for many, as is the stems' ability to stand in the vegetable patch through winter wind and frost. Fortress comes highly recommended. Incidentally, the young stems are crisp and will snap if handled unsympathetically.

Maximus I have done well with this autumn variety, even if I have found their colour a little pale in the pot. If I am going to eat sprouts, then they must be zinging with colour.
Evesham Special A hardy one this, and a heavy cropper too. Will over-winter in the snow.
Bedford Fillbasket Large sprouts of a very old variety, named after the country's commercial growing centre.
Bosworth A popular choice for many allotment holders, known for its ability to stand well throughout the coldest winter.
Red Rubine A red variety, small and mildly flavoured. I have grown these with mixed success, but their purple veins do look very beautiful on a frosty morning.
Revenge Very hardy, though the name might be more appropriate for a Jerusalem artichoke. Mid to late winter.

A sprout in the kitchen

There are two forms of interest here: the button-like sprouts and the bushy heads from the top of the stalk.

If you haven't bought your sprouts in a net from the supermarket or a paper bag from the greengrocer's, then pull them from the stalk, working from the bottom up. There may be a few tatty outer leaves that need trimming away. I suggest you don't cut a cross in the bottom like my Granny did. It makes for a soggy sprout. If you worry about the outer leaves overcooking, cut each sprout clean in half. They will cook in a minute or two that way. Small sprouts are prized for their mild flavour.

Sprouts like to dance around in lots of rapidly boiling water with a very little salt. Too much salt will make them mushy, as will any attempt to keep them waiting. Serve them up immediately they are tender.

The pong of sprouts – fetid, stale, institutional – takes on a considerably more welcome note if there is a turkey roasting nearby. The two are virtually inseparable after the winter solstice on December 21. After that, the smell of the cabbage's particularly pungent little brother needs something else if your kitchen isn't to suffer a whiff of sulphur. Cheese will do the job, either blue or hard and savoury, such as Parmesan or Spenwood; bacon, especially the tarry smoked versions; or the old-as-time smell of soy, ginger and anise, redolent of Chinese cooking.

There is no classic sprout recipe to match asparagus hollandaise, pommes dauphinoise, choucroute garnie or stuffed courgette flowers. The *petit chou* has never been a star and we do the best we can to make it palatable. I recommend nut or seed oils as a cooking medium, walnut oil for dressing, warm butter as a simple sauce, and bacon fat to refry them the next day. Olive oil seems awkward in their presence. A pan of Brussels sprouts, trimmed and halved and tossed in duck fat, has a mellowness to it unachievable with any other fat.

I'm not sure anything will come from slow cooking these little buttons. A quick flash in a pan with snippets of pancetta, smoked streaky bacon or shredded salami is a sound idea, as is a squeeze of orange juice in a dish of briefly boiled sprouts with a little butter and crushed juniper berry. Chestnuts tossed amongst this vegetable suffer from the Marmite effect. One either loves or hates it.

I eat the Brussels sprout as a main dish under a blanket of cheese sauce. On a cold night in February, after a walk round the garden lighting candle lanterns in the snow as we went, we wolfed down a supper of sprouts with a sauce made from blue cheese from Randolph Hodgson and Joe Schneider's Stichelton Dairy. Robust, slightly salty, a little too rich: just the food for the coldest day of the year.

I wouldn't want to curry them (or be downwind of anyone who had), or throw them into the stockpot, where they risk adding a cabbagy note.

But they can make a surprisingly delicate soup, even an exciting one if you add a little Roquefort or crisp bacon. It's the sort of soup I want to eat when my socks have ruckled down my Wellingtons after a long, slushy walk.
I probably don't need to mention that they make a stirring bubble and squeak, but will in case you find yourself staring uninspired at a bowl of cold cooked sprouts on a Monday.

On a more original note, they are a revelation served raw. Try them with a grain mustard dressing, lemon zest and walnut oil. They work if shredded finely (when they curiously resemble crepe paper), and like a good half hour's soaking in their dressing. Something with crème fraîche, soured cream or thick yoghurt would be sublime.

The heads of the stalks, sold as 'sprout tops', come as loose rosettes of leaves, often with immature 'sproutlets' attached. Treat them as you would cabbage, but with an even shorter cooking time.

To rid the kitchen of the scent of sprouts, try a candle or, better still, my trick of lighting a strip of *papier d'arménie*, the ancient French booklets of scented paper whose pages you tear out, fold like origami, then light with a match. Their heady smell of incense and old bookshops works on anything.

Seasoning your sprouts

All of the flavours that flatter other members of the brassica family apply to the sprout. Butter, bacon, cream, juniper, caraway, apple, lemon, pork all work their magic and we should add chestnuts and almonds (flaked, toasted and scattered over your buttered sprouts), too.

And...

* I do think sprouts at Christmas are non-negotiable. The family, all seventeen of them, expects them, and whether they love the flatulence-producing little things or feel distinctly non-committal, they will be secretly disappointed if they don't get them. And we are not here to do that.
* If you turn a sprout top over, you will find several immature sprouts hiding under the open rosette of leaves. A treat.
* Sprouts, boiled ham and parsley sauce. A forkful of calm and good taste if ever there was one.

A rich dish of sprouts and cheese
for a very cold night

Any blue cheese will melt into the sauce for these sprouts, but I have been using a lot of Stichelton recently, a relatively new, gratifyingly buttery cheese made from unpasteurised milk. A main course with rice or plainly cooked pasta, and a particularly satisfying side dish for boiled gammon.

enough for 4 as an accompaniment
Brussels sprouts – 750g
a little butter
Stichelton or other blue cheese – 180g
grain mustard – a tablespoon
cream – 400ml
milk – 100ml
finely grated Parmesan – a handful

Bring a large pot of water to the boil. Remove any tatty leaves from the Brussels sprouts and cut each sprout in half. When the water is boiling furiously, lightly salt it, then lower in the sprouts. Leave them to come back to the boil, then let them boil for three minutes. Drain thoroughly and put them in a lightly buttered shallow dish.

Crumble the cheese over the sprouts. Put the mustard in a bowl and stir in the cream and milk and a grinding of black pepper. Pour the seasoned cream over the sprouts and cheese, then scatter over the grated Parmesan. Bake at 180°C/Gas 4, till the crust is lightly coloured and the cream is bubbling.

Brussels with bacon and juniper

I often serve this as a main course, but it is in its element as a side dish. Its bright green and smoky-bacon notes would be interesting with grilled mackerel, or perhaps with thinly sliced cold cuts such as roast pork or beef. This is essentially a cheap dish, robust and earthy, to which you could add caraway seeds if juniper isn't your thing, or shreds of fat-speckled salami in place of the bacon, or a few croûtons to make it more substantial.

enough for 4 as a side dish
Brussels sprouts – 400g
smoked bacon – 250g, the fattier the better
juniper berries – 20

Put a pan of water on to boil in which to cook the sprouts. Remove any tatty outer leaves from the sprouts, then drop them into the boiling water. Bring back to the boil and simmer for three or four minutes, till they are bright and crisp. Drain in a colander.

Fry the bacon in a non-stick pan till crisp and golden. Meanwhile, slice the sprouts in half. Once the bacon is ready, remove and drain on kitchen paper. Add the sprouts to the pan – they will pick up all the crusty bits left in the pan by the bacon.

Crush the juniper berries with the flat of a knife blade or a pestle – you only need flatten them. Add them to the sprouts, along with a light grinding of salt and some black pepper.

Meanwhile, cut the bacon into pieces no smaller than a postage stamp. When the sprouts are starting to soften but are still bright in colour, return the bacon to the pan for a few minutes. Serve sizzling hot.

A salad of sprouts, bacon and pecans

Raw cabbage, especially the tight, white variety, would be good here if the idea of raw sprouts doesn't grab you.

enough for 2 as a light lunch dish

for the salad
smoked streaky bacon – 5 rashers
Brussels sprouts – 200g
a large carrot
spring onions – 2
shelled pecan nuts – 2 tablespoons

for the dressing
natural yoghurt – 200g
groundnut oil – 2 tablespoons
walnut oil – a tablespoon
parsley – a small bunch

Grill the bacon till lightly crisp. Drain on kitchen paper, then cut into wide strips. Trim the sprouts and slice them very thinly. Scrub the carrot and peel it into long shavings with a vegetable peeler. Finely slice the spring onions. Toast the pecan nuts in a dry, non-stick pan for a couple of minutes till warm and fragrant.

Put the yoghurt into a bowl, beat in the oils with a small whisk or fork and season with salt and black pepper. Chop the parsley leaves, discarding the stalks, and stir in. Toss the sprouts, carrot, spring onions, bacon, pecans and dressing together. Check the seasoning and serve.

Sprouts, sprout tops, lentils and chicory

enough for 2
Puy or similar small lentils – 125g
red chicory – 2 long ears
sprout tops – 2 heads
small Brussels sprouts – a handful

for the dressing
sherry vinegar – 2 tablespoons
walnut oil – 2 tablespoons
sunflower or groundnut oil – 2 tablespoons
sugar – a pinch
Dijon mustard – 2 teaspoons

Rinse the lentils and put them on to boil. They should be ready in fifteen
to twenty-five minutes, depending on their age. Drain them in a colander.

While they are cooking, make the dressing. Dissolve a tiny pinch of salt
in the vinegar, then beat in the oils, sugar and mustard. As soon as the lentils
are drained, toss them in the dressing.

Slice the chicory into thin rounds. Shred the sprout tops (I like to make
them about the width of pappardelle), then blanch them in lightly salted
boiling water. Remove after a few seconds and flash under cold running
water. Do the same with the sprouts, blanching them for a little longer.

Toss the greens, chicory and lentils together.

Some good things to add

* Cubes of feta cheese.
* Crumbled blue cheese, such as Roquefort or Cashel Blue.
* Paper-thin slices of coppa, speck or salami.
* Chunks of fried apple (toss cubes of peeled apple in hot butter till golden).
* Slices of raw pear.
* Sprouted mung beans.
* Slices of hot butcher's sausage or black pudding.
* Rashers of crisp bacon (of course, but I can never resist them with anything
  from the cabbage family).

Sprout tops with sesame seeds and oyster sauce

Sprouts tops share a luxury of growth and strong flavour with many of the Asian greens. One cold day in November I married them to an impromptu sauce of essentially Chinese ingredients. It worked. The tricky bit was working out what, in future, they needed to share a plate with. A slice of gammon steak; a piece of lamb's liver; a fillet of mackerel, its skin crisped on the grill; a pile of sticky rice with some finely sliced wind-dried sausages; a grilled mushroom the size of a saucer. All will work. Eminently.

enough for 4 as a side dish
garlic – 2 cloves
ginger – a 60g knob
groundnut oil – 2 tablespoons
oyster sauce – 3 tablespoons
rice wine – 3 tablespoons
soy sauce – 1 tablespoon
sugar – a pinch
sprout tops – a large handful
golden sesame seeds – 1 teaspoon

Peel the garlic, then slice it very thinly; I try to get it as thin as paper. Peel the ginger and slice thinly, then cut each slice into fine matchsticks. Warm the oil in a small pan, stir in the garlic and ginger and leave to soften for a couple of minutes. They should colour lightly.

Stir in the oyster sauce, rice wine, soy sauce and the pinch of sugar. Make it a big one. Turn the heat low, so that the mixture bubbles only very gently for about five minutes.

Wash the sprout tops thoroughly, then put into a deep pan, the water still clinging to their leaves. Cover tightly with a lid and leave to steam for two or three minutes, till bright and wilted. Toast the sesame seeds in a non-stick pan till they smell warm and nutty.

Drain any liquid from the pan of sprouts tops, then pour in the sauce. Toss the greens around gently till they are glossy, scatter with the toasted sesame seeds and serve immediately. This is one of those dishes that needs to be served as hot as you can.

Mashed Brussels with Parmesan and cream

One of the gifts of the *nouvelle cuisine* movement was the puréed vegetable. At its worst, a sad puddle of unidentifiable beige gunk; at its most successful a moreish pool of intensely flavoured, silk-textured essence. Sprouts, which marry so happily with cream, tend to look like baby food when given this treatment, so I keep them coarsely chopped instead of whizzed to a pulp. I am exceptionally fond of this little side dish.

enough for 4
Brussels sprouts – 600g
a little grated nutmeg
double cream – 250ml
Parmesan – 100g, grated

Set the oven at 160°C/Gas 3. Remove any tatty leaves from the sprouts. Cook the sprouts in rapidly boiling unsalted water for four minutes. Drain, then tip them into a food processor, along with some salt and pepper. Blitz briefly, till no more than roughly chopped, then season with a very small pinch of nutmeg. Stir in the cream and most of the cheese. Scoop into a baking dish. Scatter with the reserved Parmesan and bake for twenty-five minutes or so, until golden.

Cabbage

The dead of winter, all is silent, the world hushed by a thick covering of snow. The point in the year when strident flavours are needed: game birds, smoked bacon and dank mushrooms that have waited patiently in the fridge. It is the time for blood sausage, crisp white goose fat, red wine stews, pudding. It is now I reach for the winter spices: cinnamon, cloves, ginger, cardamom – and juniper, the dusky black berries with notes as clean and bright as a gin and tonic.

The cabbage family is suddenly allowed back into the kitchen. Each dark-green leaf somehow seems as if it will fend off our winter ills. Elephant ears of crinkled green, sparkling with dew; tight buds of young sprouts; black plumes of cavolo nero like the feathers on a funeral horse, and the dense, ice-crisp flesh of red cabbage. Strong flavours indeed.

The brassica family is large. I think of it in two quite separate forms: those we eat as leaves – the cabbages, kales and sprouts – and those we grow for their flowering heads, like broccoli, cauliflower and white and purple sprouting. The most revered is the heading side of the family, but I have much respect for the leafier greens too, and admire the quiet grace of their jade, red and dusk-blue leaves. Seen in the field under a flint-coloured sky, they are as beautiful as any rose, as complex and mysterious as any peony.

I escaped cabbage till I was in my late teens, when it came, in gently sulphurous wafts, up the stairs of my college digs. A Saturday stew pressure-cooked to within an inch of its life. Pale cabbage, mild and almost timid, cabbage without the strength to offend. It sat in shallow pools of broth with lamb's vertebrae and thick carrots, and white potatoes full of steam.

Later, a winter spent in Cornwall, sitting round pub tables for want of work, formed an introduction, a wake-up call as it turned out, to vegetables other than courgettes and peas. We bought from trestles at the farm gate, posting our money in an honesty box and taking away turnips, swedes and cabbages. In January there were sprouts, and parsnips for mashing with butter and pepper. My sister-in-law taught me to cook a cabbage. A little water in the bottom of the pan, the leaves left large and dipped into the merrily boiling water only until their colours shone and their stalks became translucent. Seconds, not minutes.

Cabbages, round heads, pointed, red leaved and green, smooth or blistered, tight or loose-leaf, are there for us when all the other leaves are out of season or come with an unfashionable seasoning of air miles.

The first primitive cabbages were bitter, their leaves loose and few. The mildness of flavour and the tight heads have come with domestication. In Gerard's 1633 *Herbal*, cabbages with 'leaves wrapped together into a round head or globe' are mentioned, but it appears they were still unusual. Having gained and lost varieties through the centuries that followed, we now have a choice between the soft-leaved spring greens, pointed summer varieties, Christmas drumheads such as the crinkly Savoys, and the hard white types that store so well through the winter. Anyone with an organic box delivery will see the styles of cabbage change as the year progresses, from soft, loosely packed heads of silky leaves in spring to the darker, coarser leaves of winter. They all have their merits.

A cabbage in the garden

Few sights in the garden are as beautiful as that of members of the cabbage family on a winter's morning, the frilled edges of their leaves encrusted with frost. Deep sea greens and misty blues, the January Kings fringed with madder rose, add a sombre, curiously Venetian note to a garden whose only other colour comes from the occasional rosehip.

I plant young seedlings rather than growing my drumheads and loose-leafs from seed, partly for want of space. They arrive, in neat bundles and trays, from a farm on Cornwall's Roseland Peninsula, which will also supply bunches of Paperwhites at Christmas. The big-name mail-order companies can send out plantlets too, and this is often the most practical way for those of us without greenhouses or much space for germinating seeds.

Those with a little room outdoors can sow their winter cabbage seeds in March and April and spring greens in July and August. There are well-known seeds, such as January King and Primo, but specialist seedsmen's lists, such as those of Thomas Etty, tempt with less obvious varieties: Mr Ellam's Early Dwarf, noted for its failure to bolt; Filderkraut for spring sowing; or Christmas Drumhead, whose modest size makes it suitable for small gardens. Scatter your seeds about a finger's width apart in fine compost in shallow seed trays. Cover with a thin layer of compost, water well and keep the compost moist. They should be up in a fortnight or so.

Winter cabbage seedlings will need to go out into the garden in July; spring cabbage in September and October. I put mine in about 30–40cm apart, giving them room to heart up but also giving myself the space to weed around them. There is nothing quite so irritating as snapping the brittle stem of a healthy plant before its prime. They will tolerate a stony soil.

Little brassica collars that sit around the base of the stem are available from garden centres, and prevent the cabbage root fly laying its eggs. I regularly see allotments where cabbages stand firm and tall all winter, keeping families in greens till late spring. Mine grow shorter than most, I know not why, but often heart up better than I deserve. A net over them in late summer is not too much of an eyesore, especially if it is dark green, and will keep off the worst of the cabbage white butterfly.

A dozen cabbage plants will keep most families going throughout the major part of the winter. And that is probably what most of us end up with after the pigeons have had their fill. Pick them when their hearts are firm and before the outer leaves get too ragged.

Varieties

Choosing carefully, you could keep yourself in cabbage all year – from the soft-leaved summer varieties through to the strident flavours and thicker leaves of the winter ones. I tend not to plant any that will be ready for picking in summer, when my beds are too full of beans and squashes, and a brassica would strike too strong a note.

Spring Greens (to sow in July and August)
Duncan A small, pointed variety.
Wheeler's Imperial Mr Wheeler's compact variety has been an allotment favourite since 1840. Dark green outer leaves and thick veining.
Offenham Flower of Spring A delicate flavour from medium-sized leaves.

Summer Cabbage (to sow in February and March)
Hispi Tight, pointed, pale green heads with a gentle flavour. A supermarket favourite because of its neat size.
Durham Reliable, popular variety with small heads that come to a point.

Winter Cabbage (to sow from March to July for harvesting from December to February) Allow thirty weeks from sowing to maturity.
Christmas Drumhead An old-fashioned variety of small, tight heads and frilly open leaves. Popular since the 1920s.
January King Large-leaved, deeply veined and often tinged with pink. Happy to stand in the freezing cold in the garden.
Protovoy Heavily blistered leaves that hold melted butter like a crumpet, dark-green outer leaves protect a paler heart; softer than January King.

A cabbage in the kitchen

From September to April, my week isn't complete without some form of *chou* on my plate. They come into the kitchen with the new school term, Michaelmas daisies and pumpkins, and go out when I dig out my short-sleeved shirts. During that time, they will appear briefly steamed and buttered; tossed with ginger, oyster sauce and soy; wrapped around sausage stuffing; and shredded in knife-sharp salads with winter roots and yoghurt.

In summer I occasionally turn to their bright emerald leaves – so much softer and smoother in the summer varieties – to accompany a piece of warm poached salmon (though I would rather have peas).

The leaves keep better as a whole head than they do once separated. Wrap the entire head in damp newspaper and store in the lower part of the fridge or in a plastic bag somewhere really cold. It will be fine for several days.

A stalk has to be really tough before I can be persuaded to remove it. I love its juicy crunch and rarely follow written instructions to discard it. The contrast of soft leaves and crisp stalk is part of the vegetable's appeal. Generally, the leaves behave better on the plate if cut up a little. I keep them as large as I sensibly can, though will sometimes make them more acceptable to polite eaters by rolling several leaves together tightly, then shredding them finely with a heavy cook's knife. The more demure of my friends can then twiddle them round their fork like fettuccine.

Seasoning your cabbage

I sometimes don't season my greens at all, taking them from their steam and squeezing a lemon over them instead. The juice brings all their sweetness to the fore.

Cream Has a calming effect on the more strident flavours, working especially well with nutmeg.

Juniper The vegetable's most appropriate seasoning, the bitter, gin-flavoured spice teasing out all the leaves' sweetness. A must with red cabbage.

Caraway A very Germanic tone and one that is too often neglected here; the warm, musty notes lend an ancient, almost medieval character to the white variety. Toast the seeds first. Your kitchen will smell like a Berlin baker's.

Ginger Use freshly grated.

Gin Steam the shredded leaves, covered in foil, in a roasting tin with a little butter, water, crushed juniper berries, shredded dill and a shake of the gin bottle.

Mushrooms Use as a stuffing, or as partners in a stir-fry.

Soy Dark soy, added late to a stir-fry, lends a mellow saltiness to any brassica. Even better with broccoli than with cabbage.

Vinegar White wine vinegar gives a sourness that is acutely refreshing with the white varieties. A good vinegary slaw can be a perfect thing on a piercingly cold winter's day. I tend to use red wine vinegar with red cabbage but I'm not entirely sure why.

Dill Finely chopped dill fronds bring a northern European tone to the leaves. Works best with white, rounded varieties.

Anchovies Finely chopped, melted into hot oil over a moderate heat, then use to dress dark green winter leaves.

Mustard Include mild versions in a cream sauce for a gratin and in dressings with walnut oil for a salad.

And...

* Any part of the pig works neatly with this group. A quick lunch of mine when I am at my desk is grilled bacon, blanched greens, toasted unsalted cashews, sprouted seeds and a dressing of oil and vinegar.

* Slow-cooked Chinese pork dishes, the sort you simmer with onions, garlic, soy and rice wine, always benefit from a pile of blanched leaves on the side, even if they aren't Chinese.

* Cabbage, simply steamed, has a lasting affinity with gravy. The two perform a perfect piece of chemistry – particularly when the gravy is exceptionally hot and sits in the craters and dimples of the cabbage leaves.

* Cabbage soup has been the last resort of crash dieters for decades. It works. But it works even better as a restorative after a cold or when you are generally in need of something both cleansing and soul enriching. I make a bowl of stock (home-made if I have it, powdered bouillon if not), then add a chopped tomato or two, a spoonful of canned (rinsed) flageolet or haricot beans, some finely shredded cabbage, crushed garlic and masses of coriander leaves and fresh mint.

* A good cabbage will squeak with freshness. To keep it that way for as long as possible, I wrap it in newspaper or I stuff it into a plastic bag – the type that seals when you press the edges together – spray water from a mist-sprayer in the bag and keep it in the salad-crisping section at the bottom of the fridge. I have had small cabbages keep in perfect condition for a week that way.

Simple steamed cabbage

Wash the leaves thoroughly in cold water, then tear them into manageable pieces. Bring a finger's depth of water to the boil in a large pan. Fill a steamer basket with the cabbage and then, when the water is boiling angrily, lower it and cover with a lid. It will cook in the steam in three or four minutes.

Boiled cabbage

The words hang heavy, wretched with disappointment. In reality, few things edible cheer me up more than a plate of cabbage freshly lifted from the steam, the colours clear and bright, the leaves singing with life. I add nothing save lemon and sometimes black pepper, coarse from the grinder. As a rule, my cabbage isn't boiled or even steamed, only blanched. Dipped briefly into boiling water, the leaves cook more quickly, and seem to stay a livelier colour than when they are steamed. The water must be deep and at a rollicking boil. A little salt can go in, though I often forget, and then the leaves. No lid. I leave them for a minute or two. They won't look ready but they will be by the time you have grabbed the oven gloves with which to lift the pot to sink and drained them. Vibrant, exhilarating even, when placed on a stark white plate.

If naked vegetables don't stir your juices, then a drizzle of balsamic vinegar, a dusting of grated Parmesan, a puddle of almost-melted butter, or a coating of mustardy French dressing just might.

White cabbage with oyster sauce

The brassicas are much revered in Chinese cooking, and dealt with elsewhere in this book, but the white cabbage, with its waxy leaves and crisp stalks, makes an excellent candidate for seasoning with the saltier accompaniments. On cold, rather grey days, the sort of day when nothing much happens, I often crave robust, dominating flavours – perhaps in a quest to inject some vigour into the occasion. Strident greens tossed in lip-tingling oyster sauce can be such a dish.

In the last four or five years, this has become one of those recipes I use as a 'knee-jerk' accompaniment – an alternative to opening a bag of frozen peas. It is excellent with grilled pork chops, though I have also eaten it atop a bowl of steamed rice before now.

half a medium-sized cabbage
groundnut oil – a tablespoon
oyster sauce – 2 tablespoons

Pull the cabbage leaves apart and wash them well. Taking two or three at a time, pile them one on top of another, roll them up, then cut into thin shreds with a large cook's knife. The width of the strips is a personal choice but I tend to slice mine about the same width as pappardelle, the widest of the ribbon pastas.

Bring a pan of water to the boil, salt it generously, then drop in the shredded cabbage. Leave at a galloping boil for a full minute. Drain and return the leaves to the empty pan. Immediately stir in the oil and the oyster sauce. Toss and serve straight away.

A crisp, sweet-sharp relish for Christmas

The sour crispness of red cabbage makes it a good ingredient for a relish. Something stirring – hot, sharp, sour, bright – to introduce to a gamey pâté or a wedge of pork pie with softly collapsing pastry. Not normally given to making pickles and chutneys, I find this startling relish manageable without feeling I am going too far down the preserving route.

> boiling water – 4 tablespoons
> tamarind pulp – 2 tablespoons
> carrots – 250g
> red cabbage – 250g
> ginger – 75g
> sea salt – 4 teaspoons
> palm sugar (or soft brown sugar) – 2 teaspoons
> hot chillies – 2, shredded
> nam pla (Thai fish sauce) – a tablespoon
> rice vinegar – 150ml
> water – 150ml

Pour the boiling water over the tamarind pulp (you can find it in Asian stores and some supermarkets). Leave for a few minutes, then strain through a tea strainer. Discard the pulp and keep the tamarind water.

Finely shred the carrots, red cabbage and ginger. Put them in a bowl with 2 teaspoons of the sea salt and the reserved tamarind water and leave overnight. Drain off the liquid and add the palm sugar, the shredded hot chillies, the remaining salt, the Thai fish sauce, rice vinegar and water. Mix thoroughly. Store in an airtight jar in the fridge. You can use it within a day or two, though it will keep for up to a week; just keep turning the jar over from time to time.

A cabbage soup

The frugality implied in the words 'cabbage soup' appeals to me just as much as the fanciful descriptions of Michelin-starred menus. The words evoke a rich simplicity where nothing unnecessary intrudes. This is indeed a soup of extraordinary solace, gratifying in its purity. The stark fact that this was a meal formed in poverty is there for all to see.

Portugal has a cabbage soup, perhaps the best known of all, *caldo verde*. It is made with *couve gallego*, a yellow-flowered kale, whose leaves are flatter and less plume like than the kale we generally buy in the shops. The other ingredients are from the store cupboard, but should include a few slices of chorizo if the soup is to have any authenticity. This soup works with any coarse-textured greens and eminently, I think, with Savoy cabbage.

> *enough for 4*
> a large onion
> garlic – 2 or 3 cloves
> olive oil
> potatoes – 3 medium sized, a waxy variety
> bay leaves – 2
> chorizo – a large piece (about 200g)
> cabbage or kale leaves – 3 or 4 handfuls

Peel the onion and garlic and slice them thinly. Warm a glug or two of olive oil in a large, deep saucepan, then let the onion and garlic soften in it over a low heat.

Peel the potatoes – I sometimes don't – then cut them into medium-sized pieces. Combine with the onion and leave to cook for five minutes before adding about a litre of water. Season with salt, black pepper and the bay leaves and leave to simmer for about twenty-five minutes, until the potatoes are ready to collapse.

With a fork or a potato masher, crush the potatoes so that they thicken the soup but remain quite lumpy here and there. Cut the chorizo into thick chunks and fry in a non-stick pan till the fat runs.

Shred the cabbage finely, then stir it into the soup and simmer for three or four minutes, until tender. Stir in the fried chorizo. I like to pass this soup round in rough, earthenware bowls.

Cabbage with beans, coconut and coriander

Early January 2008 and I am having my annual tidy up of the larder cupboard. The 'lentil shuffle' as I call it, as that is basically what the job entails. Sorting out the store cupboard always results in my making something bean or lentil orientated. I think it must remind me of just how many I have. What follows is a rather hot bean curry. You could cool its ardour by skipping a chilli or two. The greens offer a hit of cool freshness on top of the substantial and deeply spiced beans.

A speedier version, suitable for a midweek supper, can be made with canned beans. There is no real reason why you shouldn't use any dried or canned beans you wish here. Chickpeas will work well too. If I do decide to open a can instead, then I use three 400g cans.

enough for 4–6
dried haricot beans – 500g
onions – 2 medium
vegetable or groundnut oil – 2 tablespoons
garlic – 3 cloves
green cardamoms – 8
coriander seeds – 2 teaspoons
yellow mustard seeds – a teaspoon
cumin seeds – a teaspoon
ground turmeric – 2 teaspoons
chillies – 3 small, hot
chopped plum tomatoes – two 400g cans
a pinch of sugar
coconut milk – 250ml
fresh coriander – a large handful
a lime, maybe 2

for the greens
leafy soft green cabbage, such as spring greens –
   a good handful or more per person

Soak the dried beans in cold water overnight. The next day, boil the beans till tender in deep unsalted water. Drain and set aside. (If you are using canned beans, rinse them under cold running water, then set aside.)

Peel the onions, cut them in half and slice them thinly. Add them to the oil in a large, deep pan and let them soften, colouring lightly, over a moderate heat. This often takes longer than you might imagine, a good fifteen minutes at least. Peel and chop the garlic and add to the onions.

Crack the cardamom pods open and extract the tiny seeds. Crush these coarsely, using a pestle and mortar or a very heavy rolling pin, then stir them into the softening onions. Crush the coriander seeds and then the mustard, and add them to the onions with the whole cumin seeds, ground turmeric, a generous seasoning of salt, and black pepper. Cook, stirring regularly, for at least five minutes, so that the spices toast in the heat.

Meanwhile, seed and finely chop the chillies and add, with the chopped tomatoes, 400ml of water and a pinch of sugar, followed by the cooked beans. Leave to simmer gently over a low heat, with the occasional stir, partially covered with a lid, for about thirty-five to forty minutes.

Mix the coconut milk into the sauce, simmer for a further five minutes, then add the coriander leaves and the lime juice. When the curry is almost ready, make a tight fist of the greens and shred them quite finely. Steam or blanch briefly, then add to the curry.

A quick cabbage supper with duck legs

A preserved duck leg from the deli has saved my supper more times than I can count. Cased in its own white fat and crisped up in the oven or in a sauté pan, these 'duck confit' are as near as I get to eating ready-made food. One January, arriving home cold and less than a hundred per cent, I stripped the meat from a couple of duck legs and used it to add protein to an express version of one of those lovingly tended cabbage and bean soups. The result was a slightly chaotic bowlful of food that felt as if it should be eaten from a scrubbed pine table in a French cave house. An extraordinarily heart-warming supper, immensely satisfying. An edible version of the sort of people one refers to as 'the salt of the earth'. I am certain no one would have guessed it hadn't spent the entire afternoon puttering away in a cast-iron pot.

enough for 4 as a main course
haricot beans – two 400g cans
a leek – a large, thick one
smoked streaky bacon – 6 rashers
duck fat, groundnut oil or butter – a tablespoon
garlic – 2 cloves
a large carrot
potatoes – 4 small (about 250g in total)
vegetable stock (or whatever there is to hand) – 600ml
confit duck legs – 2
cabbage – a quarter, or a similar volume of spring greens
open-textured country-style bread – 4 slices

Empty the beans into a colander and rinse them under cold running water.

Halve the leek lengthways and chop it roughly, then rinse very thoroughly to remove any trapped grit. Slice the bacon into thick strips and warm it in a deep, heavy-based pan with the fat or butter. Add the chopped leek and let it soften. Neither leek nor bacon should be allowed to colour.

Peel and slice the garlic, scrub the carrot and chop it into small dice, scrub the potatoes and cut them into large chunks, then add all to the softening leek. Pour over the stock and bring to the boil. Lower the heat so that the liquid simmers gently and leave until the potatoes are tender – a matter of twenty minutes or so.

Meanwhile, put the duck legs in a shallow pan with a lid and let them cook over a moderate heat till nicely warmed, about fifteen minutes. Strip the meat and skin from the duck and tear it into long shreds, but don't wipe off the fat; it will add warmth and a silky fattiness to the soup. Shred the cabbage leaves and stir, together with the duck meat, into the soup. Simmer for five or six minutes.

Toast the bread, tear into large pieces and put a handful in the bottom of each bowl. Ladle the broth and meat into the bowls.

Winter cabbage, juniper and cream

February 2008. The garden is all frost and cabbages. Here and there the occasional fat seed head, some purple sprouts on bending stalks, and piles of sticks that I have pulled off the trees that overhang the vegetable patch. The earth is crisp underfoot. Soup days.

The winter cabbages, especially Savoy and Protovoy, are blistered with webs and hollows that seem made to hold a sauce of some sort. At its simplest, this could be melted butter or hot bacon fat, but a cream sauce seems an especially attractive idea on a cold day, adding suavity to a coarse flavour and at a stroke tempering the leaves' stridency. The juniper in the spiced cream that follows makes this a perfect accompaniment to ham or roast pork, though I have been known to eat it with brown rice as a main dish in itself.

enough for 4 as a side dish
cabbage – 400g
black peppercorns – 2 teaspoons
juniper berries – 2 teaspoons
butter – 25g
double cream – 200ml

Separate the leaves of the cabbage and shred them into finger-thick strips. I find the easiest way to do this is to pile the leaves on top of one another, then roll them up and shred them with a large knife.

Bring a pan of water to the boil, salt it lightly and add the cabbage. Let it boil for barely a couple of minutes. You want the leaves to be tender enough to eat but still bright green and perky.

Meanwhile, crush the peppercorns and juniper berries lightly with a pestle and mortar, or with a heavy object on a chopping board. Drain the cabbage, return the empty pan to the heat and melt the butter in it. Toast the crushed spices in the butter for a minute or two until fragrant, then pour in the cream. Leave to bubble for a minute or so, until it starts to thicken slightly, then season with a very little salt and tip in the drained greens. Toss them in the spiced cream till lightly coated. Serve straight away, while the sauce is still piping hot and creamy.

A winter slaw

There is much that appeals about the crude crunch of a winter slaw, white, purple and moss green, eaten under a grey and watery sky. The snap of raw cabbage under the teeth can be exhilarating, especially when there is some sharpness in the dressing. I use yoghurt sometimes, or a vinaigrette with lemon instead of vinegar, and occasionally introduce a fiery flash of blood orange or even grapefruit. The pink variety works particularly well. The crucial point is that this salad has a clean bite to it. The idea of gummy mayonnaise and the traditional coleslaw doesn't really enter into my head any more.

White cabbage, or maybe a slice across the brain-like interior of the red version, shreds of celeriac, long gratings of carrot and the occasional ice-white chevron of fennel regularly appear in my recipe. Several times each winter I find myself tossing in a ribbon of grated beetroot, added at the last moment so it fails to send its trail of blood through the ivory-white celeriac. A little bleeding of the ingredients can be quite beautiful but it is best not to mix too much, unless pink is your thing.

To the raw vegetable base, I will often add a caper or two, a handful of toasted almonds, a pinch of poppy seeds the colour of torrential rain. I might add sesame or pumpkin seeds or jewels from a pomegranate. If a herb is included, it is most likely whatever happens to be to hand, but preferably dill, echoing the chill of Scandinavia, or flat-leaf parsley torn from its stem but not chopped. If luxury is wanted, then a little crème fraîche can be stirred in with the yoghurt and olive oil that I use as a quick, light and ultimately flattering dressing.

If protein is needed, I edge the plate with cuts of salami, coppa or Parma ham straight from the deli slicing machine (my local cuts it thin enough to read a book through, then rolls it in cellophane so that each piece has a distinct curl to it, like an almond tuile). On a whim, I flick crisp gherkins, the tiny ones, in with the shredded roots, or fat, tadpole-like caper berries. Adding such piquant ingredients is a good wheeze with cabbage, to the point where I occasionally include some blue cheese too, such as Spanish Picos or Beenleigh Blue. They work in a similar way to the sourness that makes sauerkraut so tantalising on the tongue.

The exact contents will depend on the roots and brassicas I use as the backbone. There may be walnuts or pecans, particularly if I have included celeriac; almonds, sometimes smoked or salted, especially with red cabbage; sprouted aduki or lentils, though never alfalfa, which forms soggy nests amongst the layers of crisp cabbage. Cavolo nero, blanched for twenty seconds in boiling water, then dunked into iced water and shaken dry, is a regular once the frosts have set its flavour.

The dressing is invariably a 200g tub of goat's or sheep's yoghurt stirred through with three or four tablespoons of olive oil, a scattering of chopped dill or parsley, and maybe the grated zest of a blood orange or perhaps a Sicilian lemon. Freshness and a snap of acidity are vital with a salad of roots and cabbage.

A slaw of red cabbage, blue cheese and walnuts

The dressing is enough for four and will keep in the fridge for several days.

per person
a quarter of a red cabbage
half a medium-sized bulb of fennel
a Russet apple
a little lemon juice
a medium carrot
blue cheese, such as Harborne, Cashel or Beenleigh – 150g
walnuts – a handful
a rib of celery

for the dressing
mild red wine vinegar – 2 tablespoons
smooth Dijon mustard – 2 teaspoons
groundnut oil – 3 tablespoons
walnut oil – 2 tablespoons
a pinch of caster sugar

Shred the cabbage and fennel. Cut the apple into quarters, discard the core, then slice finely. Toss the apple slices immediately in a little lemon juice to stop them discolouring. Shred the carrot into matchsticks (or grate it very coarsely). Slice the cheese thinly. Toast the walnuts in a non-stick pan till they smell warm and nutty. Thinly slice the celery.

Make the dressing by mixing the vinegar and mustard with a little salt and black pepper. Beat in the groundnut and walnut oils, then taste and add a little sugar if necessary.

Toss the salad ingredients together gently, so you don't break up the cheese too much. Divide between plates and drizzle over the dressing.

A word about red cabbage

Red cabbage owes its lack of popularity to its hatred of boiling water.
It bucks the cooking method so dear to the British heart. It pickles nicely
with allspice and malt vinegar and is the one member of this family that
will wait for you once it has been cooked.

There is little wrong with the age-old method of cooking it, finely
shredded, in a pan with a little flavourless oil, plus some juniper, wine
vinegar and perhaps some cubes of apple. The flavours go rather well
with pork and the milder game, and the colour is always cheering.
As a larder staple, it keeps well too, staying in good nick in the fridge
for a week or three.

I can't say I have ever grown this one, preferring to take my chances at
the greengrocer's. Though I do make a smart pickle with carrots and red
cabbage for goosing up a coarse pâté (see page 141). I also serve the vegetable
hot, with shards of smoked bacon and a Russet apple in its midst. So good
natured to store, simple to prepare, crisp to eat and colourful to look at.
Its lack of popularity is a puzzle to me.

Red cabbage with cider vinegar

There will be quite a bit of this left over for the next day. Lovely reheated
with cold ham.

> *enough for 4*
> a small red cabbage
> a little olive or groundnut oil
> juniper berries – 8–10
> cider vinegar – 3 tablespoons

Shred the cabbage finely, cutting away and discarding the hard core, rinse
thoroughly, then drain. Heat a couple of tablespoons of oil in a wok or
deep saucepan and add the red cabbage. Turn it in the oil, raising the heat
if nothing much is happening, till the colour is bright – a matter of a minute
or two.

Squash the juniper berries roughly, maybe with the flat of a heavy
knife blade or a pestle. You don't want them so much a powder, simply
well bruised. Add them to the cabbage with most of the cider vinegar and
a seasoning of salt and pepper. Leave the cabbage to cook, covering with
a lid and tossing occasionally. It will take seven to ten minutes to become
tender but with some crunch left to it. Give it another five to ten minutes
if you prefer it soft, which is actually when it is at its best. Freshen the taste
if necessary with the last of the vinegar.

Turkey breast steaks, prune gravy, red cabbage

As cuts of meat go, the turkey breast steak is a relatively new one and will please those who like their protein neat, mild and fat free. This addition to the meat counter has its advantages for a quick supper. It can be sizzled in butter with a few aromatics (bay, black pepper, thyme sprigs and a curl of orange rind tend to cheer it up). Turkey still reeks of Christmas, but the white meat less so than the legs, which always smell like a roasting Christmas lunch.

Red cabbage makes a satisfactory accompaniment. Go further, with a few prunes and a bottle of Marsala, and you have something approaching a joyful Sunday lunch, though without a bone to pick.

enough for 2

for the gravy
an onion
a thick slice of butter
a small carrot
a stick of celery
plain flour – 2 tablespoons
soft, stoned prunes – 200g
a few sprig of thyme
bay leaves – 2
dry Marsala –200ml
light stock or, at a push, water – 500ml

for the turkey steaks
a little butter
turkey steaks – 4, about 125g each
a few leaves of thyme

Peel and roughly chop the onion. Put it in a pan with the butter and let it soften. Scrub and dice the carrot and celery and add to the onion. Let the vegetables cook till soft and lightly coloured. Stir in the flour and let it turn a pale biscuit colour, then chop the prunes and add them with the thyme and the bay leaves. Immediately pour in the Marsala and stock. Turn the heat down to a simmer and leave to bubble quietly for twenty minutes.

To prepare the turkey steaks, melt the butter in a large, shallow pan. Season the steaks with salt, black pepper and the thyme leaves (don't skip the thyme). When the butter sizzles, lay the steaks in the pan and let them colour on the underside before turning them over and continuing on a gentle heat till tender. They should take about eight minutes, depending on their thickness. Remove to warm plates and serve with the hot prune sauce and the red cabbage that precedes.

A gratin of white cabbage and cheese

All of the brassica family have an affinity with cream and cheese, yet it is those grown for their heads rather than their leaves that seem to get the comfort of dairy produce. Cauliflower and broccoli have long been served under a blanket of cheese and cream, but less so cabbage and the leafier greens. The reason, I have always assumed, is that the cabbage would be overcooked by the time the sauce has formed a crust in the hot oven. In practice, the 'white' cabbages that sit on supermarket shelves like rock-hard footballs can be put to good use in a gratin. Their leaves and stalks are juicy when blanched in boiling water and the thicker leaves hold up very well under a sharp cheese sauce, flecked with nutmeg and hot, white pepper.

I mostly use a cabbage gratin as a friend for a piece of boiled gammon or bacon, especially one that has been simmered in apple juice with juniper berries and onion, but sometimes we eat it as it comes, as a television supper, like cauliflower cheese. My suggestion of Cornish Yarg is only because I have used it here to good effect. Any briskly flavoured cheese is suitable.

enough for 4 as a side dish
milk – 500ml
cloves – 2
a couple of bay leaves
butter – 30g
plain flour – 30g
a little nutmeg
double cream – 100ml
Cornish Yarg cheese – 100g, grated
a medium-sized white cabbage
breadcrumbs – a large handful, maybe two

Bring the milk, cloves and bay almost to the boil, then turn off the heat.

Melt the butter in a saucepan and stir in the flour. Let it cook for a minute or two over a moderate heat, till it smells nutty. Pour in the milk and stir until it has thickened and any lumps have dissolved. If it remains stubbornly lumpy, then you had better get out the whisk. Season with salt, pepper (white would be a nice touch) and a grating of nutmeg. Stir in the double cream and the grated cheese. Set the oven at 180°C/Gas 4.

Bring a generous pan of salted water to the boil. Cut the cabbage in half and then into thick slices, like wedges of cake. Dunk the cabbage into the boiling water for a minute or two and then drain.

Lay the cabbage pieces in a shallow ovenproof dish. Pour over the sauce, then scatter over the breadcrumbs. Bake for roughly forty-five minutes, till the crust is patchily golden, the edges bubbling enticingly.

Carrots

Not for me the pile of buttered carrots on the plate. Too sweet, too orange (too bloody cheerful more like it). But the carrot's place is assured in my kitchen as the bringer of earthy sweetness, a backbone vegetable on which to build layers of flavour.

The heirloom cultivars so popular in the Middle Ages are more my style: more earthy, I suppose, and their colours – white, yellow, purple-black, violet, burgundy and plum – are softer. The colours of bruised flesh. But early carrots were, like the wild ones, thin affairs until the early 1600s, when Flemish gardeners finally produced a fatter, brighter carrot. The sandy soils of Belgium and Holland are much appreciated by this vegetable; indeed, most modern cultivars probably originate from the Dutch Long Orange. Now the varieties of antiquity are in demand again, their colours are intriguing in a salad with brown mustard seed, lemon juice and much, much parsley.

India provides a good hunting ground for recipes (though the vegetable is said to have been domesticated first in Afghanistan). Grated with toasted cumin seeds; stir-fried with red chillies and turmeric; a bright pickle spiky with ginger and softened with garam masala; the grated roots stirred through a brown rice pilaf with the rich warmth of ground cardamom. Indian cooks understand how to tame the monotone sweetness of the carrot (the Italians once ate it as a dessert, with honey) while making it sing with vitality and freshness.

After peas, carrots were the only truly acceptable vegetable to me as an eight year old. But even then there were rules. If they were to pass my lips, they had to be cut into small dice, the same size as peas, and preferably appear at the same time, so they could share a fork. The frozen mixture of the two by Bird's Eye must have been manna from heaven for my mother. If they appeared whole, or even the size of a cork, the offending vegetable would be guaranteed to set off a quivering lower lip.

When I was thirteen, my father gave me a strip of ground to work for myself, complete with a painted sign bearing the legend, 'Nigel's Garden'. I planted carrots, cosmos and candytuft. In contrast to the rich, fecund soil adjacent, where he grew strawberries and wigwams of scarlet runners, mine was stony and dry, partly shaded by an ancient pear tree, its fruit too high to reach. In July the ground became hot enough to fry eggs.

The carrots were thin, and many broke off as I pulled them. Their fragile flowers trembled in the wind. In winter, they were too firmly rooted to pull and the size of parsnips. My dad had to prise them out with the garden fork, whilst my stepmother poked them around the chicken that she would boil and plate up with mashed potato and parsley sauce.

None of the restaurants I ever worked in served carrots. They were backroom boys (to my eyes, carrots are unquestionably male), there to provide a balance for the piquant, gherkin-flecked sauce that accompanied paupiettes of veal, or in heroic chunks in a casserole of young lamb with needles of rosemary and curls of orange peel. But they were never stars.

I arrived at a Lake District hotel one spring, one of a ring of country-house hotels that had sprung up around the lakes in the 1980s. Daffodils shone through the rough grass that led down to the lake and I was taught to make pastry by the open window, so I could smell the green prickle of spring as I rubbed the butter into the flour. (Despite the obvious preciousness, this was the point at which I discovered that cooking can be so much more than just a way to make a living.)

The draw here was not so much the rooms, which were more luxurious elsewhere, or the formal garden, whose tubby stone putti looked ill at ease with the surrounding meadows, but the view across to Langdale Pike, which provided a suitably theatrical backdrop to the six-course, no-choice dinners. It seems crazy now to have offered a main course (roast beef, lamb in hay, local duck) surrounded by never less than six differently cooked vegetables (cabbage with gin and juniper, parsnip purée with pine kernels, red cabbage with apple, deep-fried cauliflower, courgettes with toasted almonds, straw potatoes) but they were assembled with care and thought and were rarely less than delicious. I make the parsnip purée to this day.

Carrots were much in evidence. Their sweetness no doubt went with the gilded cherubs that hung from the ceiling and the primroses that adorned the plates. If one could ever love the sugariness of a carrot, surely it would be here. The roots shone like stained-glass windows on the overcrowded plates: a cake of carrot and potato slices baked with fresh herbs; a purée of carrots with toasted cumin seed; grated carrots with walnut oil and orange zest; soups of carrot and orange, carrot and apple, carrot and beetroot and a much copied one of carrots and coriander leaf became trademarks. Good ideas all, but now I look for ways to temper their excessive sweetness. I could live without the carrot as a vegetable. But I very much value it, with onions, celery and bay, as an earthy aromatic.

A carrot in the garden

Carrot leaves and flowers have an almost fairy-like delicacy to them, belonging to the same family as lovage, fennel and angelica. I allow a few to blossom in the garden simply for the fine beauty of their lace umbrella of flowers.

This garden's soil was initially too heavy for a carrot crop, which would be happier on the sandy soils further south. Five years of digging in a compost of bracken and horse manure has now lightened it to the point where I feel a row or two of roots might survive. They dislike lumpy soil too, which makes them fork, so I break up the soil into a fine tilth, like that of a crumble topping, a week or so before planting the tiny seeds. For a spring crop, you should sow outside in late autumn, then cover with horticultural fleece. For early summer pickings, sow in early spring, as soon as the ground has warmed up a little. It needs to be about 7°C.

Few seeds are more diminutive than that those of the carrot family and they tend to grow in close tufts, which need thinning if the roots are to fatten properly. I find thinning tedious – I'd rather do almost anything else in the garden – but there is little choice. They need to end up about 10cm apart. Thinning in showery weather will prevent any passing carrot fly taking interest, as will discarding any thinnings rather than leaving them lying around. The second batch and their miniscule roots can be eaten as a treat.

Carrot fly is a problem on allotments and gardens alike but my box hedges and a simple plastic tunnel seem to disguise the leaves from the fly's sharp eyes (the insects fly very close to the ground).

A carrot diary

April 27 Carrot seed likes warm soil, so I wait till the weeds start to sprout before sowing. This year I plant the Early Nantes variety close to a row of onions in the hope that the alliums' smell will deter the carrot fly. More experienced gardeners say it works a treat. Two weeks after germination, when the fronds are just showing above the soil, a fox cub climbs into the tunnel for a snooze and squashes them flat. I start again.

This time two rows each of three varieties go in, each covered with a cane cloche secured to the ground by an iron spike or two. Three weeks later and the delicate fronds are up, already sporting tufts of the familiar bushy leaf. Throughout the early summer, small carrots, perfect for a salad or eating as a vegetable accompaniment, less so for a stew, are there for the picking.

Late July and early August The plumes of leaves are coming thick and fast. The painstaking job of removing every second or third carrot continues until they are 10cm apart. There is no alternative but to get down on hands and knees for this.

September 24 Some small but pleasingly formed specimens coming out now. The violet carrots are larger than the others – about the size of a small finger – but tougher and less sweet. The fact that they appear more 'carroty' than even the organic ones may well be because they are rushed to the pot within the hour. Sometimes less. I continue picking right the way through the early winter and past Christmas, despite having the first October snow (2008) for seventy years.

Varieties

I am not fond of the modern, blunt-ended Amsterdam carrot. It is what I call a supermarket vegetable. I much prefer the traditional tapered maincrop varieties, such as Autumn King, even though the pointed end will be almost inevitably trimmed off. Modern cultivars often seem sweeter and less earthy too. I grow the older varieties, introduced in the 1800s.

James Scarlet Intermediate Dates from 1870, a long maincrop variety with a good girth and earthy flavour. Sow in May, use by Christmas.
St Valery A medium-sized, particularly sweet root of exceptional length (though not on my soil) and slightly paler than most.
Chantenay Short, cylindrical and fast growing, a very sweet variety. The non-brittle stems make these well suited to selling in bunches with their stalks intact.
Early Nantes Yes, a bit of a stumpy end rather than an elegant point, but as rich in flavour as an early carrot can get. I plant this virtually coreless variety in April.
Purple Dragon Purple skin and golden flesh. A tough chew, but heartbreakingly beautiful. Cut into rounds, they resemble sweeties, with a ring of papal purple around an orangey-yellow core.
Paris Round A sound choice for an early crop if your soil is lumpy or stony.
Autumn King Maincrop, a good choice if you have sandy soil, so its long taproot can go down unhindered by stones and clay.
De Djerba A root from Tunisia in shades of violet, black and orange.
Violet Scarlet flesh with a violet skin.

A carrot in the kitchen

The fat maincrop carrot is probably at its most useful as the sweetening element in a composite dish – a stew, soup or 'many layered' thing. Along with onions, leeks and bay leaves, carrots often form the backbone of a recipe, exchanging flavours and introducing a firm ground on which to build. A small piece is good on the fork with boiled beef, and wonderful against the sharp edge of a soused herring. Young spring carrots lack earthiness and are probably best crunched raw in lieu of a biscuit, or included, thinly sliced, in a salad. They grate to a slush.

My weekly supply of carrots arrives in a sealed plastic bag, caked in wet Devonian mud, where they would, if necessary, stay crisp and juicy for a week. Each Friday afternoon, I split the newly arrived bag, rub off the mud with a scrubbing brush (they make a terrible muddy mess of the sink), then place the clean, wet roots in the salad crisper at the bottom of the fridge, lined with wet kitchen paper. Throughout the coming week, I pick at them, dipping them into tubs of shop-bought hummus or grating their flesh into a salad with lemon juice, dill or torn parsley.

Seasoning your carrots

Carrots appreciate being matched with members of their own family, working well with a little caraway, chervil, cumin, parsley, coriander or dill.

Chervil The leaves, like wisps of lace petticoat, are effective when stirred through a bowl of grated carrot dressed with lemon juice and black pepper.
Coriander The carrot's best friend, in salad, in soup and in a stir-fry with spring onion and matchsticks of ginger.
Caraway Adds a musky note to a carrot loaf or a bowl of soup to eat with treacly rye bread.
Cumin Toss the steamed roots with toasted cumin seeds or add them to a soup on a winter night.
Lemon juice A startling addition to a carrot salad that will also quell the excessive sweetness. Lime works well too, especially when you introduce chillies and coriander leaf.
Mustard seeds The heat and sweetness make exciting bedmates.
Sugar Absurd, but in reality a pinch seems to bring the earthy flavour, often lost to the sugary notes, to the fore.
Orange Zest, juice, even cut into chunks and roasted, the vibrant parts of the orange marry neatly with our favourite root, working in harmony with its sweetness and lifting its earthiness in the same way it does with beetroot. The vivid orange of both fruit and vegetable is not for the faint-hearted, but there is no better way to cheer up a plate of grilled lamb's liver and onions.

And...

* If you cut the stems of carrots and leave the roots in the soil, they keep very well for weeks. You can leave them there until you need them unless you live in an exceptionally cold part of the country.
* Keep the ground around home-grown carrots well weeded. They dislike competition.
* Manure will cause the roots to fork. I tend to add it the season before I sow. Keeping growing carrots moist will help keep their scent down, confusing the carrot fly. As will planting onions or garlic nearby.
* The stems and leaves are of no interest in the kitchen but of great value to the shopper. You can tell how fresh your bunch is by the fronds' state of health.
* Spring carrots seem to stay crisper without their plume of leaves. Snip them off when you get them home.
* I like to store maincrop roots with their soil on. They keep better that way, ideally in the bottom of the fridge – if not, in a paper sack in the shed. Ready-scrubbed carrots turn slimy if stored in the plastic bags they are sold in. I avoid them.
* Although long, thick maincrop carrots are available all year in the shops, they are most useful in autumn and winter, when their earthy density is particularly suited to slow cooking.
* Carrots, simply steamed, are happiest with braised or boiled beef, roast lamb and unsmoked bacon joints. Maincrop carrots, mashed with butter, make excellent partners for broth-based stews of chicken or rabbit. The smallest spring carrots seem particularly at home with the mildest meats: young lamb, poussin and rabbit.
* Carrot fritters (see page 174), if not being eaten as a main dish, make a charming side dish for roast chicken.

A salad of carrot thinnings

Carrots have been one of my quiet successes. The carrot thinning salad has become a regular weekly addition throughout the summer. Root vegetables no bigger than your little finger have a charm to them that insists you leave them whole. Cooking them, in shallow water so that they steam rather than boil, takes barely a minute or two. I dress them as soon as they are out of the pan, sometimes with a light, lemony dressing, other times with fresh coriander.

To turn this into a main-course salad, add spoonfuls of ricotta or cottage cheese to which you have added pepper and some of the dressing.

enough for 4
carrot thinnings – 6 handfuls, no thicker than your little finger,
   or 2 bunches of baby carrots
small beetroots – 6
red wine vinegar – 1 tablespoon
a clove of garlic, chopped
lemon juice – a tablespoon
olive oil – 4 tablespoons
coriander leaves – a good handful (about 4 tablespoons)

Wipe the carrots and remove their stems. Don't peel the beetroot, but cut off any thick stems or tails. Put a shallow layer of water in a large, wide pan, add the beetroot, cover and steam for ten minutes, then add the carrots. Remove the beets and carrots when they are tender. Peel the beetroot and cut into thin strips, somewhat similar in thickness to the carrots.

Make the dressing by dissolving a good pinch of sea salt in the red wine vinegar, then whisking in the chopped garlic, lemon juice and olive oil. Add black pepper and toss gently with the beetroot strips and carrots. Add the coriander leaves and toss again. Serve warm or at room temperature.

A soup the colour of marigolds

It was a simple soup, ten minutes' hands-on work and barely half an hour on the stove. An onion, roughly chopped, softened in a little olive oil in a deep and heavy pan. An equal amount of carrots and yellow tomatoes (I used 450g of each to make enough for four), chopped and stirred into the soft, translucent onion. A litre of water, I could have used stock, and some salt, pepper and a couple of bay leaves. It simmered for half an hour, then I blitzed it to a thick, pulpy broth in the blender. We ended up with four big bowls of rough-textured soup, as bright and cheerful as a jug of June flowers, a few chives stirred in at the table. As we licked our spoons, someone mentioned it would have been good to have it chilled. But by that time it was too late to try.

A couple of carrot salads

Slices of soft, rare lamb or beef left from the Sunday roast, their pink flesh framed with crisp, yellow fat, need a bright, fresh-tasting salad to go with them: coarsely grated carrots stirred through with a sharply citrus dressing made from equal quantities of olive oil and lemon juice, seasoned with toasted cumin seeds, roughly torn parsley leaves and glistening flakes of sea salt.

I sometimes make a knife-sharp, shockingly refreshing salad with carrots sliced wafer thin, tossed with a dressing of lime juice, pink grapefruit juice, finely chopped red chillies, torn coriander leaves and olive oil. I stir in a teaspoon or so of Thai fish sauce, other times salt. Occasionally I add a grilled pork steak to it, cut into thick fingers. The best bit is when the hot, lightly charred meat encounters the stinging dressing.

A simple 'boiled' carrot

Brush the carrots clean under running water and chop them roughly the size of a cork. Put them into a medium pan – they need to be in a single layer – with two tablespoons of water and a thick slice of butter, about 30g. Bring to the boil, cover with a tightly fitting lid, then let them cook at a moderate pace for seven or eight minutes. You need no salt, pepper or sugar.

Remove the lid and check for tenderness. The idea is that they are tender but still retain a modicum of bite. Drain and serve.

A side dish of spiced and creamed carrots

Perhaps it was the carrot loaf of the 1970s, slimmers' soups or the post-War carrot cake recipes without the promise of walnuts and cream cheese frosting, but carrots rarely offer us a taste of luxury.

Fiddling around – there is no other word – with grated carrots one day, I wondered if there would be any mileage in a dish similar to creamed sweetcorn, where the sweet vegetables are stewed with cream to give a deliciously sloppy side dish. There wasn't. Until I worked backwards and added spices to the carrots before enriching them with both cream (for richness) and strained yoghurt (for freshness). The result is one of those suave, mildly spiced side dishes that can be used alongside almost anything. In our house it has nestled up to brown rice, grilled lamb steaks and, most successful of all, sautéed rabbit.

enough for 4
carrots – 400g
garlic – 2 cloves
ginger – a thumb-sized piece
green chillies – 3 or 4 small, hot ones
butter – a thick slice
yellow mustard seeds – a teaspoon
cashew nuts – 2 tablespoons
double cream – 4 tablespoons
natural yoghurt – 4 heaped tablespoons
coriander leaves – a good handful
lime juice – a generous squeeze

Shred or grate the carrots coarsely. Peel and crush the garlic, then peel and finely shred the ginger and finely chop the chillies.

Heat the butter in a frying pan and add the garlic, ginger and mustard seeds, holding a lid over them to stop them spluttering. Add the chillies and then, as everything becomes fragrant, the grated carrots. Let them cook, with the occasional toss, for three or four minutes.

Roughly chop the cashews, toast them in a non-stick frying pan till golden, then set aside. Stir the cream and yoghurt together and fold them into the hot carrots. Immediately tip into a serving dish and top with the toasted cashews, coriander leaves and the lime juice.

Carrot and coriander fritters

Vegetable fritters, given a savoury edge with a flavoursome farmhouse cheese, are just the job for a quick lunch. Cheap eating, too. Grate the carrots as finely or as coarsely as you like, but you can expect them to be more fragile in the pan when finely grated. A watercress salad, washed, dried and dressed with olive oil and lemon juice, would be refreshing and appropriate in every possible way.

makes 6–8, enough for 2–3
maincrop carrots – 325g
a medium onion
a clove of garlic, crushed
double cream – 150ml
an egg, beaten
grated cheese, such as a good strong Cheddar – 3 heaped tablespoons
coriander leaves – a handful, roughly chopped
plain flour – a heaped tablespoon
olive oil for shallow-frying

Scrub the carrots and push them through a food processor fitted with a grater attachment. If you prefer, grate them by hand using the coarse side of the grater. Either way, you are after long, thin shreds rather than mush.

Peel the onion, finely slice or grate it and stir it into the carrots along with the garlic and a seasoning of salt and black pepper. Stir in the double cream, beaten egg, grated cheese, roughly chopped coriander and the flour.

Warm a shallow layer of olive oil in a non-stick frying pan. Drop large dollops of the mixture into the pan, a couple at a time, and fry till lightly cooked on the underside. Turn with a fish slice and allow the other side to colour. They should take three or four minutes per side. The cakes are ready as soon as they are dark gold. Lift out on to a warm plate. A sheet of kitchen roll will remove any oil. Eat immediately.

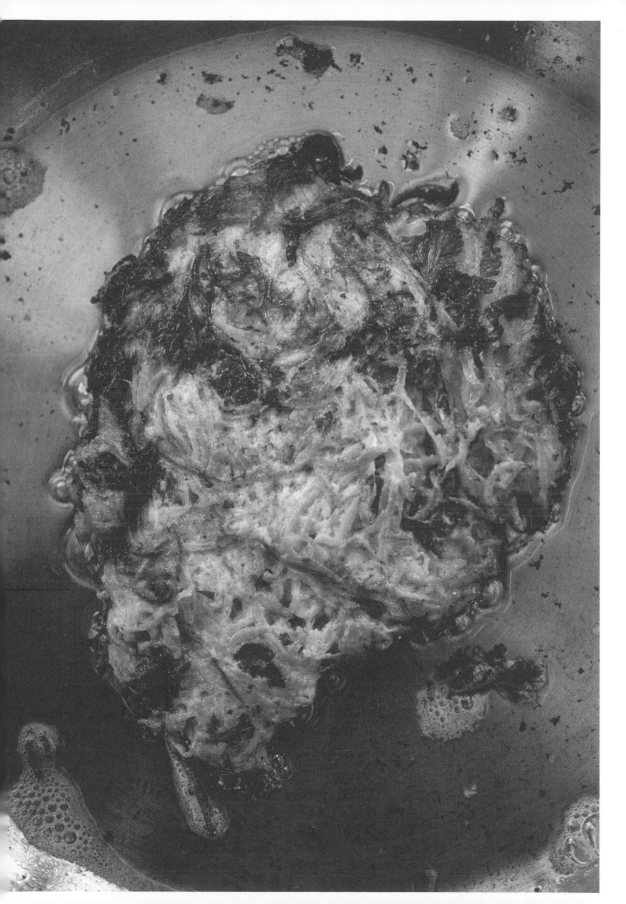

Roast lamb with mint, cumin and roast carrots

Young carrots, no thicker than a finger and often not much longer, appear in the shops in late spring, their bushy leaves intact. Often, they have a just-picked air about them, their tiny side roots, as fine as hair, still fresh and crisp. At this stage they lack the fibre needed to grate well, and boiling does them few favours. They roast sweetly, especially when tucked under the roast. The savoury meat juices form a glossy coat that turns the carrot into a delectable little morsel.

I have used a leg of lamb here but in fact any cut would work – a shoulder or loin, for instance. The spice rub also works for chicken.

enough for 4–6
leg of lamb – 1.5kg
garlic – 4 cloves
cumin seeds – 3 large pinches
mint leaves – a large handful
juice of 2 lemons
olive oil
finger carrots – 12
baby beetroots – 4
white wine or stock – a large glass

Put the lamb in a roasting tin. Peel the garlic and put it into a food processor with the cumin seeds, mint leaves and lemon juice. Add a generous grinding of salt and some black pepper. Blitz to a coarse paste, adding enough olive oil to make a spreadable slush, thick enough to cling to the lamb.

Massage the roast well with the spice paste, spreading it over the skin and into the cut sides of the flesh. Set aside in a cool place (preferably not the fridge) for an hour, basting occasionally with any of the paste that has run off.

Preheat the oven to 200°C/Gas 6. Scrub the carrots and beetroots. If they are small, you can probably get away with a rinse. Either way, be careful with their skins, which are tender at this point in their life. Put the meat in the oven and roast for forty-five minutes to an hour, tucking the vegetables in around it after twenty minutes. The cooking time for the lamb will depend on how you like it done; forty-five minutes should give you a roast that is still pink and juicy inside. Remove from the oven and rest the meat for a good ten to fifteen minutes before carving and serving with the mint béarnaise below.

If you want to make a gravy, transfer the meat and carrots to a warm place, put the roasting tin over a moderate heat, then pour in a large glass of wine or stock, or even water, and bring it to the boil. Stir with a wooden spoon, scraping away at the tin to dissolve any stuck-on meat juices. Let the gravy bubble a little, check it for seasoning (it may need salt and pepper), then keep it warm whilst you carve the lamb.

Mint béarnaise sauce

a small shallot
white wine vinegar – 3 tablespoons
black peppercorns – 6
mint leaves – 2 tablespoons, stalks reserved
egg yolks – 2
butter – 150g, soft, almost melted

Peel and finely chop the shallot, then put it in a small saucepan with the vinegar, peppercorns and the stalks from the mint leaves. Bring to the boil and watch it while it reduces to a tablespoon or so. Put the egg yolks into a glass bowl and place it over a pan of very lightly boiling water. The bowl should sit snugly in the top of the pan. Whisk the reduced vinegar into the egg yolks, holding back the debris in the pan, then slowly add the butter a little at a time, whisking almost constantly till it is thick and velvety.

Roughly chop the mint leaves and stir them in, then taste for salt and pepper. Check that the sauce doesn't get too hot. It will keep warm till the lamb is cooked, with the occasional whisk, over the pan of water with the heat switched off.

A bright-tasting chutney of carrot and tomato

I tend to use this chutney as a relish, stirring it into the accompanying rice of a main course. It is slightly sweet, as you might expect, but tantalisingly hot and sour too. Scoop it up with a poppadom or a doughy, freckled paratha (I have been known to use a pitta bread in times of desperation). On Mondays I sometimes put a spoonful on the side of the plate with cold meats.

makes 1 large jar
tamarind pulp (available from health-food shops and Indian grocers) –
2 tablespoons
carrots – 4 good-sized, scrubbed or peeled
vegetable oil – 2 tablespoons
garlic – 2 cloves, crushed
black mustard seeds – half a teaspoon
hot red or green chillies – 2 small, finely chopped
tomatoes – 6 small-medium, cut into quarters
palm sugar (jaggery) or soft brown sugar – 2 tablespoons
spirit vinegar – a tablespoon
green cardamoms – 6

Cover the tamarind pulp with 100ml boiling water, smash the brown, date-like goo into the water with a fork or spoon and leave it for twenty minutes. Push the softened paste and its liquid through a small sieve (I use a tea strainer) with the back of a spoon. Discard the seeds and solids.

Cut the carrots into thin, almost hair-like strips. The simplest way to do this is with an attachment disc of a food processor (the one you might use for coleslaw, say).

Warm the vegetable oil in a saucepan, then add the garlic. Add the mustard seeds and let them cook for a minute or two until they pop, then add the chillies. Once the chillies have started to soften, a matter of a minute or two, stir in the carrots and continue to cook for three or four minutes. Add the tomatoes, palm sugar, tamarind liquid, the vinegar, the whole cardamoms, lightly crushed (you just want the pods to open and the seeds to be revealed) and a grinding of salt. Continue cooking gently for ten minutes, until the carrots are showing signs of tenderness; I think they should be still a little crunchy. The chutney will keep in the fridge, sealed in a Kilner jar, for a few days.

A carrot cake with a frosting of mascarpone and orange

You could measure my life in health-food shops. It is to them I turn for the bulk of my store-cupboard shopping, from parchment-coloured figs and organic almonds to sea salt and cubes of fresh yeast. Their shelves are a constant source of inspiration and reassurance. It is also where I first came across organic vegetables, long before the supermarkets saw them as a money-spinner or the organic box schemes would turn up at your door. It was these pine-clad shops, with their lingering scent of patchouli, that introduced me to the joys of the organic swede.

To this day I wouldn't go anywhere else for my lentils and beans, though I can live without the crystals and self-help manuals. There is something endlessly reassuring about their rows of cellophane-encased dates and haricot beans, their dried nuggets of cranberry and jars of organic peanut butter. And where else can you get a joss stick when you need one?

Health-food shops rarely used to be without a carrot cake on the salad counter, usually next to the blackcurrant cheesecake and the deep wholemeal quiche. Good they were, too, with thick cream cheese icing and shot through with walnuts. I never scorned them the way others did, finding much pleasure in the deep, soggy layers of cake and frosting. This was first published in *The Observer* five or six years ago, and rarely does a week go by without an email asking for a copy to replace one that has fallen apart or stuck to the bottom of a pan. Few things make a cook happier than someone asking for one of your recipes.

enough for 8–10
eggs – 3
self-raising flour – 250g
bicarbonate of soda – half a teaspoon
baking powder – a teaspoon
ground cinnamon – a teaspoon
salt – a pinch
sunflower oil – 200ml
light muscovado sugar – 250g
carrots – 150g
juice of half a lemon
walnuts – 150g

for the frosting
mascarpone cheese – 250g
Philadelphia cream cheese – 200g
unrefined icing sugar – 150g
the grated zest of a medium orange
walnut halves – a handful

Set the oven at 180°C/Gas 4. Lightly butter two 22cm cake tins, then line each with a disc of baking parchment.

Separate the eggs. Sift together the flour, bicarbonate of soda, baking powder, cinnamon and salt. Beat the oil and sugar in a food mixer until well creamed, then introduce the egg yolks one by one. Grate the carrots into the mixture, then add the lemon juice. Roughly chop the walnuts and add them too.

Fold the flour into the mixture with the machine on slow. Beat the egg whites till light and stiff, then fold tenderly into the mixture using a large metal spoon (a wooden one will knock the air out).

Divide the mixture between the two cake tins, smooth the top gently and bake for forty to forty-five minutes. Test with a skewer for doneness. The cakes should be moist but not sticky. Remove from the oven and leave to settle for a good ten minutes before turning the cakes out of their tins on to a wire cooling rack.

To make the frosting, put the mascarpone, Philadelphia cheese and icing sugar into an electric mixer and beat till smooth and creamy. It should have no lumps. Mix in the orange zest.

When the cake is cool, sandwich the halves together with about a third of the frosting. Use the rest to cover the top and sides of the cake. I don't think you need be too painstaking; a rough finish will look more appropriate here. Cover the top with walnut halves.

Cauliflower

If any vegetable was made to sit under a blanket of smooth cheese sauce, then this is it. As you pour your creamy béchamel, mornay or hollandaise over its chaste white curds it will stay there, caught amongst the gentle bumps, clouds and hollows of this, the pinnacle of the brassica family. You know, for once, that this is a recipe that was always meant to be.

The perfect cauliflower (a cauli somehow just has to be perfect; there is no excuse for one of second rank) has a snow-white head, unblemished, its florets so closely packed that you can barely separate them. These curds, as they are known, should be hard, tight and milky white. Even before you swaddle it in white sauce, it is a vegetable of peace and quiet beauty. A cauliflower's leaves, long and soft like the ears of a hare, curl over as if to protect its shy, white head from fierce sun or a hoar frost. The longest leaves are often cut off for practicality's sake, but there should be some still present when we buy, if only so we can gauge its freshness.

If I am being honest, the cauliflower is far from my favourite vegetable. Sometimes I think it wouldn't bother me if I never saw one again. Yet I occasionally long for a simple white bowl of cauliflower cheese on a frosty day, especially when it has been made with love, and the sauce has been improved with bay and clove and the cheese is of the robust sort that makes the veins on the roof of your mouth stand out. If there is snow on the ground, then even better.

Cauliflowers, white, ivory, cream, green or violet, are available for most of the year. The extraordinary Romanesco, a variety turreted like a fairy castle, is there much of the time, too. As well as the summer and winter types, there are intermediate ones that keep the shops supplied without so much as a blip. But I don't want any sort of flowering cabbage in the summer. Later on, this is a vegetable that I am happy to turn into a gratin for the last outdoor lunch of the year, a pale soup for a snowy winter's day, or a crisp salad with soured cream and poppy seeds. All-year-rounder it may be, but for me it's a going-back-to-school type of ingredient.

Some historians put the home of this difficult-to-grow member of the cabbage family as Cyprus. Whatever, it came to us towards the end of the sixteenth century, possibly via Italy and Spain. Christopher Stocks, author of *Forgotten Fruits* (Random House, 2008), suspects it could have 'quietly crept in' some time between the publication of Thomas Hill's *Gardener's Labyrinth* in 1577 (where it isn't mentioned) and Gerard's *Herbal* in 1597 (where it is).

Yes, I think the cauliflower would creep quietly in. Its chaste, slightly coy presence makes this a vegetable that would never shout its qualities. At its heart is a gentle cabbage flavour, mild and sweet when young, when you can also cook it without a smell lingering in the kitchen. Aged caulis are rather sad. The curd darkens to the colour of old piano keys, the texture becomes grainy (Alice Waters calls it 'ricey') and the florets spring apart. You can still use such a specimen for soup. There's a good one below with mustard and strong cheese to give it some bite.

A cauliflower in the garden

The cauliflower is regarded as a bugger to grow, or at least to grow well. Carol Klein calls it sensitive. It likes sun and a deep, moisture-retentive soil with a pH between 6.5 and 7.5. The soil should never dry out. The fuss continues with demands for a bed manured the autumn before sowing; an insistence on not growing your crop in the same spot two years running; the need to shield its curds from bright light by folding the larger leaves over the top, and even then you may well have to net them from the pigeons. This is indeed a vegetable for the committed gardener.

So, a challenge. Those who rise to it, rather than running off to Waitrose, will need to get the seed for summer varieties sown after Christmas in a greenhouse. If you are pretty much slug and pigeon free, you can plant winter and summer varieties in the spring directly where they are to grow or in modules, transplanting them when they are large enough to deal with without risk of damage to their delicate young leaves. They will need a good 60cm between plants. Both sun and intense cold will darken the heads, so keep them covered by the plumes of leaves that tower over the curds. You may need to break one in order to bend it over the modest white heart.

With luck and a fair wind, you could have a vegetable to be truly proud of. I have never grown one good enough for a soup, let alone a show. But I will keep trying.

Varieties

Well-organised growers manage to keep themselves in cauliflower all year round, following early summer types with autumn and winter heading varieties.

All Year Round A variety that lives up to its name. Slow to mature and will stand happily in the cold.

Summer Heading Sow under glass any time from Christmas till February or directly into the soil in April and May. Transplant to their final position in early summer, harvest in late summer and early autumn.

Beauty A good long season.

Nautilus Reliable, and tolerant of less than perfect conditions.

Snowball Small head of curds with long, pert ears of beautiful blue grey. A little delicate, but has a good reputation as a fine early-season variety.

Igloo (how could you resist?) Good for use as a mini-cauliflower, planted closer than usual, and will head up in July.

Autumn Heading Sow in modules in April and May, transplant in mid- summer, harvest in late autumn.

Skywalker A true autumn cauliflower. Vigorous, with tall leaves to protect the white curds.

Graffiti Violet curds that are sweeter than most. Might win over cauli-phobes.

Kestel Very white curds appearing late summer to early autumn. A lot of allotment holders seem to like this one.

Winter Heading Sow in May or June for harvesting in November and December.

Cendis The variety I know best. A reliable choice for the organic gardener.

White Dove Sow in May and June for a late winter crop. You could be picking in February. Good, dark green leaves to protect against frost.

A cauli in the kitchen

Yes, cauliflower cheese, but so, so much more. A cauli, snapped cleanly into florets, briefly steamed, then lightly battered and deep-fried is pleasing enough, but quite sensational when you dip the sizzling dumplings into a heart-pumping accompaniment of red chillies and lime juice, or spoon over a lemon-spiked green sauce.

Cauliflower's mild, almost creamy quality is what makes it such a successful contender for the spice treatment. Coriander seed, cumin, green chillies, paprika and fresh ginger complement rather than mask this brassica's natural blandness. Throw garlic, onion, even curry spices and garam masala at it and its flavour will still shine through.

We have our cheese sauce, the Indians have their aloo gobhi, the Spanish their fried florets scattered with paprika, capers and vinegar. All of which are worth eating. Yet this vegetable has lost out in recent years to the more cheerful coloured broccolis and sprouting brassicas. There was even a recent media campaign to halt its decline. My own take is that we now like our vegetables to shriek their healthy credentials in green, orange and red.

There was a vogue for cooking cauliflower whole. Yes, an entire head, coated in a pale cheese sauce, its saw-edged leaves poking up around the edge, is a quietly beautiful sight. But I would rather break mine up a bit, making it easier to cook more evenly and less of a trial to serve. Of could it just be that you get more sauce doing it my way?

There is very little to preparing this one for cooking. Just snap the white head into florets, rinse as you think fit, and it is ready for the steamer or a deep pan of hot water. Once inside, there is barely time to blink before its ivory stems soften. Few things in our shopping basket are easier to overcook.

The idea of raw cauliflower tends to polarise opinion, but it is worth trying the florets, crisp, mild and white, tossed with a dressing of soured cream or yoghurt mixed with chopped herbs such as parsley and tarragon. A scattering of steel-blue poppy seeds is rather beautiful against the white curds.

Seasoning your cauliflower

Cream Few vegetables, save possibly spinach, take to cream so well.
Nutmeg Cut the nut-shaped spice in half and grate it finely and abstemiously over warm cauliflower, or add it to a sauce. Easy to overdo, nutmeg needs using with caution.
Cheese The stronger cheeses marry well and the Cheddars especially. Parmesan was made for this brassica. Blue cheeses are worth trying too, especially the shyer ones like Stilton. Roquefort types are a tad too bold for such a subtle partner.
Soured cream You can make the salad mentioned above with raw florets tossed in soured cream and poppy seeds as an accompaniment to smoked salmon. It has the clean snap of a winter's day about it.
Parsley A lovely, peaceful herb with which to season the white curds. But do try dill and tarragon too.
Anchovies Chop them into an olive oil dip for raw florets.
Olives Green especially, scattered amongst a salad of lightly cooked cauliflower, lemon juice, olive oil and capers.

And...

* The white curd of a growing cauliflower is very sensitive to weather conditions. Although protected by the leaves, it can suffer discoloration when it finds itself in stressful situations. Blazing sun and heavy rain will take their toll on the quality of the florets, as will constant touching by the proud gardener. Best keep our hands off till cutting time.
* You can store a cauli for up to a week in the fridge. Wrapping the head in plastic will prevent it drying out.
* Wash a cauliflower briefly, then shake it gently dry. It doesn't like to be left soaking.
* The leaves are not to be despised. I leave the smaller ones attached.
* A squeeze of lemon in the cooking water will keep a cauli white.
* In the sixteenth century, this vegetable was known as 'Cyprus cabbage'. Its smell when cooking can be surprisingly pungent. I find a drop of olive oil and a bay leaf in the water produce an aroma both savoury and enticingly vegetal, whilst being distinctly less cabbagey.
* As a vegetable accompaniment, simply boiled and rolled in soft, salted butter, cauliflower is a perfectly charming partner for white fish, lamb, ham and roast or boiled beef. It has a certain calm purity to it.

A luxury cauliflower cheese

I enjoy making a bit of a fuss about cheese sauce. The difference between a carelessly put together sauce and one made with care and love is astounding. Taking the trouble to flavour the milk with bay, clove and onion, allowing the sauce to come together slowly to give its ingredients time to get know one another, and enriching it with a little cream will result in a sauce of twice the standing of one seasoned only with speed and sloppiness. There is much humble satisfaction in a simple dish, carefully made.

enough for 4 as a side dish, 2–3 as a main
milk – a litre
a bay leaf
a small onion
2 cloves
butter – 50g
plain flour – 50g
double cream – 4 tablespoons
good, strong farmhouse Cheddar – 100g, grated
a large cauliflower
finely grated Spenwood or Parmesan – 4 tablespoons

Pour the milk into a saucepan and drop in the bay leaf. Peel the onion, spike it with the cloves and add to the pan. Bring to the boil. As soon as the milk starts to rise in the pan, turn it off and leave to sit for ten minutes, whilst the bay and cloves work their subtle magic. Set the oven at 220°C/Gas 7.

Melt the butter in a heavy-based saucepan, tip in the flour and let the mixture cook, stirring regularly, till it is biscuit coloured and smells warm and nutty. Pour in the warm milk (leaving behind the onion whilst taking the bay leaf with you) and let it come almost to the boil. Stir as it thickens, seasoning with salt and pepper, and resorting to a whisk if you need to beat out any lumps. It is less trouble than a spoon. Turn down the heat and let the sauce simmer peacefully for a good fifteen to twenty minutes. Stir in the cream and the grated Cheddar, then correct the seasoning with more salt and pepper.

Break the cauliflower into large florets. Bring a pan of water to the boil, salt it lightly, then drop in the florets. Leave at a merry boil for three or four minutes, till they will take the point of a knife without too much pressure. Drain them carefully so they don't break up, then tip them into a baking dish. Pour over the cheese sauce, fishing the bay leaf out or not as you wish, then scatter the surface with the grated Spenwood or Parmesan. Bake for twenty minutes or so, till the sauce has formed a patchily golden crust and is bubbling languidly around the edge.

A soup of cauliflower and cheese

You could measure my life in bowls of soup. Each New Year's Day brings a pot of lentil soup (a good-luck symbol throughout much of Europe); pea and mint soup is to celebrate early summer; cabbage soup for colds and crash diets; parsnip soup for frosty weekends; chicken broth to cleanse my soul. You probably don't want to know about the parsimonious soup-stew I put together from the weekly fridge tidy.

I do believe in the power of soup to restore our spirits and to strengthen and protect us. Steaming, frugal, yet curiously luxurious, soup replaces many a meal in this house. With a good loaf on the bread board and fresh salad in the bowl, I have no shame in serving soup to visitors (only amusement in watching them looking round in vain for a main course). I first came up with the idea of this soup years ago, and have watched it do the rounds, yet it has never made it into any of my own books till now. It has something of the Welsh rarebit about it.

> *enough for 4–6*
> butter – 50g
> an onion, roughly chopped
> garlic – 2 cloves, crushed
> a cauliflower – broken into florets
> bay leaves – 2
> crème fraîche – 200ml
> grain mustard – 1 heaped tablespoon
> Gruyère, Cantal or strong Cheddar – 120g, coarsely grated
>
> **to finish**
> dark rye bread – 2 slices
> grated Gruyère – 1 heaped tablespoon

Melt the butter in a large, deep pan. Add the onion and garlic and fry until soft, but don't let them colour. Boil the cauliflower in about 850ml water till tender (about eight to ten minutes). Add the bay leaves to the onion, then add the cauliflower and its cooking water. Bring to the boil and add sea salt and black pepper. Cover and simmer for fifteen minutes, until the vegetables are truly soft. Remove the pan from the heat, discard the bay leaves and allow the soup to cool slightly. Then, in two batches, purée the soup in a blender. Pour the mixture back into the pan and stir in the crème fraîche, grain mustard and grated cheese. Bring the soup slowly back to a simmer.

To finish, toast the bread on both sides, cover with the grated cheese and let it melt under a hot grill. Cut into triangles and float them on the soup.

A fried cauliflower

enough for 2 as a principal dish
a medium cauliflower
sunflower or groundnut oil for deep-frying
gram flour – 3 tablespoons
paprika – half a teaspoon

for the salsa verde
parsley leaves – a generous handful
mint – 6 bushy sprigs
basil leaves – a handful
garlic – 2 cloves, crushed
Dijon mustard – a tablespoon
capers – 2 tablespoons, rinsed
olive oil – 6 tablespoons
lemon juice – 2 tablespoons

Break the cauliflower into florets. Boil in deep, salted water for a couple of minutes, then drain thoroughly.

To make the sauce, chop the herbs quite finely, but not so small they look like tealeaves, then stir in the garlic, mustard and capers. Pour in the olive oil slowly, beating with a fork. Stir in the lemon juice and season with sea salt and black pepper. Be generous with the seasoning, tasting as you go. The sauce should be bright tasting and piquant.

Get the oil hot in a deep pan. Toss the cauliflower with the gram flour, a little salt and pepper and the paprika. When the cauliflower is coated, fry in the hot oil till crisp – a matter of three or four minutes or so. Drain on kitchen paper before serving with the sauce.

A mildly spiced supper of cauliflower and potatoes

If a cauliflower is happiest under a comfort blanket of cream and cheese, we can run with the idea, dropping the cheese and introducing some of the milder, more fragrant spices such as coriander and cardamom into the cream instead. With its toasted cashew nuts and crisp finish of spiced fried onions, this is a mild dish, so I see no reason to soften the blow with steamed rice, preferring instead to eat it with a crunchy salad of chicory and watercress (or some such crisp, hot leaf), using it to wipe the sauce from my plate.

> *enough for 4*
> onions – 3 large
> groundnut, vegetable or sunflower oil
> garlic – 4 cloves
> ginger – a thumb-sized lump
> ground coriander – a tablespoon
> ground cumin – 2 teaspoons
> cayenne – half a teaspoon
> ground turmeric – half a teaspoon
> tomatoes – 3 medium
> water – 600ml
> potatoes – 3 medium
> a large cauliflower
> unroasted cashew nuts – a good handful
> green cardamom pods – 6
> garam masala – a tablespoon
> crème fraîche– 150–200ml
> coriander – a small bunch

Peel the onions, chop one of them roughly, then let it soften with a tablespoon or two of oil in a deep pan over a moderate heat. Halve and thinly slice the others and set aside. Peel the garlic cloves, slice them thinly then stir into the softening onion. Continue cooking, without browning either the onion or the garlic. Peel the ginger, cut it into fine matchsticks, then add to the onion and garlic.

Stir the ground coriander, cumin, cayenne and turmeric into the onion. Let them fry for a minute or two, then roughly chop the tomatoes and add them to the pan. Add the water and bring to the boil. Season with salt and a generous grinding of black pepper. Cut the potatoes into large pieces (as if for boiling) and add them to the pan. Lower the heat and leave to simmer for fifteen minutes before breaking the cauliflower into large florets (about 40g each is good) and adding to the sauce. Quickly toast the cashew nuts in a small, non-stick frying pan till golden. Tip them into the pot, cover with a lid and continue to simmer for fifteen to twenty minutes.

Meanwhile, fry the reserved onions in a little oil in a shallow pan till deep, nutty gold. Whilst they are cooking, crack the cardamom pods, scrape out the seeds, crush lightly and add to the onions. Continue cooking for five minutes or so, then, when all is gold and fragrant, remove and place on kitchen paper.

When the cauliflower and potatoes are tender to the point of a knife, stir in the garam masala (the spices in it are already roasted, so it needs very little cooking) and the crème fraîche. Simmer for a minute, then serve topped with the reserved cardamom onions and the roughly chopped or torn coriander leaves.

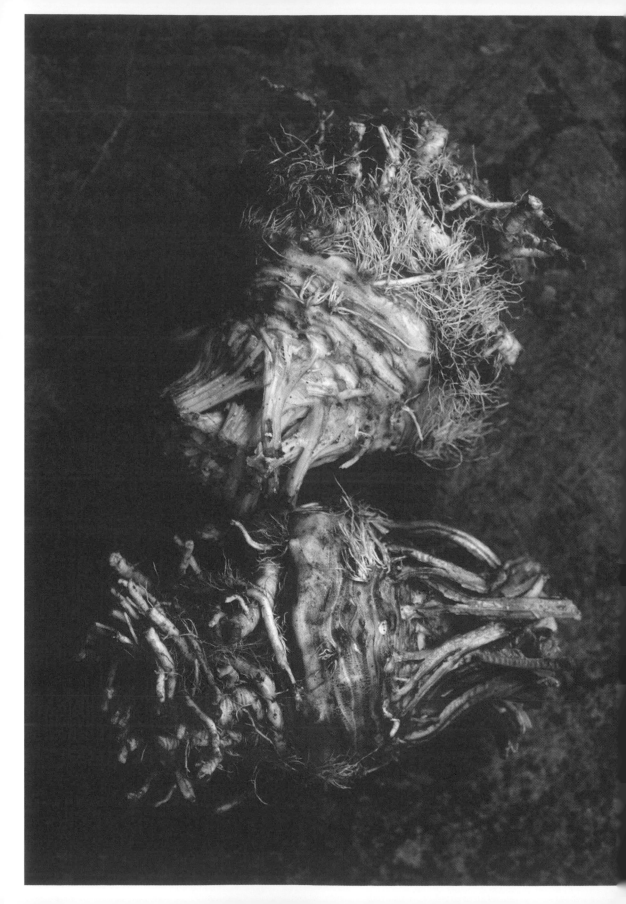

Celeriac

Knobbly, whiskery and impenetrable, its roots curled round its feet like a viper's nest, celeriac poses something of a problem for the newcomer. There are no crisp leaves to entice, no sweet juice to stir our passion, no perfume to inhale with closed eyes. In fact, no real clue at all to its reason for being. *Apium graveolens* seems an appropriately sombre botanical name.

Brush off the encrusted soil, hack away at the thick, warty skin and you have a clean, crisp bulb with the scent of freshly cut celery. Once you breathe in its cool notes of aniseed, hazelnuts and clean, sweet earth, your gnarled root starts to develop distinct culinary possibilities. A soup yes, an ice-crisp salad with apples and jagged splinters of bacon maybe, a possible candidate for the roasting tin. Opportunities slowly start to present themselves.

This member of the celery family is often referred to as 'turnip-rooted celery', as if that would do it any favours. The thin green stalks and their tuft of leaves that sprout from the bulbous root resemble the plumper, juicier ones of their better-known cousin, but they have all the bitterness of the wild variety. Put them on the compost. Most celeriac from the greengrocer's comes shorn of its stalks anyway.

The modern varieties are less rustic looking than the celeriac of old. They have been bred to possess a smoother skin, without the tangle of roots at the base, and are of a decent enough size that you need only one to make a pile of buttery mash for four. Progress of a kind. That said, you still need to use a knife rather than a peeler to gain admission.

But why would you bother when celery is so readily available and user friendly? The answer is in the root's subtlety, its failure to dominate a stew or a soup in the way that one stalk too much of celery can, and its ease of growing. That you can mash and roast it should alone answer the question. I also value the craggy one for its keeping quality, and the chance of having a long-life vegetable other than butternut squash in the house.

In some parts of the country celeriac root is known as 'celery knave' or 'celery knob', the latter sounding even more unfortunate than cauliflower ear.

Celeriac in the garden

To the gardener, celeriac has several advantages over its leggier cousin, the principal one being its robustness. A row of celery-root will keep happily in the ground over winter, or will store patiently in a cool garage. There is none of the blanching or earthing-up process associated with celery, much less disease and less demand for attention.

This is not a fussy vegetable (nor could it afford to be with those looks), and it will quietly do its thing in the most awkward corner of the vegetable patch. Full sun or partial shade, a soil of clay or sand, it will even withstand a bit of a drought later in its growth, but the fattest, whitest bulbs will come from well-manured, well-watered soil in good sun. If you can water it almost daily during its early stages, then all the better.

The seeds are tiny, and you should get them in early, by the end of March at least. Start them in small pots in a warm place, scattering the seeds over the surface of the compost, then covering with a very fine layer of vermiculite. They need to be kept at at least 15°C to germinate – unusually warm for a vegetable seed. Transfer to larger pots when the seedlings are showing a good pair of leaves.

Don't shock the youngsters by putting them straight into cold soil, but get them used to the thought of a life outdoors by bringing them out during the day, then back in at night, for a week or two. Mid May and June is probably early enough to plant out, each seedling about 30cm apart and with some slug protection such as a copper ring or a moat of coarse sand.

Water is essential until the plants have a chance to get settled; a wet summer has its uses, and it is a good idea to add a mulch around the plants to retain as much of it as possible. The idea is to get the plants well and truly established before the real heat of summer hits.

As they grow, the swollen stem bases will sit proud of the soil. If you have planted one of the older varieties, pull the lower leaves off over the summer to prevent your harvest getting too knobbly. As autumn approaches, cover the exposed crowns with soil to keep their flesh white. Many growers leave their celeriac in the ground over winter, tucking it under a loose blanket of straw if there are long, icy periods.

Varieties

It is not so much the flavour that varies with the variety but other factors, such as appearance and ease of growing.

Monarch Probably the smoothest. A newish variety that discolours less than the older ones when cut.

Giant Prague The one they grow at Heligan. Reliable and charmingly knobbly.

Brilliant White flesh, quite craggy to look at, but good keeping qualities.

Prinz A knotty heirloom variety considered very fine by aficionados.

Celeriac in the kitchen

The French probably got there first with celeriac remoulade – the classic salad made by dressing coarsely grated raw celery root with a mustardy mayonnaise. They spotted the nutty, mineral notes that set it apart from sweeter roots such as carrot and parsnip; even if you cook it there is much less sugar here. They realised that these mineral notes and its earthy quality are its trump cards (they appear almost nowhere else in the vegetable world) and that they are best captured with the bite of vinegar or lemon juice.

A sticky mayonnaise or robust vinaigrette, made on the rough side with a coarse hit of white or red wine vinegar, will show the raw bulb at its best. I'm not sure anything is to be gained by using a posh, timid version, though some berry vinegars have worked for me. To that you can add mustard, as much or as little as you like, and maybe some walnuts, whose nutty qualities bring out the same in the celeriac, just as a spoonful of honey brings out the sweetness in a roasting parsnip.

This is one root that makes a sloppy mash and needs an equal amount of potato if it is to stand in a cloudlike mound. I'm not sure it matters, but others seem to think so. Celeriac mash with a plainly roasted pheasant is an autumn treat, especially with a curl or two of fat-marbled bacon. In a visual and textural sense it is difficult to serve with roast chicken if you are also having bread sauce. A dash of lemon in the cooking water will prevent a grey mash.

I have no doubt that the most delectable roast celeriac is that which has been blanched in boiling water first (be generous with the salt). The inner core of each piece becomes meltingly tender and, though the outside never crisps quite as tantalisingly as a potato, it is still more than worth the trouble. Not giving them five minutes in boiling water first throws up the risk of them drying out as they roast.

As good as this branch of the celery family is when mashed or roasted, I have had the most heartening results when I have sliced it, then baked it in a slow oven with a moistening of stock and a knob of butter. You can pair it with another vegetable – pumpkin is a good one – or leave it by itself. Either way, it emerges soft and earthy.

I try not to waste any vegetable. Even throwing them in the direction of the compost fills me, albeit briefly, with guilt. But sometimes we just have to go with it. Whereas celery has just a few stalks and leaves to trim, this needs a good strong cook's knife to cut away the rough skin and tuft of stem. You could put the trimmings in the stockpot, where they will be of genuine use, but I doubt anyone will grumble if you sneak them into the compost.

Seasoning your celeriac

Lime juice An idea from Sarah Raven. The juice brings excitement to a salad of grated celery root and caraway seed.

Apples Use the two together in a soup or grated in a salad. I find the Russets work best, but then I'm deeply biased in favour of our rough-skinned apples.

Mustard Yes, in a classic remoulade, but also as a seasoning for soup or in a walnut oil and lemon dressing.

Celery seeds Not the overkill you might expect. The seed's musky flavours lend depth and mystery.

Honey A little in a salad dressing is good here, as is a spoonful tossed with hot roast roots in the roasting tin.

Thyme Not the easiest to match to a herb, celeriac nevertheless enjoys the company of woody herbs such as thyme and rosemary and is, I think, lacking something when there's no parsley present.

Lemon Apart from making the flavour sing just that bit louder, a shot of citrus will halt the oxidation process, keeping your grated roots white.

Walnuts The raw bulb, grated and dressed with either mayonnaise or an oil-and-vinegar, marries well with the flavour and texture of walnuts, even more so with cobnuts if you can catch their milky selves during their short season in early September.

Vinegar Rough vinegar lifts the bulb's white flesh to a more interesting level, especially the more astringent white wine varieties. Tarragon-infused vinegar works too (there's the aniseed connection), as does a slightly rasping red wine version. Celeriac likes it rough, but don't rule out the fruit versions such as raspberry. A shake over celeriac chips is a good thing in the way that fish-shop vinegar does such wonders for chips.

And...

* As vegetables go, the length of time from sowing to harvest is among the longest: thirty weeks for celeriac as opposed to twelve for carrots and fourteen for courgettes.
* The nutty notes signal the possibilities of this root working well with cheeses, and especially at the blue-veined level. Stir crumbled Stichelton, Stilton, Cashel Blue or Roquefort into a celeriac soup; serve the wafer-thin slices of the root with a lump of Picos and a long, green, mild pickled chilli; spread a creamy Gorgonzola on fingers of raw celeriac.
* A soaking in lemon juice not only keeps the flesh white but also has the effect of tenderising the starch too.
* It is difficult to think of a meat with which celeriac doesn't fit, but pork and beef are usually more appreciative than lamb.
* Celeriac mash is good with game birds, the denser and darker fleshed the better.

Celeriac remoulade – a contemporary version

Crème fraîche or strained yoghurt offers many of the qualities of mayonnaise but with a cleaner, more piquant character. Beating in a small amount of olive or walnut oil will nudge it towards the perfect coating consistency of a classic mayonnaise-type remoulade dressing. Using these tart alternatives lends a lightness, too.

enough for 4 as a side dish
the juice of half a lemon
celeriac – about 500g
a raw medium beetroot
crème fraîche – 4 heaped tablespoons
grain mustard – 2 teaspoons
a little olive or walnut oil
parsley – a small handful of leaves
walnut halves – a scattering

Squeeze the lemon into a mixing bowl. Peel the celeriac, then grate it coarsely. A food processor with the coarse grater attachment is easier than trying to do it by hand. Tip into a mixing bowl and toss gently with the lemon juice to keep it from discolouring. Grate the beetroot and add it to the celeriac, but don't mix it up just yet.

Put the crème fraîche in a small bowl, stir in the mustard and a little salt and black pepper. Gently mix in enough oil to make a coating consistency – probably about 2 or 3 tablespoons. Roughly chop the parsley leaves and add to the dressing. Mix gently with a small whisk or fork, then fold into the shredded vegetables, mixing only lightly, so that the beetroot doesn't send everything pink. Toast the walnuts lightly in a small, non-stick frying pan, then scatter them over the salad.

A simple salad of celeriac and sausage

Many of my most pleasing suppers have been one-off, chucked-together affairs made with whatever was to hand. A question of making do. I rarely write them down, assuming that no one else will be interested in something that simply filled a hole with whatever happened to be around at the time. This was one of those meals, taken as lunch in early March when the cupboard was pretty bare, but I thought I would pass it on for its frugal, done-in-a minute quality and as yet another opportunity to do something with the celeriac that turns up in the organic veg box.

enough for 2
celeriac – about 500g
plump, garlicky butcher's sausages – 4
groundnut oil – 3 tablespoons
walnut oil – a tablespoon
lemon juice – a tablespoon
smooth Dijon mustard – 2 teaspoons
flat-leaf parsley – a small bunch

Peel the celeriac, dipping it into cold water containing a drop of lemon juice as you go. Cut into pieces about the thickness of a two-pound coin. Bring to the boil in a pan of deep water, add salt, then cook for seven to ten minutes, until knifepoint tender.

Meanwhile fry or grill the sausages as you think fit, then cut them into thinnish slices and drop them into a salad bowl. If they crumble, all to the good. Make the dressing with the groundnut and walnut oil, lemon juice and mustard, whisking the ingredients together with a grinding of salt and pepper. Chop the parsley and stir it into the dressing (the parsley is essential here, I think).

Drain the celeriac. Now toss carefully with the sausage and the dressing.

A remoulade of celeriac and smoked bacon

As much as I appreciate the traditional rendition of the sort of celeriac remoulade you might get in a Parisian brasserie, I also like to shake it up a bit. Including the ham, or even bacon, in the salad rather than serving it alongside gives the meat a while to get to know the other ingredients, becoming more than just an accompaniment. An alternative to bacon would be shreds of smoked venison or Parma ham, or maybe smoked mackerel.

Radish sprouts are stunningly coloured sprouted seeds with a spicy heat. Enterprising wholefood shops and supermarkets have them, or you can sprout your own in a salad sprouter. If they evade you, you could use any sprouted seed here.

enough for 2 as a light main course

for the dressing
crème fraîche – 250ml
the juice of half a lemon
grain mustard – 2 tablespoons

for the salad
parsley leaves – a large handful
celeriac – about 500g
smoked bacon – 8 rashers
radish sprouts or mung bean sprouts – 50g

Mix the crème fraîche, lemon juice and mustard together and stir in a little salt and black pepper.

Roughly chop the parsley. Peel the celeriac and shred it coarsely. I find this easiest with a food processor and a coarse grater attachment. Grill the bacon till it is starting to crisp and the fat has turned gold, then cut it into pieces the size of a postage stamp. Stir the celeriac, radish sprouts, parsley, bacon and dressing together. Serve while the bacon is still hot.

Steamed pork in an aromatic broth, celeriac purée

Knuckle is not an easy piece of meat to carve. I just do the best I can, cutting the soft meat away in pieces and laying them in a shallow bowl or deep plate. Then ladle the thin, aromatic broth around it.

enough for 4
pork knuckle or spare rib chops on the bone – 2kg
spring onions – 10
a lump of ginger – 75g
garlic – 4 cloves
groundnut oil – 2 tablespoons
sugar – 2 tablespoons
dark soy sauce – 2 tablespoons
rice wine – 3 tablespoons
salt – a level teaspoon
a whole star anise
five-spice powder – a teaspoon
crushed dried chillies – a teaspoon
a stick of cinnamon
stock – a litre

for the celeriac purée
a large head of celeriac
butter – 50g

Fill a large pan with water, add the piece of pork to it and bring to the boil. Simmer for five minutes, then lift out the pork and set aside, pouring away the cooking water. While the meat is simmering, trim the spring onions, discarding the darkest part of the green stalks, and chop them. Peel the ginger and cut the flesh into matchsticks. Peel and finely slice the garlic.

Put the pan back on the heat and add the oil. Warm it over a moderate heat, then add the spring onions, ginger and garlic and leave to soften, stirring so they do not colour. Lower in the piece of pork.

Add the sugar, soy sauce, rice wine, salt, star anise, five-spice powder, crushed chillies and cinnamon stick and then pour in the stock. Bring to the boil, turn the heat down so that the cooking continues at a comfortable simmer, then cover with a lid. Leave to cook gently for an hour, checking occasionally that there is plenty of liquid left in the pan. Turn the meat over, so that the other half is now under the broth, cover and continue cooking for a further hour.

Peel the celeriac, chop it up and boil in deep, salted water till tender. It should be ready in about twenty to twenty-five minutes. Drain thoroughly and put into a food processor with the butter and some black pepper. Whiz to a smooth purée.

To serve, put a big spoonful of celeriac purée in the middle of a large, shallow bowl. Carve the pork into rough slices (it will fall apart as you do so) and lay it on the purée. Pour a ladleful or two of broth around the outside and serve. You'll need spoons for the broth.

A pot-roast pheasant with celeriac mash

Pheasant and celery get on rather well. I sometimes put thick ribs in with the aromatics for a pot-roast bird, and have included shredded celery in a salad of cold pheasant with Little Gem lettuce and walnuts. Celeriac seems to be one of the most successful mashes to serve with the mildly gamey flesh of this bird (parsnip is good, too).

enough for 4
olive oil – 2 tablespoons
pancetta cubes – 150g
oven-ready pheasants – 2
garlic – 2 cloves
sage leaves – 4
dry Marsala – 200ml

for the mash
potatoes – 4 medium to large
a whole head of celeriac
butter – 50g

Set the oven at 180°C/Gas 4. Warm the oil and the cubes of pancetta in a large, heavy-bottomed casserole set over a medium heat. When the pancetta fat starts to colour, add the pheasants and brown them lightly on all sides.

Peel the garlic cloves and slice each one in half lengthways. Add them to the pot with the sage leaves, then pour in the Marsala. Let it come to the boil, cover the casserole with a lid and put in the oven for forty minutes. Turn the pheasants once during cooking.

To make the mash, peel the potatoes and celeriac and, keeping them separate, cut them into large pieces, as you would for boiled potatoes. Put them in separate pans of cold water and bring to the boil, starting the potatoes ten minutes before the celeriac. As soon as both are tender, drain them, mix the potatoes and celeriac together and mash with the butter. I do this with a potato masher, followed by a good whipping with a wooden spoon, but you could do it in a food mixer if you don't mind the washing up.

To serve, divide the mash between four warm plates. Lift the pheasants from the casserole and put them on a chopping board. Using a heavy cook's knife, cut each one in half lengthways (this sounds scary if you have never done it before, but you will find one good push should do it). Place half a bird on each pile of mash, then spoon over the hot juices and pancetta from the pan.

A baked cake of celeriac and parsnips

Once the snowdrops are out and the buds on the trees start breaking, I have usually have had enough of mashed, roasted and baked roots and am gasping for the fresh greens of spring. As the root season draws to a close, I find a dish of parsnips and celeriac, thinly sliced and slowly baked, makes a pleasant enough change. Sweet and yielding, this is both an accompaniment and a vegetable dish in its own right. I have used the quantities below as a main dish for two before now.

enough for 4
onion – a large one
parsnip – 500g
celeriac – 500g
butter – 85g
thyme leaves – a teaspoon
vegetable stock – 100ml

Peel the onion and slice it into thin rounds. Put them in a large mixing bowl. Peel the parsnips and celeriac and cut them into very fine slices. A sharp knife will work, but you could use a mandolin or the appropriate disc on your food processor (it's the one at the very back of the drawer). However you go about it, your slices should be almost thin enough to see through. Toss them with the onion.

Set the oven to 190°C/Gas 5. Melt the butter in a shallow ovenproof pan, then add the vegetables, layering them neatly or just chucking them in as the mood takes you, seasoning with the thyme leaves, pepper and salt as you go. Be quite generous with the salt. Now pour the stock over the top.

Cover with a circle of greaseproof paper or kitchen foil, pressing it down well on the top of the cake. Bake for about an hour and ten minutes, until tender to the point of a knife. Remove the cover, turn the heat up to 220°C/Gas 7 and bake for a further ten minutes, until the top has coloured and crisped a little.

A crunchy celeriac and blood orange
salad for a frosty day

There is something uplifting about refreshing food eaten on a frosty day.
What follows is a light, fresh-tasting salad that makes your eyes sparkle.

enough for 4
small kohlrabi – 2
a blood orange
the juice of half a lemon
capers – 12
olive oil – 3 tablespoons
raw beetroot – 2 small
celeriac – a 200g wedge
spring onions – 3
flat-leaf parsley – a handful

for the dressing
thick yoghurt (I use sheep's) – 200g
olive oil – 3–4 tablespoons
garlic – a small clove, crushed

Slice the kohlrabi thinly and divide the slices between four flat plates.
I don't think you have to peel them, but you can if you wish. The slices
should be very thin, otherwise the whole thing loses its delicate quality.

Peel and thinly slice the blood orange and place on top of the kohlrabi.
Add a pinch of sea salt to the lemon juice, stir in the capers and olive oil,
then spoon it over the sliced kohlrabi. Set aside for a good half hour.

Peel and coarsely shred the beetroot and celeriac. Finely shred the
spring onions and toss all together with the parsley leaves. Mix the yoghurt
and olive oil, stir in the crushed garlic clove and add a pinch of salt and
black pepper.

Pile the grated vegetables on the kohlrabi and add the dressing.
Mix together as you eat, to retain the fresh crunch of the raw vegetables.

Celery

More than any other, celery is the vegetable I associate with Christmas. The Fenland-grown white stalks are at their peak then, with more earthy, mineral notes than the green celery we see for the rest for the year. They possess more of a crunch too, and less water. Balance a crumb of Stilton on a single stalk and you have the essence of the season on your tongue.

I am thankful enough for the green stuff. Translucent, juicy, commonplace, its fresh-tasting ribs make a cool contrast to a musky hummus or a smoky *moutabal*. I use a stalk as one might a spoon, in place of hot pitta, to scoop up the sloppy, garlicky sauces.

Celery comes to us from the wild 'smallage', a thin, tough and stringy member of the carrot family that was used as both a herb and a medicine. The flowers are tiny and white, like fairy parasols, their scent strong and unmistakable. The Italians look the most likely to have bred the thicker, milder-tasting stalks we know now, some time around the sixteenth century. They appeared here in Britain a century later.

Christmas celery, with its flatter, ice-white stalks was something we put on the table in a jug of cold water at home, which had the effect of crisping it up nicely. A trick I use to this day. White celery comes with strings, which perversely I like, but which puts many people off. It is rare to find green celery with strings and when you do, they are less tough and tend to snap rather than sticking in your teeth.

It has to be said that of all the vegetables I have grown, cooked with or talked about, celery is the most unpopular. For every person I have met who turns their nose up at swede or claims not to think much of parsnips, I must have come across twenty who reckon they 'hate' celery. A lifelong fan, I almost feel like starting an appreciation society. I like vegetables that remind you that they come from the soil, and few do that as uncompromisingly as this one. At least, the white stalks do; I'm not sure some of the imported green stuff has ever been near real earth.

A well-made celery soup is the voice of calm. I stir in blue cheese to give it some bite. Having once been virtually the only soup offered on hotel lunch menus, it has now almost disappeared. I still make it though, and there is a good working recipe below. You can bake the stalks too, and serve them with pot-roast pheasant, the recipe for which is in *Appetite*.

Celery in the garden

I have no doubt that a standing trench of celery is a beautiful sight on an allotment, an achievement to make any grower puff out his chest, but such an undertaking would defeat even the most enthusiastic home-grower. I have never grown celery, and what is more I probably never will. Celery is a crop for only the most committed of gardeners. Even the modern 'self-blanching' varieties such as Loretta and Celebrity, for which there is no need to dig a trench, are beyond this gardener-cook.

Celery's copious demands mean that growing a row is either a non-starter or an obsession – unlike everything else in this book, there is nothing in between. Your seed will need both warmth and light, and may be slow to germinate. Seedlings must be grown at a minimum of 10°C and young plants will need protecting with fleece. You will be required to dig a trench, cosset your young plants with plenty of water and keep on almost permanent slug patrol, as they find the fleshy stalks as irresistible as a delphinium. There is mid-season mulching to do and the late-season earthing up – the notorious blanching – that will keep your stalks pale and crisp. And don't even ask about the celery fly. When the great Alan Titchmarsh refers to growing celery as 'decidedly challenging', I think one gets the message. I regard growing it as beyond the simple realms of this book, written for the enthusiastic amateur. But don't let me put you off. If you fancy trench warfare, go for it.

Celery in the kitchen

Celery is the place where vegetables and aromatics meet. Its principal use in my kitchen is as a way to get hummus into my mouth if I am not in the mood for bread (or more likely, there simply isn't any) but a close second is when it joins bay leaves and onion as the aromatic foundation of a stew or a soup. For this alone, it is worth its place in the shopping bag.

In a stew, braise, sauce or soup, celery is often used as part of the base, with onion, garlic, carrot, bay leaves and sometimes thyme sweated in butter, to produce a backbone on which to build up flavour. These base notes will vary according to which country you are cooking in – the Spanish will add tomato, the Italians more garlic – but a small amount of celery, perhaps a single stalk in a recipe for six, is usually present. The stalks can turn bitter when they colour, so it is best to keep the heat moderate, and add them after the onion and garlic have started to soften.

Heads of celery are rarely used as a vegetable in their own right. A shame, because they can be made into a particularly juicy and sweet main course when baked in a cheese or herb-flecked sauce or poached in stock. Like chicory, celery doesn't conform to the boiled-and-buttered knee-jerk treatment so beloved of the British cook, so it needs a little more thought. I make a good celery soup, and a warming gratin too, but I know I am unusual in giving this vegetable so much of a starring role.

Elizabeth David was fond of celery, pointing us in the direction of a dip of mashed anchovies, olive oil and vinegar and towards a slightly more interesting idea with a garlicky version of hollandaise sauce, both for raw stalks. I think we have all moved on a bit now, but her idea of stewing the roughly chopped ribs in a shallow pan of butter and oil for fifteen minutes and finishing them with a spoonful of good chicken stock is still valid. A lovely dish with pheasant or other game, or pork chops.

Seasoning your celery

Aniseed Any of the aniseed herbs – tarragon, dill, chervil and fennel – has the effect of bringing out the stalks' better points.

Anchovy Difficult to use the two together, but an anchovy mayonnaise for a celery-based salad is a possibility, as is adding a crushed fillet or two to an oil and vinegar dressing.

Parsley A lovely combination with celery.

Mushrooms A good friend.

Walnuts There is a lot of crunch going on when the two are combined, but nevertheless their flavours are more than happy together.

Cheese Use for a marriage made in heaven. Any cheese is a worthy suitor, but especially the soft, Brie-like varieties and most of all the blues.

Celery salt Made from crushing sea salt with celery seeds, this is a faintly bitter aromatic to enhance any celery-based dish and also a worthwhile seasoning for other vegetable-based recipes. It is the principal seasoning for a Bloody Mary.

And...

* Celery is good with game in any form: stuffed around the bird in a pot roast, included in a salad of cold pheasant and apple, or served as a vegetable beside roast venison or a casserole of pigeon.
* White celery often has strings running down the length of its ribs. Remove them by grabbing them at the root end between thumb and knife blade and pulling down.
* Celery provides the earthy note in the base for a stew, marrying perfectly with the sweet notes of the carrot and the savoury ones of the onion, but adding a few dill seeds will make it more prominent. A good one for true celery lovers.
* Cooking the heads whole is not really an option, as soil gets trapped at the root end of each stalk. Slicing them in half lengthways allows you to rinse out any grains of soil before cooking. The green ones are easier to deal with than the white.
* Celery is one of the few vegetables to emerge from the canning process virtually unscathed. Though only from the cook's point of view rather than the cheese-eater's.
* Most of our commercial white celery is grown on the Fens, where the plants love the deep, black soil and moist climate. This is the Rolls-Royce of celery and worth looking out for from October till the New Year.
* The leaves cut from the top of the stalks make an interesting addition to a salad, particularly ones containing apples or cheese. I tend to munch them while I'm chopping the rest.
* Rather than serving celery snapped off into stalks, it is an idea to cut the entire head, still joined at the root, in half lengthways, then again into three, so that you get a long 'wedge' rather than a single stalk. This way, you get the crisp outer ribs and the tender inner ones all at once.
* Adding a lump of celeriac to a celery soup will intensify the flavour and add body.

A dish of baked celery and its sauce

When making a sauce to blanket a dish of boiled celery ribs, I like to harness the mineral quality by using the celery's cooking water in with the milk. It deepens the flavour and, together with parsley, establishes the vegetable's earthy flavour. Celery blanched in deep water, smothered with a duvet of slightly bland and salty sauce and given a crust of breadcrumbs and cheese is certainly worth eating. I have suggested making a crust for the celery and its sauce with Parmesan and breadcrumbs, but there is much success to be had with Berkswell, the sheep's milk cheese from the Midlands. Despite being a rather different cheese from Parmesan, it has a similar fruitiness.

enough for 6
celery – 2 plump heads
a small onion
bay leaves – a couple
milk – 250ml
butter – 45g
plain flour – 40g
Parmesan – a couple of handfuls, freshly grated
flat-leaf parsley – a small bunch
fresh breadcrumbs – a large handful

Snap the heads of celery into individual ribs (a strangely satisfying task), then wash, trim and neaten them where necessary. Lay the ribs in a large, flameproof baking dish or saucepan and pour in enough water barely to cover them. Peel and thinly slice the onion, then add to the dish with the bay leaves, a little salt and some black pepper. Poach over a low heat, with the water at a gentle bubble, till the celery is tender to the point of a knife.

Set the oven at 180°C/Gas 4. Remove the celery, onion and bay with a draining spoon and lay them in a large, shallow baking dish or roasting tin, leaving the hot cooking liquor behind. Warm the milk in a small pan. In a separate pan, melt the butter over a moderate heat and stir in the flour. Continue cooking, stirring pretty much continuously, till you have a pale, biscuit-coloured paste – it will smell warm and slightly nutty. Add 350ml of the cooking liquor from the celery followed by the warmed milk, a small ladleful at a time, until you have a smooth sauce. Stir in three-quarters of the Parmesan and turn the heat down so that the sauce simmers quietly for a good fifteen to twenty minutes. Chop the parsley not too finely, stir it into the sauce, then taste and correct the seasoning (I try to bear in mind that I will be adding more Parmesan shortly, which will be a little salty).

Pour the sauce over the celery. Mix the remaining grated Parmesan with the breadcrumbs, then strew over the top. Bake for forty minutes or so, till the sauce is bubbling enticingly.

A soup of celery and blue cheese

Long associated with the finale of the Christmas meal, Stilton and celery is a fine combination and there is every reason to turn it into a soup. I'm not sure it matters which blue cheese you use but the saltier types tend to be more interesting here. A good Stilton will work well enough, but something with more punch – say Picos, Roquefort, Stichelton or Cashel Blue – would get my vote, as would good old Danish Blue. Cream is usually a given with celery soup, but I am not sure you need it.

enough for 4
celery – a large head
an onion
celeriac – half a head, about 250g
butter – a thick slice
chicken stock – a litre
a bay leaf
blue cheese – 125g

Give the celery stalks a really good wash, then chop them roughly. Peel and roughly chop the onion and celeriac.

Melt the butter in a deep pan, tip in the chopped vegetables and let them cook for about twenty minutes, until soft. Pour in the stock, put in the bay leaf and bring to the boil. Season with salt (remember that you will be adding a salty blue cheese later), then lower the heat to a simmer and leave for half an hour, stirring occasionally.

Put the soup through a blender or food processor till really smooth. It may need a little longer than most other vegetables. Check the seasoning and ladle into warm soup bowls. Crumble the cheese into the soup at the table and stir until it is partially melted.

A simple sauté of chicken and celery

Some steamed or boiled potatoes, slightly fluffy at the edges, would be my choice of accompaniment here, with a plate of large, soft lettuce leaves for mopping up the juices.

enough for 2–3
chicken joints (thighs, drumsticks, whatever) – 6
butter – 50g, and some more to finish the sauce
olive oil – 2 tablespoons
garlic – 3 cloves, peeled
half a head of celery
parsley – a small bunch

a glass of Noilly Prat or other white vermouth
lemon juice

Season the chicken all over with salt and black pepper. Melt the butter in
a shallow pan and pour in the olive oil. Put the chicken in, skin-side down,
and allow to colour lightly, then turn it over. Keeping the heat moderate,
add the whole peeled garlic cloves and cover with a lid. Leave to cook for
about forty-five minutes, checking regularly.

Break the celery into ribs and cut into short lengths. Once the chicken
has been cooking for twenty minutes, add the celery. Continue cooking till
everything is tender. Chop the parsley leaves; you will need a good handful.

Remove the chicken and celery to a warm place. Pour the vermouth into
the pan and let it boil, scraping away at the sticky goodness at the bottom
of the pan with a wooden spatula and stirring it into the bubbling
vermouth. Leave over a high heat to bubble down a bit. It will never
thicken, but will become slightly syrupy. Whisk in a thick slice of butter, say
50g, and the chopped parsley. Freshen with a squirt of lemon juice if it needs
it. Return the chicken and celery to the pan, continue for a couple
of minutes till all is hot, and serve.

A gentle vegetable dish of old-fashioned grace

Heads of celery, braised in good chicken stock, are a reminder of the elegant
days of hotel dining rooms and railway dining cars. A flashback to times
before chefs were ever talked about, let alone 'celebrities', and the head
waiter rather than the kitchen ruled the roost. Braised celery is what I want
to eat with roast turkey and the trimmings.

enough for 4
celery – 2 heads
chicken stock – 200ml
butter – 50g
garlic – a fat clove, peeled and flattened
Madeira – 3 tablespoons

Set the oven at 180°C/Gas 4. Trim the bunches of celery, leaving the stalks
attached at the root end and cutting each head down to about 20cm in
length; keep the trimmings for stock. Cut each head in half lengthways.

Heat the stock. Melt the butter in an flameproof dish and gently fry the
heads of celery over a low heat without letting them colour. Add the garlic
and Madeira, then pour over the hot stock. Cover with a piece of buttered
greaseproof paper or a lid, then bake for forty-five to fifty minutes, till the
celery is tender.

Chard

The garden sleeps. Here and there the white tear of a snowdrop, a late Crimson Bengal rose glazed with frost, a paw print deep in the snow. The few cabbages are battle scarred from the wind and freezing rain, their leaves like green-blue lace. If I had to live from this little garden I would starve.

Tucked behind the yew hedge that separates the vegetable patch from the rest of the garden, the dark green is suddenly shattered by a row of chard as bright as a jar of boiled sweets. Their maroon and bottle-green leaves, veins as thick as pencils, lie fallen from the cold, but their stalks – ruby, apricot, saffron and ivory, and one the colour of seaside rock – glow as if lit by candles.

Swiss, ruby and rainbow chard are one of the few vegetables that remain in this plot in deepest winter, while I let the soil take a rest. The earthy, mineral notes of chard are detectable even in the youngest sprouting seed but get stronger as the leaves age. I have eaten the jewel-coloured stems at every stage of their maturity, from when they are as young and fragile as mustard-and-cress right through to the point at which the stems are so old and thick that they need to be cooked separately from their leaves, lest the latter fall apart. Yet it is only relatively recently that I had even heard of this member of the beetroot family.

Cousin to spinach, along with purple orache, the wild 'fat hen' and, oddly, samphire, this handsome vegetable gets its name from its thick, wide, heavily ridged stems, known as 'chards'. It owes its modern-day popularity to the organic box schemes, which have keenly embraced its general good nature and cut-and-come-again qualities.

Commercially grown chard has changed since I first came across it in the mid-1990s, in that it is being picked younger, while the stems are more supple and less strident in flavour (there is sometimes a hint of bitterness in the older 'chards'). Rarely now do I spot the wide, flat stalks of white Swiss chard that took forever to cook and had strings you had to peel away, like old-fashioned celery. Almost gone are the days when you had not one but two vegetables: the stalks to braise and the leaves to steam.

This is a vegetable taken further up the deliciousness ladder simply by picking it earlier. Immature leaves the size of your thumb are a true earthy delight in a salad. The honourable exception is Fordhook Giant, a magnificent sight on the allotment, its leaves like huge green waves. It is still grown by those who value its generous stalks.

Chard in the garden

It is a rare moment, perhaps when I have been overenthusiastic in clearing the vegetable beds on a winter's afternoon, when there is no chard in this garden. Once the seedlings have got away there is no stopping them, and I can pick the odd handful throughout the winter. Chard can be a good friend to the gardener–cook when there is no one else to play with.

I have had more success with sowing in seed trays and transplanting the finger-high shoots into the garden than I have had with direct *in situ* sowing. It seems a slug can spot the tiniest blood-red seedling from six feet. Chard likes moist, quite rich soil. I dig in a shovel or two of compost every spring. If your chard lacks lustre, add a little nitrogen.

I sow in April and May, a mixture of Jacob's Coat or Bright Lights and the single-colour rhubarb chard, no more than a centimetre deep. You can sow in July and August for plants to carry you through the winter. Once established, chard plants seem to thrive on neglect. At least mine do. But they will bolt in very hot weather, though less dramatically than spinach. In theory, a good frost will kill them, but mine often shrug off a cold snap, even more so if I remember to put a wicker cloche over them.

There are two ways to pick chard: either as a salad leaf when the plants are still small (if you cut no less than a centimetre away from the soil, they will re-sprout) and after eight weeks or so, when the leaves are fully mature and the ribs firm and thick. Picking the outside leaves first gives the inner leaves a chance to fatten up. They will keep for several days, wrapped in newspaper in the bottom of the fridge.

A chard diary

Late May, early June I scatter the seed both into seed trays and over a square patch of ground that measures little more than a stride either way (I could have sown it as early as April or as late as August). A fortnight later, both the seeds in the tray and those in the ground continually sodden from endless rain have sprouted in clumps that look like cress, their red and yellow stems already plainly visible.

Just a fortnight or so after they first emerged, some of the larger leaves, now the size of a teaspoon, are ready to pick and add to a salad, but those in the seed trays are more prolific. The seeds grown in the open air have suffered at the hands of the snail population and the heavy rain.

So small, yet still with that distinctive earthiness that chard does so well, they end their short life with mild, crisp leaves of Little Gem lettuce, sliced, white-tipped radishes and roughly broken shards of feta cheese – a simple salad of salty, earthy, hot and mild notes that didn't require, or at least didn't get, any dressing whatsoever.

Early July I transplant the tray-grown seedlings into open ground.

Late July, early August Vast plumes of leaves with stems in shades of ivory, ruby and a piercing yellow are coming non-stop. Like the sweet peas that stand beside them, the more you cut the more they come. The trick is to pull a few from each plant. The transplanted seedlings have generally fared better than those planted directly in the soil.

Mid August The fox cubs visit one evening, curling up in the chard bed and crushing the crisp stems and leaves. The next day I cut off the leaves in the hope of a come-again crop.

Late September Up and running again.

November Some of the leaves have gone to seed, but I am still picking the larger ones for the kitchen. Rarely has a packet of seeds given me so much for so little.

Varieties

Swiss Chard Classic variety with green leaves and very wide, flat stems. Sometimes known as silver beet.

Wavy Leaf What it says on the packet.

Rhubarb Chard Green-maroon leaves, vermillion veins and stems. Slightly less hardy than the others.

Bright Lights Green leaves with veins and stems of raspberry pink, blood red, saffron, orange and yellow. Similar to Jacob's Coat and Rainbow mixtures.

Oriole Deep gold veins, very dark leaves.

Fordhook Giant Large, flat white stems, curling green leaves. This is one to cook leaves and stalks separately.

Chard in the kitchen

When my first bunch of wide, white stalks and their plume-like leaves turned up in the weekly organic box I had little idea of what it was. In true British style I boiled it, admiring the crunchy, deeply mineral flavour of its stalks but despairing at the over-cooked and watery leaves.

Next time, I cooked the leaves and their stalks separately. Actually that is not entirely true. I twisted off the leaves and steamed them like spinach with melted butter and lemon juice, putting the stems back in the fridge for another day. A week later I guiltily turfed out the wilted, stringy things I had completely forgotten about. Then, just as I thought I had got away with it – the waste and the humiliating lack of inspiration – another bloody bunch arrived.

Treated with respect, both are good to eat: the stems keep their crunch even during slow cooking and the leaves can be almost as tender and silken as spinach. They are less sharp than spinach, tougher too, except when they are very young. Swiss chard has deepest emerald-green leaves and thick, cream-coloured stalks. Ruby chard has translucent red stems and green leaves whilst the almost maroon-brown leaves of rainbow chard are shot through with cream, yellow, orange and red veins and stems, making this one of the most extraordinarily cheerful-looking vegetables you can have in the kitchen.

Anyone signed up for a weekly organic vegetable box will know that chard makes a regular appearance. Some might say too regular. The stems are interesting cooked in a way that celery – which they vaguely resemble – rarely is, and can, with olive oil, lemon juice and garlic, be of real interest. In the kitchen, chard is also at home in a bean soup, heavy with thyme, garlic and tomato.

Even under a blanket of richly savoury cheese sauce (a little cayenne wouldn't go amiss here), the stalks keep their character and are better than you might expect alongside a piece of gammon or even a pork chop.

The ivory stems seem to be crisper and cleaner tasting than the red, yellow and orange. But I could be wrong.

Vegetables tend to prefer oil or butter as a cooking medium but these stalks are happy with either. I generally use olive oil out of habit, but softened butter on the verge of liquidity, given an edge with a squirt of lemon, is very appropriate. Like leeks or celery, this is one for fairly gentle cooking. Nothing much will come from roasting the ribs, and they can become bitter when browned.

Seasoning your chard

Lemon juice and peppery olive oil As a dressing for warm leaves and stalks.

Cream Especially as an ingredient in a gratin.

Mustard In conjunction with cream, or as a principal ingredient in a dressing for the stalks.

Nutmeg Perhaps as a seasoning in a gratin.

Anchovies Chopped and cooked to a pulp in olive oil, then used to dress leaves and stalks.

Parsley Seems to calm the excessive mineral notes of older stalks, especially when used with lemon juice and olive oil.

Cheese I go for the stronger varieties, but particularly the long-matured Cheddars.

And...

* I have boiled chard briefly in deep water, cooked it in shallow water under a lid in the way most people cook spinach, and steamed it over boiling water. To be honest, there's not a lot in it, but the colours tend to stay brighter in boiling water. A big plus when you are using rainbow varieties.

* If the stems are very wide or tough, they really do need to be cooked separately from the leaves. As a rule of thumb, I cook the two parts separately if the stalk is more than a good finger's width.

* When I do decide to cook the stems and leaves separately, I cut the stalk a centimetre or so below where the leaf starts. The stem is still very tender at this point but will help the leaf keep its shape better during cooking.

* In a gratin-type recipe, the chard leaves need a good squeeze to rid them of their water. If you don't do this, they will ooze liquid as they bake and water down the sauce.

* Yoghurt, fromage frais and mascarpone are all suitable as a dressing for freshly cooked chard. I add a trickle of olive oil too, and maybe a scattering of paprika.

* Tatty outer leaves can be left in the ground over winter. They will protect the more fragile leaves coming up in the middle of the plant.

* Raw chard is really worth trying, but only when the leaves are small. They are exceptionally sweet until they get above the size of a teaspoon, when they start to develop their characteristic earthiness. You might like to add them to a watercress or other small leaf salad and dress them with nothing but raindrop-sized splashes of olive oil and some crisp, salty croûtons hot from the pan.

* I have never known chard stalks, no matter how thick, take longer to boil or steam than three or four minutes.

A chard gratin

The first time I cooked the stems separately from the leaves, I cut them into short lengths, boiled them till almost tender, then drained them and laid them in a buttered shallow dish. Covered with a classic cheese sauce, dusted with grated Parmesan and baked till the top was golden, they made a perfectly fine gratin.

A better gratin, this time with grain mustard

enough for 4
chard stems and leaves – 450g
grain mustard – a tablespoon
double cream – 400ml
grated Parmesan – a good handful

Cut the chard leaves from the stems. Chop the stems into short lengths, then cook briefly in boiling, lightly salted water till crisply tender. Dip the leaves in the water briefly, till they relax. Drain and put them in a buttered shallow dish. Put the mustard in a bowl and stir in the cream and a grinding of salt and black pepper. Pour the seasoned cream over the stems and leaves, cover with grated Parmesan and bake at 180°C/Gas 4 till the top has a light crust the colour of honey.

A soup of lentils, bacon and chard

On the right day, a deep bowl of lentil soup is all the food I need. The homely, almost spare quality satisfies me in a way fancier recipes cannot. The undertones of frugality, poverty even, are avoided by rich seasonings of unsmoked bacon, herbs and good stock. The backbone of earthiness is given a fresh topnote with mint and lemon juice. You can keep your beef Wellington.

enough for 4
a large onion
olive oil
garlic – 3 or 4 cloves
unsmoked bacon or pancetta – a good handful, chopped
flat-leafed parsley – a small bunch
chard – a large bunch
Puy or Castelluccio lentils – 250g
stock or, at a push, water – 1 litre
a lemon
mint – a small bunch

Peel the onion and chop it finely, then let it soften in a deep pan over a moderate to low heat with a little olive oil. Peel the garlic, slice it thinly, then add to the onion with the chopped bacon or pancetta. Chop the parsley and stir it in.

Wash the chard thoroughly, set aside four beautiful stalks and their leaves, then separate the remaining stalks and leaves. Chop the stalks roughly and set the leaves aside. Add the chopped chard stalks to the onion and bacon and continue cooking,

Wash the lentils thoroughly, then stir them into the onion and bacon. Pour over the stock or water and bring to the boil, skimming off any froth that comes to the surface. You can add a bay leaf or two if you like. Turn the heat down so that the lentils simmer merrily, then almost cover the pot with a lid and leave till they are tender, but far from collapse – about thirty minutes, depending on your lentils.

Tear the reserved chard leaves up a bit. Tip them into the soup. Steam the reserved whole leaves and stalks till tender.

Season the soup with salt, black pepper, lemon juice and the mint leaves, tasting as you go. Ladle the hot soup into warm bowls, add the steamed chard and serve with more lemon and mint for those who want it.

Chard with olive oil and lemon

Perhaps because of the thickness of its stalks, or the unruly tangle of leaves on the plate, chard always manages to exude a rustic quality. It is not really a vegetable for 'fine dining'. Blanched and seasoned with young, mild garlic and a squeeze of lemon, the stems and leaves become a useful side dish for any big-flavoured main course.

Allowed to cool, they also work with cold roast meats, thickly torn chunks of mozzarella, wedges of warm savoury tarts or coarse-textured 'country' pâté. In other words, a distinctly useful thing to have in the fridge.

enough for 2 as a side dish
white-stemmed chard – 450g
young garlic cloves – 2 or 3 small ones
extra virgin olive oil – 3 tablespoons
a lemon

Cut the white stalks from the leaves and keep both separate. Wash them thoroughly in cold water, rubbing any soil off the stalks with your thumb. Rinse both leaves and stems thoroughly.

Put a large pan of water on to boil, salt it and add the chard stalks. They will take three or four minutes to cook and should still retain some bite, rather than be softly tender (you could steam them if you prefer). Scoop out the stalks and drain them. Bring the same water back to the boil and add the leaves. They will need barely two minutes. Take them out when they are tender but still bright green. Tip away the water, wipe the pan and return it to the heat.

Peel the garlic and slice it finely, or chop it if you prefer. Pour the olive oil into the pan and let it warm over a low heat. Toss in the garlic and stir it so that it softens without colour. Tip in the drained chard leaves and stalks and gently fold them over in the warm oil and garlic. Grind over a little black pepper and sea salt, then cut the lemon in half and squeeze half over the greens.

Serve immediately, with the rest of the lemon on the side.

Potato cakes with chard and Taleggio

Bubble and squeak can be as simple as the traditional leftover cabbage and potato fry-up or somewhat more sophisticated, with the introduction of cheese, smoked pork, fish or other vegetables. The bells-and-whistles versions can often successfully disguise the fact that your supper is made from stuff you found at the back of the fridge. Keeping the potato pieces quite rough makes the texture more interesting.

makes 4, enough for 2
chard leaves and (only) the finer stalks – 200g
basil – a large bunch
olive oil – 75ml
lemon juice – 2 teaspoons
Taleggio, Wigmore, Waterloo or similar semi-soft cheese – 150g
cooked potatoes – 400g, roughly mashed
plain flour – a tablespoon
parsley – 4 tablespoons, chopped
cornmeal (polenta) – 6 tablespoons
olive or groundnut oil – a little for frying

Wash the chard thoroughly, then steam or boil till the stalks are tender. Drain well. Whiz the basil leaves and their stalks and the olive oil in a food processor, then stir in a pinch of salt and the lemon juice. Set aside. Roughly chop the chard, leaving four beautiful leaves on one side.

Cut the cheese into small pieces and mix with the roughly mashed potatoes. Season generously with salt and black pepper, then stir in the flour, parsley and chopped chard. Divide the mixture into four and shape each one into a rough patty about the diameter of a digestive biscuit. Tip the cornmeal on to a plate, then turn the patties in it to coat.

Warm a thin layer of oil in a non-stick frying pan. Lower the patties into the oil and cook for about four minutes on each side, till golden. Leave briefly on kitchen paper to drain whilst you dip the reserved chard leaves in the frying pan, just to warm them through. Serve the cakes topped with the chard leaves and a trickle of basil oil.

A shallow tart of chard and cheese

Cheese is the saviour of chard, as a crisp crust, a seasoning for soup, a luscious sauce, bringing out its qualities while introducing a note of luxury. Often, the bolder the cheese the more interesting the result, so a well-matured British cheese is a wise choice for something like a shallow chard tart. As a sort of double-whammy, I add cheese to the pastry as well as the filling.

enough for 6 or more

for the pastry
plain flour – 250g
butter – 100g, cut into small dice
a sharp farmhouse Cheddar – 35g
thyme leaves – a teaspoon
an egg, lightly beaten

for the filling
red or rainbow chard – 270g
spring onions – 4 thin ones
large eggs – 2
double cream – 300ml
Cheddar – 50g, grated
Pecorino, Spenwood or Parmesan – 40g, grated

Put the flour into a mixing bowl and add the butter. Rub it into the flour until it resembles coarse breadcrumbs (you can also do this in a food processor). Grate the cheese and stir it in along with the thyme, a pinch of black pepper and the beaten egg. Bring together to form a soft ball, adding a little milk if necessary.

Lightly flour a work surface. Roll the pastry out and use it to line a 30 x 23cm non-stick baking tray (if your baking tray isn't non-stick, brush it with a little butter). Press the pastry carefully into the corners and trim the edges, then chill for a good thirty minutes. Don't be tempted to skip the chilling period, otherwise your pastry will shrink in the oven.

Set the oven at 200°C/Gas 6. To make the filling, blanch the chard in a little boiling water until soft and tender. Drain and squeeze as much of the water out with your hands as you can, then roughly chop the chard. Finely slice the spring onions and add to the chard with a seasoning of salt and pepper.

Lay a piece of foil or greaseproof paper in the pastry case, weighing it down with baking beans (I sometimes find a piece of silver foil is heavy enough to do the job without the beans, though not so greaseproof).

Bake for fifteen minutes or so, till the pastry is firm, then remove the paper and return the pastry to the oven for five minutes, till dry to the touch.

Put the chard into the pastry case. Beat the eggs and cream till well mixed and season lightly. Scatter the grated cheeses over the chard and pour over the egg and cream mixture. Bake for twenty to twenty-five minutes, till the pastry is crisp and the filling has set.

Chard with black pepper and cream

The purity of a leaf and its edible stalk, lightly steamed and served 'naked', is always somehow life enhancing. But occasionally I want a more sensuous treatment (a welcome lift in times of recession).

The spiced cream with juniper and peppercorns recipe that I occasionally use with green leaves makes them a particularly sound accompaniment for grilled or roast pork, or for poached ham or chicken, but I also find it perfectly acceptable with brown rice as a main dish in itself.

> *enough for 4 as a side dish*
> chard – 400g
> black peppercorns – 2 teaspoons
> juniper berries – a teaspoon
> butter – 25g
> double cream – 150ml (a small pot will do)

Shred the leaves into thick strips. Cut the stalks in half widthways. Steam the leaves and stalks till tender, bright green and perky, then drain.

Meanwhile, crush the peppercorns and juniper berries lightly with a pestle and mortar, or with a heavy object on a chopping board.

Melt the butter in a saucepan and toast the crushed spices in it for a minute or two, until fragrant. Pour in the cream and leave to bubble for a minute or so, until it starts to thicken slightly. Season with a very little salt and tip in the drained leaves and stalks. Toss them in the spiced cream till they are lightly coated. Serve straight away, whilst the sauce is still piping hot and creamy.

The Chinese greens

There are moments when I long for a plate of steamed greens. This may be after the summer solstice, when I have had one too many salads, or in late autumn, when the kitchen has been inundated with sweet roots. Perhaps I have had too many rich meals in a row. But there are times when I want nothing more than emerald-green shoots, in quantity, brought still steaming and virtually unadorned to the table.

The greens I obsess over most, the leaves I will take an hour's bus journey simply to get my hands on, are usually the Chinese brassicas. The gai lan and pak choi, the choy sum and mizuna leaves are ones I never seem to tire of, despite the singularly unadventurous way I tend to prepare them. Steamed, drained, tossed in hot oyster sauce, their bold green simplicity excites and pleases me.

No green shoots are more succulent or refreshing than those of gai lan or choy sum, and whilst I value them for their soft leaves and mild mustard flavours, I reserve most of my esteem for their fleshy stems. These are the greens you see being packed up into fat bunches in the back lanes of Chinatown, the ones that come to your table tossed in chopped garlic. Greens whose extreme juiciness tempers their traditional hot or salty seasonings.

I like to think of these faintly mustard-edged leaves as the future of our home-grown winter vegetables – they thrive in the cool and are a verdant shock in the dark days of March – but they are hungry feeders, who require not just good but excellent soil in which to grow, and are heavily reliant on our most precious resource, water. Succulence comes at a price.

I have given up trying to grow the plump, joyously crisp pak choi because of its ability to seduce a snail from twenty feet, but the long-stemmed gai lan and the yellow-flowered choy sum are worth dedicating our most humus-rich soil to.

Nothing good will come from getting too fancy with these greens. They bask in simple treatment and become shy when long lists of ingredients appear. The real moment of glory for the Chinese brassicas is when they team up with high-octane dressings such as salty oyster sauce, searing chillies or chopped and sizzling garlic. The marriage of mild, juice-filled stems and hot, simple flavourings is reason enough for their place in the vegetable patch.

Chinese greens in the garden

Given the right conditions, these brassicas will grow very quickly but I have not found them to be the easiest of tenants. They are greedy, so you need to add manure to the beds the summer before you sow and then be prepared to add high-nitrogen fertiliser as they grow into mature plants. They are very thirsty too, so you can expect to get the watering can out regularly. The young plants have shallow root systems, so like a bit of mulching too, to keep the ground moist as the weather heats up.

I find they respond better to being grown in modules and transplanted when they are a few inches high than they do sown directly into the soil (I suspect my soil isn't fine or moist enough for them). Small coir pots are excellent to get your seedlings going.

The leaves of the young plants are delicate and dislike heavy rain, so growing under cloches is ideal. Sow again in autumn (I put them in after the peas come out), and with luck and a bit of protection they will stand throughout the winter. Although they are from the same family as sprouts and Savoy cabbage, they lack their coarseness, instead offering the sort of subtlety we expect from a spring shoot.

I have had little success with pak choi, whose juicy stems attract any number of marauding snails 'popping out for a Chinese'. Gai lan has proved less demanding and can be made to last for several weeks if you pick the main shoot, allowing secondary shoots to appear from the stems.

Preparing the bed with organic matter the summer before you plant is essential unless your soil is naturally exceptionally fertile. Raised beds will help to keep snails at bay and a spraying of nematodes such as Nemaslug during warm weather will be worth the expense.

Choy sum

You see bundles of these greens and their tight yellow buds all over Chinatown. Their soft-textured, oval leaves are nice enough but it is the fleshy stems that are the real attraction. I steam the whole thing, buds and all, till they are bright and will easily take the point of a knife, then toss them with a little oyster sauce.

The flowers should be only just starting to open. Avoid any with yellowing leaves or fully blossoming flowers. You will need quite a bit of space to grow these yourself, but a row or two would be a beautiful addition to your patch.

Pak choi

These spoon-shaped annuals have not been easy for me to grow and I regard them as one of my failures. Mine come in a bag from Chinatown or from the farmers' market, where they tend to be stragglier than the usual squat form. Their USP is their mild flavour and juicy stems, plus their ability to calm a pungent sauce. You eat every bit, the stems, leaves and flowers.

Grown in China since the fifth century AD, they come in several varieties, ranging from ones with green or white stems to others whose leaves are as long as rabbits' ears. I find the compact ones easiest to deal with and, for no reason other than their colour, prefer the all-green ones. Their neatness appeals to my enhanced sense of order and, despite their ability to reach 30cm in length, I tend to ignore any that are longer than 15cm.

The plump stems – they narrow towards the leaves – are decidedly crunchy and easy to overcook. They need barely five minutes in a steamer, maybe less. The faint hint of mustard rescues them from accusations of blandness. When the leaves are small, about the size of a teaspoon, they are refreshing in a salad, though they are generally eaten cooked. Sometimes the stems and leaves are cooked separately, the thick stems being added to the wok before the leaves.

Gai lan

Also called kai lan and Chinese broccoli, these long-stemmed, blue-green leaves are possibly the most delicious of all the cabbage family. Known as 'mustard orchid' in China, they have an elegance on the plate and a gentility too rare in the vegetable world. It is surprising that they are not more popular here, being crisp, green, quick to cook and mildly flavoured. The purple variety (zi cai tai), like climbing beans of the same hue, tends to lose its colour once it meets hot water.

I treasure them and their crisp stems lightly steamed and placed on an oval plate with a slick of oyster sauce, let down with a little stock and oil. Some shredded ginger warmed with the oil, oyster sauce and a pinch of sugar would be heaven. Roughly chopped, the stalks make a very good stir-fry with garlic, beef steak, oyster sauce and spring onion.

Sow seed in mid to late summer for autumn and early-winter harvesting. You can plant seedlings out in the autumn that will last all winter. Once the plant is about 15cm tall, you can snip out and eat the main shoot, then break off and harvest the side shoots as they appear. It is slower growing than choy sum. The flowers, caught just as the yellow buds are opening, are charming in a salad of dark green leaves.

Mizuna

I have always thought of spiky, rocket-like mizuna as Japanese but it actually originates in China. The leaves are feathery and open and have an airiness to them that lightens a salad. I sometimes wonder if there could be a prettier edible leaf. They take a bit of chewing, but they are rarely anything but tender, even when they get to the size of a spoon. The oldest leaves might need cooking.

Mizuna is the current darling of the trendy salad bag, though its flavour is on the mild side. I use it principally in salads, to add body and a frilly texture to the mix, but it can be stir-fried very successfully too. Once it hits the heat, the characteristic spikiness is somewhat lost, and I can't help thinking of it as best in a salad. Like rocket, too much can tickle the throat and cause you to cough.

The plants, which form a bushy clump, can be vigorous and don't mind moderate shade. They rarely bolt, which is an unusual quality for a brassica. You can sow the seed in spring and be picking – albeit small leaves – three weeks later. They have shallow root systems so I use a seed tray lined with newspaper and some fine, organic seed compost. The little leaves love it. I have left sowing till late summer and been picking till the frosts. If I had more indoor space I would grow this leaf all year, but they are happy enough on a windowsill if it is just small, salad-ready leaves you are after.

Once the leaves are the size of a teaspoon, the plants can go out into the garden and be left to form unruly clumps.

Mibuna

I mention this only because it is growing in popularity and is one of the most versatile cut-and-come-again leaves. It is very easy to grow and can be cut four or five times – the new growth being more resistant to frost and cold than the fully matured leaves. Related to mizuna, it has long, softer-edged leaves, with none of mizuna's feathery quality. You should be able to pick a few of the larger leaves about six weeks after sowing. They can grow up to 15cm in length and have a pleasing, almost mustardy warmth to them, which gets stronger as the plants age. I prefer them lightly cooked rather than in a salad.

Sow from spring to late autumn. I have not had much luck transplanting young seedlings into the ground (though that may just be me) and I recommend you sow them directly where they are to grow.

Chinese mustard greens

This is a huge family of leaves of different shapes and textures, only a few of which are available in the UK, even in seed form. They originate from the Himalayas, spreading first to China and then to India and beyond. Whatever their size or shape, they have in common their prominent mustard flavour. Although I can handle them in a salad when the leaves are small (I especially like the small mauve-blushed Osaka Purple leaf), they are generally best either steamed or added to a stir-fry.

The young growth of the mustard family has a sweetness to it that is missing in the older specimens, which get hotter as they get nearer to bolting. This is the leaf that takes you by surprise in harmless-looking mixed salad bags, the one that burns your tongue. But most of them provide a gentler heat, and especially so when they are torn up and used in a wok. They come in various guises, some with large, tight heads of wavy-edged leaves, others with long leaves, and still others like huge, unruly iceberg lettuces.

I grow these in shallow seed trays, planting both Osaka Purple and the jagged-edged Green in Snow. The first is very much a cut-and-come-again variety, for adding in small quantity to a salad. The latter germinates quickly and offers lots of small, hot leaves to tuck in a sandwich. The small leaves are peppery and fun when matched with something cool, like soft white bread, but can be eye-wateringly hot if left to reach their full, 30cm-long potential.

Chinese greens in the kitchen

'Useful in a stir-fry' is one of those cop-out sentences that make this writer's blood boil. Except in this case it is true. No other member of the greens family takes so well to the intense heat and feisty seasonings associated with this way of cooking. The stems cook quickly, while the leaves soften and take up the garlic, ginger, chilli and liquid seasonings that are the heart and soul of the everyday Chinese or Vietnamese stir-fry.

I sometimes steam my Chinese brassicas lightly before they meet the stinging sides of the wok. It tends to produce a juicier result. The downside is that the extra water contained in a cooked stem of pak choi turns to steam in the pan and will lower the temperature of the wok, which is the last thing you want, so any pre-cooked greens should be well drained.

You can eat the smaller leaves of all the Asian brassica family as saladings, or wait a few weeks and then steam them. I find a large bamboo steamer placed over a wok of boiling water is the ideal way to cook them. Then I toss them in a mixture of oyster sauce and garlic, or chilli sauce.

Outside the salad bowl, the steamer and the stir-fry, there isn't much I would want to do with these vegetables. Using them in European recipes feels awkward. Rather like trying to make carbonara with Chinese noodles.

Seasoning your Chinese greens

All the flavours we associate with Asian cooking – chillies, ginger, garlic, fish sauce, soy, oyster, hoisin and chilli sauces – work perfectly with these greens. Any European ingredients, such as butter, are somehow just plain wrong.

And…

* Buy or pick only those with more bud than open flowers.
* The Chinese who sell these honourable vegetables have a habit of squashing them into a tight bundle, resulting in leaves that look squashed. This doesn't mean they are not fresh. The slender stems and their delicate leaves will be fine when they are cooked.
* The mustards tend to get hotter when they are deprived of water.
* Mizuna and mustard leaves aside, the Asian brassicas will keep in good condition for several days. Pop them into a plastic bag or newspaper and store them in the bottom of the fridge.

A Vietnamese stir-fry

Of all the flavours that seem to bring out the rest of the cabbage family's earthy greenness, few work as effectively as those of Southeast Asia. Ginger, spring onion and garlic have a natural affinity with chlorophyll-rich vegetables of any sort, but the saltiness of the fish sauces with which Thai and Vietnamese cooks season their food does much for cabbage leaves. I often serve this with roast duck, which appreciates such seasoning, or as a side order for a mushroom stir-fry hot with chillies and soy.

enough for 2 as a side dish
Chinese greens or small cabbage leaves – 12 stems or small leaves
garlic – 2 large cloves
ginger – a thumb-sized piece
spring onions – 6
groundnut oil – 2 tablespoons
nuoc mam or nam pla (Vietnamese or Thai fish sauce) – a tablespoon

Put a saucepan of deep water on to boil and salt it lightly. Wash the greens thoroughly. Peel the garlic and ginger, finely chop the garlic and shred the ginger into matchstick-like strips. Trim the spring onions and cut each into two or three.

Warm the oil in a shallow pan or wok. Toss the garlic, ginger and spring onions in the oil till deep gold, verging on being lightly browned and fragrant. Drop the greens, whole or shredded as you wish, into the boiling water. Leave for only a minute or so before draining. Pour the fish sauce in with the garlic and ginger – it will spit and sizzle – then toss with the greens and eat.

Chinese broccoli with garlic and oyster sauce

Any of the brassica family is good to go here. Most successful are gai lan (kai lan) and choy sum.

enough for 2 as a side dish
Chinese broccoli – 8 stalks
garlic – 3 cloves
shallots – 2
a little oil
oyster sauce – 3 heaped tablespoons
Shaoxing wine – 3 tablespoons

Steam the greens over hot water. Meanwhile, peel and finely chop the garlic and shallots. Fry them for a minute or two in a little oil. Stir in the oyster sauce and the wine and bring to the boil. Let the resulting sauce reduce for a minute, maybe two, then pour it over the steaming-hot greens.

Prawns, leaves and limes

Pak choi or, better still, gai lan will be perfect here. Eat it hot and spluttering from the pan.

enough for 2
Chinese greens – 150g
ginger – a thumb-sized piece
lemongrass – a large stalk
small, hot red chillies – 2
spring onions – 2
groundnut or vegetable oil – 2 tablespoons
large raw prawns – 500g
lime juice – 50ml
nam pla (Thai fish sauce) – 50ml
sugar – 2 teaspoons
coriander leaves – a large handful
basil leaves – a large handful

Do the prep first, because everything happens quite quickly once you start cooking. Wash the leaves and remove any tough stems. Peel the ginger, then grate it or cut it into small, matchstick-like shreds. Remove the tough outer leaves of the lemongrass and very finely shred the tender heart. Finely chop the chillies, removing the seeds if you prefer cooler spicing. Finely shred the spring onions.

Warm the oil in a wok or shallow pan. Add the ginger, lemongrass, chillies and spring onions and stir-fry for a couple of minutes, till the ginger starts to colour. Drop in the prawns. As they turn opaque and colour lightly, add the lime juice, nam pla and sugar. When all is sizzling and fragrant, add the greens, turning them over in the pan as they start to wilt and darken. As soon as they are tender, add the coriander and basil leaves and serve immediately.

Squid with greens and basil

I often come home from Chinatown with a squid and a bag of choy sum. The fishmonger will have done most of the dirty work for me, leaving me to give the body sac a final rinse before slicing. Squid is ideally suited to this quick, high-temperature cooking.

enough for 2
Chinese greens – 2 large handfuls
large red chillies – 2
ginger – a thumb-sized piece
prepared squid bodies and tentacles – 400g
nam pla (Thai fish sauce) – 2 tablespoons
soft brown sugar – 2 teaspoons
lime juice – 2 tablespoons
vegetable oil – 2 tablespoons
basil leaves – a large handful

Blanch the greens in boiling water for a minute or two. Drain and set aside, chopping the stems roughly.

Halve the chillies, remove the seeds and slice the flesh thinly. Peel the ginger and grate or shred it finely. Wash the squid, dry it thoroughly with paper towels, then cut the bodies down one side and open them out. Wipe them clean (sometimes they have bits of yuck attached). Cut into large pieces and score each one carefully with the point of a sharp knife. Mix the fish sauce, sugar and lime juice together.

Warm the oil in a wok or frying pan, then add the chillies and ginger. When it sizzles and the ginger starts to colour, add the squid bodies and tentacles. Fry for two minutes, until the edges of the squid start to colour, then pour in the fish sauce mixture. Take care, as it will spit and pop.

Continue frying briefly, then add the lightly chopped greens. Toss in the basil leaves, let them wilt, then eat immediately, from two warm bowls.

Climbing beans

It's the second week of August, the air heavy with the smell of overripe figs from the tree on the terrace. Golden mirabelles hang like glass beads at the far, dark end of the garden. Only the distant laughter of a child breaks the oppressive silence.

The dark bronze stems of the beans I planted in late spring are curling their way up their frame, looping around the dead sweet pea husks that a neater gardener would have taken out. The buds of Cosse Violette – the beans I grow every summer – are shining an intense violet amongst the green leaves. The beans, some of which ripen whilst others are still in bud, are a dusky purple-black. I will admit to finding the marriage of violet, deep green and inky black one of the most beautiful and tranquil a garden has to offer.

The term 'climbing' beans covers both the 'French' bean in all its colours, and the longer, wider runner bean. 'French' beans, introduced to Britain by the Huguenots, are the more refined cousins of our much-loved cottage-garden runner bean. They have names like Rocquencourt, Fin de Bagnol and Chevrier Vert, are a little less resilient, and need more careful nurturing early in life. Instead of the stinging scarlet of the runner, their flowers are ivory, cream and soft lavender. Not that any of this makes them better of course, only different.

Pleasing as they are to eat, if I am honest, I grow French beans as much for their beauty as for their usefulness in the kitchen. I am unsure exactly why we have taken to the green bean rather than the yellow. There is much gentle beauty in a dish of butter-yellow pods glistening with almost-melted butter and a few grains of black pepper. Oval Yellow China, St Esprit Jaune and Mont d'Or are varieties worth seeking out. Eyes closed, they taste very little different from a green one, but their beauty is threefold.

The runner bean (*Phaseolus coccineus*) is flat and slightly coarse to the touch. I regard hearing its loud snap as one of the highlights of the British summer, just as others do the crack of a cricket ball on willow. The French beans (*Phaseolus vulgaris*) are mostly round and shorter than the runner, and come in all sizes, from the pencil-thin Blue Lake to the plump and knobbly borlotti. Their skins can be green, yellow, purple or mottled like a bird's egg. Some, such as borlotti and Cream Splash, can grow to over 20cm, the seeds clearly visible through the bean's skin.

I particularly mention the borlotti as it is the bean I am asked about more than any other. Its cream and bright-pink speckled pods make it one of the most beautiful of all the beans. Inside, the jade and pink seeds have a singular fresh greenness to them. They are increasingly being seen as something to eat fresh rather than dried, which is how many of us know them best. I grow them, sharing a frame with purple beans or maybe a climbing miniature pumpkin such as Munchkin. I should mention that this bean is one variety that needs a good hard boil for ten minutes. When borlotti are undercooked, some people find them indigestible.

Climbing beans in the garden

No peony, full-blown rose or wandering clematis could ever bring me as much delight as the sight of a cane wigwam of beans. There is much childish delight in making one too, tying the thin ends of the long, sturdy canes with tarred string; getting the thick ends equidistant in the ground; the constant shaking to test how secure they are; and that proud moment when all is complete. Passers-by might see you as a dedicated gardener, but only you know you are secretly seven years old again and making a den.

While I am not sure a vegetable patch is worthy of the name without its pointed frame of scarlet-flowered runners, it is a fact that this bean was first grown for its flowers rather than for the table, and Native Indians still eat their roots as well as the long, flat bean itself.

I have been besotted with the sight of beans growing up rickety canes since I was a kid. The bean fields of the farmer next door were my hiding place as an eleven-year-old, sitting cross-legged amongst the heart-shaped greenery and its vivid blossoms for hours on end. We knew them as 'scarlet' runners, but their flowers can be anything from red and white (Painted Lady) to pure ivory (Desirée).

I built my first wigwam for beans one day after school, on the precipitous slope of the family vegetable patch, with odd canes of assorted lengths. An unimaginably difficult task handed out by my father. Now I build them on the flat, each cane 6cm or so apart, one in the middle of each of my vegetable beds (and last year another, less secure than usual but just as useful, in a giant terracotta pot). Such tall, thin frames make sense for the gardener with limited space. The plants, which hate wind, protect one another as they huddle together, and take up less space than those grown in a long row.

One June, as I travelled from the station in a country taxi, the driver asked me, 'Have you got your beans in yet?' It seemed an odd question to ask a perfect stranger. He then proceeded to tell me how he dug a square hole, two spades deep, in early spring, filled it with shredded newspaper, which he watered and covered with a layer of 'well-rotted 'orseshit', then piled rich garden soil on top of that. He felt that the newspaper held water and that the beans then thrived without much need for the hosepipe. He was right, and I have done it ever since. Though I fancy my 'two spades deep' is more like his 'one'.

Climbing beans of all sorts need warmth. They will germinate in soil above 12°C. I sow mine in pots of seed compost in May and start them in the cold frame. Prior to that, I just used my kitchen windowsill until all danger of frost had passed. They grow quickly enough for you to consider a late planting, say at the end of July. French beans are happy to ramble over a wicker cloche (I once saw them growing through a large rose). I pick the round climbing beans while they are still no longer than a finger, and up to pencil thickness.

Runners, named for their ability to climb, are much longer and heavier and need a strong frame. They were introduced to England by Tradescant, King Charles I's gardener, who also brought us my beloved cottage-garden phlox. The dark red roses growing in pots outside my back door are named for him.

My beans, the prolific Scarlet Emperor, Viola Cornetti or Cosse Violette and Blue Lake, are a follow-on from the sweet peas that start to go downhill around the summer solstice. Last year, when my borlotti beans failed to germinate, a neighbouring Connecticut squash gratefully squatted in their place and utilised the frame till the first frosts turned its stems to slush.

In all the years I have grown beans this way, it was Christopher Stocks, in his book *Forgotten Fruits* (Random House, 2008), who first brought to my attention the fact that runner beans climb clockwise, whilst all other beans clamber up in the opposite direction.

A bean diary

May 5 I plant four varieties of climbing bean in seed compost in deep pots: the French, sulphur-yellow Merveille de Venise, the sultry, purple Cosse Violette, the mysterious Black Knight that arrived by mistake, and the Scarlet Emperor runner bean that grows in virtually every cottage garden in Europe (in the United States their flowers are said to attract the hummingbird). Well watered, the seeds sit in the open cold frame for ten days or so before I notice their tips peeping through the black soil. Few seeds germinate at so satisfying a pace.

May 20 I put sticks up the stems as soon as they are tall enough to bend. I don't tie them; they generally hold on of their own accord.

June 1 40cm tall, their stems entwined like necking swans, the beans go into the prepared ground, four plants around each side of the climbing frames. The French Merveille de Venise, with long leaves like iron-age arrows, is planted in a deep terracotta pot around a tepee of long, bamboo canes, just as I have seen them growing on a barge in Venice. The others go into the garden, the Cosse Violette shares a bed with jewel-stemmed chard, globe artichokes whose leaves look as if they are glistening with frost, and Dahlia Black Monarch, whose flowers are of a deep, arterial red. Each bean has its long white root tucked deep into the soil and well watered, then surrounded by spent coffee grounds to ward off the garden snails. As usual, some seeds are tucked in amongst the growing plants to extend the season well into the autumn.

August 8 Much is starting to ripen. We continue to pick through to October.

Varieties

French beans
Expect to start picking eighty days after planting.

Cosse Violette A good tall bean, with a long cropping period. I pick until the first frosts. Similar to Purple Tepee.
Blue Lake An easy-to-grow variety, stringless and, despite its name, green. I like seedsman Thomas Etty's catalogue note that Blue Lake originated with the Native Indians on the banks of the Missouri.
Merveille de Venise A flat yellow pod, rather like a yellow runner bean. I sometimes entwine its yellow stems amongst those of the Cosse Violette.
Neckargold A straight, round yellow bean.
Anellino Giallo Elegantly curls back on herself, like a giant comma.
Aiguillon Like Blue Lake, this is a true haricot vert, waxy green, long and pencil thin.
Rose d'Eyragues A parchment-hued bean with splashes of rose. A rare form from Avignon I am desperate to grow.

Also worth trying are Coco Noir, a beautiful, earthy black bean (just saying the name is enough for me); the Prince, which is both stringless and flat podded; and Blauhilde, a long, purple-black bean that can also be left and eaten as 'flageolet'.

Runner beans
Usually ready about ninety days after planting.

Painted Lady An ancient variety introduced in the seventeenth century and occasionally known as York and Lancaster.
Red Rum Reliable and early to mature.
Scarlet Emperor Copious orange-red flowers from black and purple speckled seeds. My favourite runner.
White Emergo Slimmer pods than most and quite prolific.
Czar White-flowered runner from the nineteenth century.

Also worth looking out for are the almost-stringless Butler, Polestar (keep well watered) and Pickwick, a somewhat dwarf variety good for small gardens.

Climbing beans in the kitchen

What we are eating here is an immature bean, which we can enjoy pod, barely visible beans and all. Runner beans are harvested slightly nearer maturity, so the pink bean inside the pod is quite visible. At the market, it is worth trying one before you buy. They toughen if left on the vine too long. Some require their edges peeling – a task known as 'stringing' the beans. Runners need 'topping and tailing', which simply means they need their ends cutting off before cooking, as do the French. However, though I totally see why no one wants to eat the knobbly stalk end, I tend to leave the elegant tail ends intact. They are tender and sweet and I see no real reason to remove them.

Beans are a pleasure to grow, to witness in flower and to pick. There is much happiness to be had in rummaging through the leaves in search of the elegant, dangling pods. I often eat a plateful with a roast tomato sauce. All red, green and yellow, like a kid's painting.

Too much is made of undercooking. The flavour, what there is, develops only once the bean is tender, so a crisp green bean cooked for seconds rather than minutes is all very well, but it will never have the flavour of one that is cooked till it bends. A perfect bean should have some bite to it, but be incapable of standing to attention. I take a sample out of the pan every now and again. They will probably take only three or four minutes if the beans are young and the water boiling merrily. They are done when dark emerald green and visibly starting to relax.

There are few ingredients that can do anything for a French bean, and even fewer for a runner, but a little chopped shallot, melted butter or a crushed clove of young garlic are all worth a try. Olive oil does it no favours other than in a salad, with sun-scorched tomatoes, torn mozzarella and basil leaves. Nasturtium flowers look gorgeous, the orange and red petals falling like paint splatters over a dish of freshly cooked green beans, but add little in terms of flavour. But who cares when you have painted such a picture?

Purple beans such as Blauhilde and Viola Cornetti lose much of their colour once they hit boiling water. Sometimes they turn completely green. But that is all they lose, though there is little to say about the flavour of French beans – purple, yellow or green. What matters is youth and texture.

If enough ripen at once or I have picked some up from the farmers' market, I throw them into boiling water to which I have added a little salt, then drain and toss them in soft butter and very, very finely squashed garlic or chopped shallot. I have been known to use spring onion. Anything else would interfere with their subtle 'green' flavour. They rely on a cook with nothing more than a stopwatch. Imagination is unwanted here.

And...

* Some runner beans have a thin string down each long edge that needs removing before you slice them. If you insert a knife at the stalk end and pull along, the string will sometimes pull off easily. Other times, you need to slice it off. Much depends on your beans.
* Strings running down the edge of a runner bean are not necessarily a sign that the bean is old (though it often can be the case). It may just be the variety. Generally though, the younger a runner bean is picked, the less stringy it will be.
* About 15–18 cm is the right length to start picking your runner beans. French beans should be picked well before they get to that length.
* If a runner bean doesn't snap when you bend it, then it is probably past its best.
* The smooth, flat green beans in the supermarket imported from Kenya are not runners, but a form of French bean.
* There is nothing you can do to stop purple beans turning green in the cooking water.
* French beans can sometimes squeak as you eat them, especially if you undercook them. I rather like this attribute, but those who find it disturbing might like to toss them in butter. It quietens them down.
* If you can see the seeds clearly bulging through the pod, then it is probably on the tough side.
* Any French bean thinner than a pencil will need only two to three minutes in boiling water or a steamer. Runners need three to four.
* The flavour of round climbing beans becomes deeper the longer you cook them, but at the cost of loss of colour and texture.
* There is a point in the climbing French bean's life when it is past being tender enough to eat as a whole bean, 'pod'n'all', but not yet plump enough to be podded and dried. This is the 'flageolet' stage. The beans can be popped straight from their shells and boiled. Wonderful tossed with olive oil and lemon juice and eaten warm.

Warm chicken with green beans and chard

As much as I like big flavours, I sometimes want something more gentle, a little genteel even. French beans lend themselves to such cooking.

enough for 2
chicken – 2 plump breasts
a little oil
rosemary – a bushy stalk
French beans – 200g
chard – 12 thin stems and their leaves
tomatoes – 6 small ones, cut in halves or quarters
   depending on their size
a few nasturtiums, if you wish

for the dressing
a small shallot
lemon juice – 3 tablespoons
olive oil – 6 tablespoons
mint – a small bunch

For the dressing, peel and chop the shallot very finely. Put it into a screw-top jar with a good pinch of salt, the lemon juice, olive oil and the leaves from the mint, lightly chopped (discard the stalks). Screw on the lid and shake the jar to mix the dressing.

Brush the chicken with oil, season with salt and black pepper and scatter with the finely chopped rosemary needles. Grill or roast until cooked right through and the skin is golden. Set aside for ten minutes, perhaps with a mixing bowl over the top to keep it warm, saving any cooking juices that come from it.

Trim the beans, cut the chard stalks into similar lengths and remove and reserve their leaves. Boil the beans and the chard stalks in boiling water till tender – a matter of two or three minutes in each case (I prefer to do this in two pans, as the red from the chard water darkens the beans, but it is up to you). Dip the leaves into the water for thirty seconds. Remove and drain. Tip the dressing into a bowl, then add the drained green beans, chard leaves and stalks, the tomatoes, and the nasturtium flowers if you are using them. Divide the salad between two plates or lovely white bowls. Cut the chicken breasts into thick slices – about four each – and place on top of the salad.

Beans in the steamer

I have said elsewhere that I often prefer green vegetables boiled rather than steamed, but I find the opposite with beans. There is something about the bean family's flesh that works exceptionally well in the steamer. I trim my beans, then cook them in a covered steamer basket over boiling water. I find this way they keep their colour and the flavour is often better. Steamed runners work especially well.

French beans with shallot butter

Boil your beans, nicely trimmed as you think fit, in lightly salted water, or steam them if you prefer. They need about four minutes or so; they should be dark green and bend a little. Meanwhile, melt a little butter in a shallow pan, stir in some finely chopped shallot and let it soften without colouring. Dribble in a little white wine vinegar, then drain the beans and toss them with the shallot butter.

Beans and cheese

Parmesan and beans sounds an unlikely coupling but I recommend it. Pecorino, a young one, is a possibility here too, or one of the hard sheep's cheeses British cheese makers are getting so good at.

> green, purple or yellow French beans or runners
> butter
> Parmesan

Trim the beans (I suggest a good handful per person), then boil them in deep, salted water or steam over boiling water.

Have ready some almost-melted butter and some grated cheese. As you lift the beans from the water, toss them in the butter and cheese.

Another way with beans and cheese

For each fat handful of French beans, I allow about 75g of cheese, such as Wigmore, Waterloo or any of the other white-bloomed, melting-textured cheeses. If I can get nothing 'local', then I use Taleggio or Camembert. Cut the cheese into small pieces. Immediately the beans are cooked and drained, toss them with the little cubes of cheese. The heat from the beans will melt the cheese so that it forms a thick, savoury dressing.

A chicken lunch for a searingly hot summer's day

Roast a chicken, perhaps with olive oil and lemon, and set it aside to cool. I don't think it should be cold, just vaguely warm. Make an aioli or mayonnaise. Cook freshly picked green beans in lightly salted water. Use a spoonful of the cooking water to thin the mayonnaise to the consistency of thick cream. Drain the beans and toss them in the thinned mayonnaise. Eat them with the cold roast chicken. The moist, just-warm chicken, lightly cooked beans and garlicky mayonnaise come together perfectly.

A crisp salad of climbing beans, fennel and Parmesan

enough for 2
French beans – 200g
a medium fennel bulb
small, hot salad leaves, such as rocket and watercress –
    4 double-handfuls
white bread – 2 thick slices
oil for frying the bread

for the dressing
tarragon vinegar – a tablespoon
Dijon mustard – a teaspoon
an egg yolk
olive oil – 100ml
grated Parmesan – 3 tablespoons, plus a block of Parmesan for shaving
lemon juice – 2 teaspoons

Trim the beans and boil them in lightly salted water, or steam them, till tender. Drain them under cold running water. Cut the fennel bulb in half and shred finely. Make the dressing by whisking the vinegar, mustard and egg yolk together with a little salt and black pepper, then beating in the oil followed by the grated cheese. It should be thick and creamy. Squeeze in the lemon juice, stir, then set aside for a few minutes.

Put the salad leaves in a large bowl with the cooked beans and the fennel. Cut the bread into small squares and fry in shallow oil till golden on all sides. Drain on kitchen paper. Toss the leaves and beans lightly with the dressing. Pile the salad on to two plates and shave pieces of Parmesan over with a vegetable peeler. I usually do at least eight per salad, depending on my dexterity with the peeler. Tip the hot croûtons over the salad and eat straight away, whilst all is fresh and crunchy.

Green beans, red sauce

The smell you get from slicing freshly picked runner beans and the warm, herbal notes attached to the stalk of a tomato are, to my mind, the very essence of summer. Put those scents together and you have a recipe that is pure pleasure to make. A dish that could only mean midsummer – something to eat with cold salmon, a slice of crab tart or a plate of grilled sardines.

> *enough for 2*
> tomatoes – 500g
> olive oil
> bay leaves – 2
> a little red wine vinegar
> runner beans – 450g
> grated lemon zest

Put the tomatoes into a roasting tin or baking dish; they should fit snugly in a single layer. Pour over enough olive oil to wet the fruit and to form a thin layer at the bottom of the dish. Season generously with salt and black pepper, tuck in the bay leaves and sprinkle a little red wine vinegar over (a teaspoon will do). Now leave in a hot oven (200°C/Gas 6) for about thirty minutes, until the skins have started to blacken here and there and there is much juice in the dish.

Crush the tomatoes with a fork, check the seasoning and correct it with a little salt and pepper if necessary.

Trim the beans and slice them thinly. Steam for three or four minutes, till tender but still crisp and bright, then toss them with the tomato sauce. Grate some lemon zest over the hot beans and their sauce.

Courgettes and other summer squash

The summer squashes, mild tasting, elegant, gently hued, are here from June until late autumn, when the hard-skinned winter varieties take over. Canary-yellow, green and almost snow-white, they can be eaten skin, seeds and all. Summer squashes appear in farmers' markets, allotments and seedsmen's catalogues not just as the well-known long courgette but as butter-yellow crooknecks, squat patty pans the shape of a Shaker pie, green golf ball-sized Ronde de Nice and, as the season takes its bow, plump, elephantine marrows.

Any tender-skinned variety can be used in place of the ubiquitous courgette (so good when picked shiny and crisp from the plant), though the very small, round varieties may be a challenge to stuff. Try sheep's cheese and basil rather than mince. Their charm is in their quiet colours and gently bending shapes, and the patty pans, crimp-edged like an apple tart, are heartbreakingly cute, but I would be hard pressed to spot much of a difference in flavour.

What interest there is relies on the creamy taste of those picked very young, or the refreshing green quality of those cooked in olive oil with a final spritz of lemon. But we are not talking big flavours here; just the calm, non-confrontational food that you might wish to eat on a summer's day in dappled shade. That thought alone is enough to have had me planting courgettes each spring for a decade, in pots, garden beds and even on the compost heap.

It is curious that we have taken up the French term courgette over the Italian zucchini. The latter is extraordinary – a lyrical word full of life and passion when said with an Italian accent, unlike the flaccid-sounding 'courgette'. I use the Italian at home when there is no one around to twitter about pretentiousness. My seeds come from Italy, as do the pots in which they germinate, the varieties themselves are Italian (Genovese, Romanesco, Bianco di Trieste) and I mostly cook them in the Roman manner, yet apparently I must give them the French name. Throughout what follows I interchange the names randomly and without apology. What is more, as they are technically a fruit, but eaten as a vegetable, so too I swap the terms about to suit myself. Pedants will have a field day.

Lunchtime in Florence, a decade ago. We sit at a simple table set with a white cloth, thick plates and tumblers for wine glasses. A dish is brought and placed in the centre of the table, unasked for but gratefully accepted. The gift is two battered zucchini flowers, huge golden clouds the size of my hand and still hissing from the fryer. At their side sits half a lemon wrapped in frost-white muslin.

We squeeze the lemon from on high and use a pinch of sea salt from the open saucer on the table. The batter shatters to send squirts of hot zucchini juice through our mouths. No garlic, no stuffing of Parmesan or ricotta, no herbs. Just a fragile (female) flower and its immature fruit encased in the lightest, crispiest, saltiest batter.

What followed was mostly pedestrian, but how could it not be, when the show had already been so successfully stolen? To this day, I have eaten very few courgettes in Italy that haven't been fried in some way, many in rustling slices on an earthenware dish, others cooked slowly in oil, always olive, with basil and garlic, or stuffed with the lightest ricotta and crisped in boiling oil.

My first encounter with a stuffed courgette was in Greece, at a harbourside restaurant without the help of a printed menu. Instead we wandered, stupefied by the searing heat, into the kitchen to point at whatever we liked the look of amongst an array of dented tin dishes of lukewarm, sleepy food. Courgettes lay slumped together stuffed with rice, raisins, oregano and pine kernels, their filling jaundiced with saffron and finely mashed preserved lemons. Just as welcome was the sight of a sloppily tepid stew with aubergines, tomato and onion that required little or no effort to eat.

Unlike spinach, broccoli and tomatoes, the nutrient level of a courgette is relatively low (the winter squashes have a rich supply of beta-carotene). Neither are they high on flavour, generally getting by with a little help from their friends, garlic, lemon and tomato. Their popularity cannot be solely down to their ease of chopping. Yes, they stuff neatly enough, are refreshing in a crisp, tempura-style batter and make a particularly fine fritter with salty cheese and dill (see *The Kitchen Diaries*) but will they stand up in their own right?

Those who dismiss the summer squashes, and there are many, might like to try a freshly picked crookneck, golden or classic striped courgette cooked lightly in olive oil till the flesh is translucent, seasoned with a generous pressing of a lemon, some sea salt and a handful of torn basil leaves. Their charms will beguile even those who have previously written them off as all water (well, they are 90 per cent). Moving on from the traditional rice stuffing and ratatouille-type melange, I offer a citrus-flavoured salad, a basil- and tomato-scented quick supper, a sauté with bacon and a hearty lentil filling for the larger specimens.

A courgette in the garden

The squash family thrives on rich, moist soil and bright sunshine. Those grown on my compost heap, slightly shaded by a mirabelle plum tree, tend to produce more leaves than fruit. I have had as much success in pots as in the veg beds and conclude that the family is not fussy as long as you can keep it warm, well watered and out of reach of slugs and snails who will, given the chance, feast on the fleshy stems like a panda on bamboo.

The flat, oval seed goes on its side into small pots of light compost no earlier than May. I keep it warm and slightly damp on a window ledge or outside in the cold frame till the young plants are a hand high, then carefully transplant them to a warm patch in the garden, a spadeful of muck dug in a week or two before (generous amounts of very well rotted manure will help the soil retain the essential moisture). You can also sow straight outdoors, but I find the snails tend to make a beeline for the downy-stemmed seedlings. The plants are ringed with coarse sand and a copper band to ward off the snails, and, if there is a spare one, a glass cloche to protect the young shoots from rain, wind and clumsy fox cubs.

Squashes have a habit of sulking, then suddenly, when your back is turned, producing more fruits than you know what to do with. The patty pans are better behaved in this respect. I find that cutting any squash with a knife is preferable to tugging at them, which can easily weaken the stems of the main plant. Being soft skinned, they will not keep like the winter squashes, but a few days in the fridge will do little harm.

Each plant will contain both male and female flowers. Like birds, the cock flower has the more dramatic plumage. It is the larger male flower that is most suitable for stuffing, the smaller female one that produces the fruit. The male flower can be seen tied in bunches in Italian markets, like great golden throats. They are picked early, before they have time to fertilise the female flowers. Their job done, the male flowers flop, then shrivel.

Varieties

For ten years or more, I have grown Striato Pugliese, a bright green, striped courgette with good flavour, and now and again, the delicate eau-de-nil, scallop-edged Peter Pan.

Gold Rush An early, heavy-cropping courgette-style squash with a crisp texture that some say is redolent of mushrooms.

Lebanese White Bush, White Egyptian Beautiful, almost white variety, shaped like a small aubergine, this is the one for Middle Eastern dishes. Looks coolly elegant with mint.

Ronde de Nice Bright green, round squash, good for stuffing (Sally Clarke has a sumptuous recipe with cream, ceps and rosemary). Suitable for small gardens due to its compact habit.

Costata Romanesca Heavily ridged, pale green fruits with good flavour (for a courgette). Mine always produce a lot of male flowers of exceptional size, so ideal for stuffing. Generally sweeter than the dark green varieties.

Green (or Black) Milan Smooth, long, dark and handsome.

Sweet Dumpling Tubby, cool mint green with darker stripes and freckles, this late-season squash is cute for stuffing. Harvest in October.

The zucchini diaries

Mid April Three Striato d'Italia plants arrive in the post. I have previously grown them from seed (follow the suggestions in the winter squash chapter on page 488) but this year I decided to try plug plants instead. Their juicy stems seem so fragile as I pot them up in rich compost in long, plastic pots. They settle in the cold frame, well watered.

Late May I plant them out, a tad later than I had hoped, in a bed that gets much sun. The plants are already top heavy and have to be supported with sticks. I put in seeds of Caserta and Cocozelle too, a variety that promises to be more of a marrow than a courgette.

Early June I pop a spadeful of manure in the holes before lowering in half the plants. The others I transfer to a large terracotta pot, a backup I suppose, in case it turns out to be too soon to set them free in the garden.

Late June Suddenly the leaves seem to have grown to the size of sunflowers, their edges sharp and hairy. Like teenagers, watery vegetables seem to erupt into adulthood overnight. The flowers are profuse now, and the size of an outstretched palm. Some have no fruit underneath, but a couple of others have the first signs of a striped green courgette plumping up under the vivid yellow flower.

July 15 I pick the first pair of courgettes. One is perfect, the other charmingly bent at the end. They are firmer and crisper than those from the shops and more brilliantly coloured. We cook them in shallow Tuscan olive oil with nothing but salt and a squeeze of lemon.

August 2 The fruits are coming regularly now, each one taking about ten days to ripen. I pick them small, no larger than my index finger. Once a fortnight I give them a drink of liquid fertiliser, avoiding the leaves.

August 3 I am sitting on the back step gazing at Caserta in its wide terracotta pot. The marbled lime and acid green leaves jagged as the teeth of a saw; the flowers a rich saffron yellow. A rare plant, more decorative than d'Italia, Romesco or Black Milan. Of its fruit, I know nothing yet.

August 25 Every time I open my eyes, another cheeky fruit is waving itself explicitly at anyone who passes.

October 5 Nought but a marrow left, though the flowers are still coming, their deep-golden petals looking beautiful in the early autumn vegetable beds. None is frost hardy, and clearing away the soggy tangle of blackened stems one frosty December weekend is always strangely pleasing.

A courgette in the kitchen

In an ideal world, the courgette you buy in the shops or at the market would come complete with its cheerful yellow flower. The blossoms, opening at dawn, last only a day, and in the relentless sun in my garden even less, collapsing in a soggy blob by nightfall. No wonder the shops never have them for sale with their golden trumpet attached. Yet I have seen them sold that way on the canal boats in Venice and in small greengrocer's shops in the backstreets of Florence too. Occasionally they pop up at the farmers' market here, a rare and showstopping find.

The shops here don't always treat what they sell with as much care as they do in Italy. The zucchini, with its stripes and speckles, dots and dashes, is a fragile fruit, its soft skin easily scarred by careless handling, yet they tend to be chucked around quite roughly in the shops. A recently picked courgette has a gloss to it, and a clean, freshly cut, slightly hairy stalk. They look perky. There should be no scratches or blemishes. If you like the look of what you see, then squeeze it gently. If it is anything but firm, let it go. A flaccid courgette is pointless. A recently picked one will keep well in the fridge, or in a cool place wrapped in newspaper, for up to a week. They lose their gloss as they age. A dull courgette is an old courgette. Inside, the seeds should be barely visible. Big seeds are a sure sign of ageing vegetables.

Few courgettes are picked at a tender age, when they are barely the size of your index finger, but I think they should be. That is when they are probably at their best – glossy, toothsome and with a mild, creamy flavour. Left too long on the plant or in the vegetable rack, they become dull, thick skinned and woolly, but still edible enough if you scrape out the seeds with a teaspoon and bake the rest slowly with garlic and tomatoes.

The lone Great Dish in the courgette's repertoire is *fiori di zucchini fritti*, the single flower dipped into very light batter (I make mine with fizzy mineral water) and deep-fried, then served with sea salt and a wedge of lemon. Often, they are stuffed with an almost ethereal filling of ricotta flavoured with grated lemon zest and chopped basil. This is their moment of glory. But they are also fine when stewed with tomatoes and garlic, or stuffed with rice, pine kernels and sultanas, or part of a plate of roasted vegetables with garlic and thyme tucked amongst them.

You can bake a courgette (with anchovy and breadcrumbs), stuff it (with minced veal, prosciutto and Parmesan), or grate it, fresh from the garden, into a salad dressing. In the Trentino area of Italy, land of mushrooms and *tortelli di patate* – the crisp potato pancakes that accompany so many of the local dishes – they make thin slices of the fruit held in a fragile pancake of egg and grated Parmesan, known as *frittata di zucchini*. Note the habit of baking and frying. Nothing good will come from cooking any of this tribe in boiling water.

Courgettes share a family name, *Cucurbita pepo*, with marrows, summer squashes and pumpkins. They are all made up of a large percentage of water, with mild flesh and, when young, an edible skin. They are worth trying grated and tossed with hot olive oil, young thyme and a squeeze of lemon. The dish takes just ten minutes, unless you grate too fast and need to hunt out a plaster. I have found myself daydreaming while grating a large batch of courgettes.

While most summer squash will ripen in the languid, half-hearted warmth of a British summer, they need feverish heat in the kitchen if they are not to collapse into blandness. I prefer courgettes cut into finger-thick strips, like fat chips, rather than rounds. Why? Because cut that way they retain a little more body and crispness.

For an ingredient with such a high percentage of moisture, the courgette grills surprisingly well. Sliced into ribbon-like strips down its length, briefly salted and rested in a colander to remove excess liquid, then patted dry and cooked over charcoal, it will take on a profound nuttiness. But it needs a good dressing of fruity olive oil, lemon and fresh herbs. By which I probably mean basil.

The courgette has long played a defining role in the Middle Eastern kitchen. Both sumptuous feasts and simple family dinners often include a dish of stuffed courgettes, limply tender, collapsing under the weight of their filling. Traditional stuffings, varying from family to family but often including tomatoes, spring onions and rice, are seasoned with mint, lemon, cinnamon, golden sultanas and sometimes sumac, the purplish lemony-flavoured berries. In my book, this is food for the gods.

Seasoning the summer squashes

Basil For tearing up and scattering over crisply fried courgettes
or for peppering up a tomato and courgette fry-up.
Lemon Squeeze some over crisply fried slices of zucchini.
Garlic Because it just works.
Tomato For vegetable stews and thick, bean-speckled soups.
Sultanas Strange one this, but the plump, golden dried fruits work well
if included in a stuffing with pine kernels or tossed in a sauté with parsley
and lemon juice.
Mint Toss with sliced courgettes before and after baking with olive oil.
The dried herb works surprisingly well in stuffings.
Dill For including in cakes, salads and pickles.
Olives and olive oil The saltiness of olives brings out all the sweetness in
a courgette. My own preference for cooking all summer squash is olive oil,
whilst butter seems more appropriate to the winter varieties.

And...

* Sow the seeds on their sides. When sown flat, the water sits on their surface
  and they can rot.
* I get the best results when I am generous with the water and the manure.
* The yellow courgettes seem to have a softer skin than the green, and need
  gentler treatment in the pan. They tend to break up more easily.
* Unusual squashes don't always tell us whether they are thin-skinned summer
  varieties or thicker autumn ones. Tapping the bottom with your knuckles is
  a good clue. If it sounds hollow, then it is usually a 'keeper'. Silence means
  it's one that should be used quickly.
* The smaller the courgette, the denser its flesh will be. It's the older
  specimens that have a loose, woolly texture.
* Deep-fried courgettes or their flowers make a refreshing first course with
  a little hollandaise or thinned garlic mayonnaise, but I often use them as
  an accompaniment to a lamb steak, or maybe a nice piece of beef rump.
  Deep-fried courgette slices are sensational with steak béarnaise.
* Don't even think of freezing a glut of squash. They lose all their magic.
  Make chutney instead. Better still, pass them round.
* As a rule, I find the round, crookneck or patty pan summer squashes
  can be substituted for courgettes in any recipe. The flavour won't be
  exceptionally different but they can look very beautiful on the plate.
  The larger seeds present in some of the smaller patty pans are entirely
  edible. As the fruits get bigger, so do the seeds inside.
* All the summer squashes are good with fish. Lightly sautéed, courgettes are
  a suitably timid accompaniment to sea bass, haddock and pollack.

Fruit and nut filling for baked courgettes

The ideal here would be the pale, plump courgette varieties you find in Middle Eastern grocer's shops. I visit one near London's Edgware Road that even has them ready prepared, their seeds removed for stuffing, and packed into little plastic crates. If these torpedo-shaped squashes escape me, and they often do, then I use the ubiquitous type, halve them lengthways and scatter the filling loosely over the top rather than making a clumsy attempt to stuff them.

The classic courgette stuffings of the Middle East vary from family to family but usually include cooked rice or minced lamb, or occasionally walnuts, pine kernels or hazelnuts stirred into softened onion and then lightly seasoned with allspice, tomato purée and parsley. The effect is a moist filling of elegance and pleasing predictability.

I sometimes want something more unusual. A stuffing that intrigues as much as it pleases.

enough for 4
a small to medium onion
olive oil
fresh white breadcrumbs – 50g
dried apricots – 50g
pistachios – 40g
couscous – 150g
vegetable stock – 250ml, boiling
thyme leaves – a tablespoon or so
the grated zest of a small lemon
parsley – a handful, chopped
courgettes – 8 medium to large

for the sauce
a small bunch of dill
a small clove of garlic
white wine vinegar – 2 tablespoons
olive oil – 3 tablespoons
yoghurt – 200g

Peel the onion, chop it finely, then let it soften with a little olive oil in a shallow pan over a medium heat. Stir in the fresh breadcrumbs. Chop the dried apricots and the pistachios, then add them to the pan. Remove from the heat. Set the oven at 180°C/Gas 4.

Tip the couscous into a heatproof bowl and pour over the boiling stock. Pour in a small glug of olive oil, then cover with a plate. Set aside for about ten minutes.

Add the thyme leaves, lemon zest and chopped parsley to the breadcrumb mixture, then season thoroughly with salt and black pepper.

Once the couscous has soaked up all the liquid, stir it into the stuffing with a fork (this helps to keep the grains separate). Slit the courgettes in half from stem to tip and lay them snugly, cut-side up, in a shallow dish. Scatter the stuffing over the courgettes, cover the dish with foil or buttered baking paper and bake for twenty-five minutes.

Whilst the courgettes bake, chop the dill, crush the garlic and stir in the vinegar and olive oil. Beat in the yoghurt with a small whisk or fork. Serve with the baked courgettes.

Zucchini on the grill

Young summer squash of any sort grill rather well, but better if you salt them first, so that they relax rather than harden over the heat. As soon as they are lifted off the bars, I toss them in dressing, keeping them moist and silky. A side dish, and very good with mozzarella or feta.

enough for 2–4
courgettes – 4 medium
the zest and juice of a lemon
olive oil – 3 tablespoons
a small bunch of basil leaves

Wipe the zucchini and slice thinly along their length. I like to make them no thicker than a pound coin. Put them in a colander in the sink. Grind over a little salt and leave for half an hour. Once they are covered with little beads of moisture – as if they have broken out into a flop sweat – pat them dry and put the slices on the grill. Let them brown lightly in stripes on the underside, then turn them over and brown the other side.

Meanwhile, make the dressing. Grate the zest from the lemon into a mixing bowl. I do this finely and lightly, as any white pith will make the dressing bitter. Add the lemon juice, then beat in the olive oil with a fork or small hand whisk. Add a pinch of salt and black pepper. Roughly tear the basil leaves, depending on their size – I like to leave small ones intact. Lightly crush them in the hand to release the oils, then add them to the dressing.

As each slice of zucchini becomes ready, drop it into the dressing and mix gently so that the slices become completely soaked. Set aside for ten minutes for the flavours to marry and the vegetables to soften slightly.

Spiced courgette and carrot fritters

Small squash deep-fry particularly well, offering a refreshing, almost juicy contrast to the ethereally crisp batter. This is one of those recipes – pancakes are another – that I tend to make when there are just two of us, and we can eat our sizzling fritters at the stove while the next one cooks. I find I get a much crisper result if I don't overcrowd the pan.

makes 6 or 8
a large carrot
a large leek
courgettes – 2
a large red chilli, seeded
shredded coriander leaves – a tablespoon
garlic – 2 cloves, chopped
self-raising flour – 100g
bicarbonate of soda – half a teaspoon
garam masala – 2 teaspoons
ice-cold water – about 175ml
oil for frying

for the chilli sauce
natural yoghurt – 150g
red and yellow chillies – 2 or 3 small hot ones
cumin seeds – a teaspoon
coriander leaves – a handful, roughly torn

Put the yoghurt for the sauce into a bowl. Seed and finely chop the chillies, then stir them into the yoghurt. Toast the cumin seeds in a dry non-stick pan, then, as they start to smell warm and dustily nutty, stir them into the sauce with the roughly torn coriander.

Cut the carrot and leek into fine strips about the length of your finger. Cut the courgettes and chilli into very fine slices. Put all the vegetables and the coriander and garlic into a bowl. Put the flour, bicarbonate of soda, garam masala and a generous amount of salt and pepper into another bowl, then beat in enough cold water to make a smooth but sticky batter. Add the vegetables and toss thoroughly.

Heat up the oil in a deep pan. Carefully drop large tablespoons of the mixture into the hot oil, about four dollops at a time. Fry for three or four minutes, till they are puffed and golden. Serve hot, with the chilli sauce.

A supper of courgettes, tomatoes and basil

2008 saw not only my usual terracotta pots of Striato d'Italia on the back steps but also a trailing variety known as Caserta, a pale fruit the colour of mint ice cream, with darker stripes. The light-skinned varieties such as Clarion, Di Faenza and the almost ivory Lebanese White Bush look particularly delicate and summery when sautéed in butter and olive oil with a handful of herbs thrown in at the last moment, the scent of late summer hitting you as you spoon over the pan juices. Perhaps that should be swoon.

Squashes of every variety love a tomato. Occasionally you could argue they need it too. Late last summer, just as the beans were forming on the poles in the vegetable beds, I made a last-minute, rough-edged supper with little more than a few courgettes and a couple of tomatoes. It was done in fifteen minutes flat. There are many who would insist on skinning and seeding the tomatoes for this, but not only do I think it unnecessary here, it also means missing out on all their rich juices and scrunchy seeds.

enough for 4 as a side dish, 2 as a principal dish
courgettes – 5 medium
olive oil – 3 tablespoons
tomatoes – 4 medium to large
basil leaves – a handful, torn
lemon

Cut the courgettes into thick fingers. I think they work best about the size of thick, homemade chips. Warm the oil in a deep pan and let the courgettes cook over a moderate heat for six to eight minutes or so, till they start to soften.

Chop the tomatoes roughly and add to the courgettes with the torn-up basil leaves, salt, pepper and a good squeeze of lemon. Stir, cover with a loose-fitting lid and leave to simmer for ten to twelve minutes, until the courgettes are totally tender and the tomatoes have cooked down to a basil-scented saucy slush. The colours should be bright, the courgettes softly yielding but not browned. Sponge up the sunny-tasting juices with bread.

A quick way with courgettes

This one is very useful when you need a vegetable in a hurry: you cut them into short pieces and toss them into a pan of hot olive oil, leave them to the tenderness fairy, then, when they are golden at the edges, season with lemon juice, salt and black pepper. Add a scattering of hand-torn herb and you have a ten-minute vegetable dish of surprising freshness and refinement. A mound of brown rice at their side and you have supper, albeit one without protein.

A Thursday night supper

Thursdays are when we tend to make the best of a bad job, a supper prepared from whatever is left in the fridge (usually bacon or pancetta and a long-life vegetable of some sort). This is when we clear out the fridge before the Friday organic box and the Saturday trip to the market. Whilst a winter rummage usually ends up as soup, a regular summer supper involves a hot frying pan, some smoked bacon and a couple of courgettes.

I cut the bacon into cubes and let it cook with a little olive oil in a shallow pan. As the fat turns from white to gold, I dice a few courgettes and drop them in with a grinding of salt. An occasional stir, enough to stop them sticking but not so much that they fail to colour, and then some salt. The dish is ready when the vegetables are tinged with gold, the bacon dark and smokily fragrant. I put it on a plate with a final drizzle from the olive oil bottle and some easily torn bread such as ciabatta. Sometimes I will add a few thyme leaves with the squash, a little rosemary at the beginning of cooking, or some basil at the end.

A lemon- and garlic-scented side dish

Middle Eastern cooking is flecked with the cool pepperiness of fresh mint. Italian, and especially Sicilian, cooks include mint with zucchini, often in tandem with garlic and lemon. I find mint invigorating with all summer squashes and often make a dish where they (patty pan is particularly suitable) are cooked in olive oil with mint and the merest hint of garlic. It is very good with grilled fish.

enough for 2
small courgettes – 400g
garlic – 2 cloves
olive oil – 3 tablespoons
mint leaves – a good handful
flat parsley leaves – a small handful
the juice of half a lemon

Cut the courgettes in half lengthways and then into short lengths. If they are real babies, you could simply halve them.

Peel the garlic and roughly chop it. Warm the olive oil in a shallow pan. Add the chopped garlic, let it fry for a minute over a moderate heat, then add the courgettes. Let them cook in the oil, turning them occasionally, until they are lightly golden and tender. Add the whole mint leaves and parsley leaves. Turn up the heat, pour in the lemon juice and let it bubble briefly. Crumble over a little sea salt.

Courgettes and green lentils to accompany slices of dark and interesting ham

Green lentils and bacon has long been a salad worth making. I will occasionally fold in some shards of crisp, olive-oil-drenched toasted ciabatta or lots of whole parsley leaves. A couple of years ago I started moving the whole thing up a notch by putting the lentils against a few pieces of exquisite Spanish ham and adding a certain smokiness with wide slivers of courgette, their edges blackened from the grill. This has become a late-summer lunch I can't get enough of.

enough for 4

for the salad
courgettes – 4 medium
small, dark green lentils – 150g
olive oil – 2 tablespoons
parsley – a good handful, roughly chopped
very thinly sliced jamon – 100g

for the dressing
red wine vinegar – a tablespoon
sherry vinegar – a tablespoon
olive oil – 4 tablespoons
a small clove of garlic, crushed
spring onions – 4

Slice the courgettes into long, thin ribbons about the thickness of a piece of lasagne. Put them in a colander with a scattering of salt and set aside in the sink or on a plate for a good half hour, longer if you have it.

Cook the lentils in boiling, lightly salted water till tender but retaining a nutty bite. They are usually ready in fifteen to twenty minutes, but I start checking them after ten or so. I think it's essential that they keep their shape and don't soften. Drain them in a colander.

While the lentils are cooking, make the dressing by mixing the vinegars, the oil and the crushed garlic together with a little salt and black pepper (I like to dissolve the salt in the vinegar first before adding the oil). Thinly slice the spring onions and stir them into the dressing. As soon as the lentils are drained, toss them in the dressing and cover.

Mix the olive oil with the roughly chopped parsley. Get the grill hot. If you prefer, a ridged griddle pan will do.

Rinse the salt from the courgettes, pat them dry, then cook them on the hot grill till their flesh starts to soften and they have charred a pleasing golden brown here and there. As you remove each from the grill, toss it in the olive oil and parsley. Divide the lentils and courgettes between four plates, and eat with the ham.

A salad of raw courgettes, lemon and toasted Parmesan

I was once rebuked for putting raw courgette in a salad. Rather than tasteless, I found them to be nutty and pleasingly lactic. Having had my wrist slapped, I forgot about the idea for several years.

In the wet July of 2008, I spent a rare hot afternoon at Petersham Nurseries in Richmond, filling the car boot with wine-coloured pelargoniums and pots of thyme for the back steps. Lunch was in the hands of Skye Gyngell, whose food I find tantalising and delicately balanced. Her menu included a salad of raw courgette. I felt vindicated. Perhaps I had been before my time. Skye had used courgettes the size of my little finger, sliced lengthways and layered in a fragile pile with the vegetable's own flowers – eaten raw – and a dressing of basil oil and lemon zest. The real revelation was the pepperiness of the flowers and the extraordinary creaminess of the young courgettes. They had the quality of freshly picked wet walnuts, something they possess only when very young and fresh from the vine.

The accidental marrow

The marrow is a handsome vegetable (one could say proud) and even more so when it appears at harvest festival propped against a jam jar of pink, red and yellow dahlias. It looks good in the golden light of a church window on an autumn afternoon, rather less so in your own vegetable rack.

Whilst I have never got into the whole show bench vegetable scene – the marrow was born to sport a rosette – it is fun to find them in the garden, lurking under the giant leaves like a beached tugboat. It is only as I try to cut through its shell with a not-so-sharp kitchen knife that I begin to regret the marrow's presence in the kitchen.

In the oven, the flesh softens to a buttery consistency, then collapses into a juicy slush. I like this for its refreshing quality, and for the delicate way it picks up the hint of garlic or tomato, tarragon or ginger that it is cooked with. Others feel the marrow's wateriness is a quality they can live without. The traditional recipes involving minced meat in a coat of white sauce that one can trace back to the eighteenth century leave me cold, but once you bring in sweet-sharp tomatoes, young garlic, toasted pumpkin seeds, matchsticks of ginger or a fistful of coriander leaf and lemon, you are in for a pleasant surprise. The golden rule is to season well and bake but never boil.

I have never deliberately grown a marrow. In 2005 I grew several by accident, having overlooked a courgette or two that grew like Topsy to give a courgette suitable for cooking as a marrow. The two are botanically different, but an inflamed courgette can be cooked as a marrow if it is not woolly inside, though it will lack the keeping quality of a true marrow.

Their names charm: Badger Cross, Tiger Cross, Green Bush. Their mottles and stripes have turned my organic box into a scene from a country show. I have eaten them baked with olive oil and butter (the marrow, for some reason, seems happier cooked with butter than olive oil, though I have no idea why), with sweetcorn and parsley, with lentils, basil and peas, and yet I have never planted one. If there is ever a marrow in my kitchen it is by (happy) accident.

A lentil stuffing for a cheap supper

A marrow for supper will generally coincide with the leaves turning on the trees, the first early morning mists, new school uniform. Their bulk and their bargain-basement price ensure that they will make a cheap supper. For this, we love them. This filling – earthy, sloppy and much nicer than mince – is good for pumpkin too.

> *enough for 4*
> small brown or green lentils (Puy are perfect) – 200g
> a medium-sized marrow (or pumpkin)
> olive oil
> shallots – 2 large, or an onion
> garlic – 2 large cloves
> tomatoes – 6 medium, or 20 cherry tomatoes
> chilli sauce, such as harissa
> green leaves, such as spinach or chard – 2 handfuls
> grated Parmesan – 2 tablespoons

Set the oven at 180°C/Gas 4. Bring a pan of water to the boil in which to cook the lentils. Add them to the water and leave to simmer, I think rather vigorously, until you have tender lentils. On this occasion they should be soft rather than *al dente*.

Cut the marrow in half lengthways but do not peel it; the rind will give it some support. Scoop out the core and put both halves into a roasting tin, then brush with olive oil and put in the preheated oven. Leave the marrow until tender and translucent – about twenty minutes – then remove from the oven. You could, alternatively, steam it.

Meanwhile, peel and slice the shallots and garlic and soften them in a saucepan with three tablespoons of olive oil. Chop the tomatoes, peeling them if they have tough skins (dunk the whole tomato into boiling water, then peel off the skin after a few seconds), and add them to the pan. Let them cook a while, till they are soft and mushy, then stir in your chilli sauce. I use a couple of teaspoons of harissa here. The amount will depend on which chilli sauce you have around and how hot you like your lentils to be. Remember that the marrow will soften the heat. Pour in just enough water (I use barely a teacupful) to make a slushy sauce and be generous with the salt and black pepper.

Drain the cooked lentils, then stir them into the onion and chilli sauce. Tear the spinach or chard leaves into small pieces and stir them into the lentils. Bring to the boil, then cover and leave to simmer over a low heat till the greens are silky soft. Spoon the lentil mixture into the hollows in the marrow, scatter with the grated Parmesan, cover with foil or greaseproof and bake for twenty minutes.

Baked marrow, minced pork

A contemporary take on the mince-stuffed marrow. This economical supper stands or falls by the way the mince is cooked. The real flavour here comes from the caramelisation of the sugars in the meat. To make the most of this, I have the oil at quite a high temperature as I add the mince, then resist the temptation to stir or turn the meat too soon. Continual movement will result in 'wet' rather than crisp-edged, golden mince.

enough for 2 as a main dish

for the marrow
young marrow or large courgettes – 750g
garlic – 2 cloves, crushed
mint leaves – a handful
olive oil
the juice of half a lemon

for the pork
dill – a small handful
parsley – a small bunch
garlic – a couple of cloves
red chillies – 2 small, hot
olive oil
minced pork – 450g
the grated zest and juice of a lime

Halve the marrow and remove the seeds and fibre. I peel it only if the skin is particularly thick (if a fingernail lightly pressed against the skin fails to leave a wound, then it is unlikely ever to be tender enough to eat). Cut the flesh into thick chunks and toss in a roasting tin with the crushed garlic, mint leaves, a couple of generous glugs of olive oil and the lemon juice. Set aside for an hour.

Set the oven at 180°C/Gas 4. Bake the marrow for forty-five minutes or so, till soft and tender. Roughly chop the dill and its stalks, the parsley leaves and the garlic. Finely chop the chillies, removing the seeds if you like a milder effect.

To cook the pork, get a couple of tablespoons of olive oil smoking hot in a shallow pan, then add the meat. At this point, I don't turn or stir it, however tempting, till the underside has had a chance to colour and crisp. Turn when you can to brown the other side. Add the dill, parsley, garlic and chilli. Let the mixture cook over a high heat, till all is fragrant, sizzling and golden. Season generously with salt and black pepper, then stir in the lime juice and zest. Serve with the baked marrow.

Jerusalem artichokes

I almost missed the dusty brown wicker basket with its cargo of palest-ivory artichokes. Rolling them over in my hand and brushing the loose soil from them with my thumb, I wasn't even sure if they were artichokes at all. Slender and smooth, with the smell of fresh earth, they lacked the warts, knobs and tight crevices that I associate with the root vegetable known for its capacity to produce velvety soups and triumphant wind. They had long tails and whiskers, too. When I got them home in their brown paper bag it was like washing baby mice under the cold tap.

I steamed the artichokes unpeeled, then browned them in a shallow pan of butter and oil, parsley and a last-minute shot of lemon juice.

I had expected the usual earthiness, and the introduction of lemon juice only went on to highlight that, but what surprised was the warm nuttiness of the little tubers and the pleasing roughness of their skins. The outside was all texture, like eating walnuts, the inside a mouthful of ivory-hued, fudgy delight, with a whiff of the artichoke hearts with which they are often confused.

Beside them in a small pile were several slices of cold roast pork as thin as paper and three long shards of crisp crackling, its skin blistered with golden bubbles. No condiments save the buttery, walnut-coloured juices and a scattering of burnt bits from the pan. Rarely has a meal of cold meat and vegetables been so satisfying, its sepia tones perfectly suited to the grey of a cold November day.

Despite its dullness of hue, the artichoke is a member of the sunflower family, and may take its name from the Italian *girasole* – because of the flowers' habit of moving with the sun. There is another line of thought, which I prefer, that the name is from Terneuzen, the third largest Dutch port and home to the flying Dutchman, from where they were first imported to Britain. While either explanation makes sense, this artichoke's homeland is neither Holland nor Jerusalem but North America.

Jerusalem artichokes make you fart. This has probably cost them more than a few friends, but they have so much going for them, both as a vegetable for the allotment – their height makes an efficient windbreak for more tender vegetables such as spinach or peas – and in those legendary smooth cream soups, that I do everything I can to encourage people to try them. I have been known to add them quietly to a mixed vegetable soup and not tell anyone. Perhaps quietly is not the right word.

And whilst the odd bay leaf in the cooking water or a thorough peeling may (or may not) calm their side effects, it really is just a case of learning to love them.

A Jerusalem artichoke in the garden

Once the stems are fully grown and the flower buds open, the artichoke's connection to the sunflower is unmistakable. The flowers are delicate, others might say pathetic, so I dig in a few Velvet Queen sunflowers amongst them to add a touch of opulence to their section of the garden. Their thick stalks and spreading roots take up quite a bit of space, which is why it is best to grow them near the back of the vegetable border. In a windy autumn, their stems may need tying back.

Prolific is a word I heard more than once before I planted my own artichokes. You get a lot going on underground from planting time in January and February (you can put them in as late as May) through to what can be a copious harvest in late autumn and winter. Many gardeners trim the flowers and the tallest of the shoots in midsummer to encourage the plant to plough all its strength into the slowly fattening tubers. I find this neither necessary nor aesthetically pleasing.

The tubers over-winter well enough in deep ground (pile soil on top if you think they might be too near the surface) and keep better there than in the house. If your ground freezes and you do need to bring them in, they will keep well if the air is a little damp. The bottom of the fridge is ideal.

I am looking out at mine as I write, their swaying stems and rich, tobacco-brown winter foliage stands striking against the row of golden hornbeam that does its best to shield the garden from the worst of the west wind. The tallest and most elegant of vegetable plants, even in repose.

Topinambors, as the French and Italians know them, thrive on rich soil and sunshine and the slugs are partial to their tender new shoots, but they have few other demands. They will grow on a shady site, and even suffer neglect from the watering can. A patch will last for years if you wish it to, though replanting regularly will, say the experts, give you smoother tubers. And whilst everyone seems determined they will become a weed if you fail to clear the ground properly, I can think of worse weeds to deal with than one that will bring me soup of such solace.

An artichoke diary

February 23 A paper bag of beige tubers dusted with fine, black soil arrives on a winter morning, when the earth is white with frost. Artichokes will survive shade, and I decide to grow them close to the thick yew hedge that acts as an impenetrable boundary for the vegetable garden; a patch where little has previously even survived, let alone flourished. I fork the area lightly. The soil is rich but light, and surprisingly less claggy than it has been in past years. The recent frosts have broken down the soggy clods into something altogether more friable.

The tubers are Fuseau, unusually smooth, each with a pink nose at the pointed end. Ten small holes, 15cm deep and a good 20cm apart, are to be their home. I put them in nose up, then cover them with soil and a forest of hazel twigs to give any inquisitive foxes a poke in the eye.

April 16 First signs of life, here and there a furry shoot pokes through the soil like the ears of a startled hare. I run out with the coffee grounds and organic slug pellets.

May 4 Tufts of matt green leaves sprout from stems white with hairs, their edges cut as if with pinking shears.

May 15 Eighteen inches high, the hairy stems and their long ears are leaning away from the hedge and towards the light, as befits their other name, the sunchoke. I tie them up with strong brown string.

November 9 The stems are taller than a man, and sway back and forth in the wind. The leaves have almost blackened with the first frosts, and are leaning across the path. They rustle as you push past them on the way to the compost. An eerie sound on a dark evening. If they were in a more exposed site, such as an open allotment, I would cut the stalks down and lay them over the soil to keep the tubers cosy through the winter.

November 17 The garden fork goes in and I lift out a huge root dripping with twenty or more long, smooth tubers. It is one of many, but I take only half of them, leaving enough behind to sprout next year.

Varieties

Not many, but I recommend Fuseau for a smooth, delicately flavoured tuber; Stampede for a knobbly variety with the look of a Henry Moore sculpture, and Dwarf Sunray for those who prefer not to peel their 'chokes.

A Jerusalem artichoke in the kitchen

The smoother varieties and those with fine, pale skins often need nothing more than a good wash under running water. The knobbly ones are likely to hold on to their mud like a rabbit holds on to its coat. I take a scrubbing brush to them; it's often the only way to get the soil out from the deeper notches and dimples. Once you break the skin you are in trouble, and will need the action of lemon juice to stop the white flesh browning. A bowl of acidulated water will do. Resist the temptation to peel them and instead celebrate the vegetable's wholehearted earthiness.

You can eat them raw, thinly sliced and tossed with parsley, nut oil and the juice of an orange or lemon, or perhaps with shredded salami and again, more parsley. Artichokes like to be steamed or cooked in butter. Simmered only with stock or water, a soup of Jerusalem artichokes can give the impression of having been laced with cream, even when the only dairy produce it contains is a knob of butter.

Peeled, they are likely to turn to wet mush in the pan, so I scrub them instead. You can boil them with a little lemon in the water, but better, I think, to steam them in a colander set over merrily simmering water, in which case their flesh is less likely to collapse. Marry them to parsley, to lemon (to emphasise their earthy qualities) or to seafood and anoint them with butter. But the real trick is to bring them to tenderness in stock instead of water. Chicken or vegetable broth, and a careful eye for any signs of approaching tenderness, will reward you with a soup that has both sweetness and body. The tubers love a good chicken stock above all, and simmered together they will produce a soup far superior in terms of flavour and texture than mere water alone will ever produce. Boiled in water, they sometimes take on a disinfectant note.

If you are cooking them in oil or butter, they will benefit from five or six minutes in the steamer first. This will tenderise the innards, leaving less risk of them toughening in the frying pan.

When I first came across a recipe that married the root with scallops, I assumed it was an affectation – a plea from a chef desperate for attention. Who else could have contrived a terrine of thinly sliced scallops and artichokes framed with sprigs of chervil? Then, a while later, I came across a mention of artichokes with prawns; then a soup, a salad, a posh restaurant dish that again brought together the earthiest of tubers and the most delicate of seafood. Warily, I tried them. Wonderful. The most successful partnership seems to be with scallops, particularly if you include the crescent-shaped corals.

Seasonings for the artichoke

Parsley The most fitting of all herbs, earthy but fresh, a perfect match. Fold a handful, roughly chopped, into an artichoke salad, or more finely chopped into a soup. To my taste, the two are inseparable.
Lemon The best way to keep the vegetable from turning grey, but also as a welcome shock of freshness and light to balance the mineral tones.
Orange Finely grated and added to a dressing in an artichoke salad. Use with care.
Butter Even a thin slice added to oil for frying or roasting is rewarding.
Hazelnuts and almonds Toast and scatter over the surface of a soup; include in a warm salad of artichokes and young spinach leaves.
Walnuts and their oil Add toasted walnuts to artichoke soup; toss them into a salad of artichokes and lemon; use the oil to dress the warm tubers straight from the pan.
Bay leaves A must in artichoke soup.
Cream It is not always a necessary addition to soup, but even a mere swirl of double cream will introduce a little gentility into the proceedings. Till later, of course.
Scallops, prawns Steam your artichokes and toss them with freshly cooked prawns or queen scallops, a mass of hashed coriander and a dressing of olive oil and lemon juice.

And...

* The tubers first appear in the shops in late autumn, continuing throughout the winter, and should snap crisply. I avoid any that bend.

* I find artichokes keep best with a little of their soil attached – or at any rate unscrubbed – wrapped in newspaper, in the bottom of the fridge. A cold garage or shed will work just as well. Home growers, such as myself, will find they keep freshest when left in the soil.

* Peeling isn't always necessary. A good scrub is often enough. I chuck any trimmings in the stockpot.

* Once the artichokes have been trimmed, the discoloration of their white flesh can be halted not only by the usual lemon juice but also with a dash of wine vinegar in the soaking water. You won't taste it in the cooking.

* The extraordinary affinity that the artichoke has for prawns and scallops is at its most simple and charming in a soup of puréed artichoke with a scattering of lightly fried scallop on top.

* Purées or mashes of artichoke work beautifully with almost any white fish, but sautéed hake, parsley sauce and mashed artichokes is especially pleasing.

* Nutty, firm-textured cheeses – think of the Cheddars and Dales varieties, along with the Beaufort, Gruyère and farmhouse Gouda-style cheeses – partner this root more successfully than the strongly flavoured, softer varieties, which tend to bring out its bitterness.

* Though they are good enough with pork, the sweet, mild flavours of the roasted roots make a particularly fine contrast to the exceedingly savoury pan-stickings of a joint of beef.

* Wind is almost inevitable. Just go with it.

A salad of raw artichokes

The juicy crunch of a raw artichoke bears many of the qualities of a water chestnut. Few ingredients pack such snowy crispness. I use them in a parsley-flecked salad to add a snap to baked pork chops, but have also offered them at a Saturday bread'n'cheese lunch of Cornish Yarg and Appleby's Cheshire. Lemon is essential if the peeled tubers are not to discolour.

> *enough for 2*
> a medium lemon
> olive oil
> walnut oil
> Jerusalem artichokes – 400g
> parsley

Make the dressing first. Dissolve a good pinch of salt in the juice of the lemon, twist in a few turns of the peppermill, then whisk in enough olive and walnut oil to make a thickish dressing. I usually find two tablespoons of each is about enough. You want the lemon to really sing rather than sit quietly in the back row. Peel the artichokes, then slice them thinly, using a vegetable peeler. They will be almost transparent. I usually let the shavings of artichoke fall into the dressing so that they don't discolour.

Chop the parsley, but not too finely, then toss gently with the salad. Add any of the ingredients below or not, as the mood takes you.

Good things to add to your artichoke salad

* Hazelnuts, skinned and toasted.
* Toasted walnuts.
* Thin slices of grilled scallop.
* Peeled prawns.

A warm salad of artichokes and bacon

'Monday cold cuts' is a key dish in our house: it shows our intent to use every scrap, to make the most of what we have, but it also gives me a break. It is one meal I don't have to think about other than sharpening the carving knife. The appearance of thin slices of cold meat on the first day of the week also gives me a chance to consider a side dish more interesting than a baked potato. Sometimes I bring out a bubble and squeak, fried in my old cast iron pan, or some leftover mashed root vegetables warmed in a bowl over hot water with a knob of butter; other times it's red cabbage, shredded with pickled walnuts as black as coal. Another favourite is a warm salad of some sort of root vegetable, fried or steamed, then turned in a mustardy dressing.

enough for 2
Jerusalem artichokes – 500g
smoked streaky bacon – 200g
olive oil – 3 tablespoons
walnut oil – a tablespoon
lemon juice – a tablespoon
grain mustard – 2 teaspoons
flat-leaf parsley – a small bunch

Peel the artichokes, dipping each one into cold water containing a squeeze of lemon juice as you go. This will stop them browning. Pile into a steamer basket or colander and steam over boiling water until knifepoint tender.

Meanwhile, cook the bacon in a non-stick pan till lightly crisp – you probably won't need any fat – then cut into finger-thick strips and drop into a salad bowl. Make a dressing with the olive oil, walnut oil, lemon juice and mustard, whisking the ingredients together with a seasoning of salt and pepper. Chop the parsley and stir it into the dressing (the parsley is essential here, I think).

Slice the artichokes thickly, I like them quite chunky for this recipe. Over a moderate heat, warm the pan in which you cooked the bacon, then add the sliced artichokes, letting them cook till nicely coloured on both sides. Now toss them carefully with the bacon and the dressing.

Serve with cold roast beef or chicken.

Roast artichokes

Scrub the artichokes, say four or five per person, then slit them in half down their length. Warm a thick slice of butter and a glug of groundnut or sunflower oil in a roasting tin. Put the artichokes in, cut-side down. Crack open a whole head of garlic, squash 2 or 3 cloves per person with the flat of a knife – just enough to break the skin – then chuck them in the tin.

Roast for twenty-five to thirty minutes in a hot oven (200°C/Gas 6) until the underside of the artichokes is crusty. Squeeze over the juice of half a lemon, maybe more, and a handful of roughly torn parsley.

Jerusalem artichokes with walnut oil and lemon

Having discovered the delights of raw artichoke with lemon and walnut oil, it was only a matter of time before the ingredients took the leap into the pan. A main course of artichokes is probably more than most gentle people could take, so I use this as something to cuddle up to a main course. It is very good with smoked mackerel.

enough for 4 as a side dish
Jerusalem artichokes – 750g
butter – 75g
walnut oil – a tablespoon
an open-textured loaf such as ciabatta – 4 slices
lemon juice
parsley leaves – a handful, roughly torn

Wipe, scrub or peel the artichokes as you think fit. Steam in a colander balanced over a pan of boiling water, or simply cook in boiling water, till just yielding to the point of a knife. Drain.

Melt the butter in a shallow, heavy-based pan and add the walnut oil. When the fat is sizzling, add the artichokes and a generous grinding of salt. Leave them to colour, then shake the pan or stir them to colour the other sides. Tear the bread into wide hunks and tuck them amongst the vegetables. Leave to colour here and there and soak up the pan flavours. Squeeze over a little lemon juice to lift the general earthiness, then toss with the parsley and eat.

A pan fry with duck fat and bay

Jerusalem artichokes share with the potato an ability to drink up both dressings and the fat in which they cook. Roll a still-warm steamed artichoke or potato in a sharp oil and vinegar dressing and it will soak up the liquid like a sponge. It is this quality that makes them a candidate for cooking in luxurious mediums such as bacon fat or, better still, duck fat.

This contemporary twist on the sautéed potato is, as you might expect, something with which to garnish a steak. An ice-crisp salad of winter leaves (chicory, radicchio, frisée, maybe) would slice the edge off its richness.

enough for 4 as a side dish
Jerusalem artichokes – 1.5kg
a lemon
duck fat – 3 generous tablespoons
thyme – a couple of sprigs
bay leaves – a couple

Bring a deep pan of water to the boil. Scrub the artichokes, removing the most awkward of the lumps and bumps and dropping them into a bowl of water into which you have squeezed a little lemon juice. Steam the artichokes for seven minutes till almost tender. If they break a little, then it is all to the good.

Melt the duck fat in a shallow, heavy-based pan and, once it starts to sizzle, add the thyme leaves and bay leaves. These are not an affectation – their effect is subtle but essential. Put the artichokes in the pan in one layer and season with salt. Leave to cook till the roots are crisp, golden and tender, shaking the pan from time to time. They should be ready in thirty to thirty-five minutes.

A Middle Eastern seasoning for an earthy roast

December 2007 and a net of ivory and pink artichokes has turned up in the organic box, as knobbly as a bag of vertebrae. We have had them twice out of the garden already this week and I am not sure whether to laugh or cry. Sound and clean, they have a pink blush to them that makes them appear more delicate than they probably are. They tempt, though, and I decide to roast them to serve with the sliced cold ham and jar of fruit jelly in the fridge.

The tubers get a brief once-over under cold water, which makes their soft colours shine like young flesh, then I put them on the chopping board and whack each with a tin of chickpeas. I could have used a rolling pin to break the rough-sided tubers but I like the squat heaviness of the tin in the hand – it feels like the right tool for the job. The idea is, I suppose, to crack each one open so that the roughly broken insides as well as the skin might caramelise in the oven's heat.

For no particular reason, I decide to follow the earlier roast artichoke recipe but to season the sweet, earthy roots with the piquancy of a couple of chopped pickled lemons, a teaspoon of crushed coriander seeds and the throat tickle of large, coarse, parsley leaves. The contrast with the pan-cooked ones with fresh lemon I mentioned previously is striking.

A new artichoke soup

I have long made a simple artichoke soup by adding the scrubbed tubers to softened onions, pouring over stock and then simmering till the artichokes fall apart. I often add a little lemon juice, bay leaves and sometimes a thumb of ginger. I blitz it in the blender, then stir in lots of chopped parsley. Some might introduce cream at this point but I honestly don't think it's necessary. The soup is velvety enough. It has become a staple in this kitchen over the last few winters; its warm nuttiness is always welcome on a steely-skied January day.

Late in the winter of 2008, possibly having had one day too many of what Beth Chatto calls 'dustbin-lid skies', I changed the soup's tone by adding a stirring of bright green spinach. As often happens, it came about by accident – a bowl of creamed spinach left over from a boiled gammon lunch – added to the soup just to use it up. The magic in this soup is in the marriage of earthy cold-weather food and a shot of mood-lifting chlorophyll. Spring is obviously stirring.

enough for 4–6
large leeks – 2
butter – 40g
Jerusalem artichokes – 450g
bay leaves – 2
light stock or water – a litre

for the spinach
butter – a thick slice
large spinach leaves – 500g
crème fraîche – 2 heaped tablespoons
nutmeg

Finely slice the white and palest green part of the leeks, wash thoroughly in plenty of running water, then drain. Melt the butter in a heavy-based saucepan, add the sliced leeks, then leave to soften over a low to moderate heat for fifteen to twenty minutes. They need to remain green and white and shouldn't brown at all. I find the easiest way to achieve this is to place a disc of greaseproof paper on top of the leeks, followed by the pan lid. A regular stir will help.

Rinse and roughly chop the artichokes and add them to the leeks. Continue cooking for a few minutes, then add the bay leaves and stock or water and bring to the boil. Turn the heat down so that the soup bubbles gently, partially covered with the lid. It will take about twenty-five minutes before the artichokes are tender. Blitz the soup in a blender till smooth. I should probably remind you not to overfill the blender jug. Pour into a bowl.

Make the spinach cream: melt the butter in the artichoke pan and add the spinach. Turn it from time to time till it softens. Press the spinach against the side of the pan and drain off the liquid. Do this thoroughly. Tip into the blender and add the crème fraîche, a tiny pinch of ground nutmeg and a little salt and blitz.

Warm the artichoke soup (it may be hot enough already if you have worked quickly), spoon into soup bowls, then add a couple of spoonfuls of the spinach to each bowl and mix the two lightly together as you eat.

A casserole of artichokes and pork for deepest winter

A damp January morning (2006) and a walk round the vegetable patch
reveals only two herbs in reasonable condition: rosemary, which loses some
of its potency in winter, and parsley, most of which has collapsed in a dead
faint to the ground. I value both enormously, feeling even now that they
have an edge on the imported basil and spindly thyme in the shops.
Both respond well to earthy winter cooking.

Chilled to the bone (I find it's the damp that gets to me more than the
temperature), I come in and use the parsley where it really matters: in a pan
of braised artichokes and pork sausage, whose brown depths I freshen up
with Italian lemons and, at its side, some crisp and chewy greens.

enough for 4
pork sausages – 8 really good ones
olive oil
onions – 4 medium
garlic – 2 cloves
small mushrooms – 250g
Jerusalem artichokes – 500g
a large lemon
fennel seeds – a teaspoon
light stock or water to cover – about 500ml
flat-leaf parsley – a small bunch, roughly chopped
steamed cavolo nero, spring cabbage or purple sprouting, to serve

Brown the sausages all over in a little oil in a deep casserole. Set aside.
Peel the onions and cut them into thick segments, then add to the pan in
which you browned the sausages, pouring in a little more oil if you need
to. Let the onions soften over a moderate heat till they are tender enough
to crush with a wooden spoon. Don't hurry this; it should take about fifteen
to twenty minutes. Peel and finely slice the garlic and add it to the onions.
Halve the mushrooms and add them too.

Peel or simply scrub the artichokes, then cut them in half. Add them to
the pan, pushing the onions aside, and let them colour slightly. Now tip the
sausages back into the pan. Cut the lemon into fat chunks and tuck them in
along with the fennel seeds and a good seasoning of salt and black pepper.

Pour over enough stock or water to cover and bring to the boil. Turn
the heat down and simmer for about thirty minutes, until the vegetables are
truly tender. If there is too much liquid, turn up the heat and let it reduce
a little. Stir in the parsley, check the seasoning and eat with the greens.

Kale and cavolo nero

From a distance, huge undulating pillows of green and dusky blue. Close up, coarse, frilly leaves with a tough central rib. In the mouth, richly textured, a little chewy, sweet and slightly bitter. Kale is both pleasingly humble yet vibrant and big flavoured, a forerunner of the full-headed cabbages we know today.

The leaves are long, plume-like and run from the mildly serrated through to the heavily fringed and indented. They are so beautiful they could be grown as an ornamental, while their texture can be softer than spring greens or so tough you feel like a donkey chomping at thistles. Much depends on the variety.

Since earliest times the kales have kept us going during the hungry gap from January to March. So important was the crop that the Romans referred to the month of February as Kalemonath. It was often the only leaf crop standing in late winter – good enough reason for them to be thought of as a survival vegetable, something to chew our way through when the land is bare, but our attitude is changing. Kale has gone from a food of poverty to one of supreme trendiness. Much of its current popularity has to do with the leaves' high vitamin content and the fashion for growing your own – kale is an easy and reliable crop. The plants are relatively pest free too, which is partly why they are the winter darlings of our organic farmers (though they are apparently the very devil to pick in quantity).

There are four kales of real interest: red Russian, which is a soft silver green edged with pink; black, which is better known as cavolo nero; curly kale, whose leaves are almost as tightly clenched as old-fashioned parsley; and the late, flat-leaved form often called Hungry Gap.

Where we might harvest a cabbage for its entire head, kale leaves tend to be picked individually in a cut-and-come-again fashion. At least they are on my patch. Sometimes, especially from organic box growers, they arrive in a whole, gracefully arching bunch. While fans like me get overexcited at the sight of a crate of curly kale leaves at the market in January, I should probably mention that others find this member of the brassica family rather coarse and difficult to deal with.

I am heartily grateful that what was once consigned to cattle (and still is at the end of the season, when the herds are allowed into fields of unsold crops) is now the most fashionable of all the green vegetables. Some of its new popularity is due to the publicity the leaves have received for their apparent cancer-fighting abilities, more to the new varieties whose bitter notes have been somewhat bred out, but I suspect the true breakthrough was down to Ruthie Rogers and Rose Gray at the River Café. Their full-bodied bean soups, richly laced with garlic and Parmesan, often feature the black-green kale we know as nero de toscana, cavolo nero or black palm cabbage. I like to think it is down to them that you can now pick up a bag of black cabbage, albeit mild and ready-trimmed, in the more enterprising supermarkets.

Cavolo nero was the first of the cabbage family to be planted in my garden and I welcome its presence in the bone-chilling patch after New Year, when it stands, embarrassingly ragged but curiously elegant, against the frost-white soil. Those frosts, incidentally, sweeten its character. Its long, blue-black leaves are pretty much all that is left on my vegetable patch in February. Well, that and Jerusalem artichokes. A combination best avoided by the easily embarrassed.

Kale in the garden

The fancier-leaved forms of kale are the most hardy and the most pest resistant. The softer, wavy-leaved plants are slightly less hardy and will attract the attention of the cabbage white butterfly. I throw a net over mine in summer, removing it only when the weather is too cold to entice a butterfly out to play.

You can grow plants from seed either *in situ* or in seed trays, moving them on to small pots and then, when they are feeling strong enough, to the garden. Sow from April to June in order to harvest in late winter. Sown under glass or on a windowsill, your seedlings should be through in ten days or so.

At six to eight weeks old, the seedlings should be sturdy enough to transplant. I use a dibber to make a deep hole, then lower the young plant in. A thumb will do. About 40cm is usually enough between the plants, certainly in my garden. Rather than pushing the soil back into place with my hands, I puddle water in from a watering can and leave them to sort themselves out. I put a stick in, to which I should tie them, but I find the heavier, more indented leaves generally hold on without any help from garden string. They hook themselves round the stick. The plants need regular watering but are less capricious than other cabbages, even tolerating a little shade, and will withstand any amount of frost. Some varieties, such as Russian kale, don't show their true colours till the air is cold enough. Few sights, vegetable or otherwise, are more breathtaking than a patch of Russian kale in the snow, its leaves the hauntingly beautiful dusty greens and faded pinks of an old tapestry.

Varieties

Dwarf Green/Blue Curled Exceptionally hardy, positively thrives in the cold.

Frosty A very curly form, growing taller than most.

Winterbor The young leaves are tightly curled and frilled, opening to a somewhat flatter leaf as they mature. The pale blue-grey of Paris at dusk. I have much success growing this variety.

Hungry Gap Robust, reliable, heavily curled leaves.

Winter Red Flat type with gently frilled edges. Colours well once the frost is here.

Redbor Deeply frilled, dark pink form. Pleasing colour in the winter vegetable patch.

Red Russian Pink-purple veins and rose edges to sweet and tender leaves. Only colours up in exceptionally cold weather.

Nero de Toscana What the Italians mean when they say cabbage. Long, almost black, blistered leaves with wide stems. Strongly flavoured, will withstand virtually any amount of cold. A very popular variety with my snails.

Kale in the kitchen

I particularly look forward to the arrival of the greens we pick by the leaf rather than by the whole head. Flat leaved from the garden; deeply curled from the box scheme in Buckfastleigh; purple stemmed from the market in the East End. It enriches my life even before I put it in the pot. Just heaped into the sink, the leaves are handsome against the stainless steel. Once the icy water collects in droplets, glistening like diamonds in their frills and waves, I feel uplifted, invigorated.

I have shocked people by adding curly kale, tugged from its stalk in stamp-sized nuggets, to a salad. It works if the produce is young and there is grilled bacon involved, or slivers of speck or salami or chorizo, and if the dressing has a dab of mustard in it. Lemon, too, will make your lunch sing, but not in the same salad as bacon. You can dip the leaves into deep boiling water and come up with an accompaniment of vivid purity – wonderful on a bowl of white rice with a drizzle of toasted ginger and soy – or you can steam and toss it in almost-melted butter and lemon juice.

Kale lends itself to many of the same treatments as cabbage and several of the oriental greens. It is worth checking out those sections in this book and using the softer-leaved kales in their place. The tough kales – robust, literally bouncing with health – need careful handling. With their tough stalks, they are apt to get stuck in your teeth. At least, they do in mine. In my kitchen, the leaves are shredded, stalks and all, and plunged into boiling, unsalted water before being chucked into a smoking pan of oil, garlic, sliced red chillies and shredded ginger. Tossed briefly, then quickly out on to warm plates. The chillies get stuck in the leaf folds and offer occasional and unexpected fireworks in the mouth. Either that, or I tear the leaves from their thick stems, trudging the latter to the compost heap the next day.

Seasoning your kale

Cream, mustard, juniper, caraway, bacon and the other flavours so happy
to co-exist with the headed or sprouting brassicas are appropriate here, but
there are a few others that seem to work especially well with the strong-
leaved kales.

Eggs A softly poached egg dropped on to a plate of steamed kale makes
a quick and cheap supper dish.
Anchovies Chopped finely and 'melted' into warm butter, then tossed
with the greens.
Ham Stridently flavoured leaves work well stirred into soups made with
ham stock.
Vinegar Use to temper kale's more ribald notes. Use it generously in
a dressing for steamed or raw (young) kale.
Potatoes Work well in a soup with the tougher leaves. Add chunks
of garlicky sausage too.
Lemon A pacifier.

And...

* Bacon is not the only cured pork to get on with the kale family. Cured
  sausages, chorizo, speck and coppa all marry well, as do pancetta and lardo,
  the preserved pork fat from Italy. Apart from making good additions in
  their own right, they will all soften over heat to form an excellent cooking
  medium in which to toss the leaves.
* The kales become bitter as they age. Stick to the smaller fronds if this
  worries you.
* I have met people who put raw kale in their smoothies (gawd luv us).
  They did look exceptionally healthy.
* We are now starting to see kale all year round in supermarkets. Rather than
  bemoan the merging of the seasons as I usually would, I feel pleased that the
  lowly ancestor of the cabbage is getting more popular. Though I still think
  it looks out of place in July.
* Steamed kale, energised with a squirt of lemon, is an acceptable side dish
  for most of the fishes, especially the gelatinous skate and the cheap and
  rather more sustainable mackerel.

A soup-stew of beans and cavolo nero

The soup-stew, a bowl of spoon-tender meat, beans and aromatics that partly collapse into the surrounding stock, is one of the suppers I hold dearest. More often taken as lunch, this is food that feeds the soul as much as the belly, enriching, calming, quietly energising. This is the cooking on which to lavish the cheapest cuts going, the fatty, bony lumps that butchers sell at reduced prices: mostly cuts from the neck and lower legs. Ingredients whose sole purpose is to give body to the liquid in which they cook.

A knuckle end of Parma ham would be a sound addition here, if your local deli will sell you one. Most will charge very little. Butchers are an excellent source of ham bones with much meat attached. Failing that, I use a lump of gammon, complete with its thick layer of fat.

> *enough for 4–6*
> dried beans, such as cannellini, butterbeans or borlotti – 250g
> bay leaves – 2
> olive oil
> pancetta in the piece – 150g
> large onions – 2
> carrots – 2
> garlic – 2 large cloves, chopped
> tomatoes – 400g, chopped
> water or vegetable stock – 1 litre
> a small butternut squash or pumpkin
> a meaty ham bone or knuckle of Parma ham
> a short length of rind from a lump of Parmesan
> flat-leaved parsley – a handful, roughly chopped
> cavolo nero – 2 large handfuls, or half a small cabbage, cut into wedges

Soak the beans overnight in deep, cold water. Drain, tip them into a large, deep saucepan and cover them with fresh water. Bring to the boil, then remove the froth from the surface with a draining spoon. Drop in the bay leaves and a tablespoon or so of olive oil and leave to boil merrily for forty-five minutes to an hour, until tender (older beans tend to take a little longer). Add salt to the water about twenty minutes before the end of cooking. Drain and set aside. (I sometimes put a shot of olive oil over them at this point to prevent them sticking together.)

Cut the pancetta into short lengths or fat cubes, put them in a deep pan with a couple of spoonfuls of oil and set over a moderate heat. Peel the onions, halve them and slice them thinly. Once the pancetta has begun to sizzle, add the onions and stir them from time to time until they soften.

Scrub the carrots, cut them into large dice and add to the onions with the garlic. Let everything soften without colouring, lowering the heat as and when you need to. Add the tomatoes and let them soften and melt a little into the other vegetables before pouring in the water or stock. Peel and roughly chop the squash or pumpkin and stir it in.

Now is the time to add the ham bone and Parmesan rind. Either one will make a huge difference to the finished flavour. Bring the soup almost to the boil, then turn down the heat so that it simmers gently. Cover with a lid but set it askew, so that some of the steam escapes. Leave to simmer, with only the occasional stir, for an hour and a half, by which time the soup should be thick, rich and heavy.

Add the beans to the pot along with the parsley and cabbage leaves. Continue cooking for ten to fifteen minutes. Serve with grated Parmesan.

Black cabbage and bacon – a fry-up

A fantastic little recipe, cheap, simple and fast. I usually have some bread with this, if only to rub round the plate afterwards. This is best on very hot plates.

> garlic – 2 cloves
> butter – a thick slice
> mildly smoked bacon or pancetta – 150g
> cavolo nero – 4 handfuls

Peel the garlic and chop it finely. Let it soften fragrantly with the butter in a shallow pan over a sprightly heat.

Cut the bacon into chunks or thick strips, whatever tickles your fancy, then let it fry with the garlic till its fat is pale gold. If the cavolo nero leaves are large, tear them up a bit, then add to the sizzling bacon and toss in the garlicky fat. As soon as the leaves relax, tip them and the fat on to hot plates.

Young kale with lemon and garlic

I often take bright young leaves and their sprouting shoots, cook them briefly in boiling water, then toss them into sizzling butter seasoned with garlic and lemon as an accompaniment for grilled pork belly, a roast fillet of lamb or a nice piece of fish. That said, it still takes up more room on the plate than the meat.

Red Russian kale, which I often cook in this way, is finer boned than the curly plumes we know so well. The heavily laced leaves have a fragility to them, and wilt quickly after picking. For all their gentility and mauve-pink blush, they still carry something of the coarseness of the stronger stuff.

enough for 2 as a side dish
kale or any tender young greens – 2 large handfuls
butter – 30g
olive oil – a little
garlic – 2 cloves
lemon zest – a little
the juice of half a lemon

Wash the greens and set them aside. Bring a pan of water to the boil, salt it lightly and cook the greens for no longer than a minute or two. They must retain their crispness and vigour. Drain and set aside.

Meanwhile, warm the butter and oil in a shallow pan, peel and crush the garlic and soften it in the butter and oil. Add a little grated lemon zest (a couple of teaspoons should suffice), then, as the butter starts to froth, squeeze in the lemon juice. Lower in the greens and toss them gently in the hot, lemony garlic butter. Correct the seasoning and serve immediately.

Kale with golden raisins and onions

Even though much of the bitterness of this cultivar has been bred out, some extra sweetness is often welcome. Casting around for something sweet to scatter over a plate of steamed kale, I suddenly remembered the Sicilian habit of adding golden raisins to soft, sweet onions. The contrast between the leaves and their seasoning is strangely comforting. Quite when you might eat this is debatable. We first ate it with treacly rye bread and Gruyère cheese, next to fillets of smoked mackerel. It is tricky to know where it would sit most comfortably.

enough for 2
kale or cavolo nero – 2 large handfuls
a medium onion
olive oil
sultanas, golden raisins – 3 tablespoons

for the dressing
a blood orange
white wine vinegar – 2 tablespoons
extra virgin olive oil
capers – 2 tablespoons

Wash and trim the leaves. Peel the onion and slice it thinly into rings. Pour a thin layer of oil, say a couple of tablespoons, into a shallow pan and leave the onion there to cook for fifteen minutes or so, till soft and sweet. It will need the occasional stir to stop it browning beyond a pale honey colour.

While the onion cooks, squeeze the orange juice into a small bowl, add the wine vinegar, then beat in up to five tablespoons of olive oil, to give a sweet-sharp dressing. Stir in the capers and a grinding of black pepper. Steam the greens briefly.

Pour the blood orange dressing into the pan with the onion, shake in the sultanas and tip over the leaves.

Chicken broth with pork and kale

Kale is just one possibility for bulking out this supper of pork balls and broth. I use it because I like the fullness of its leaves with the smooth pork balls. You could use any member of the greens family, and particularly Savoy cabbage. The important bit is not to overcook the greens.

enough for 3–4

for the pork balls
minced pork – 400g
small, hot chillies – 2
spring onions – 4
garlic – 2 cloves
parsley – 6 bushy sprigs
mint – 6 bushy sprigs
a little oil

for the soup
chicken stock – a litre
kale leaves – 125g

Put the pork into a mixing bowl. Finely chop the chillies and add them with their seeds to the pork. Chop the spring onions, discarding the roots and the very darkest tips of the leaves, peel and crush the garlic and add with the spring onions to the pork. Pull the parsley and mint leaves from their stalks and chop roughly, then add to the pork mixture with a generous seasoning of salt. Mix thoroughly, then roll into about sixteen balls.

Warm a shallow film of oil in a non-stick pan and add the pork balls, letting them cook until they are nicely toasted all over.

Pour the stock into a saucepan and bring to the boil, season carefully with salt and black pepper, then lower in the pork balls. Turn down the heat and let them simmer for five to seven minutes, till they are cooked through.

Whilst the balls are cooking, pull the kale leaves from their tough stalks and cook them briefly – about one or two minutes only – in boiling salted water, then drain (don't be tempted to cook them in the stock). Lower the kale into the soup and serve immediately.

Leeks

The leek is the vegetable of clear, white winter skies and kitchen windows fugged up with condensation. It is garden soil glistening blue with frost; grainy potato soups the colour of antique linen; itchy socks that have ruckled down the back of your Wellingtons, toes numb with cold. I like the gardener's expression, 'a good stand' of leeks, and that the upper green part is called a flag. For that is what they do, stand and wave, when all else in the garden or allotment has collapsed in a tangle of crisp, brown stems.

The leek is the onion's refined sister, brought here by the Romans, for the times you want the latter's silken texture but less of its bold sweetness. The white stalk is especially delicate, tender, succulent, subtle, but unlike more extravagant cooks I make use of the coarser green leaves too (in soup, mostly, and in chicken stock). Musselburgh is the one I grow. Renowned for its long, green leaves, it's an essential ingredient in cockie-leekie.

Although of the same family, the leek has none of the sugary stickiness you get in a slowly baked onion. Less rugged and hearty, the slender green one turns up not as the backbone of a rustic dish but in an altogether subtler role. It is linked with gentle, even genteel, cooking, such as chilled vichysoisse in a fine china bowl, leeks vinaigrette, leeks mimosa (steamed, chilled leeks with finely grated hard-boiled egg yolks the colour of primroses) and Scotch broth to heal the sick.

As a farm crop, leeks are back-breaking work. They cannot be machine harvested and rely on hand picking in freezing weather. A sobering thought as we tuck into our steaming bowl of leek and potato soup.

A leek in the garden

You can sow leek seeds under cover in early spring, planting them out in early summer. Having limited indoor space, I buy mine as immature plants in May and June for harvesting from late autumn through to next spring. I rarely pick before November. These 'plugs' require a nice, deep hole – use a pencil if you have no dibber – and should be lowered in without crushing the fragile roots. The plants need around 15cm between them. Rather than filling the hole around their stems with soil, pour water in from the watering can and let them sort themselves out.

Young leeks need plenty of water but, once established, they are good natured and undemanding. More than enjoying a drop now and again, they like a thorough soaking every fortnight or so. During the growing season, pile earth up around the shaft of the leek; this will encourage extra-long growth of the white part that is so useful in the kitchen.

Unlike onions, which have to be lifted and dried, leeks will stand in the patch all winter. Pick as you need them.

A leek diary

Leeks wallow in moist, dense soil. They don't like their long, white roots to be waterlogged in cold weather, but will take a bit of shade if they must. A good frost usually sees off the rust to which they are prone.

July 22 The 'leeklets' that arrived a month ago, wisp-like in their plastic tray, are now almost pencil thick, and I plant them, the splayed width of my hand apart, in a partly shaded, damp bed near the medlar tree. As usual I'm growing the old Scottish variety, Musselburgh, a blue-green-leaved leek of mild flavour and medium size that should plump up by late autumn and still be standing in the new year.

I make deep holes, a good 15cm deep, with an oak dibber, then drop the young leeks into the hollows, taking care not to bash their roots. Instead of pushing the soil in around them, I 'puddle' them in as is traditional, filling the hole around each leek with water from the watering can instead.

August 1 A sultry morning, still and strangely ominous. The foxes have dug up the leeks, leaving them and their fragile roots scattered over the garden like bits of green and white string. I replant them all, cursing.

Throughout the autumn, the shafts continue to thicken, the leaves change from green to blue. They get the odd watering and an occasional stroke.

January 31 A stand of leeks means a great deal to me at this point in the growing year. Little else is around, and I love the way they stand proudly through heavy frosts and even deep snow. A midnight walk up through the vegetable patch reveals leeks sparkling in the frosty night air, as if sprinkled with sugar. I normally start digging them up, one or two at a time, around now. I have only a few, and to be honest they are not very straight, but they will last me through till the finger-thick ones arrive once more at the market.

Varieties

Leeks for winter and spring eating
Sow in spring, plant out in June and July.

Musselburgh A late Scottish variety from before 1834, known for its mild flavour and long, thick stalks.
Blue Solaise A French variety known for its hardiness and its ability to stand in the garden in good condition for longer than most. Wonderful blue-green flags.
King Richard A slender, long-shafted early variety. Plant in April for August pulling. Will keep well until after Christmas.
St Victor Established French variety with distinctive blue leaves. Very hardy and very late; plant out in July for pulling the following late winter/spring.
Siegfried Late-maturing, tough old thing, especially suited to chilly areas of the country. Invaluable for those with long, cold winters.

Leeks for summer and autumn eating
Sow indoors in winter, plant out in April.

Toledo A popular, late leek with a long shaft.
Pandora An early, well-flavoured variety for autumn eating. Will stand a bit of frost, but not a hardy leek.
Varna A tall, slim leek suitable for summer eating. Mild enough to eat in salads like a spring onion if picked small enough.

A leek in the kitchen

Leeks are a little more demanding of the cook. Whereas an onion caught around the edges by a bit of overcooking will take on a welcome rustic note, a leek scorched is a leek ruined. You cannot rescue a pan of browned leeks. Their flesh should remain pearlescent, which is why I cook them with a gentler hand than I would an onion: in a taller pan, over a lower heat, covered not only by a lid but with a disc of greaseproof paper, albeit carelessly torn, that ensures the vegetables steam rather than fry.

When they have been steamed or softened in butter, leeks are very pleasing with eggs, especially in a soufflé, stirred into scrambled eggs or caught within the tender folds of an omelette.

A leek is what you reach for when a fish dish requires a touch of onion. Fish pie, made with haddock and mussels, climbs to a different level when you add the fish to a tangle of lightly stewed leeks. Creamed leeks with grilled scallops is a very fine dish. Leeks are more appropriate – less overbearing, subtler, more integrated – than onions in a fish soup.

The leek collects grit between its layers as it grows. No other vegetable needs such careful attention in the sink. No cursory rinse here, but a thorough cleansing in ice-cold water to extract every last speck of trapped grit. I peel back and discard the outer layer, which is often tough, then slit the leek down its length, stopping shortly before the root. First I hold it under the cold tap, opening the layers out like a fan, then swish it around in a bowl of cold water. If I am washing shredded leeks, then I leave them to sit in water for a few minutes, to give the fallen grit time to settle at the bottom of the bowl.

It is butter rather than oil that brings out the best in this member of the allium family, which is another reason to keep the heat low. Their pale green leaves love cream too, and I often stir a spoonful or two into a pan of shredded and softened leeks to go with a grilled gammon steak or to slide into the crack of a baked potato. Wonderful, too, with mackerel, especially when its skin is charred black from the grill. Oil, with the exception of that in a French dressing, does very little to enhance the flavour or texture of this vegetable.

Seasoning your leeks

Butter The preferred cooking medium for all leeks, thin or fat.
Cheese Most cheeses have an affinity for any member of the onion family. Use saltier sheep's cheeses for the crust of a leek gratin or to amplify the flavour of a sauce.
Blue cheese In a soup, gratin or sauce. The more strident cheeses work better than the timid.

Aniseed Tarragon, chervil and fennel all flatter the flavour of a leek stew or soup.

Bacon Add diced bacon to a leek soup; wrap rashers around blanched leeks before sliding them into a gratin; add snippets of grilled streaky to a leek tart.

Chicken Of all the meats you can partner with this allium, chicken seems the most comfortable. Particularly in broths and stews or baked together in a pie.

Potatoes Perhaps most famously married in a soup, the two can also be baked slowly with a little stock, or the leeks used as a stuffing for a baked King Edward.

Mint The most useful herb next to parsley when cooking with this elegant vegetable.

And...

* The deeper the trench you dig, the longer your leek will be. Exhibitionist growers have been known to employ old drainpipes to get the length they need.

* Short, fat leeks are hardier than more elegant strains, which is why our own tend to that shape rather than to the slim ones from warmer European climates.

* Washing a leek can be a peaceful, if finger-chilling task. Split the leek right down the shaft, splay out the layers and rinse long and carefully under running water. Leaving a split leek in cold water will make it curl.

* The top part of the green flag is usually too coarse to interest anyone but a keen composter, but further down, where the colour starts to soften, it is worth using if you cook it slowly enough with plenty of butter or stock. Tough leaves really should be added to the stockpot.

* It is worth trying a leek instead of an onion in many classic onion dishes. The result is often more delicate.

* If I'm honest, I use leeks so much because onions make me cry and I don't have to peel them.

* A lovely way to present this vegetable is to cut the stalk and pale green bit into short lengths, then simmer it, covered by a lid, with a generous slice of butter, a glass of white wine and a spoonful or two of water. Leave until it is soft and knifepoint tender. Leeks, butter and wine are a threesome that deserves to be better known.

* You can grill leeks of small to medium girth with great success. I prefer to blanch them for a couple of minutes in boiling water first, then place them on the grill or grill pan till their sides start to colour. Dress with olive oil and squeeze lemon over whilst they are still warm.

Potato soup with leeks, black pudding and parsley

The potato and the leek are happy bedfellows, as anyone who has eaten a good vichysoisse will know. Softer than potato and onion, more graceful than a chowder, warm potato and leek soup has a peaceful, almost soporific quality. A silky, cool-weather soup that somehow manages to taste creamy and rich with only the smallest amount of butter and no cream in it.

enough for 4–6
large leeks – 2
butter – 40g
medium celery ribs – 4
floury potatoes – 400g
light stock or water – 1.5 litres
parsley – a small bunch, chopped
black pudding, boudin noir or morcilla – 250g

Discard the toughest of the leaves from the leeks, then cut the tender white and palest green flesh into thin rounds. Rinse thoroughly under running water to remove any trapped grit, then add them to a heavy saucepan with the butter. Let them cook over a low to moderate heat for a good fifteen to twenty minutes, without letting them colour, till they are soft enough to crush between your fingers.

Once they have started to soften, you can finely slice the celery and add it to the pan, then peel and chop the potatoes and stir them in too. Cover the pot with a lid and let the vegetables sweat and soften without colouring, then pour in the stock or water and bring to the boil. Turn the heat down so that the soup bubbles gently and partially cover it with a lid. It will take about twenty-five minutes for the potatoes to become truly tender. Blitz the soup in a liquidiser or put it through a mouli, stir in the chopped parsley and check the seasoning.

Cut the black pudding into slices and grill till crisp. Ladle the soup into bowls and float the slices of pudding on top.

A chowder of mussels and leeks

Onions have always had a slightly awkward relationship with fish. They seem particularly ungainly and rough edged alongside the white varieties or shellfish. Shallots work better, with their milder notes and less significant dose of sugar, but of all the alliums it is the leek that marries most successfully. The white of the leek has an elegance and subtlety that is unlikely to overpower any fish you put it with. In a soup or pie, it dances with the piscine ingredients where an onion would tread on their toes.

Chowder is traditionally a hearty bowl of food. The one I make with mussels and bacon is a short step away from the big clam and potato numbers I have eaten in Boston, in that it is somewhat lighter and less creamy, but it is still essentially a big soup for a cool day.

> *enough for 4*
> leeks – 3
> smoked streaky bacon – 150g
> butter – 40g
> mussels – 1kg
> white vermouth – 2 glasses
> potatoes – 450g
> double cream – 200ml
> bay leaves – a couple
> thyme – 4 sprigs
> parsley – a few sprigs, chopped

Thinly slice the leeks and rinse them very thoroughly. No vegetable holds its grit like a leek. Cut the bacon into short, thin strips and put them into a deep, thick-bottomed pan with the butter. Let the bacon colour lightly over a moderate heat. Turn down the heat, add the leeks and cover with a lid. Leave them to cook for twenty minutes or so, with an occasional stir, until they are soft and sweet – they should not colour. Remove from the heat.

Check the mussels and pull away any beards. Discard any mussels that are broken, open or exceptionally heavy. Put them in a large pot, pour in the vermouth and cover tightly with a lid. Place over a high heat till the mussels have opened (a matter of minutes), then remove each mussel from its shell.

Peel the potatoes and cut them into large dice. Put them in a saucepan with 400ml of the mussel cooking liquor, drained through a sieve. Add the cream, bay, thyme and a little black pepper (no salt). Bring to the boil, then reduce the heat so that the potatoes simmer gently for about ten minutes.

Add three-quarters of the cooked potatoes to the leeks and bacon. Put the remainder in a blender with the cream (pick out the herbs first) and blitz briefly till smooth (too long and it will turn gummy). Pour into the pan and add the mussels and parsley. Bring all to the boil and serve.

Braised lamb shanks with leeks and haricot beans

Users of *The Kitchen Diaries* may feel they recognise this recipe. Previously I have always made it with cubed lamb, but I recently tried it with lamb shanks and left it overnight before reheating it. The presence of the bone and fat and the good night's sleep have made such a difference that I thought it worth repeating here. You could make it a day or two in advance to good end.

enough for 4
dried haricot beans – 300g
bay leaves – 3
olive oil
small lamb shanks – 4
large leeks – 4, trimmed
butter – a thick slice, about 60g
garlic – 2 cloves
thyme leaves – a tablespoon, chopped
plain flour – a tablespoon
light stock or water – 650ml
the juice and zest of a lemon
a handful of parsley, chopped
a handful of mint leaves

Soak the beans overnight in cold water. The next day, drain them, put them into a deep saucepan and cover with fresh water. Bring to the boil, skim off the froth, add a bay leaf and a drop or two of olive oil and simmer for about forty minutes. Turn off the heat and leave them in the water.

Warm a glug of olive oil in a deep casserole. Season the lamb shanks all over with salt and black pepper, then lower them into the pan. They should sizzle when they hit the oil. Turn the meat from time to time till it has coloured nicely on all sides (we are talking pale honey colour rather than deep brown). Remove the meat from the casserole and set aside on a plate to catch any escaping juices.

Set the oven at 160°C/Gas 3. Cut the leeks into chunks roughly the length of a wine cork, wash them thoroughly, making sure no grit or sand is trapped in their many layers, then put them in the casserole together with the butter, keeping the heat low. Cover with a piece of greaseproof or baking parchment, then cover with a lid (the paper will encourage them to cook in their own steam rather than brown). Leave them to cook till they have started to soften, a good twenty minutes or so. You will need to give them an occasional stir.

Remove and discard the paper. Peel and thinly slice the garlic and add it to the pot with the thyme and the remaining bay leaves. Sprinkle the flour over the top and continue cooking for three or four minutes, stirring occasionally. Pour in the stock or water, then drain the beans and add them too. Season with salt and pepper.

Return the shanks and any collected juices to the pan and bring to the boil. Cover the casserole with a lid and place in the oven for an hour and a half or until the lamb is completely tender. Sometimes it takes two hours. You should be able to remove it from the bone with little effort (then again, it shouldn't actually be falling apart). Remove from the oven, stir in most of the lemon juice and zest, parsley and mint, then scatter the rest.

Leek and cheese mash

A good side dish for Monday's cold cuts. The quantities are deliberately vague because of the nature of leftovers. A recipe for which we must use our instinct.

a large leek
butter
leftover mashed potatoes
cheese – anything you have around that needs using

Wash and chop the leek, then let it cook in a generous amount of butter, covered with a lid and a piece of greaseproof paper if you wish, till soft. Season with salt and then scoop into a shallow ovenproof dish.

Tip the mashed potatoes on top of the leeks. Level them a little without packing them down too tightly. Dot small knobs of butter over the surface, cover with grated or crumbled cheese, then bake in a hot oven till the cheese has melted and the potatoes are heated through.

A soup of roots, leeks and walnuts

Good cooking often comes from simply going with what is around at the time. Ingredients that are in season at the same time tend to go together – in this case, the last of a hat trick of leek soups made with all that is left in the depleted winter vegetable patch.

enough for 4–6
large leeks, with plenty of green – 2
butter – 40g
medium celery ribs – 4
Jerusalem artichokes – 400g
light stock or water – 1 litre
parsley – a small bunch, chopped

for the spice mix
coriander seeds – a teaspoon
shelled walnuts – 30g
ginger – a 30g lump
groundnut oil – 4 teaspoons

Discard the toughest of the leaves from the leeks, then cut the tender white and palest green flesh into thin rounds. Rinse thoroughly under running water to remove any trapped grit, then add them to a heavy saucepan with the butter. Let them cook in the butter over a low to moderate heat for a good fifteen to twenty minutes, without letting them colour, till they are soft enough to crush between your fingers.

Once they have started to soften, you can finely slice the celery and add it to the pan, then peel and chop the artichokes and stir them in too. Cover the pot with a lid and let the vegetables sweat and soften without colouring, then pour in the stock or water and bring to the boil. Turn the heat down so that the soup bubbles gently and partially cover it with a lid. Cook for about twenty-five minutes, until the artichokes are very tender.

Grind the coriander seeds to a fine powder with a pestle and mortar, then add the walnuts, mashing them briefly to a pulp. Peel the ginger and slice it thinly, then cut it into thin matchsticks. Warm the oil in a shallow pan, add the ginger and fry for about thirty seconds, till it is golden and crisp. Toss in the crushed walnuts and coriander, let them sizzle briefly, then tip on to kitchen paper.

Blitz the soup in a liquidiser or put it through a mouli, stir in the chopped parsley and check the seasoning. The soup should be mild and almost nutty tasting. Ladle into bowls and top with the spice mix.

A tart of leeks and cheese

There is a point in the year, usually after the Christmas decorations have
been put away, when the house gets too cold to sit still in without a wrap
around you. I have always kept a cold house, hot rooms make me feel
unhealthy, but sometimes the only way of getting warm here is to eat.
Carbohydrate-rich meals, such as the tart of leek and cheese and pastry
I made on the coldest day of the year, warm you in a way few others are
capable of.

> *enough for 4*
> waxy potatoes – 650g
> medium leeks – 3 (about 750g)
> butter – 50g
> crème fraîche – 200ml
> Cheddar – 180g, grated
> a little freshly grated nutmeg
> puff pastry – 500g
> beaten egg for glazing

Set the oven at 200°C/Gas 6. Bring a large pan of water to the boil. Peel the
potatoes and cut them into slices as thick as a pound coin. Salt the boiling
water, add the potatoes and let them simmer enthusiastically till tender –
they can be almost falling apart. Drain and tip into a large mixing bowl.

Meanwhile, remove the greenest part of the leeks and discard it.
Slice the white and pale green part into rings, then rinse thoroughly under
running water. Melt the butter in a saucepan and add the leeks. Cover with
a lid and cook over a low to moderate heat till thoroughly tender; this will
take a good twenty minutes. Put the leeks in with the drained potatoes, then
add the crème fraîche and grated Cheddar. Season with salt, black pepper
and nutmeg.

Roll the pastry into two rectangles approximately 32 x 24cm. Lay one
on a non-stick baking sheet. Pile the filling into the centre, then brush the
edges with beaten egg. Lay the second piece of pastry over the top and press
the edges down. Trim around the edges, then pinch firmly to seal. Brush the
top with beaten egg and cut equally spaced slits across the width of the top
piece of pastry. Bake till the pastry is crisp and golden, about forty to forty-
five minutes.

Spring leeks, broad beans and bacon

In spring, the young leek is a welcome sight with its stick-thin body and compact green flags, particularly after the thick winter ones with their frozen cores. They are worth steaming and dressing with a mustardy vinaigrette or, as here, using as a base for a broad bean and bacon lunch. We sometimes have this in the garden, with inelegant wodges of bread and sweet Welsh butter.

enough for 2 as a light lunch
young, slim leeks – 3 or 4
green streaky bacon or pancetta rashers – 6
butter – a thick slice
a clove of garlic, peeled and squashed
broad beans – 1kg (weighed in the pods)
tarragon leaves – 2 loosely packed tablespoons, chopped
flat-leaved parsley – a handful, chopped

Put a deep pan of water on to boil. Wash and thickly slice the leeks. Remove the rind from the bacon rashers and cut each rasher into finger-thick strips. Warm the butter in a shallow pan and add the strips of bacon. Let the bacon colour lightly in the hot butter until its fat is starting to turn pale gold, then add the sliced leeks and the garlic clove. Partially cover with a lid and leave the leeks to soften but not colour.

Whilst the bacon and leeks are cooking, pod the beans and add them to the boiling water. Salt the water and let the beans cook for four or five minutes, till tender. Drain and rinse in cold water till cool enough to skin. Leave the tiniest of beans unskinned, but it is probably better to skin anything larger than a thumbnail – just squeeze each bean between thumb and finger and pop it out of its skin.

When the leeks and bacon are soft and fragrant, stir in the tarragon, parsley and the drained and skinned beans, then season. Stir gently, allow to heat through for a minute or two, then serve on warm plates.

Pork, leeks and green peppercorns

To our list of ingredients that balance the leek's (and onion's) tendency towards sweetness, we can add green peppercorns. Outside the anise-scented emporiums of Chinatown they are difficult to track down in their fresh state, but bottled ones in brine are perhaps even better here. Deep-winter stuff, this. Some fresh, crisp greens might be appropriate with it, some winter salad leaves or maybe a plate of lightly cooked spinach. Whatever, I do recommend some plain, steamed potatoes to balance the general richness.

Green peppercorns in brine are available in tins or bottles from good grocer's shops and delicatessens.

enough for 4
leeks – 650g
butter – 40g, plus a little more
cubed pork – 500g
mushrooms – 500g
plain flour – a heaped tablespoon
stock – 500–600ml, hot
bay leaves – 2
parsley – a small bunch
green peppercorns in brine – 4 teaspoons
double cream – 140ml

Trim the leeks, discarding the dark, outer leaves. Slice the leeks about 2cm wide and wash thoroughly. Warm the butter in a large, heavy-based casserole, add the leeks, then cover with a lid and leave to cook slowly for ten to fifteen minutes. You want them to end up bright and almost tender but without colour. Lift them out and set aside.

Return the pan to the heat, let it get a little hot, then add the pork. Let it colour lightly on all sides, then remove and add it to the leeks.

Set the oven at 150°C/Gas 2. Cut the mushrooms into halves or quarters, then fry them in the casserole till they are golden and slightly sticky. Add a little extra butter if they need it. Return the leeks and pork to the pan, scatter over the flour and leave it to cook for a minute or so. Slowly pour in the hot stock. Stir in the bay leaves and a grinding of salt and black pepper. Bring slowly to the boil, then cover with a lid and transfer to the oven. Leave for fifty to sixty minutes to cook its way quietly to tenderness.

Chop the parsley and stir it into the casserole with the peppercorns and cream, then either return it to the oven for five minutes or heat through on the hob. Check the seasoning and serve with steamed, unbuttered potatoes (see below).

The potatoes

Either steam or boil large, floury potatoes, then drain them. Put them back on the stove over a low heat for a few minutes, so that they are completely dry, then gently shake the saucepan back and forth so the edges of the potatoes 'bruise' and crumble slightly. Eat them with the casserole, mashing the floury, crumbly spuds into the sauce from the casserole with your fork.

Chicken with leeks and lemon

To balance the sweetness of leeks, we can use a little white wine vinegar, especially tarragon, or lemon juice. The addition of either removes any risk of the dish cloying. The recipe that follows is one of my all-time favourites for a good, easy, midweek supper. What especially appeals is that although the sauce tastes rich and almost creamy, it has no butter or cream in it at all.

enough for 4
olive oil – 2 tablespoons
chicken thighs – 8
medium leeks – 4
dry vermouth such as Noilly Prat – a glass
the juice and zest of a lemon
chicken stock – 500ml
parsley – a small bunch

In a large casserole, warm the olive oil over a moderate heat. Add the chicken pieces, skin-side down, and cook until pale gold in colour. Wash the leeks thoroughly, shake them dry, then cut them into pieces the length of a wine cork. Lift the chicken out of the pan and add the leeks. Cover and let them cook gently until they are soft but relatively uncoloured. Whatever happens, they should not brown. Once they start to soften, add the vermouth, the zest and juice of the lemon and the chicken stock. Bring to the boil, return the chicken and its juices to the pan, season with salt and pepper, then cover and simmer for about twenty minutes.

Chop the parsley, taste the sauce for seasoning and stir the parsley in.

A risotto of leeks and pancetta

Like asparagus, leeks produce a particularly subtle risotto. The crucial point is not to let them colour. Cook them over a low heat, with a lid on if you wish, or maybe with a piece of greaseproof paper on top. Either way they must not brown.

> *enough for 2*
> medium leeks – 2
> butter – about 50g, plus a walnut-sized lump to finish
> arborio or other risotto rice – 300g
> Noilly Prat – a glass
> chicken stock – a litre, hot
> thin rashers of pancetta – 6
> grated Parmesan – 3 tablespoons, plus more to finish

Wash the leeks thoroughly, splitting them down their length and rinsing under a running cold tap, then slice them finely. Melt the butter in a wide, high-sided pan over a low heat and add the leeks. Let them soften without colouring, stirring from time to time.

Stir in the rice, then pour in the Noilly Prat. Let the mixture boil until the alcohol has evaporated, then tip in the first ladleful of hot stock. Continue stirring, adding the stock as and when the rice has absorbed almost all of the previous ladleful, till the rice is plump, tender and yet has a little bite left in it – a process that will take about twenty minutes. Meanwhile, grill the pancetta, or cook it in a non-stick frying pan (no oil necessary), until truly crisp. Cut into pieces about the size of a large postage stamp, leaving a couple of rashers whole. Fold the cut pieces into the risotto.

Stir in the walnut-sized lump of butter, adding the 3 tablespoons of Parmesan as you go. Divide between warm dishes and finish with a piece of pancetta and more grated Parmesan.

Little cakes of leeks and potatoes

This sounds too spartan a recipe to be true but, when cooked slowly in butter, the leeks take on a deep sweetness that makes these cakes so much more than the sum of their simple parts. They are great with grilled bacon or cold roast beef.

makes about 12 cakes, enough for 4
medium potatoes – 5
large leeks – 2
butter – 50g
milk – 100ml
vegetable or groundnut oil for shallow-frying

Peel the potatoes, then boil them in deep, salted water. Trim and rinse the leeks, discarding the dark outer leaves, and slice them thinly. Melt the butter in a shallow pan and cook the leeks in it over a low heat, stirring from time to time, till they are soft and melting; they should be ready in twenty minutes or so. If they colour they will turn bitter, so cover them with a lid or a piece of greaseproof paper.

Bring the milk to the boil in a small saucepan, then switch off the heat. When the potatoes are tender, drain them, put them back on the heat for a minute, covered with a lid or a tea towel, to dry out, then mash them with a potato masher, pouring in the warm milk as you go. You are after a thick mash, not a sloppy one, so stop adding milk when the consistency is thick enough to make into patties. Stir in the leeks and season generously.

When the mixture is cool enough to roll, shape it into rough patties. Don't be tempted to make them perfectly smooth; they will be all the more interesting if they are a little rough.

Heat some oil in a shallow pan. When it is hot, slide in the patties, not too close together, and let them colour lightly on both sides. They will cook quite quickly, about three or four minutes on each side. Lift the patties out with a fish slice and drain briefly on kitchen paper.

Onions

I regard a baked onion as a fine but humble supper. It will probably have been steamed first to keep its flesh juicy, then left in a low oven to bake with a little butter and salt until its translucent, golden layers are at the point of collapse. Its edges may have caught and even blackened here and there, and the few juices may come embellished with a little cream and grated pecorino or perhaps our own Spenwood. There will be hand-torn bread, and maybe some lightly cooked spinach at its side. Oh and a glass or two of wine, something quite velvety, would do nicely.

Onions are often described as the backbone of a stew, a sauce, a casserole. I think of them more as the heart of a dish, their vital activity rarely considered, quietly beating away in the background. They provide sweetness, mellowness, depth, warmth, tenderness, suavity and body, and seem to have a steadying influence on all the other ingredients. This is why the way in which we treat them in the pot is crucial. Why we must never hurry the onion's slow progress towards sweetness or burn its delicate edges or, worst of all, fail to cook them enough. Get the onion part of a dish right and you are halfway towards a good supper. Get them wrong and no amount of cooking and clever stunts can quite put matters to rights.

Anyone who has cooked a stew without a member of the allium family knows how they settle a dish and, in the case of a casserole, give it a sense of being. We have always cooked with them – they appear in our oldest recorded recipes and may well have come to us with the Romans. Certainly they were widely used in the Middle Ages. We briefly supplied most of our needs ourselves, with Bedfordshire the centre of production. Now, with most of the supplies coming from Egypt or China, the only way to get our hands on a locally grown onion is to bring them back from the farmers' market or grow them ourselves. A row or two in the garden gives us the chance of cooking with a traditional old school Ailsa Craig, named after the craggy island off the Scottish coast, or a Red Baron.

From a purely aesthetic angle, a soldierly row of neatly tied onions sitting proudly on dry autumn soil is a sign of a well-ordered allotment. Onions will not do well grown higgledy-piggledy in a badly tended site, and tend to struggle amongst weeds. Hating the hoe – their roots lie too close to the surface to rely on this easy way to weed – they require more hands-on care than you might expect.

The onion is probably the one vegetable that even the most thoughtful food shopper tends to take for granted. We are not helped by the fact that onions are almost never labelled with their variety. Growing our own introduces more possibilities for getting to know this aromatic bulb in all its forms than picking one up from the cornershop or supermarket. There are soft-fleshed Spanish onions, sweet enough for eating raw in a Cheddar sandwich but whose keeping qualities are low; hard, crisp-skinned golden onions for general cooking and long winter storage; red onions, for where a mixture of strong flavours and intense sweetness is required; shallots for when mildness is key – in a sauce, for instance; and long, thin spring onions for crunching raw in a salad. One might say an onion for almost every culinary occasion.

An onion in the garden

Decent onions, firm, sweet and unblemished, are available in almost any shop that sells food. They are a mainstay of the organic box, a stalwart of the farm shop and delicatessen and part of the wallpaper in every greengrocer's in the land. The question is, why would anyone want to grow their own?

Those of us lacking much in the way of outside space have to be ruthless about the plants we grow, and onions are often the first we cross off the list. I grew them initially as a way to deter slugs – they hate all members of the allium family – but soon found that the space they took up was too valuable. Onions are generally grown from 'sets' – immature onions – though they are more cheaply grown from seed. The sets for an early-autumn crop are sent out in early spring. They need to be planted right up to their necks, about 15cm apart. Small varieties can be closer, with 5–10 cm between them, but in either case just the tip should be visible. Any more and they will be pulled out by the pigeons.

Onions like a cool start to the year, in rich but not freshly manured soil (do it the autumn before), and plenty of sun later on. Their pet hates are being waterlogged or choked by weeds that nick their nutrients. It is essential that the bulbs have a good amount of space between them for airflow. Cramped, wet conditions will encourage rot and bolting. Avoid watering much once they are established.

In the cool part of the season, the bulbs will send up green shoots, then, as the weather warms, the bulbs themselves slowly fill out. The onions are ready to pick once the leaves start to yellow in late July or August. They store well, but they need to dry out before we put them away for winter. Pull them out of the ground with the help of a garden fork so that the roots come too, and leave them in a dry place for a day or two before storing. Make sure that the air can get round each bulb and they are not touching one another. If the weather is good, it will help to do this out in the sun. Bring them into store only when they feel dry in the hand and the skin is crisp.

Golden onions will keep for months in a cool, very dry place, red ones slightly less. They will go mouldy in humidity. Tying the dried leaves together in the style of a French onion seller is a good way of storing them, as is keeping them (don't laugh) in a pair of tights hanging from the ceiling. Sprouting in spring is natural, but a sign that the bulbs are past their best.

Varieties

Suppliers often give two choices for the home grower: packets of seed or 'sets', the immature onions that are grown from seed planted the previous summer. More varieties are available as seed than as sets, but many find sets more reliable. I grow from immature plants.

Red onions
The red onion has gained in popularity over the last decade, offering a mild character, rather sweeter than the yellow. It cooks to a slightly disappointing murky purple and lacks the savour of the traditional golden onion. It generally keeps less well. Simmered slowly with oil and thyme, red onions break down to a sweet 'marmalade' that is good with cheese.

Red Baron Everyone seems to swear by this sweet, reliable red onion.
Rossa Lunga di Firenze Mild, slightly elongated onion that can be eaten raw.

Golden onions

Senshyu Yellow Slightly flattened, yellow-skinned mild onion for August planting. Overwinters well, ready in June. I have had much luck with this one.
Santé A popular choice for spring planting.
Ailsa Craig Mild, large variety, an excellent all-rounder. Originating in Scotland, it is also a popular 'showing onion' for those who think growing is something to do with getting a rosette.
Sturon Mild, reliable, round onion.

An onion in the kitchen

The golden skin of an onion will lend a warm, amber glow to a stock, keep a baked onion moist and prevent a boiled one falling apart in the water, but most of the time a recipe will tell us to peel it.

I was taught to peel an onion whole, in the old-school manner, by slicing off both root and tip and peeling away the skin with an oversized cook's knife. Now I do it my own way, by cutting the onion in half from root to tip whilst still in its skin. It is then easy to prise off even the most tenacious skin. I use a very small, sharp knife too. Cooking isn't about rules, it is about whatever makes the cook feel comfortable.

Unless we are baking our largest alliums whole or boiling them for stuffing (with anchovy, parsley, lemon and ricotta, maybe), we need to decide whether to slice or chop them. Much will depend on how you want them to look in the finished dish. A tangle of hair-like slices and melted cheese is essential to a classic onion soup. Thickly cut, meltingly soft slices are what you want in a baked onion salad; *imam bayildi*, the famous stuffed aubergine of the Middle East, needs onions chopped in such a way that they will easily melt into a silken pulp. Whether I am chopping roughly for a beef stew or finely for a rosemary and breadcrumb stuffing, I keep the root intact for as long as I can. It holds the layers in place and stops them slithering around.

It is worth mastering the chopping of an onion. Apart from the physical pleasure of holding a knife, its thick handle cushioning the cold sharpness of the steel, an onion swiftly chopped with a knife of almost surgical sharpness is less likely to end in tears. Heavy work with a blunt blade will bruise the vegetable's cells and send a fine spray of juice into your eyes.

The villain of the piece is lachrymator, the chemical that sets our tear glands off. Not everyone is affected to the same extent. It sometimes seems as if every cook save me has a tried and trusted method to sabotage the work of the evil lachrymator. I find peeling onions such torture that I often choose a recipe that uses leeks instead. Some of the ways other sufferers might like to try include:

Peeling them under the hood of an extractor fan.
Chilling the offending onions in the fridge to slow down the release of their oils.
Slicing from root end along.
Removing the skin under running water.
Holding a piece of bread in your mouth to absorb the lachrymator.
Wearing swimming goggles.

In my experience, none of these seems to make any difference at all. Much depends on the season and how old an onion is. Fewer tears are shed in summer.

During cooking, an onion will behave differently according to the variety and the time of year. In summer, onions contain more water and tend to steam in the pan, taking longer to caramelise. If you absentmindedly cook them with the lid on, you will end up with a pan full of juice. They may brown less successfully, too, because their sugars are less concentrated, and should you lack the time to let the juices evaporate, you will end up with a watery mess.

A soup, a sauce or a risotto generally starts with the chopping of an onion and its slow journey towards tenderness in hot butter. Including bacon fat or olive oil will add flavour whilst lessening the risk of the onion burning. Only when the onion is glossy and the colour of honey can we add garlic, celery or tomato and any spices or herbs. To add the garlic at the same time as the onion would risk it browning too much (fine in Chinese cooking but not what you want for a risotto).

Older onions, those that feel heavy for their size or seem particularly reluctant to shed their skins, are often piercingly strong. Offensively pungent onions can sometimes be tamed with cold water or vinegar. A short soak in iced water will often quell a sliced onion's anger so successfully that it can be eaten raw. Cut no thicker than garden twine, raw onion can be rustically satisfying in a doorstop sandwich with sharp Cheddar and soft white bread. Finely diced bullies destined for a salad dressing can be calmed by five minutes in a puddle of red wine vinegar.

Cooked long and slow in earthenware, steel or cast-iron pots, onions are often enriched with olive oil and butter, thyme, garlic, parsley, and not mere bacon but expensive, faintly herbal pancetta. This scented base will act as a backbone around which we can build a dish with meat or beans or both, to which we can add diced root vegetables, mushrooms or spices and moisten with stock, wine or water. The onion is the aromatic foundation stone on which the cook can build. A level floor capable of taking any amount of our creativity and imaginative cooking.

Seasoning your onions

The twiggy herbs, such as rosemary, thyme and bay, have an elemental pull towards the onion, as do beef stock, white wine and butter. Onions and cheese have a longstanding affair with one another, especially the more piercingly flavoured farmhouse varieties. Onions flatter all meat and poultry and have a deepening effect on the flavour of most vegetables. So useful and versatile is the onion that it would probably be easier to say what doesn't go particularly well with it. I say probably, because it is surprisingly difficult to think of anything, at least in a savoury sense.

A few special partnerships

Cream Add double cream and a spoonful of Dijon mustard to a pan of caramelised onions to make a luxurious sauce for steak.
Woody herbs Add thyme and rosemary to softened onions, then scatter them over a focaccia dough with olive oil and flakes of sea salt. A slow stew of butter, onions and woody herbs is a sound base for all manner of recipes.
Anchovy Chopped finely and stirred with onion till it melts, this salty little fish balances the bulb's inescapable sweetness. Add to potato gratins and bean dishes.
Butter Onions cooked slowly in butter take on a mellow sweetness. Oil, duck or goose fat, and beef dripping are often used too, but butter is the only one that seems to have a sweetening effect.
Parmesan It is difficult to think of two ingredients more flattering to one another.

And...

* Twigs laid over newly planted onion sets will deter birds from pulling them out or squirrels looking for something to play ball with.
* I buy onions by feel. They should be hard, the skins crisp and showing no signs of sponginess round the shoulders. Any with mildew or a mouldy smell should be dismissed. I don't buy if they are sprouting or damp to the touch. Greengrocers are prone to throw them around, upending the traditional orange net bag into the onion bin, but that doesn't mean they won't bruise. The care with which the French have long wrapped theirs in trailing strings, using the dried leaves like twine, is more like the consideration we should show them. A bruised onion will rot.
* Dark-skinned varieties store better than pale ones.
* The green shoot that appears inside an ageing onion is simply the leaf forming for the next planting. Many people find it indigestible and bitter.
* The darker your storage, the longer your onions will keep from deteriorating.
* Avoid putting a cut onion in the fridge. It will taint everything that is in there, especially the milk.
* The marriage of sweet onions and salty ingredients is particularly pleasing. Try the obvious anchovy or Parmesan mentioned above, but feta and olives are also worth bearing in mind.
* Shallots are an invaluable addition to a salad. I chop them into fine rings, letting them sit in the vinegar for a while before I add the oil and pepper.

A few words about shallots

Refined in flavour and possessing an extraordinary elegance, the shallot has a milder taste than the onion. Its golden skin and the flesh beneath tend to have a pink blush, and it is usually easier to peel. Shallots are often flat sided from where they have grown together in a huddle.

High-level restaurant cooking is this allium's natural home, as a base for classical French sauces, but they are worth giving a more down-to-earth treatment too. I cook them slowly in a shallow pan with butter and thyme, leaving them to soften and take on a coat as sticky as treacle. A little sugar, a trickle of balsamic or sherry vinegar and just a little salt is all that is needed in the way of seasoning. Grilled fish welcomes this accompaniment, as do cold roast meats, especially slices cut from a joint of pork.

The larger form, often sold to the shopper as 'banana shallots', is good roasted, when the flesh softens meltingly inside the crackling skin.

Fried onions to accompany liver or steak

Onions were never a big deal at home when I was a kid. One or two turned up in the occasional stew, floating in the languid stock along with thickly sliced carrots, parsnips and a bay leaf, but they were not stalwarts of our kitchen.

In my teenage years I was finally introduced to the liver and onions so hated by most of my school friends, the onions cooked lovingly in our battered aluminium frying pan, blackened from years of Sunday fry-ups, till they took on the colour of varnish and their flesh turned from acrid to a deep, honeyed sweetness. I took to this marriage of the intensely savoury meat and sugary-sweet onions straight away, though more for the glistening alliums than the pan-fried organ.

My first attempts at cooking onions to match those luscious little nuggets I had been enjoying at home failed for lack of a heavy-based pan and a little patience. The gorgeous, caramel-edged stickiness of a fried onion needs time in which to develop. A quick ten minutes in the thin frying pan that accompanied my crummy bedsit was never going to work.

To make perfect fried onions, you need a shallow, heavy-based pan. The temperature should be low to moderate and the onions should be allowed to soften slowly. Winter onions, which contain less water, will produce a sweeter and deeper gold result. Summer onions, full of water, will produce rather a lot of liquid, which will have to be evaporated away by turning up the heat.

The essence of frying onions is to let them soften in an unhurried manner with only the occasional stir to stop them sticking. You want their sugars to caramelise on the bottom of the pan; it is what gives fried onions their characteristic gloss and sweetness.

enough for 2–3
large, golden onions – 3
butter – a thick slice
oil – a small glug

Peel the onions. Cut them in half from root to tip, then slice each half into thick segments. Melt the butter in a shallow pan, add the oil and then the onions. Leave to cook over a low heat till the onions are sweet and soft enough to squish between thumb and forefinger. Salt only at the end of cooking, otherwise they will fail to soften.

There is no hurrying this. Turning the heat up will result in the onions browning, and what you are after is onions that are deep honey-gold rather than the colour of creosote. Stir them as they soften so they do not stick, but not so often that they fail to leave a glossy, sticky residue in the pan. There will be much flavour there.

The fusion of onions, beef and beer

Cooking onions slowly and without colour produces an aromatic backbone to a dish that is less sweet than one where the sugars in the onion have been allowed to caramelise. To do this successfully, I keep the heat low and stir the pot regularly. This is not something for the impatient cook. They need a watchful eye if they are not to colour, and can take up to twenty minutes or so to become a pale, translucent gold. They are ready when each piece is easily squashable between finger and thumb.

My early casseroles were complex, made up of layers of onion, celery, carrot, bay, thyme, red wine and meat juices, simply because that was the way I was taught to make them. It is what comes from learning to cook in cookery schools and restaurants rather than at your mother's knee. It has taken a while for me to appreciate the simpler style of slow-cooked stew such as the Lancashire hotpot and the French *pot-au-feu*.

Beer and onions is a merry little friendship. It works in hotdogs, the ploughman's lunch and Flemish beef casseroles. The Belgians often use beer instead of wine, stock or water. As it cooks, it loses its alcohol content but adds a characteristic sweet-sharp note that is difficult to introduce in any other way.

A simple stew of onions, beer and beef

This extraordinarily deep-flavoured stew is one for a day when there is frost on the ground. The inclusion of apple sauce isn't quite as daft as it sounds, and there is much magic to be found at the point where the sharp apple sauce oozes into the onion gravy. Boiled potatoes as big as your fist, their edges bruised and floury, are the ideal accompaniment.

enough for 4
butter – a thick slice
stewing beef in the piece – 750g
large onions – 2
thyme – a few sprigs
plain flour – 2 heaped tablespoons
Trappist beer – 2 small bottles
bay leaves – 2 or 3
redcurrant or apple jelly – a tablespoon

for the apple sauce
apples – 5–6, the sharper the better
butter – a walnut-sized knob
sugar – a little to taste
ground cinnamon – a knifepoint

Set the oven at 180°C/Gas 4. Melt the butter in a large casserole to which you have a lid. The heat should be quite sprightly. Cut the beef into four pieces, each nicely seasoned with salt and black pepper, then lower into the lightly sizzling butter. Let the meat colour on one side, then turn it over. Peel, halve and thinly slice the onions while the meat browns. Once coloured, remove the meat to a plate and lower the heat.

Add the onions to the pan, with the leaves from the thyme sprigs, and cook over a low to moderate heat until the onions are soft and pale gold.

Stir in the flour and leave until it is the palest biscuit colour, then pour in the beer and add the bay leaves. Once the sizzling has subsided and it is approaching boiling point, return the beef and its juices to the pan and lower the heat. Season with salt and black pepper, cover with a lid and place in the oven. Leave for a good hour to an hour and a half.

Peel the apples for the sauce, core them and cut into rough chunks. Put them into a pan with a little water and the butter and bring to the boil. Turn down the heat, cover with a lid and leave to cook to a sloppy mass. Sweeten with a little sugar and the ground cinnamon, then beat with a fork or wooden spoon till smooth.

Lift the lid from the casserole and stir in the jelly. Check the seasoning, adding salt, pepper and jelly as you go. Serve with the apple sauce.

A classic meat and onion pie

Onions make an important contribution to the filling of pies, providing a sweet balance for the savouriness of the meat and a necessary change of texture, too. A meat pie with no onions would be hard going.

I rarely make a meat pie. It is one of those recipes I reserve for a cold autumn day, when it's too wet to go out.

enough for 4
rump steak, cut into large bite-sized pieces – 750g
thyme – 4 sprigs
rosemary – 2 bushy sprigs
bay leaves – 2
red wine – 2 glasses
ox kidney – 450g
plain flour – 2 tablespoons
butter – a thick slice
medium onions – 2, chopped
chestnut mushrooms – 250g
beef stock – 450ml
puff pastry – 350g
a little beaten egg

Put the steak into a china or stainless-steel bowl, add the thyme, rosemary and bay and pour in the red wine. Cover with cling film and refrigerate overnight.

Set the oven at 200°C/Gas 6. Cut the kidney into large, bite-sized pieces removing any fat or sinew. Toss it in the flour with the drained steak (reserve the marinade). Melt the butter in a deep pan and add the floured meat. Let it sizzle for a minute or two. As soon as it is lightly browned on all sides, add the onions, letting them soften for a few minutes, then the mushrooms, cutting them into quarters as you go. Pour in the reserved marinade and the stock, season with salt and pepper, cover with a lid and leave to simmer for a good hour and a half, till the sauce is like a thick gravy. Allow to cool.

Put the filling into a pie dish, or divide between four small dishes. Roll out the pastry, then cut off strips to cover the rim of the dish. For the large pie, you may need to put a pastry funnel, eggcup or tumbler in the dish to hold up the pastry. Brush the rim of the dish with beaten egg and press the pastry strips into place. Now brush that with beaten egg, then lower the pastry lid or lids into place. Cut a slit in the top for the steam to escape and bake for forty to fifty minutes, till golden.

An onion rabbit

Of all the hot snacks I knock together, it is this unctuous topping of onions, thick toast and highly seasoned melted cheese that pleases most. The onions need to be left to cook, with the occasional stir as you pass, for a good fifteen minutes or so. They are ready only when they are truly soft and golden – there is no short cut. The leftover cold beer solves the problem of what to drink with your meal.

makes 2 rounds
small to medium onions – 2
butter – 35g
Cheddar – 150g
plain flour – 1 heaped tablespoon
dark beer – 125ml
milk – 75ml
English mustard – 1–2 teaspoons
thick slices of brown bread – 2

Peel the onions and cut them into rings or thin segments. Let them cook slowly in the butter over a low to moderate heat for fifteen minutes or so, till they are softly sweet and pale gold. While the onions are softening, grate the cheese.

Stir the flour into the onions with a wooden spoon, letting the mixture cook gently for a few moments, then slowly stir in the beer, followed by the milk. You should have a thick sauce. Stir in the mustard and a grinding of black pepper, then introduce the grated cheese.

Get an overhead grill hot. Toast the bread lightly on both sides on a baking sheet. Spoon over the rabbit mixture and leave under the grill for a few minutes, till the crust is scorched here and there.

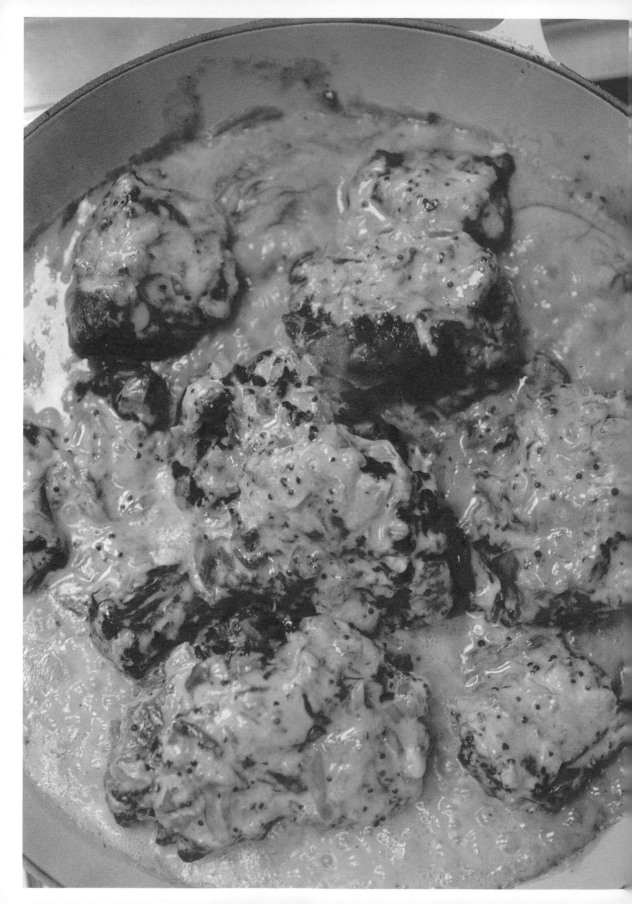

A stew of oxtail and onions for a cold night

The animal's tail has a gentle life, the occasional swish in a buttercup-strewn meadow, and I like to think that is reflected in how we choose to cook it. Oxtail is a meal of almost soporific qualities. It will not be hurried towards tenderness any more than the animal will be hurried along a country lane. After a long, slow baking with a lot of finely sliced onions and a little aromatic liquid, the velvety fibres will fall away from the bone in brown and pink flakes. Some spinach, very lightly cooked and served without butter, will flatter the meat and melt into the creamy sauce.

> *enough for 4*
> olive oil
> oxtail – 1.75kg
> large onions – 2
> 3 bay leaves
> a glass of white wine
> double cream – 300ml
> smooth Dijon mustard – a tablespoon
> grain mustard – a tablespoon

Warm a little olive oil in a heavy casserole. Season the oxtail all over with salt and black pepper. Lower into the oil and leave to colour on all sides. Meanwhile halve, peel and thinly slice the onions, whilst occasionally turning the meat so that it gilds lightly and evenly. Remove the oxtail from the casserole and add the onions, letting them soften a little but not colour.

Hide the meat amongst the onions, tuck in the bay leaves and pour over the white wine. Lay a piece of buttered or oiled greaseproof paper over the top, then cover with a lid. Bake at 160°C/Gas 3 for two and a half hours, checking now and again that it is not dry. If it is, add a little more liquid.

Lift the lid and remove the meat to a warm dish. Pour off any obvious fat from the pan, then stir in the cream and the mustards and check the seasoning. Bring to the boil on the hob and bubble hard for five to ten minutes to reduce the quantity, stirring in any pan-stickings as you go.

Spoon the mustard sauce over the oxtail and eat immediately.

Roast lamb, couscous, red onion

Onions are used in most stuffings, both lightening the rice, couscous or breadcrumbs and introducing sweetness. As they melt down, they keep the filling moist.

Ask the butcher to prepare your shoulder of lamb for stuffing. When the bone is removed, it provides a neat pocket that will hold just the right amount.

enough for 6
a large red onion
olive oil
fine couscous – 90g
boiling water – 200ml
golden sultanas – a handful
ground cumin – half a teaspoon
ground cinnamon – 2 large pinches
a shoulder of lamb – about 1.3kg, prepared for stuffing

Peel and thinly slice the onion, then let it soften in a little olive oil over a moderate heat, stirring from time to time. It is ready when soft and golden. Put the couscous in a bowl, pour over the water and leave for ten minutes. Set the oven at 220°C/Gas 7.

Fluff the couscous with a fork to separate the grains. Stir in the softened onion, the sultanas and the spices. Season generously, then stuff the mixture into the pocket inside the lamb. Pull the meat over the stuffing and seal with a skewer or tie with string.

Place the meat in a roasting tin, scattering any spare stuffing around the outside and rub a little olive oil over the fat. Pour a glass of water into the roasting tin and place in the oven. Roast the lamb for twenty minutes, then lower the heat to 200°C/Gas 6 and continue roasting for forty minutes, until the fat is crisp and golden and the juices run clear when the meat is pierced with a skewer. Remove from the oven and leave to rest for ten minutes before carving.

Grilled gammon, baked onions

This is a lovely dish, homely, old fashioned and what I call 'great-grandmotherly'. I sometimes find white sauces a bit heavy, so I have lightened this one by using half stock to milk. In practice this means adding just a teaspoon of Marigold vegetable stock powder dissolved in 250ml water, but you could use real stock if you have some.

The sauce is worth seasoning generously, with salt, pepper, grainy mustard, bay leaves and a (mild) grating of nutmeg. I leave the bay in even when the sauce is finished and poured over the onions. It adds much in the way of subtle flavour.

Should you not fancy grilled gammon, then I would still urge you to make the onions – they would be good even on their own, perhaps with a mound of buttery mashed potato or, better still, golden swede with lots of butter and pepper.

serves 2, with second helpings of onions
medium onions – 6
butter – a thick slice (about 30g, if you are weighing)
plain flour – a heaped tablespoon
light stock (see above) – 250ml, hot
milk – 250ml, hot
bay leaves – 3
nutmeg
grain mustard – 2 teaspoons
parsley leaves – a small handful
a little oil
gammon steaks – 2, about 150–175g each
dried oregano

Set the oven at 180°C/Gas 4. Bring a deep pan of water to the boil. Peel the onions, add them to the pan, then turn down the heat and let them simmer until they are tender enough to take the point of a kitchen knife. This will only be a matter of twenty to twenty-five minutes or so. Drain them and discard the water (don't try using it in the sauce, the flavour can be too strong).

Put the pan back on the stove, melt the butter in it and stir in the flour, keeping the heat low to moderate. Let the flour and butter cook for a couple of minutes, stirring often so the mixture doesn't burn, then turn up the heat, pour in the stock and milk and whisk together for a minute until there are no lumps.

Season the sauce with salt and black pepper, the bay leaves, a gentle grating of nutmeg and the mustard. I cannot emphasise enough the importance of these seasonings: they add depth and savour to the sauce and make the whole dish 'work'. Let the sauce simmer gently for a good ten minutes or more, stirring regularly so that it does not catch on the bottom.

Cut the onions in half from stem to tip – take care, they are slippery – and place them flat-side down in a shallow baking dish. I use an oval enamelled gratin dish. Chop the parsley, but not too finely, and stir it into the sauce, then scoop the lot over the onions. Their caps will probably be poking out, but no matter, just bake for forty to forty-five minutes till the sauce is bubbling.

Turn off the heat, but leave the onions in the oven whilst you cook the gammon. If your grill is, like mine, in the oven, then move the onions to the bottom and put the grill pan two-thirds of the way up, so that it blocks the onions from the grill (if you prefer, you can cook the gammon on a hob-top grill).

Oil the steaks lightly and season them with pepper, a very little salt and a light sprinkling of oregano. Now grill them for three or four minutes on each side, till golden. Serve the grilled gammon with the baked onions and their sauce.

Shallots with raisins and cider vinegar

I have eaten these onions, at once caramel sweet and pickle sour, with bread and cheese, and that is really what I meant them for. But they also make a sticky accompaniment for a roast – maybe a fillet of lamb or pork – and are good on the side with cold roast beef, kept pink and sweet. I serve them warm rather than hot or chilled.

enough for 4 as a side dish
shallots – 30
olive oil – 2 tablespoons
butter – a thick slice
a clove of garlic
thyme – 4 bushy sprigs
cider vinegar – 3 tablespoons
raisins or sultanas – 2 tablespoons
light muscovado sugar – 2 tablespoons

Set the oven at 190°C/Gas 5. Peel the shallots. Warm the olive oil and butter in a small roasting tin or baking dish. Peel the garlic and slice it thinly, add to the butter, then put in the shallots and the thyme leaves, stripped from their stems. Add the cider vinegar, an equal amount of water, the raisins or sultanas and the muscovado sugar. Season with salt and black pepper and bake for forty to fifty minutes, stirring once or twice, till the shallots are sticky and sweet-sour. They should be soft enough to crush between your fingers and thumb. If they are browning too quickly, then cover with tinfoil.

Lentil soup with lemon, pancetta and mint

One of those soups that doubles as a main course, earthy, filling and beefy. The soup relies on the onion to add depth and body.

serves 4
onions – 2 small or 1 large
olive oil
garlic – 3 or 4 cloves, sliced
unsmoked bacon or pancetta – a good handful, diced
flat-leaf parsley – a small bunch
Puy or Castelluccio lentils – 250g
stock or, at a push, water – a litre
spinach – 2 large handfuls
a lemon
mint – a small bunch, leaves torn

Peel the onions and chop them finely, then let them cook over a moderate to low heat with a little olive oil, the sliced garlic and the diced bacon. It should all be golden and fragrant. Chop the parsley and stir it in.

Wash the lentils thoroughly, then stir them into the onions and bacon. Pour over the stock or water and bring to the boil, skimming off any froth that comes to the surface. You can add a bay leaf or two if you like. Turn the heat down so that the lentils simmer merrily, then almost cover the pot with a lid and leave till they are tender but far from collapse – about thirty minutes, depending on your lentils.

Wash the spinach thoroughly and tear it up a bit. While it is still wet and dripping, put it into a shallow pan over a high heat and shut the lid tightly – you need to cook it in its own steam. After a minute or two it will be limp and bright emerald green. Lift it out, squeeze it dry, then divide it between four warm bowls.

Season the soup with salt, black pepper, lemon juice and the torn mint leaves, tasting as you go. Ladle the hot soup on top of the spinach and serve with more lemon and mint for those who want it.

Onion soup, Madeira and Gruyère toasts

I relish the frugality and bonhomie of a bowl of onion soup. This is slightly richer and thicker than the one in *The Kitchen Diaries*, possibly for colder weather. I don't often use flour to thicken a soup but in this case it produces a particularly velvety texture.

enough for 4
butter – a good thick slice
large onions – 3, sliced
bay leaves – 2
plain flour – 2 tablespoons
white wine – 250ml
chicken stock – 1 litre
Madeira – 3–4 tablespoons
sourdough bread – 8 small slices
Gruyère – 75g, thinly sliced

Melt the butter in a heavy-based saucepan, add the sliced onions and the bay leaves and let them cook, without colouring, over a medium heat. You want them to be soft and slightly sticky, which will take a good twenty-five minutes. When they are ready, stir in the flour, cook for a minute or so, then pour in the white wine, followed by the stock. Bring to the boil, season with salt and black pepper, then turn the heat down so that the soup simmers and leave it, with just an occasional stir, for thirty minutes. Add the Madeira and continue simmering for five to ten minutes.

Toast the bread on one side, then cover the other side with the sliced Gruyère. Check the soup for seasoning, then spoon into heatproof bowls. Float the slices of bread on top and place under the grill for a couple of minutes, till the cheese has melted.

Baked onions

Banana shallots (sometimes known as torpedo), the most generously proportioned and mild tasting of the shallot family, roast superbly, their translucent flesh almost melting inside their skins. I have eaten them this way with creamy goat's cheese mashed with herbs (thyme, tarragon, chives) and with a lump of good, mouth-puckering Cheddar too. Yet they will also stand as a vegetable. I think it worth including them here for that alone.

banana shallots – 4 per person
olive oil
thyme sprigs
a little cheese, such as Caerphilly or Cheddar

Put the oven on at 190°C/Gas 5. Bake the shallots in their skins, with a light drizzle of oil and a few sprigs of thyme, for about thirty minutes, till soft to the touch. Test one; it should be meltingly soft inside.

Put the shallots on serving plates, cut into each shallot, then pour in a drop or two of olive oil and add a few thyme leaves and a few thin scraps of cheese. Press together until the cheese softens. Push the onion from its skin and eat while hot.

Baked onions, porcini and cream

These are *the* onions to have alongside a few slices of rare roast beef. The marriage of flavours is superb. If they are to be truly tender and silky soft, it is crucial to take them as far as you dare in the pre-cooking stage, before you scoop out the centre and stuff them. They need to be boiled for a good half an hour, depending, of course, on their size. Any layers that are not supple and easy to squash between your finger and thumb should be discarded.

There is no reason why these onions with their mushroomy, creamy filling couldn't be served as a main dish. You would need two each, I think, and maybe some noodles, wide ones such as pappardelle, on the side, tossed in a little melted butter and black pepper.

enough for 4 as a side dish
dried porcini mushrooms – 15g
medium to large onions – 4
butter – a thick slice
garlic – 2 small cloves, crushed
thyme – 5 sprigs (you can use dried thyme at a push)
double cream – 200ml
grated Parmesan – 40g

Put the porcini in a small bowl and cover with warm water. Peel the onions, then boil them in deep, salted water for about thirty minutes, until they are tender and the layers will come apart when pulled. They mustn't be hard in the middle. Drain them, slice the top off each one to give a flat edge, then put them in a small baking dish, one in which they will fit snugly. Using a teaspoon, scoop out most of the inside of each onion without splitting the sides and base.

Chop half of the scooped-out insides (you can discard the other half, you won't need it) and warm it with the butter and crushed garlic in a small, shallow pan. Drain and chop the porcini, pull the thyme leaves off their twigs and chop them finely, then add both porcini and leaves to the onions and continue cooking, stirring from time to time. As the onions continue to soften and colour and the mixture starts to smell interesting, pour in the cream, season with salt and black pepper and remove from the heat.

Stir in most of the grated cheese, then spoon the stuffing into the hollows of the onions. Add the remaining cheese on top and bake at 200°C/Gas 6 for twenty minutes, till bubbling.

Couscous, red onions, parsley, pine kernels

I have eaten this for supper with a spot of harissa sauce stirred in (let down with a little water) but that is not really the idea. It is meant as an accompaniment to grilled lamb or fish, or perhaps some spicy meatballs. Instantly comforting, and as soothing as a pashmina.

enough for 4 as an accompaniment
couscous – 100g
large red onions – 2
olive oil
bay leaves – 3
pine kernels – 35g
flat-leaf parsley – a small bunch

Put the couscous in a bowl, sprinkle with a cupful of water and leave for ten minutes.

Peel the onions and cut them into thin slices. They should be no thicker than your little finger. Warm a little olive oil in a heavy frying pan — just enough to cover the bottom – then add the onion rings and bay leaves and cook till golden brown. Do this over a low heat, and expect it to take a good fifteen minutes, maybe longer. That way they will soften without burning and caramelise to a sweet, deep golden colour. Cook them too quickly and they will take on a bitter note.

Put the couscous into a steamer basket lined with a damp new J-cloth or into the top of a couscousier, suspended over a pan of boiling water. Steam for ten minutes, then remove and sprinkle with a little more water and a shake or two of olive oil. Let it swell for five minutes, then return it to the steamer for ten minutes.

Stir the pine kernels into the onions and let them colour lightly. Chop the parsley leaves and stir them in too, with a seasoning of salt and black pepper. As soon as it is tender and fluffy, tip the couscous into the onions and stir.

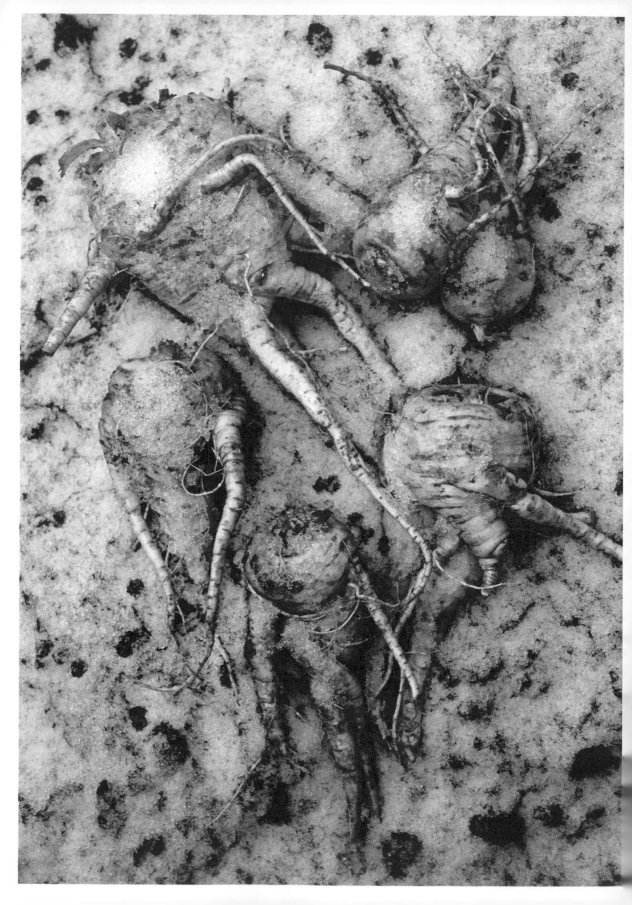

Parsnips

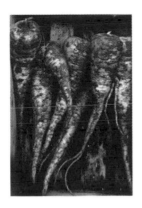

The soil-encrusted root, gnarled like the bark of an old tree, hides a creamy flesh that is both earthy and sweet. Snapped in half, it smells of freshly dug ground. Roasted in butter, it smells of warm heather honey. I value the parsnip for its gentle sweetness, its happy marriage with the crusted edges of a piece of roast beef, and the velvety soup you can make even from its woody core. Steamed, mashed and softened to a purée with warm cream, the frugal root becomes a deceptively luxurious accompaniment to roast lamb. Baked in a slow oven with cream and the milder spices – cumin, nutmeg, a few specks of mace – the parsnip makes a sensual supper on a day when you are expecting someone to arrive home cold and sodden.

Medieval cooks, to whom sugar and honey were expensive, were glad of its sweetness. The plump varieties we enjoy now did not appear till the 1850s, a deliberate attempt to improve upon the wild one with its thin, strong-tasting tail. I buy my first bag in autumn to eat with a curl of Cumberland sausage and a bottle of cider, the last some time around April, when I have had my fill of sugary roots.

I haven't always loved the parsnip. It is extraordinary that a child so fond of sugar managed to find no comfort in the sweetest of all the root vegetables. But then I mostly knew the parsnip as the yellow chunk amongst the orange, brown and white ones in a Wednesday neck of lamb stew. The whispering cloud of sweet mash, the fluffy chip and the slice of sugary root bathed in spices and cream were all parsnip recipes I would meet up with only later in life.

Almost more than any other vegetable, the parsnip is linked to cold climates (you will see beetroot on sale in warm countries but rarely parsnips). As a kid, I would dawdle in the woods on my way home, particularly on Sunday afternoons in winter, when the hazels were bare and the twigs underfoot were as brittle as icicles. I would sometimes pretend to be lost, though in truth I never really went so deep into the trees as to lose sight of the glow from the cottages that lined the main road. Somehow, an imaginary adventure made arriving home to the smell of roast beef and baked apples all the sweeter. My dad insisted that the odd parsnip should be tucked in amongst the potatoes that sat, gently crisping, round the Sunday roast. The woods around Knightwick are still there, though now they have more elder and are no longer threatening or even exciting. To this day, I find parsnips are at their most welcome after a cold walk, and I too hide the odd parsnip amongst the Arran Victory and Maris Pipers in the roasting tin, a sugary surprise for those who fail to check what is on their fork.

It is worth making sure that everyone is happy with this arrangement. Whilst the parsnips take on the juices of the roast and turn a pleasingly chewy gold, they don't meet with everyone's approval. Especially when they are disguised as a potato.

It was 'Gaudy Bohemian' Molly Parkin and the cookery doyenne Jane Grigson who saved the parsnip from a life of endless stews. The writer, celebrity and fashion editor Molly Parkin ('two ex-husbands, nine ex-fiancés and a galaxy of glorious lovers') invented a recipe from which the sleepy root has never looked back. Parsnips Molly Parkin is initially an unconvincing-sounding dish made up of layers of tomatoes, parsnips, brown sugar and cream. It tastes less sugary than it sounds. We first bumped into one another (the recipe that is, not Ms Parkin and I) when I was given the task of producing a daily vegetarian option in a busy metropolitan café. Original, profitable and really rather delicious, the recipe gathered fans to the point where we barely dared take it off the menu. For all its richness, the idea is still valid, though I think it is probably better as a side dish. The cream and the acidity of the tomatoes make this a sound enough accompaniment to anything you might serve with a classic potato dauphinoise. It's a good dish with a roast shoulder of lamb and one of the few times tomatoes can be said to go successfully with root vegetables.

A less jazzy treatment involved the late Jane Grigson's 1960s idea of stirring a cautious amount of curry powder into a parsnip soup. Warmly sweet and with a curious depth, the soup has become a modern classic and is one I make, with endless variations, to bolster us on a winter's day. These two treatments took the humble root to another level of sophistication altogether.

Parsnips did rather well out of the period that saw a panoply of peasant foods adopted by chefs looking for 'beyond the pale' ingredients with which to surprise and amuse their customers. While the Jerusalem artichoke fared best of all, the parsnip was not overlooked. I once ate a roast fillet of lamb sliced and arranged in a spiral (you know the sort of thing) encircled by a purée of parsnip scattered with pine kernels. Back at home, where the cooking tended to be somewhat less precious, I served a mound of the mashed roots gussied up with a little cream, grated nutmeg and toasted pine kernels alongside a roast leg of lamb. It has remained a favourite to this day and deliciously gets rid of the wizened roots from the larder.

Today the parsnip is the darling of the organic movement, which values its solid reliability and the ease with which it wards off predators. The brown roots are a stalwart of my organic box from November to April. Most of us have usually had enough of them long before Easter. The mash turns up both in gastropubs alongside lamb shanks and in avant-garde splatters across Michelin-starred plates. In my kitchen they are often seen in the company of thyme, mustard, cream and curry spices.

A parsnip in the garden

You probably only need to know that the parsnip's umbrella-like flowers are a pale mustard yellow if you have planted them next to the carrots – whose flowers are white – and forgotten to label them. They must look charming against their native chalk and limestone soil. Yes, they are a weed. As a plant, *Pastinaca sativa* lacks the carrot's delicacy of form (its leaves are coarse, like lovage or celeriac) but in the kitchen it has a charm and shyness that can make the bright orange carrot look a bit crass.

I have never grown them, enjoying reliable supplies from the organic box delivery or from the farmers' market (those from the Fern Verrow stall at Borough Market are hauntingly beautiful). Arriving dirty, with their long rat-tails intact, they are tougher skinned than the polished ivory roots from the greengrocer's or the supermarket, which, like sheep, have had their tails docked (in truth, the thin roots are useless and tend only to dry up in the oven). Two- and three-pronged parsnips, whilst amusing the shopper, are given withering looks by show gardeners, who blame a split root on heavy or badly prepared soil. Me, I rather like their random shapes and forked tongues. There is little enough to make a cook smile in February.

Those who grow their own seem to favour the long-rooted varieties such as Excalibur, Gladiator and Javelin (one is led to assume the varieties were all named by men), appreciating their generous yield and resistance to canker. Home gardeners and allotment holders need some patience here.

The seeds take forever to germinate, and are usually sown in late winter and early spring in rows about 30cm apart. They like their feet in deep, sandy soil (you can get away with shallow soil if you plant a stubby variety such as Evesham). My rich clay would smother them. Lumpy soil will make the roots turn a corner. A vigilant gardener will thin the seedlings to a good hand's width apart, then water them when and if they remember. The parsnip is quite tolerant of drought, so useful for the forgetful gardener.

The old wives' tale about this vegetable tasting better after a good frost or two has sound foundations. In practice, the frost turns the starch into sugar, giving a more rounded flavour. Older gardeners have told me they really need four or five hard frosts to make a difference. I am tempted to suggest we leave them in the ground till the roast beef is in the oven, but they can be frustratingly difficult to extract if the ground is frozen.

Varieties

I have never seen parsnips sold under their varietal names. 'It's just a parsnip, guv.' If we want to know which is which, we apparently must grow our own. As a cook, I remain unconvinced that there is a huge difference between one and the other, but allotment holders and farmers may know better. Besides Excalibur, Gladiator and Javelin, other varieties you might like to grow are:

Hollow Crown Named for the way in which its stem seems to be sunk deep into the top of the root, this is one of the oldest varieties in cultivation, if not the oldest. Paler flesh than some, and mellow rather than 'in your face' sweet.

The Student Grown initially from wild seed, this thick variety was the work of one James Buckman, professor of geology, natural history and botany at the Royal Agricultural College, who donated his prize seed to Suttons in 1860. Painfully slow to germinate.

A parsnip in the kitchen

The hidden treasure here is sugar. To get the best out of this vegetable, you need to caramelise the sugars present in the flesh and introduce an element of richness with butter, cream or spices. There is little excitement in a plainly boiled root.

Simmering in water till they yield slightly to the touch will soften the starch. It's generally a good idea to do this before roasting or baking, otherwise they tend to become a boring chew. Shocking them in sizzling butter or a mixture of butter and oil helps to get a good crust going. Slow roasting, with the occasional turn, should achieve a tender, nuttily flavoured vegetable that is pleasurable in small quantities. Two or three cork-sized lumps per person are usually enough.

Where the 'snip reaches glorious heights is when you tuck a handful around the Sunday roast, when the roasting juices get a chance to caramelise with the roots' own sugars, or if you bake them in layers with cream to which you have added a few spices. Thickly sliced, they have the ability to soak up the cream and develop a soft, undulating crust similar to potatoes cooked à la dauphinoise. The combination of sweetness, spice and cream is extraordinary.

There are still many who fail to get the point of this overblown wild root. Others have questioned why I give it such high billing in my kitchen. In its defence, the parsnip possesses a rare quality that will introduce body to soups, stocks and stews. Lamb stew without a touch of parsnip always seems to have something indefinable missing. The vegetable has a grounding, steadying effect and seems to bring the other aromatics together.

As a mash to accompany a chicken casserole, a pork roast or a pile of butcher's sausages, parsnip makes a fine alternative to the usual potato. The inherent sweetness is a good contrast to the umami notes of the meat and its glossy, sticky skin. That mash, if made dry enough, can be used as a base for parsnip patties flecked with parsley and bacon or as a thick crust for a shepherd's pie. For which you might like to see my recipe in *Real Cooking*.

Roasted, the root will provide the necessary sweet note to balance a meal that might otherwise be monotonously savoury. The occasional mouthful of sugary root, its edges browned and tacky with caramelised sugar, is entirely at home with roast beef and pork.

A soup of parsnips – bland, sweet, calming – is pleasing on a grey day. A version with apple is surprisingly 'unsweet', especially if you add a crisped rasher or two of bacon.

A fried parsnip can also be a good thing. The trick is to blanch chunks of the vegetable first in boiling water, then fry them in deep groundnut oil. The resulting sweet, hot chips are tempting when dipped into hollandaise sauce, especially if it contains more than the classic proportion of lemon juice.

One of the curious facts about the parsnip is how it shines all the more brightly with the addition of a bit more sugar. In theory this should be too much of a good thing. In practice it is what the root needs if we are to see it at its best (which is, after all, why we are here). A scattering of demerara sugar before baking, a spoonful of runny honey or maple syrup before the chopped roots meet the roasting tin, is all it takes.

When parsnips are sold away from the scrubbed and sanitised supermarket shelves, some shoppers find the sight of this long root and its casing of soil less than inviting. I disagree, but then I like to buy my veg dirty. Once home, it will keep best in its protective layer of earth. If it has been scrubbed, keep it in a cool, dry place; the bottom of the fridge will do. In the kitchen the parsnip needs peeling – the skin tends to toughen on cooking and will refuse to mash, or will turn to leather when roasted – and when you do you are left with a sweet, ivory-cream root with which to play. Curious, though, how a peeled and rinsed parsnip becomes as slippery as a bar of soap.

Seasoning your parsnips

With the exception of thyme and rosemary, herbs are of little interest here. Spices, on the other hand, work like a dream. As a cooking medium, butter, dripping and duck fat are more appropriate than olive oil – often the case with things grown underground.

Beef and its dripping A scattering of parsnips around the roast is invariably a good thing.
Gravy A jug of hot gravy poured over a mound of mashed roots is even better if the gravy was made yesterday and has had time to 'ripen' in the fridge. Both gravy and mash should be piping hot.
Spices Cinnamon, cumin and nutmeg added to the onions at the outset flatter a smooth parsnip soup, as will a spoonful of the mild garam masala stirred in towards the end.
Mace If there is a single spice that seems made for the parsnip it is powdered mace. In a parsnip cake, or as a knifepoint of seasoning in a creamy dauphinoise, mace's subtle, musky sweetness is extraordinary.
Butter Use to enrich a mash or for frying thickly sliced steamed roots. A fat knob added after draining will brighten even the lowliest offering of boiled roots (surprisingly luxurious when eaten with boiled gammon).
Cream It may seem altogether too bland to match such a sweet vegetable but cream will seduce when used to bake a dish of sliced 'nips. The addition of some softened onions or a little pancetta is also worthwhile.
Mustard Mild grain mustard balances the inherent sweetness in gratins and soups.

And...

* Due to their excellent storage qualities, parsnips are in the shops all year. At their best after a good frost, their sweetness is welcome in any month from October to March. They feel awkward in summer.
* I have been known to stick a box of them outside when there is frost around. They seem all the sweeter for it.
* The small, round parsnips that appear in late summer are exceptionally mild (one could say tasteless) but are good for introducing the root to sceptical newcomers.
* I have very little spare room in my vegetable patch, so I plant no parsnips. They hog a lot of space throughout summer.
* The sweetness of this root is particularly appropriate with beef and all the game birds and ravishing with offal. Mashed, it forms a sincere partnership with liver, bacon, lamb shanks and oxtail. This is not the vegetable to force into a marriage with fish. It is just plain wrong.
* The sweet mash likes some gravy to play with. I include it on the side of unctuous, sloppily sauced suppers like braised oxtail, ham and parsley sauce, lamb stew and liver and sausage hotpot.
* Parsnip chips rarely crisp as successfully as potato ones. But blanching or steaming the vegetable first, then frying it once in hot oil, then again in very, very hot oil will bring us as near as we can get.
* If you grow parsnips, they will keep splendidly in the ground till you need them. If you buy them, then try to find dirty ones. The presence of soil seems to have a preserving effect. I keep mine in a cool scullery (the coldest room in the house) in a brown paper bag. They remain in fine condition for a week or more. The fridge is fine too, even more so if you wrap them in newspaper.

The perfect roast parsnip

Amongst the potatoes there were clearly parsnips, their cut sides straighter, their colour darker and showing the odd flash of glowing, deepest yellow. There was beef, a small rib, its three wide bones sticky, its fat incandescent in the metal roasting tin blackened and buckled from a decade of Sunday lunches.

The beef was lifted out to a warm place to rest under a dome of crumpled foil and its juices left to settle. The potatoes and parsnips were emptied into a dish and briefly returned to the oven. There was a last-minute stirring of gravy on the hob, the mixing of grated horseradish root and cream in a cup, wedges of cabbage were drained and buttered. Plates clattered.

You could argue that the perfect roast parsnip had a lot of help – the gravy, the odd savoury crumb of fat from the beef, the faintest dab of heat from the creamed horseradish to kick its sweetness into touch – but it was as fine as a swollen, starchy root could ever be, both savoury and stickily sweet on the outside and softly yielding within. It had picked up the soul of the roasting juices and toasted onion in the pan.

Roasted alone with just dripping, oil or butter, plus salt and thyme leaves pulled from the branch, a parsnip can be treat enough, yet allowed to catch here and there with the other elements from the tin, the parsnip can excel. A nugget of sweet gold amongst a plate of serious savour and celebration.

Roast parsnips

I cook them in dripping or butter for preference. Groundnut oil if there is nothing else. They take forty minutes to colour interestingly but an hour will turn them into vegetable toffee. The initial steaming is worth the ten minutes' wait and the pan to rinse and dry, helping as it does to keep them moist during the roasting and preventing them from toughening up in the heat.

enough for 4
parsnips – 450g
dripping, duck fat or butter – a couple of spoonfuls

Peel your parsnips, cut them into fat lumps and steam them for ten minutes in a colander over a pan of boiling water. Warm a couple of heaped spoonfuls of fat in a roasting tin at 180°C/Gas 4, then tip in the steamed parsnips. Roast for forty-five minutes or so, till their insides are soft and creamy, their exterior gold, brown and, here and there, almost black. An occasional turn in the pan is a good thing, but too much meddling will prevent them achieving the ultimate sticky crust (the same goes for sausages, which I mention only because the two make a lovely pair). Inevitably the parsnips will have one side – that which lies underneath – darker and chewier than the others. It is part of the pleasure.

... and with thyme and maple syrup

The thyme is essential here, adding an important herbal note to the general sugar-fest. You need something savoury alongside, and nothing works quite so well as gloriously rare roast beef. Sausages come a close second.

enough for 6
parsnips – 6 large
butter – a thick slice
a little beef dripping (or extra butter)
thyme – about 8 small sprigs
maple syrup – 4 teaspoons

Set the oven at 200°C/Gas 6. Peel the parsnips and remove the tops. Slice each in half unless they are truly enormous, in which case quarters might be better. Put them into a roasting tin with the thick slice of butter and a spoonful of beef dripping (or more butter). Season with salt and black pepper, then roast for thirty-five to forty minutes, until the parsnips are soft and golden. Remove the leaves from the thyme sprigs and add them to the vegetables with the maple syrup, turning the parsnips over as you go. Continue to roast for twenty minutes or so, till the surface of the vegetables is sticky and golden, the flesh soft and sweetly tender.

... and with sesame and honey

Whatever magic it may contain (and I certainly believe it does), honey is still sugar, and it seems extraordinary to add it to an already sweet root. But for some reason it works, bringing out the vegetable's flavour and lending it a distinct depth. I can't think of any better accompaniment to roast pork.

enough for 4
parsnips – 1kg
a little groundnut oil
a little rosemary
sesame seeds – 2 tablespoons

for the dressing
honey – 4 level tablespoons
sherry vinegar – 3 tablespoons
groundnut oil – 3 tablespoons
sesame oil – a good splash

Set the oven at 180°C/Gas 4. Put a pan of water on to boil. Peel the parsnips, cut them in half lengthways and then into fat chunks. When the water boils, lower them in and simmer for ten minutes, till they show early signs of tenderness. Remove from the heat and drain.

Pour a glug of oil into a roasting tin, add the drained parsnips and toss them with sea salt, pepper and some chopped needles of rosemary. A tablespoon or so will do. Roast for about forty minutes, turning them in the pan occasionally, so that they end up with a pale, golden crust on all sides. In a dry, shallow pan, lightly brown the sesame seeds. They will take barely a minute or so to colour.

Put the honey into a small bowl and whisk in the vinegar, groundnut oil and sesame oil with a small grinding of salt and black pepper. Remove the parsnips from the oven and immediately toss them in the honey dressing, scattering over the toasted sesame seeds as you go.

How to make the silkiest purée

Parsnips make a better purée than a mash. Their fibres, coarser than potatoes or carrots, demand that extra bit of trouble from the cook, but they are easy enough to reduce to a fluffy cream in a food processor or food mixer (use the beater attachment). Butter, hot milk or a dollop of crème fraîche helps smooth the resulting starchy pulp to a soft and extremely silky purée. Beat it in with a whisk or wooden spoon to introduce air. The trick to a mash that is smooth but not wet is to steam the roots rather than boil them and a generous hand with the dairy produce.

The moment of bliss is when the parchment-coloured purée slides into hot roasting juices or gravy on the plate.

A contemporary parsnip purée

Peel and boil, rather than steam, your parsnips here. The extra water will help with the texture. When they are tender to the point of a knife, blitz them in a food processor till smooth. Tip into a bowl and beat in enough butter and crème fraîche to turn it into a shapeless purée. Season with a little smooth mustard and black pepper. Serve with grilled lamb cutlets.

A rich root and cheese soup for a winter's day

The tools for my winter gardening sessions tend to lie on the kitchen floor from one week to the next: the pruning knife, my leather-handled secateurs, the largest of the two spades, the rake. They serve as a reminder that even though the garden may look crisp and neat from the window, there is still work to be done. It is during these cold, grey-sky days that I sometimes feel as if I live on soup. Roots – fat carrots, artichokes and woody parsnips – are part of the line-up, along with onions and the occasional potato. I take much pleasure in the way something can be both earthy and velvety at the same time. Rather like my gardening gloves.

enough for 4
a medium onion
large parsnips – 2
butter – 50g
garlic – 2 plump cloves
a little flour
dried chilli flakes – a teaspoon
turmeric – half a teaspoon
vegetable stock – a litre
single cream – 100ml
mild, grainy mustard – 2 tablespoons
Cornish Yarg, or perhaps Gruyère – 100g, diced

Peel and roughly chop the onion and parsnips. Melt the butter in a large, heavy pot, add the onion and, once it has started to relax, add the parsnips.

Peel the garlic, squash it flat, then add to the pan. Cook over a moderate heat, lid on, until the onion has coloured lightly and the edges of the parsnips are mostly golden. Resist disturbing the vegetables too much as they cook: a slight browning of the parsnips here and there is essential to the flavour of the soup.

Sprinkle a dusting of flour into the pot, stir in the chilli flakes and turmeric, then cook for a minute or two to remove the raw taste of the flour. Add the stock, stir and bring to the boil. Lower the heat to allow the soup to sit at a light boil and continue until the vegetables are soft, about twenty minutes.

Pour into a blender or food processor and whiz to a creamy purée. Add the cream and mustard and salt and freshly ground pepper to taste. Drop the cubes of cheese into four warm soup bowls, then ladle the soup over. Serve immediately.

Ham with apple juice and parsnip purée

A poaching broth for fish, a chicken or a lumbering piece of ham is all the more interesting for the inclusion of a leek or two. They soften the stock, bringing the flavours of onion, carrot and herbs together.

The ham recipe here is my standard 'food for a crowd'. Poached ham slices neatly, even when it falls off the knife in chunks, and can be kept waiting patiently in its own stock without coming to any harm. I often serve it with creamed spinach. I include it here partly to show ham's affinity with parsnips and also because it's a useful recipe and I wanted to get it in somewhere. This seemed as good a place as anywhere.

I usually buy a ready-tied piece of boneless gammon from the butcher for this. It needs no soaking, but will benefit from being brought to the boil in water, drained and then rinsed before being cooked in the apple juice.

enough for 6
boneless gammon, tied – 2kg
leeks – 2
large celery ribs – 2
a carrot
unfiltered apple juice – 2 litres
juniper berries – 15
a cinnamon stick
black peppercorns – 9
parsley stalks – 6 or so
bay leaves – 2

to serve
parsnip purée (page 384)

Put the ham in a large saucepan; it should fit snugly. Cover with water, bring to the boil, then pour the water away. Rinse the ham and return to the pot.

Split the leeks in half, discarding most of the tough, dark green tops. Rinse them thoroughly under cold running water to remove any trapped grit that may be lurking between the layers. Cut the celery into short pieces and tuck them into the pot with the leeks and the whole carrot. Pour in the apple juice, adding a top-up of water if it doesn't quite cover the ham.

Lightly crush the juniper berries with the flat of a large knife, then add them to the pan with the cinnamon stick, peppercorns, parsley stalks and bay leaves. Bring to the boil, turn the heat down to a jolly simmer, then scoop off the froth that floats on top. Cover partially with a lid and leave it to get on with things for a couple of hours, checking from time to time that it isn't bubbling too fiercely or hasn't stopped altogether.

After two hours, check the ham for tenderness. Leave in the cooking liquor, the heat switched off, for anything up to twenty minutes before carving. Serve in thickish slices, drizzled with a spoonful of the hot, appley cooking liquor, with the vegetables if you wish, and the puréed parsnips.

A dish of cream and parsnips to accompany a roast

Eventually, possibly towards the end of your meal, you reach the point where the salty, herbal juices from the meat mingle with the sweet creaminess of those from the parsnips, a moment of intense pleasure.

While winter was in its death throes, and the first white narcissi were starting to peak through the damp earth, I produced this for Sunday lunch with a leg of lamb spiked with tough old rosemary twigs. We passed round a bowl of winter chicory and watercress for everyone to take handfuls with which to clean the mixture of juices from their plates.

enough for 4–6
parsnips – 450g
a knob of butter
double cream – 300ml
full-cream milk – 100ml
thyme
a lump of Parmesan
breadcrumbs

Set the oven at 160°C/Gas 3. Peel the parsnips and slice them thinly from stalk to tip. The slices should be only slightly thicker than a pound coin. Bring to the boil in deep, unsalted water, simmer for five to seven minutes, then drain carefully so that they don't break up.

Butter a large baking dish or roasting tin. Lay the sliced parsnips in the dish, neatly or hugger-mugger as the mood takes you. Mix the cream and milk in a jug and season with salt and pepper. Pull a tablespoon of thyme leaves from their stalks and stir into the cream, then pour over the parsnips. Grate over enough Parmesan and breadcrumbs to cover the surface lightly. Bake for forty to fifty minutes, by which time it should be bubbling and golden.

A soup of toasted roots with porcini toasts

Dried porcini are expensive, but even a small handful added to a soup will bring with it a wave of smoky, almost beefy notes. A general instruction with parsnip soup is to prevent the vegetables colouring, presumably to keep the soup pale, but I suggest the opposite. You want the parsnips to cook to a gentle golden colour before you add the stock; that way the soup will have a deeper flavour and a colour reminiscent of heather honey.

enough for 6
dried porcini mushrooms – a handful
onions – 2 medium
olive oil – 3 tablespoons
a large knob of butter
parsnips – 600g (2 large ones)
stock – 1.2 litres (Marigold or similar will do very well)
a stick of celery, chopped
garlic – a plump clove, peeled and squashed

for the porcini toasts
dried porcini mushrooms – a handful
the leaves from a small bunch of parsley
a small clove of garlic
walnuts – a handful, chopped
butter – 50g
interesting bread – 6 pieces, toasted

Soak the porcini in about 300ml warm water for thirty minutes.

Peel the onions, chop them roughly and put in a heavy-based pan with the oil and butter. Cook till soft and translucent, stirring regularly. Peel the parsnips and cut them into large chunks. Add them to the pan and let them colour lightly on all sides. They need to be evenly but gently toasted – a pale honey gold rather than mahogany brown. This will take seven to ten minutes with the occasional bit of stirring.

Pour in the stock, then add the celery, garlic, the porcini and their soaking water. Season and bring to the boil. Turn the heat down so that the soup simmers merrily for about forty minutes.

This is one of those soups that are best eaten smoothly puréed, so push it all through the blender till smooth. Check the seasoning; it may need more salt and pepper. Serve with the toasts below, if you wish.

To make the toasts, soak the porcini in warm water for half an hour. Squeeze dry, then chop together with the parsley and garlic. Stir in the walnuts. Melt the butter in a small pan, add the mixture and stir till warm and fragrant. Spoon on to the pieces of toast and float them on your soup.

A root vegetable korma

The kormas of India, serene, rich, silken, have much in them that works with the sweetness of the parsnip – cream, yoghurt, nuts, sweet spices. The Mughal emperors who originally feasted on such mildy spiced and lavishly finished recipes may not have approved of my introduction of common roots but the idea works well enough. Despite instructions the length of a short story, I can have this recipe on the table within an hour. For those who like their Indian food on the temperate side.

enough for 4 with rice or Indian breads
onions – 2 medium
ginger – a fat, thumb-sized piece
garlic – 3 cloves
a mixture of parsnip, swede, carrots, Jerusalem artichokes –
    1.5kg in total
cashews – 100g
green cardamom pods – 6
cumin seeds – 2 teaspoons
coriander seeds – 3 teaspoons
vegetable or sunflower oil, or butter – 2 tablespoons
ground turmeric – 2 teaspoons
chilli powder – half a teaspoon
a cinnamon stick
green chillies – 2 smallish ones, depending on their heat, thinly sliced
single or double cream – 150ml
thick natural yoghurt – 150g
fresh coriander, chopped

Peel the onions, cut them into large pieces, then blitz in a food processor till roughly minced – you don't want a sloppy purée. Peel and roughly grate the ginger on the coarse side of a grater. Peel and finely slice the garlic cloves. Peel and coarsely chop the vegetables. Roughly chop half of the cashews.

Now deal with the spices: open the cardamom pods with your nails and scrape out the seeds, then crush them to a gritty powder. Grind the cumin and coriander seeds to a fine powder.

Put the oil or butter into a deep, heavy-bottomed pan and stir in the onions, letting them soften but not colour. Stir in the grated ginger and sliced garlic, continue cooking over a gentle heat for a couple of minutes, then introduce the spices – cardamom, cumin, coriander, turmeric, chilli powder and the cinnamon stick. Continue cooking, stirring for a couple of minutes, until the fragrance of the spices begins to rise, then add the chopped root vegetables and the chopped nuts. Season with the thinly sliced chillies, salt and black pepper.

Stir in 750ml water, partially cover with a lid and leave to simmer gently for forty-five to fifty minutes, till the roots are tender to the point of a knife. Toast the reserved whole cashews.

Carefully introduce the cream and yoghurt to the pan, allowing them to heat through but not boil. Should the mixture boil, it will curdle, and though the flavour will be fine the grainy texture will be offputting. Check the seasoning, adding more salt or pepper if necessary. Scatter over the toasted cashews and some chopped coriander.

Another supper of young parsnips and sausage

At the top of the garden, past the sunny stone terrace, the little beds of vegetables and the unruly shrubs, is a thicket, less than three metres deep but just enough to give the whole garden an unkempt, relaxed feel. Here lie the compost bins with their lids of rotting carpet, green plastic bags of decaying leaf mould and four small trees of damson, hazel, mirabelle and a King James mulberry – the latter being a 'guardian' tree planted in the northernmost corner to protect the garden from the north wind. In between grow drifts of snowdrops, wild garlic sent by a friend from Cornwall and *fraises de bois*, with which this garden is littered, and whose flowers twinkle like tiny stars in spring.

The work in this part of the garden is mostly done in winter, if only because the leaflessness of the trees makes it possible to see what you are doing. It is always dark and cold here, and damp, too. I come in from turning the compost or cutting hazel twigs with my feet like ice, my fingers numb. Invariably it's a Saturday, when I have been early to The Ginger Pig for my sausages. I leave them to bake with parsnips and stock. A slow bowl of food, which often sits patiently till I come in, too chilled to the bone to do anything but eat.

> *enough for 4*
> onions – 4 medium
> groundnut oil – 3 tablespoons
> parsnips – 500g
> butcher's sausages – 6 thick, juicy ones
> thyme – a few sprigs
> chicken stock – 500ml

Set the oven at 190°C/Gas 5. Peel the onions and slice them in half from root to tip, then cut each half into six or eight pieces. Soften them slowly in the oil in a flameproof baking dish or roasting tin over a moderate heat.

While they are softening, peel the parsnips and cut them into short, thick chunks, about the length of a wine cork. Add them to the onions and leave to colour, turning up the heat a little if needs be. Remove the onions and parsnips from the pan.

Cut each sausage into three, put them in the pan, adding a little more oil if it appears dry, and let them colour. Return the onions and parsnips to the pan. It is important everything is a good colour before you proceed. Strip the leaves from the thyme and stir them in, together with the chicken stock. Bring to the boil briefly, then put in the oven to bake for thirty-five to forty minutes, until the sausages are cooked right through, the parsnips are truly tender and the stock has reduced a little.

Parsnips baked with cheese

It is often worth introducing some sort of richness to vegetables with a heart of starch. Ideal suitors include butter, cream, bacon fat and honey. Jane Grigson suggests cheese, often in the form of Gruyère or Parmesan, as do others, who have been known to roll a stiff parsnip mash in grated Parmesan and deep-fry it as a croquette. To this list I add my own, a shallow cake along the lines of a pan haggerty, made with thin slices of the root layered with grated cheese and herbs. Parsnip haggerty, anyone?

enough for 2 as a main dish, with winter salad at its side
a large onion
butter – 75g
parsnips – 2 large
thyme – the leaves from 3 or 4 sprigs
cheese – 100g, I use Cornish Yarg or sometimes Gruyère
vegetable stock – 100ml

Set the oven at 200°C/Gas 6. Peel the onion and cut it into paper-thin rings. Melt half the butter in a shallow ovenproof pan and gently fry the onion till soft and translucent. Stop before it colours.

Peel the parsnips and slice in fine discs. I like to make them so thin you can almost read through them. Tip the onion out of the pan, place a layer or two of parsnips in it, then brush with more melted butter and scatter over salt, pepper, some of the thyme and a little of the cheese. Do this twice more, ending with cheese. Pour over the stock.

Cover with lightly buttered greaseproof paper or foil, then place on a high shelf in the oven and bake for twenty-five to thirty minutes. Remove the paper and test the parsnips with a sharp knife; it should glide in effortlessly. Return to the oven, uncovered, for about ten minutes to brown. Serve straight from the pan.

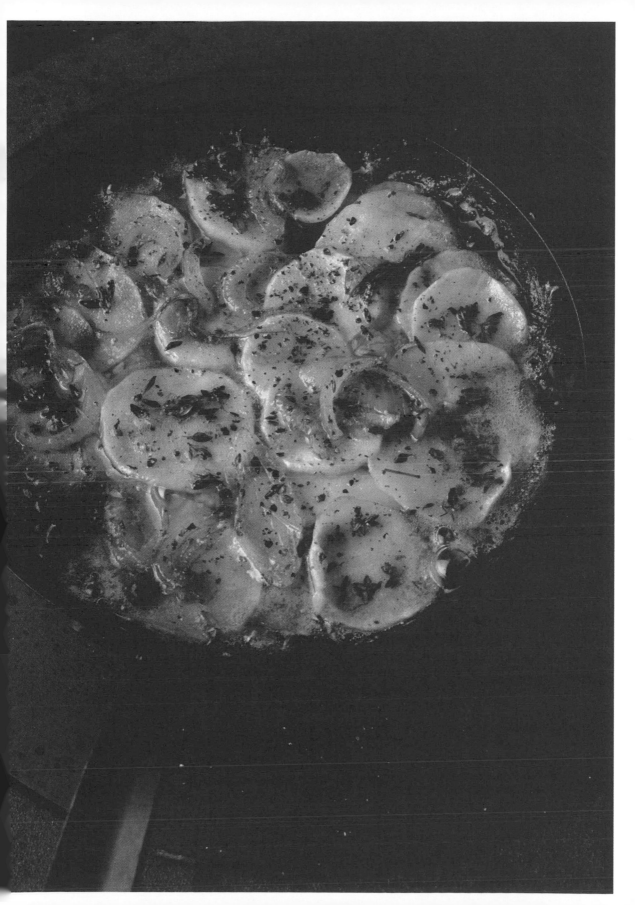

Peas

Walking around your garden or allotment at midnight is a gentle but sensuous pleasure, and never more so than in midsummer when the pea flowers, and those of the broad beans, shine as white as bone in the moonlight. Sometimes, just before I go to bed, I like to walk along the paths, the gravel crunching under my feet, taking in the eerie shadows cast by the crooked cane wigwams of climbing Viola Cornetti beans, their tendrils reaching out from the shadows. On a still night the scent of the roses is joined by that of the sweet peas – Cupani, Black Knight, the snow-white Dorothy Eckford – broad beans and jasmine. To burst a pod of peas and eat them in the dark is a sweet joy.

I am not sure how much space you need to be self-sufficient in peas, but more than any allotment or average garden can offer. No matter. The pleasure from a row or two held up with hazel canes and string, their young growing shoots whispering in the night, is enough to make the planting and potting and watering and podding worth every second of our time. And how could anyone fail to find romance in a pea called Serpette Guilloteau (named after a sickle-shaped pruning blade) or any one of the endless stories of 'mummy peas' that are rumoured to have originated – or not – in several of the Egyptian tombs? As if to fire our imaginations even further, there is an old variety named Tutankhamun.

You could, of course, open a bag. Frozen peas are a dependable delight. Though the pea has been dried, soaked and used as basic sustenance since earliest times – the poor ate them as a porridge, like a bland dhal – they have only been eaten fresh since the thirteenth century, when the Italians made them fashionable. The plants were, by all accounts, gangly specimens that required ladders for picking. Duke of Albany and the rarer Magnum Bonum are tall varieties still hanging on, being grown like runner beans, though they have generally been superseded by shorter varieties such as Hurst Greenshaft.

More peas are eaten raw than cooked in my house. They end up in salads of crab and coriander, or tucking themselves into the crevices of pale green Buttercrunch lettuce. Many are eaten straight from the pod. They don't age well, so I cook them the day they are picked, and certainly so if I have bought them from the greengrocer's. In truth, shop-bought peas can disappoint, but then maybe I'm unlucky, even though I always seek out plump pods that are bright green and unblemished.

The pea has a simple nature. In the garden, the plants like much moisture and a cool spot in which to grow; in the kitchen they can be boiled, preferably in deep, lightly salted water at a merry boil, and will cook in four or five minutes. Often less. Nothing good will come from getting convoluted with them. It is for their sweet simplicity that we value them.

The perfect pea

1970 and the lane down to Collins Green Farm is steep, on one side a meadow dotted with plantain and long-stemmed buttercups, the other a kitchen garden with broad beans, swaying hollyhocks and here and there discarded bikes with stabilisers and children's anoraks. Near the walls of the house itself is a stand of long canes, secured halfway with string, tightly bound against the wind. It is what I would expect runner beans to grow up.

The canes are full of peas, taller than usual, growing higher than even the tallest runner beans. No one knows the variety – it could well be Alderman, one of the few survivors of the many varieties of tall peas we once had, or Telegraph, Telephone or Duke of Albany, which can grow taller than a man. Being tall, they need more water than the dwarf varieties, but are less back-breaking to pick.

My trips down the lane were for bales of hay for my rabbit or for runner beans for tea, but sometimes I would come back with a basket of peas as a gift for my parents. Still wet with dew, they should have been the sweetest peas ever, but rarely matched those from the bag in the freezer.

Frozen peas never vary in sweetness or flavour. No vegetable is as successful at being bred for a consistent taste. They are never tough or sour or pallid, or just 'not the same'. The frozen pea is a testament to uniformity and reliability. Pity it so lacks romance.

A pea in the garden

Most crop twelve weeks after planting (plant in March or April, harvest in June and July), though this will vary according to variety and the conditions. You can plant outdoors in March and April if the ground is not too cold, in trenches 5cm deep and 10cm wide. Most experienced growers claim that peas do better when planted from early autumn onwards, giving an earlier and more reliable crop. They are not frost proof in the way of a broad bean, so unless you have somewhere cool and frost free to keep them till the ground has warmed up, spring planting may be a safer option.

A pea diary

April 6 I have a fancy to plant a row or two of peas, not purely for their pods but for their delicate, curling shoots and tendrils, which I find an extraordinary and enchanting addition to a salad. There is something fairylike about their presence in a bowl of early summer leaves, romantic wisps of palest green perched on top of all the other fronds and fragile greenery. The dressing must be so light as to seem almost non-existent. I wake to find a layer of thick snow has fallen during the night, turning my grubby, rundown corner of London into a scene of peace and piercing-white light. I long for these rare moments. Each shivering stamen on the white pear blossom outside the kitchen window is sparkling with flakes of freezing snow. A single set of prints tells that a brave bird came looking for crumbs early this morning.

By mid-afternoon the sun is on my back, shining so brightly I almost wish I were wearing a T-shirt, as I dib dried peas into pots of deep, wet compost. It's a risk – peas hate going into cold soil – but I am testing Douce Provence, an ancient French pea that is said to withstand frost and whose robust qualities belie the tenderness of its pods. Douce Provence is a forgotten pea, from a time when legumes were grown more for drying than for eating fresh. The habit of boiling fresh peas may well have been introduced by Catherine de Medici, whose gardeners are said to have brought them from Italy. Loving them the way we do (for some, peas are the only truly acceptable vegetable), it is a habit for which we should be more than grateful.

May 4 The plants, fragile, dull green leaves from cotton-thread stems, are already a good 2cm high. The ground they are to go in, on the cool side of the garden, has been dug, lightly manured and rested for six weeks. Now I cover it with a roll of garden fleece to keep it warm. Peas tend not to germinate in cold ground, but when the weather heats up they will value the moisture-retaining quality of cool, rich soil.

May 5 I plant Hurst Greenshaft, a more popular variety. A week later to the day, they are up too, their plump green tips unfurling. Many allotment holders will regard this as exceptionally late, peas hating the strong heat of summer, but I find they soon catch up with those you plant earlier.

May 28 Roots are showing through the bottoms of the pea pots. I move them to the bed, making two long, shallow trenches with a trowel (for want of a hoe), 20cm apart, then gently pushing each seedling into the soil, 2cm apart. Each plantlet gets its own stick, and here and there a brittle hazel twig, stripped of its leaves, to give it something interesting to climb. Chicken wire would work too, as would a cat's cradle of string. I water them in well.

May 31 Most peas of both varieties have survived, save a couple that lie in a dead faint. Several are bursting into flower. Pale, ivory-white blooms against fine, twining stems.

June 25 We pick the first peas and their tendrils, splitting the pods with a childish pop, then worrying the contents out with our thumbs. They never make it as far as the kitchen.

Varieties

Hatif d'Annonay Small bushes that need little support. Dark green pods with smooth seeds. Sow and pick early.

Amelioree d'Auvergne Early or maincrop pea with short, plump pods held on plants just over a metre high.

Pilot A tall, fast-growing pea for planting in autumn or early April.

Alderman One of the few tall varieties left, growing to six feet or more. Good flavour but won't hold up in a drought.

Early Onward Early, bushy variety with excellent flavour.

Feltham First Short-growing, very early pea, but needs picking whilst young.

Kelvedon Wonder Good flavour, a much loved favourite of many allotment holders.

Little Marvel A reliable, early-maturing dwarf pea, good for those with limited space.

Hurst Greenshaft Along with Kelvedon, one of the most popular and flavoursome varieties. Long pods and good cropping from plants about 60cm high.

Other reliable varieties are the heavy-cropping Lincoln and Onward, a delectably sweet pea that is probably the widest grown. The mangetout pea is not for me. I find it tastes more of sugar than of pea, but those who like its flat, pale crunch could do worse than grow Carouby de Maussane, sweet pea pods with brilliant purple flowers, or Dwarf Sweet Green – a variety that lives up to its name.

A pea in the kitchen

Tiny peas straight from their pods need three minutes in frantically boiling water. That's all. I never salt them. Ready-shelled fresh peas from the supermarket provide the most instant gratification in the vegetable world, but in our house rarely make it to the pot, being eaten straight from the bag like vegetable Smarties.

Peas destined for a risotto can be added at two specific points. First, just before the rice, giving them time to truly flavour the dish, and second, about five minutes before the risotto is due to finish cooking, offering a sparkle of fresh pea flavour. That way, you get both depth of flavour and freshness, but you also get two distinctly different shades of pea.

For emerald soups (of lettuce and bacon or spinach), the peas need little more than seven to ten minutes if they are added with the onion base, before the stock. They work well enough when chucked raw into the filling for a chicken or fish pie but should be cooked in boiling water before being tossed into a dish of freshly drained pasta. I don't add them to a stir-fry. They like a bit more moisture to cook in than such a recipe has to offer. Peas and chopsticks are an accident waiting to happen.

To purée them, I use a food processor or a blender, adding olive oil or melted butter to speed the process. To crush them for a rougher texture, I find a potato masher or fork helpful.

Seasoning your peas

The pea shares its Christmas card list with the broad bean, numbering bacon and smoked pork products as its best mates. It has many close friends; indeed, it is difficult to think of anything it doesn't get on with.

Pancetta Warm cubes of pancetta or smoked bacon in a shallow pan till the fat is gold, then stir in freshly cooked peas. Serve with cauliflower cheese or a similar comfort supper.

Cheese A controversial marriage this, but I stand by it. Feta, in jagged pieces, chalky goat's cheeses and thick, quivering slices of buffalo mozzarella all work well with the pea's sugary notes. Others claim that peas in a Cheddar cheese sauce as a side dish for bacon or gammon makes the heart sing, but I have yet to try it.

Lemon A revelation. Shake cooked peas in a pan with a liquid seasoning of lemon juice, finely grated zest and olive oil. A lively addition to a plate of steamed halibut, grilled plaice or fish fingers.

Lettuce The classic recipe of *petits pois à la française* involves simmering soft-leaved lettuce with fresh peas till the peas are dull green and soft. The two make a curiously moreish marriage, rich and yet homely.

Mint Yes, I know it's unfashionable. Do I care? No. This is the number-one herb for the pea, although basil comes in a surprising second. Mint goes in the water as they cook; basil is best shredded and mixed with the melted butter you will toss them in.

And...

* While it is difficult to find anything that a spoonful of peas would not grace, it is worth making sure that we experience them with some of the ingredients whose sweetness they flatter most. Young lamb, battered cod, grilled plaice, poached ham, salmon in any guise, goat's cheese are all enhanced by our little green ones.

* I often don't put the peas into the boiling water until the meat is resting on the (warm) plates. I have known the tiny petits pois variety to be done in the time it takes me to carry the plates to the table.

* Peas do like a knob of butter when they are cooked, but increasingly I find they also lap up melted bacon fat. It's a pukka marriage and you can add them, straight from the boil, to a pan in which you have fried a rasher or two of streaky.

* Peas and new potatoes don't appear on the same plate just because they share a season but because the sweet greens and nutty potatoes form a thoroughly pleasing partnership in the mouth. Some might say inseparable.

* Don't put peas in a quiche. They may go nicely with a ham or crab filling but they make the custard fall apart. Not to mention the fact that a spotty quiche looks a bit silly.

* Peas are not always the easiest things to get from plate to mouth. At home I was taught to mush them on to the back of my fork with my knife. Now no one is looking, I use my fork as a shovel. I lose fewer that way. Others, perhaps a little greedily, use a spoon. Ideally, serve them with something they will stick to, like steamed fish and parsley sauce, roast beef and horseradish, even a dab of mashed potato.

A salad of beans, peas and pecorino

Amongst the charcoal and garlic of midsummer's more robust cooking, a quiet salad of palest green can come as a breath of calm. Last June, as thousands joined hands around Stonehenge in celebration of the summer solstice, I put together a salad of cool notes: mint, broad beans and young peas – a bowl of appropriate gentility and quiet harmony.

enough for 4
shelled broad beans – 250g
shelled peas – 400g
ciabatta – 4 small slices
a little olive oil
salad leaves – 4 generous handfuls
mint leaves – a good handful
pecorino sardo cheese – 80g, in thin shavings

for the dressing
a lemon
olive oil (fruity and peppery) – 4 tablespoons
balsamic vinegar – a teaspoon

Put a pan of water on to boil, then salt it lightly. Cook the beans in this, drain them, then rinse in cold water. Put more water on and cook the peas. Drain them and mix with the beans. Both peas and beans will need barely more than a couple of minutes if they are small and sweet.

Make the dressing by dissolving a good pinch of salt in the juice of the lemon, then using a fork to beat in the olive oil, balsamic vinegar and a grinding of black pepper (alternatively put all the ingredients in a screw-top jar and shake).

Toast the slices of bread on both sides and tear them into short pieces. Drizzle a little olive oil on to each one, then shake over a light dusting of sea salt.

Toss the salad leaves and mint in the dressing, then add the peas, beans and pecorino shavings. Tuck in the toasted ciabatta and serve.

Peas with parsley and artichoke hearts

Nowhere does the flavour of two separate vegetables come together as successfully as when peas and globe artichokes are combined. There are, I believe, flavours that are destined to spend some time together, and these are two of them. Gentle and uncomplicated, a quick stew of peas and artichoke hearts makes a curiously pleasing lunch with some open-textured, flour-dusted bread.

    I have made this with both fresh artichoke hearts and the ready-prepared ones from the deli counter and I must say there is rather less difference than one might imagine.

enough for 4
olive oil – 120ml
young garlic – 4 cloves
prepared artichoke hearts – 450g
the juice of half a lemon
shelled peas – 350g
thyme leaves – a tablespoon or so
parsley – a small handful, roughly chopped

Warm the olive oil in a large pan, peel the garlic and add it to the pan. Cook over a moderate heat for a minute or two, until the garlic is fragrant but not coloured. Cut the artichokes hearts into quarters and add them to the pot with the lemon juice and peas. Throw in the thyme and continue cooking over a medium heat for ten minutes. Season with the parsley and some salt and black pepper. Continue cooking for two or three minutes, then serve in bowls, with hunks of open-textured bread.

Minted pea purée

shelled peas – 400g
mint – 4 sprigs
olive oil – 3 tablespoons

Boil the peas and mint sprigs in lightly salted water till tender, then drain. Whiz the peas and mint in a food processor with the oil till smooth.

A lamb steak with peas and mint

It's mid June and I have returned home with four lamb steaks. It's the sort of thing I buy when my mind is elsewhere. I think I was after a 'nothing-special' lunch of ease and straightforwardness, yet once the steaks and their fine frame of white fat had been brushed with olive oil and the leaves and flowers of thyme and were sizzling on the blackened garden grill, I realised I had an extraordinary treat on my hands. Instead of a mound of petits pois at the lamb's side, I blitzed the peas to a smooth purée with mint and melted butter.

enough for 4
thyme – 6 bushy sprigs
a little olive oil
lamb steaks – 4, or 12 small cutlets

for the pea purée
shelled peas – 400g
mint – 4 sprigs
melted butter – 4 tablespoons

optional
pea shoots – 4 small handfuls
extra virgin olive oil

Chop the thyme, then mash it in a pestle and mortar with a large pinch of salt. Stir in the olive oil and a grinding of pepper. Brush over the lamb and set aside for thirty minutes.

Boil the peas in lightly salted water till tender. Meanwhile, put the mint leaves, butter and a pinch of salt into a blender or food processor and whiz till smooth. Drain the peas and whiz them in the blender or processor with the mint butter until you have a thick, green cream. If you need to keep it warm, put it in a basin covered with foil in a pan of hot water.

Grill the lamb on both sides till the outside has crisped and the inside is still rose pink and juicy. Depending on the thickness of your lamb and the heat of your grill, this will take about four minutes on each side.

Divide the pea cream between four warm plates. Place the cooked lamb on top, then a handful of pea shoots on the lamb. Shake a little olive oil over the lamb and pea shoots and serve.

A salad of hot bacon, lettuce and peas

Anyone who has podded a bag of peas will know how good they are raw.
Far too little is made of their scrunchy sweetness, and I put forward the
pod-fresh raw pea as an idea to throw into salads of pale yellow butterhead
lettuce, cracked wheat or dishes of cooked broad beans. They work in their
uncooked state only when very young and small. Old peas are mealy and
sour. One rainy lunchtime in June, I put them into a simple salad of Peter
Rabbit lettuce, crisply cooked smoked bacon and hand-torn ciabatta. The
result – restrained, refreshing and somehow quintessentially English.

enough for 4
smoked streaky bacon – 8 rashers
a little oil
white bread – 150g
a large, soft-leaved lettuce
a small bulb of fennel
podded peas – 150g

for the dressing
Dijon mustard – a teaspoon
red wine vinegar – a tablespoon
olive oil – 4 tablespoons

Trim the bacon and discard its rind. Cut it into short lengths and cook in a
non-stick pan, with a little oil if necessary, till crisp. Remove the bacon from
the pan and drain on kitchen paper.

Tear the bread into small, jagged-edged pieces, discarding the crusts
as you go. Fry in the pan in which you cooked the bacon, adding more oil
as necessary. As soon as the pieces are nicely golden and blessed with the
flavour of the smoked bacon, remove to kitchen paper to drain and salt
them lightly.

Whilst the bread and bacon are cooking, wash the lettuce, separate the
leaves, tear them into manageable pieces and put them in a serving bowl.
Finely shred the fennel and toss it into the lettuce leaves with the peas. Make
the dressing by mixing the mustard, vinegar, a grinding of salt and pepper
and the oil in a small bowl or shaking them together in a small jar.

Put the hot bacon and bread in the salad, gently toss with the dressing,
then serve immediately.

Peppers

Without heat – from a grill, an oven, a cast-iron pan blackened with age – there is little point to the pepper. Raw, green and unripe, its waxy, plastic skin and lack of obvious juice offer little but crisp nothingness. Refreshing, yes, but somehow an imposter in a green salad; an annoying intruder in a Bloody Mary; an unimaginative addition to a rice dish. Wherever it appears, the raw green pepper seems uncomfortable.

Left to ripen to a sunset orange or scarlet (a few varieties remain green even when ripe), then blistered over a hot flame or baked in a scorching oven, the pepper will show us its true heart and soul. By roasting or grilling, we do more than soften it, we create sweet juice with notes of caramel, tomato, honey and smoke. The crisp shell relaxes to the texture of soft, moist flesh. Our 'crisp nothingness' becomes the most tender and sensuous of vegetables.

The variety we know intimately, the bell pepper or capsicum, was originally Mexican, though the recipes we use tend to originate in the Middle East, the Mediterranean or Eastern Europe. It is a fruit really, though we eat it as a vegetable, and a member of the nightshade family, along with the potato, aubergine and the smaller, hot chillies. In mid August we get the home-grown ones, twisted like a sultan's slipper; difficult to stuff neatly but more interesting than the bell pepper of dumpy uniformity. Horn-shaped varieties offer more of a clue to the fact that they are sisters to the chilli, but there is no heat here, just slinky, silky flesh and a shape that begs more than anything else in the vegetable rack to be used to carry a cargo of spicily seasoned grain.

Stuffing aside, the pepper's proudest moment must be when it has been grilled or baked, stripped of its blackened skin, then laid in long, blood-red strips on an earthenware dish. Moistened with a bright, fruity olive oil and seasoned with the occasional slice of new, mild garlic and some torn basil, the pepper carries with it an almost erotic pleasure.

A pepper in the garden

The pepper only just survives the British climate. Night temperatures need to be above 20°C for the seedlings to endure. In this country they will need glass to protect them, but as the bushes get stronger you can plant them outside. Mature plants do well in large pots, polytunnels, growbags, and especially with their backs against a heat-retaining wall. If you can grow tomatoes, you can grow peppers.

Experts recommend planting seed in late winter, at a minimum soil temperature of 20°C. Use a thermometer rather than making an attempt to guess. Having no indoor growing space, I have yet to grow any from seed. My plants tend to arrive as 'plugs' in late spring, and remain in 9cm pots in the cold frame till early summer. I don't pinch out the tips as others do, but give them a high-nitrogen feed at this point. I transfer them to deep, 30cm pots once their roots have filled the small pots. They spend their days and nights on the stone steps near the house, their heavy harvest and thin stems supported on sticks, soaking up the residual heat. Once the flowers appear, the plants like good ventilation and an occasional feed with liquid fertiliser (I use bog-standard tomato food). They need plenty of late summer sun, more so than tomatoes, if they are to ripen, and – if you can find such a thing nowadays – the odd sprinkle of Epsom salts to quench their thirst for magnesium.

Varieties

I buy my plug plants ready for potting on, from a catalogue that includes
the following:

Ace An unusually good-tempered variety that ripens even in the coolest
of summers.

Gourmet Snooty name, but hides a glowing, orange pepper with a good,
long season.

Gypsy Narrow, bell-shaped, orange-red pepper.

Giant Szegedi Popular Hungarian variety with high yields that will
probably need support. Its thick flesh makes it sound for stuffing.

Red Knight Early ripening and forgiving of the British summer.

Bounty Long, slender, deep-red pepper that lives up to its name.

A pepper in the kitchen

A latecomer to the British kitchen, *Capsicum annum* is still rarely used
as the principal ingredient in a meal. The 1960s and '70s were a time of
culinary adventure, a discovering and celebration of the heady flavours
of the Mediterranean and, with it, the red pepper. Elizabeth David's books,
written a decade earlier, became the blueprint for restaurants such as
the Elizabeth in Oxford and the Hole in the Wall in Bath, whose menus
consecrated the warm flavours of olive oil, aubergines, basil and ripe peppers
that are now firmly a part of Britain's diet.

From Mrs David's books and these pioneering kitchens came piperade,
a dish of eggs and sautéed peppers, which I never made, and gazpacho, a
chilled vermillion soup of finely hashed cucumber, garlic, tomatoes and red
peppers, which I did. With its raw garlic and pimento, I remember it as a
fiery, heart-pounding soup, an open window to the passionate flavours of
its homeland.

In the 1980s Britain's chefs discovered the 'coulis', a thin, brightly
coloured liquor somewhere between juice and purée, which modern-
thinking French chefs were using to accompany a piece of meat or fish.
The coulis – of anything from tomato to raspberry – was drizzled like an
edible moat around (rather than over) noisettes of lamb, fillets of salmon
and fanned-out duck breasts. In some establishments the moat itself would
be dotted with artfully turned vegetables and even flowers. A passing
culinary fad, whose positive legacy has been to encourage a lighter style of
cooking. The red pepper, perhaps because of its vibrant colour, became the
most ubiquitous coulis of all. In theory, the idea of using a thin sauce of red
pepper to flatter a filo pastry parcel of ratatouille seems sound enough. The
flavours should sit together happily but the effect was effete and contrived.
A proud fruit humiliated.

Of all the luscious, sun-soaked recipes we have borrowed from the Med, peppers Piedmontese, with its flashes of orange, pillar-box red and deep olive green, is the one in which the pepper shows us what it is truly made of. No treatment quite gets this fruit to shine like roasting it with olive oil and a hint of anchovy. I don't always include the little fish. I add basil leaves to the open halves of pepper too, so that the copious olive oil, nuggets of garlic and tomatoes tucked inside feel at home. It is a fragrant kitchen the day we have *peperoni alla Piemontese* for lunch.

Elizabeth David wrote of this vivacious dish a few years before I was born. Delia Smith made it a star of the 1990s dinner party. But in our house it is one of those dishes that appears, oblivious to fashion, in late summer and early autumn – made with the fat, barrel-shaped ripe peppers that turn up in the organic box – sometimes in the classical form, other times with a basil dressing poured in at the very end of cooking. Sometimes it shows up with a slice or two of mozzarella and on other occasions with the anchovy reinstated. It's a humble dish, yet pulsating with the flavours of another place, another climate – an edible postcard from headier, sun-soaked kitchens.

In the autumn of 1988 I went from being someone who could take or leave these red and green fruits to someone who craved them as others might a steak, and a bloody one at that. I was casting around for vegetables to roast. The peppers' startling colours caught my eye. I tucked them whole, stalks intact, in amongst the aubergines and tomatoes. They went into the oven and then by chance I forgot them (a clear case of 'out of sight, out of mind'). The dish that emerged looked at first like burnt offerings but was to change everything, opening up a whole new chapter of deliciousness.

Externally, the capsicums had blackened, one step away from charcoal. Inside, however, was a different story. Their flesh was slithery and a deep, angry red, at once smoky and sweet, and beguilingly delicious. I have 'overcooked' my peppers ever since.

Seasoning your peppers

Tomato Offers the piquancy missing in the pepper's sweet flesh. Use as a stuffing instead of minced meat.

Basil The pepper's best friend. The combination, especially when olive oil and garlic are invited along, is the essence of the Mediterranean.

Warm, sweet spices Cinnamon, cumin, cardamom and allspice work nicely in starchy stuffings, making the pepper feel very much at home.

Anchovies The salty, oily quality of this little fish has a natural affinity for the pepper.

Garlic Roasted, the caramel notes of garlic blend almost perfectly with that of the roasted pepper. Raw, they can both be indigestible.

Goat's cheese The sharp tingle of acidity in a slice of chèvre is a welcome contrast to the sweetness of a cooked pepper.

Vinegar Use a little more than usual in a dressing destined for grilled pepper. It will make the fruit's natural sugar sing.

And…

* Pepper plants are tricky to raise at home. I sometimes buy a couple of relatively mature plants from the farmers' market in early summer. They stand a better chance of survival.

* If summer is especially wet or miserable, peppers simply won't ripen. They need our sunniest corner.

* Keep the plants well ventilated and avoid putting them in a humid atmosphere. They will rot if kept too damp.

* Roast peppers in their skins, letting them go almost black. Put the roasted peppers in a bowl, cover tightly with clingfilm or a plastic bag and leave for fifteen minutes before peeling off the skin with your fingers. You will be left with pieces of soft, skinless pepper for dressing with olive oil and basil.

* Red, yellow and orange peppers are considerably sweeter than green ones. Those who usually find peppers indigestible may have no problem with the ripe, red roasted fruit.

Baked peppers for a summer lunch

My version of classic Italian baked peppers, but without the anchovies and with a last-minute stirring in of basil. There are some gorgeous flavours here, especially when the tomato juices mingle with the basil oil.

enough for 4
large peppers – 4
small or cherry tomatoes – 12–16
olive oil
basil leaves – a couple of handfuls

Set the oven at 200°C/Gas 6. Cut the peppers in half lengthways and discard the seeds and white core. Put the halved peppers, cut-side up, in a roasting tin or baking dish. Cut the tomatoes into halves or quarters, depending on their size, and season with salt and black pepper. Divide between the peppers. Pour a little olive oil into each pepper and bake until the tomatoes and peppers are lusciously soft, about forty-five minutes to an hour.

Blitz the basil leaves and about 70ml olive oil in a blender (sometimes I use a pestle and mortar), then pour into the peppers. The basil dressing will mingle with the warm tomato juices.

Stuffed peppers for an autumn day

Rice has for centuries been the obvious contender for stuffing a pepper – and indeed aubergines or a beefsteak tomato – flavoured with caramelised onions, golden sultanas and musky raisins and seasoned with capers, anchovies, cinnamon or cumin. Small grains – cracked wheat, brown rice, the underused quinoa – are eminently suitable fillings, as is any type of small bean, lentil or the plump, pearl-shaped couscous known as mograbiah. Vegetable stuffings can set the pepper alight. Piercing, cherry-sized tomatoes, such as Sungold or Gardener's Delight, or chunks of sweet steamed pumpkin offer more than just jewel colours to lift the spirits. They have a brightness of flavour very different from the humble, homely grains. They offer a change of step. A few hand-torn chunks of mozzarella and some olive oil will produce a seductive filling. Minced beef, the knee-jerk filling, somehow makes my heart sink.

Mograbiah, sometimes known as pearl couscous, takes the idea on a bit, having the comforting, frugal qualities of rice but possessing an extraordinary texture, poised between pasta and couscous. Made of wheat and sometimes known as fregola, it is available from Middle Eastern grocer's shops.

enough for 4
medium to large ripe peppers – 4

for the stuffing
mograbiah (pearl couscous) – 200g
olive oil
spring onions – 6
garlic – 2 cloves, sliced
ground paprika – half a teaspoon
the grated zest and juice of half a lemon
mint leaves – a large handful, chopped
coriander leaves – a large handful, chopped
pine nuts – 75g, toasted

for the yoghurt sauce
thick yoghurt – 200g
coriander and mint – a handful each, chopped
a pinch of paprika

To make the stuffing, cook the mograbiah in plenty of well-salted boiling water (use the same amount of salt you would to cook pasta) for about fifteen minutes, till tender. Drain and toss lightly with a little olive oil to stop the 'pearls' sticking together.

Meanwhile, finely chop the spring onions, discarding only the very darkest of the green shoots, and let them soften over a moderate heat in a glug or two of olive oil. Just before they start to colour, add the garlic, then the paprika and the grated lemon zest. Stir in the chopped herbs and the toasted pine nuts. When all is fragrant and starting to darken a little in colour, stir in the drained mograbiah and the lemon juice. Season carefully.

Set the oven at 180°C/Gas 4. Cut the peppers in half, tug out the seeds and cores and lay the halves cut-side up in a baking tin. Pile the filling into the peppers, drizzle over a little more olive oil and cover loosely with foil. Bake for about forty-five minutes, until sizzling.

To make the sauce, mix the yoghurt with the herbs, paprika and a grinding of black pepper. Spoon it over the peppers at the table.

Peppers with pork and rosemary

The deep sweetness of a roasted pepper makes it a suitable candidate for an exceptionally savoury filling. I have tried several over the years: beef with cinnamon and tomato; minced chicken, lemon and chillies; and more recently mozzarella and cherry tomatoes. Each had its merits, especially the latter with its tart juices. The latest manifestation of the stuffed pepper in my kitchen is one of highly seasoned minced pork with rosemary, Parmesan and garlic. I think of it as the best yet.

enough for 4
a large onion
olive oil – 2 tablespoons, and a little more
garlic – 2 cloves
rosemary – 3 bushy sprigs
large tomatoes – 2
minced pork – 350g
breadcrumbs – 50g
small red peppers – 6
grated Parmesan

Set the oven at 200°C/Gas 6. Peel and finely chop the onion, then put it into a large, shallow pan with the oil over a moderate heat. Let the onion soften without colouring. Peel and slice the garlic, chop the leaves from the sprigs of rosemary and add to the onion. When all is soft and fragrant, chop the tomatoes and stir them in. Continue cooking until the tomatoes have collapsed into the sauce. Season with salt and black pepper, then stir in the minced pork and the breadcrumbs. Remove from the heat.

Cut the peppers in half lengthways, remove the seeds, then lower them into a pan of boiling water and cook for six to eight minutes, until they are slightly limp. Remove them with a draining spoon and put them skin-side down in a baking dish.

Divide the pork mixture between the peppers, then moisten with a little olive oil. Scatter grated Parmesan over the top and bake for thirty-five minutes, till sizzling.

A handful of stuffings for baked peppers

* Onions softened till sweet and golden, then stirred into cooked brown rice, sultanas and toasted almonds. Season with allspice, dillweed, black pepper and cinnamon.

* Simmered green lentils seasoned with mashed roasted garlic, spring onions and mushrooms that you have sautéed till sticky. Season with sherry vinegar, lemon juice, cinnamon and parsley.

* Onions softened in butter, then stirred through with cooked pearl barley, sautéed mushrooms, chopped preserved lemon, thyme, a little garlic and parsley. Dot with butter before baking.

* Steamed couscous seasoned with fried onion, raisins, toasted pine nuts, cinnamon, ground cardamom and toasted garlic. At the table, drizzle with yoghurt into which you have stirred coriander leaf, olive oil and fresh mint.

* Mozzarella, torn into chunks, pushed into the open pepper halves with cherry tomatoes, fresh basil, olive oil, black olives and chopped anchovy, then baked till fragrant.

A Hungary-inspired stew for the depths of winter

Peppers, the red, collapsed horns in particular, are heavily linked with Hungary and its rust-coloured stews. The Hungarians make ground paprika from them too, which has become their most famous culinary export. Despite their South American origins, Hungary is where I have found the most dazzling displays of capsicums in the shops.

Two minutes, even less, from the river and the Szabadsag Bridge, Budapest's market stalls glow deep rust and gold with tins of paprika and strings of dried mahogany chillies. I love the crumbling wooden stalls of scarlet-capped mushrooms with their stray pieces of iridescent moss, wicker baskets of black sloes and small sacks of red berries, and the apparently precarious piles of peppers, Christmas red, clean white and burnt orange turning scarlet.

The long peppers that curl back on themselves have the intrigue of Aladdin's lamp but are awkward in the kitchen, tending to tip their stuffing out into the baking tin. You can roast them, though, with olive oil and lots of salt, and eat them with sesame bread torn into chunks.

The most useful, called Gypsy and the size of a fat rodent, are perfect for stuffing: with spinach and cream; translucent onions, capers, parsley and garlic; cracked wheat, green olives and toasted pine kernels; minced lamb and cumin. But mostly they are baked with a shake of the olive oil bottle and a grinding of salt till they collapse, wrinkle and melt into silken strips. You'll need bread then, in fat, rough chunks, and maybe a glass of bright beer.

From August to the close of the year is when the market has the most from which to choose. After that the peppers come dried, in long strings of tobacco, madder and soot. They shouldn't be despised. By then the stalls are mostly piled with roots and cabbages, endless sausages and wholesomely fatty pork. The paprika stalls, stacked with red and gold tins, are kitsch in a Hansel and Gretel way, their shelves covered in fastidiously ironed lace, like the old women who run them.

Gulyas, or goulash, means 'cowboy' and was traditionally cooked over an open fire. My paprika-scented pork stew – you could use beef – departs not too radically from the classical dish. I include dried mushrooms and cook it in a low oven, giving it a particularly deep, smoky flavour.

enough for 4
medium onions – 3
olive oil or dripping – 2 tablespoons
a medium-sized hot chilli
sweet paprika – a heaped tablespoon
cubed pork (shoulder or leg) – 800g
plain flour – a tablespoon
dried porcini or other dried mushrooms –
   a handful, soaked in 400ml warm water for an hour
large, mild red peppers – 2
plum tomatoes – 400g can
stock, white wine or, if nothing else, water – 200ml
caraway seeds – a level teaspoon
soured cream – 100ml
wide noodles or boiled potatoes, to serve

Set the oven at 140°C/Gas 1. Peel and thickly slice the onions and soften them slowly in the melted fat in a deep, heavy-based pan – they should be soft and crushable, and a pale, appetising gold. Chop and seed the chilli, stir it into the onions with the ground paprika and cook for a minute or two. Remove from the pan and set aside, leaving behind any fat you can. Turn the heat up a little, add the cubed meat to the pan and let it colour on all sides, adding more fat if you need to.

Return the onions to the pan, sprinkle over the flour, cook briefly, then stir in the mushrooms and their soaking liquor. Halve and seed the peppers, cut each half into three and stir them in together with the tomatoes, liquid and caraway seeds. Bring everything to an enthusiastic simmer, season generously with salt, then cover with a lid and transfer to the oven. Leave it, unpestered, for a good hour and a half. Remove from the oven, check the meat for tenderness and remove some of the fat from the surface. Pour the soured cream over the top and stir once so that the surface is merely rippled with the cream. Serve with the noodles or potatoes.

Potatoes

The flowers of the potato, delicate petals whose stamens bunch together to form a point, are amongst the most charming in the vegetable garden. Marie Antoinette wore them in her hair. The flowers of the Salad Blue are perhaps the most beautiful of all, an ethereal lavender and white, with deep orange-gold stamens often heavy with pollen. Charlotte, a soft candy pink; Kestrel, a piercing lilac and white. Summer rain and even cloud makes their flowers close and droop like a swan in repose. As dusk falls, they gently close.

Once you have seen the delicacy of the potato's blossom you feel differently about what lies beneath the soil. In late summer, when you unearth the early, pale yellow Duke of York, the ivory-skinned Pentland Javelin or the creamy Snowdrop, you do so with a certain tenderness, brushing the soil from their thin skins as gently as you might wipe the tears from a child's cheek. The idea of throwing them around the way Alf the greengrocer does suddenly seems as wrong as putting a box of eggs at the bottom of your shopping bag.

One of the more extraordinary details of my garden is its potato bed. Two metres square, surrounded by a tightly clipped box hedge, it is on the cool side of the garden and is damp enough never to need watering. Against all sensible advice, it is heavily sheltered by a six-year-old medlar tree. What is more, the soil can be heavy, a tad claggy even. And yet, potatoes work well for me here. Having such success with them has been one of the greatest joys of 'growing your own'. I would probably plant them even if I didn't eat them, if only to give them away.

So firmly do potatoes feel part of our culinary heritage that it is odd to think that we had none till they came over in the cargo holds of Spanish ships in the late 1500s. Medieval Britain had no potatoes at all (nor carrots, parsnips or many other roots) and it is hard to think of our diet without these beloved lumps of starch. *Solanum tuberosum* was first cultivated in the Andes, and was treated with suspicion when it arrived in Europe because of the flowers' similarity to those of the deadly nightshade plant. They are indeed from the same family.

That we love the potato so much is partly down to its versatility and, it must be said, its ability to fill us up cheaply. Potatoes calm and comfort, satisfy and satiate us, but in truth they have little nutritional merit. Yes, the public relations people can scrape around for the presence of vitamin C and a few minerals but the real reason we eat so many is simply because of their power to soothe and fill.

Apart from a freshly dug tuber, steamed and eaten for its earthy taste, we tend to take our tatties with fat. Boiled and buttered, mashed with milk, baked in cream, smothered in cheese, fried in oil, tossed in mayonnaise – be it a single potato crisp or a spoonful of *pommes à la dauphinoise*, fat and the potato go hand in hand. Even the celebrated Jersey gets its time-honoured brushing of melted butter or – heaven forbid – marge. Fat, in one form or another, makes the potato tempting.

The humble spud really got into its stride during the eighteenth century, and it is that period that gave us many of the dishes we still enjoy today. The French, who initially banned them, developed most of the lexicon of classic potato recipes (the Italians were slightly less gung-ho, perhaps because they had their own favoured carbs). Whilst French cooks baked them in stock, fried them to a crisp and let them tenderise in a slow oven with thick cream and garlic, we simply boiled them. Whether they were large, small, new or maincrop, we took our starchy tubers cooked in boiling, salted water.

This is one vegetable that is losing its popularity. Yes, we are eating food from other cuisines, and growing and eating many new vegetables and fruits, but the real reason is our gradual slide towards eating less starch. The nutritionists' disdain of 'empty calories' has done the spud no favours at all. They are one of the first foods to be removed from most weight-loss diets. Chips and crisps are blamed for childhood obesity rather than the more obvious lack of exercise.

I see only good coming from this movement away from having a pile of potatoes on our plate. From it will come a new appreciation of an ingredient whose qualities have long been measured only in quantity. We shall learn that this vegetable is so much more interesting than simply a 'filler', that it is something whose character can vary dramatically according to season and variety. A vegetable to be explored with a new vigour. It may yet be seasoned as much with restraint as with fat. That said, I will happily eat a plate of *pommes à la dauphinoise* with simply a green salad at its side. I just wouldn't do it every day.

Varieties

Potatoes are divided into two main groups, earlies and maincrop. The first can be referred to as either first earlies or second earlies, according to when they are ready. You can pick them as soon as the flowers appear. Maincrop potatoes, which I tend to start eating in late summer, can be dug up once their stems have collapsed and started to die down.

The variety of potato will, to a certain degree, decide what we use them for. Those with a dry texture will make a light mash or roast crisply but will fall apart in salads. Waxy-fleshed varieties will make a gluey mash but hold together in the rough and tumble of a salad. In no other vegetable are the varieties so distinct from one another. Like grapes, a tuber's flavour will be affected not only by the variety but also by the soil and the climate in which it was grown. In general, cold climates tend to produce a more interesting-tasting spud, which may well be why so many of our best-loved names hail from Scotland.

The early potatoes have a thin-skinned delicacy to them and a nutty sweetness. They are what we call 'new' potatoes, and rarely need peeling (though are very elegant when you scrape them to shed their flaky skins). Rarely larger than a hen's egg, some of them have a waxy quality that makes them appealing in a salad. They take on a pleasing fudgy texture when sautéed in butter and can even be roasted, the sticky gloss that accumulates on their young skins only adding to their pleasure.

Varieties to look for in late spring and early summer

Duke of York A Scottish variety bred by William Simi in 1891, with floury flesh and exceptionally fine flavour. A very good roaster.
Epicure Introduced in 1901 by Charles Sharp, this almost pear-shaped 'early' has smooth skin with a waxy texture and good flavour. It remains a classic in Scottish gardens.
International Kidney (called 'Jerseys' when grown there) Despite the drone of those who insist they 'don't taste like they used to', the Jersey, when properly grown and dug young, is a good, waxy little spud. Left in the ground, it becomes floury with age.
Edzell Blue Bright, violet-blue skin, white flowers and floury flesh.
Kestrel A creamy yellow, oval potato with purple-blue eyes, which roasts, fries and chips well. A joy to grow.
British Queen Another Scottish variety with a good dry texture and excellent earthy flavour. Archibald Findlay's Victorian masterpiece makes some of the best mash.
Charlotte A waxy variety with excellent flavour.
Belle de Fontenay An old French variety, kidney shaped and slightly curved, with waxy flesh. Very nice cold, when its deep flavour really shines.

Snowdrop Sometimes called Witch Hill, a white potato with slightly waxy flesh and a fine, earthy flavour. A medium-sized potato, good for boiling or roasting.

Kerr's Pink A Scottish variety with pale pink skin and floury flesh. An exceptionally fine potato for roasting and mashing.

Arran Victory An old, purple-skinned potato from the Isle of Arran, this late maincrop, bred by Donald Mackelvie, is legendary. With its violet skin and snowy-white flesh, it is the oldest Arran potato still available. Its floury flesh makes an exceptional mash, cumulus like but with plenty of body and a depth of flavour that may (or may not) come from the local habit of putting kelp on the fields.

Golden Wonder One of my favourites for frying and roasting. A russet-skinned, white-fleshed Scottish variety of great beauty. Easy to grow.

Of great visual charm are the 'blues', those extraordinary varieties that have not only blue skin, like the Edzell Blue, but also violet-blue flesh. They are tricky to find in shops, but farmers' markets provide a good hunting ground. Blue seed potatoes for growing at home are available from specialists such as Alan Romans and Carroll's. I keep a look out for Shetland Blue, Salad Blue and the rare, grey-skinned Vitelotte Noire. If their exquisite violets and indigos were matched by their flavour they would probably be better known, but they are worth having now and again just for their beauty.

A potato in the garden

I grow my own, but have only taken it up recently – twenty years later than I first grew tomatoes, ten years later than I planted my first beans. They are now one of my most successful crops, both in terms of quality and yield.

When I sowed that first grubby handful of Charlotte seed potatoes, it was as an experiment. I had no intention of making a potato bed a permanent fixture in my garden. There is too little room, and I somehow felt they were so cheap and plentiful that there was little reason to chit, plant and dig my own. There was also the idea that they are difficult to grow organically.

Once Charlotte's pink flowers had passed and the stems had grown leggy, I dug them up, half expecting to find a few moth-eaten tatties. What sat on my garden fork was a veritable nest of small, perfect potatoes, oval, golden and smelling of sweet earth. I think I was even a bit proud of myself. The following year I planted five varieties, only one of which (Pink Fir Apple) didn't do particularly well. The others were pretty much picture perfect and cooked beautifully.

Potatoes like deep, well-drained soil that gets some sun for at least part of the day. I grow mine in the shadiest beds of all, which enjoy direct sunshine only for a couple of hours around midday. It's not perfect, but they cope. The crop will benefit from a good manuring the autumn before you sow. I dig in a couple of bags after harvesting and let it enrich the soil over winter. I alternate my planting between two beds, both on the shadier side of the garden, to stop the build-up of soil-borne viruses. A gap of three years between planting on the same site would be even safer. You can also grow a small crop in deep terracotta or plastic containers. This works especially well for early, waxy potatoes. The confined space is not a problem, as they need room to spread down rather than across.

Seed potatoes can be planted directly in the soil but most people find it better to 'chit' them first. This is simply another word for letting them sprout for about a month, till they have a few short, strong shoots. I find egg boxes ideal for this, the hollows holding the potatoes securely while they sprout. They need some light, otherwise the shoots will grow long and weak, as they do when you forget them in the vegetable rack.

Once the shoots are a couple of centimetres long, and the risk of frost is over, the whole potato can be planted outside. I make individual holes about 15–20cm deep (you can dig a trench, if you prefer), then gently plant each potato with the healthiest-looking shoots uppermost. They need 30–40cm between the rows. Label the varieties clearly and write them down too (the foxes ran off with some of my wooden labels one year, so I could have been confused had I not kept a separate note).

The time it takes for your potatoes to mature depends on the variety, the weather and your location. A hundred days is about the minimum between planting and digging up. It's a good idea to plant an early variety, then a couple of others for later in the year. Generally, early potatoes are ready once the flowers appear; maincrops are ready once the flowers have faded and the tops have started to collapse.

* If you want an early crop, lay fleece or black plastic over the soil to warm it up for a week or two before planting.
* Plant with the sprouting end up.
* You can start with 'earlies' in March, covering them with deep 'earthed-up' soil or a cloche to keep the frost out.
* Potatoes like to grow in soft soil. You can use up old compost and anything from plant pots in the trench. I use the contents of last year's tomato pots.
* As soon as the shoots show above ground, pull the soil up around them to protect against late frosts. It is worth remembering that some parts of the country can experience frosts as late as May.
* A layer of horticultural fleece to cover the shoots at night is a good investment.
* You can store maincrop potatoes in paper sacks in the dark for weeks, even months. Whatever you do, keep them away from the light.
* And yes, it is true that they keep better with their soil on.

A potato diary

February 24 Five varieties of seed potato arrive from Scotland: Arran Victory, Kestrel, Golden Wonder and Pink Fir Apple. There's a rare and capricious blue one too, which I intend to grow more for its flowers than any hope of a crop.

I put the tubers to 'chit' in egg boxes – that is, to develop strong green shoots. I use the coldest room in the house for this, warm temperatures giving rise to thin, weak shoots. The tubers stay in their egg boxes until Good Friday.

April 9 I plant them out. No matter whether Easter is early or late, I do this on Good Friday. It is an ancient tradition amongst allotment holders and I have stuck to it. But then, I always trim my hedges around Derby Day too.

May 4 Almost a month to the day, the first shoots push through, teased through the wet soil by a succession of drenching showers and piercing sunshine. First up is Kestrel, with its tight tufts of hairy, bottle-green leaves. A day later I spot the first signs of the Salad Blue, dense clusters of violet-black leaves edged with a single line of green, barely visible against soil the colour of molasses. The dark leaves intrigue, exuding an air of mystery and poison. You are reminded that the potato is but a short hop from deadly nightshade, with its jet-black berries and threat of death.

I protect them from the snails and slugs with spent coffee grounds and copper rings.

May 15 Every potato is up 15 inches, standing proud against the damp soil, which is now scattered with a confetti of white medlar petals.

Late June The potatoes are in flower. Since I have previously grown only varieties with pink flowers, the violets, mauves and deep indigo shades come as an unexpected and graceful joy.

July 28 Most potatoes are ready to dig when the flowers are open. They generally keep well in the ground, so I tend to leave them there till they are needed. We start digging on July 28 (wonderful, purple-skinned Salad Blue) and continue till late October, when the last of the Golden Wonder are dug.

A potato in the kitchen

Nowhere else in the vegetable kingdom does 'the right one for the right job' matter quite so much. The texture of a potato after cooking depends on its flesh structure and water content. Some varieties have a low water content, resulting in a 'fluffy' texture when cooked and making them good for mashing, roasting and baking. They are often referred to as 'floury'. Others have a high water content, giving them a waxy feel and allowing them to keep their shape when cooked. They are especially good for gratins and salads. These are the ones to use when a recipe suggests a 'waxy' variety. Their flesh is often more yellow in colour than the 'floury' varieties. There are also many that sit on the fence and can be used for different kinds of recipes.

Seasoning your potatoes

Fat Butter, olive oil, bacon fat, duck and goose fat, beef dripping – all have much to offer the plain and floury potato. The best cooking medium seems to me to be duck or goose fat, or beef dripping.

Cheese Sharp, piquant cream cheeses, robust, mouth-puckering British farmhouse Cheddars, melting cow's milk cheeses with rind the colour of snow – all marry beautifully with potatoes. I sometimes break little nuggets of soft cheese over a boiled and softly floury King Edward or Maris Piper, then squash the melting cheese into the spud with my fork.

Spices Cumin, turmeric, chilli, ground coriander and the spice mix garam masala do much for a floury variety. Aniseed-flavoured spices (fennel seed, star anise) less so.

Herbs Rosemary, thyme, bay, parsley, coriander, tarragon and mint are the most obvious, and it is indeed difficult to find any herb that does not contribute something to potatoes. Despite my comment about aniseed, chervil is delightful with the new and very waxy. Unusually, sage gets a look in too. Normally too pungent for use with vegetables other than onions, this musky-tasting leaf finds a friend in a slow-cooked potato. Chives are especially good when the potato is eaten cold, in a salad or perhaps a chilled soup.

Cream The flesh of both floury and waxy varieties will, to differing extents, soak up cream or milk. Be it mash (floury) or slow baked (waxy, in a gratin), the effect of this vegetable combined with cream is thoroughly calming.

All meat, game and most fish are happy to share a plate with potatoes in pretty much any form, though I can't say I have ever managed to marry them with crab particularly successfully. Smoked and pickled fish are at their most comfortable with a potato salad at their side. Ask any Scandinavian.

Mashed potatoes

The perfect mashed potato is one that manages to be both fluffy and buttery at the same time. Too much butter will make it heavy; too little and it will fail to satisfy. The mixture of starchy carbs, butter and, sometimes, warm milk produces what is possibly the most soporific vegetable dish of all.

Mashed potato is often at its most blissful when we use it to soak up gravy or sauce. For many, it is the ultimate side dish for ham and parsley sauce, or rich stews whose gravy can seep into the mound of starch. Generally, the richer the sauce with which it is served, the less butter I put in. Mash is also used as a crust for fish pies or minced lamb or beef, and as the backbone of a fishcake.

Traditionally, a floury potato is used. The high percentage of dry matter in large, white potatoes produces a fluffy, light result. Beaten hard with an electric mixer or a wooden spoon, a floury potato will hold air and produce a mash of extraordinary volume.

In recent years, a new style of mash has become popular using waxy-fleshed varieties, which produce a creamy, almost purée-like finish. Mixing is kept to a minimum, as the starch grains would turn gluey if beaten as much as when using a floury potato. Introduced by restaurant chefs to anchor their griddled scallops to the plate, this mash is too rich and buttery to have in great steaming clouds with your sausages but is very soothing under a hunk of roast cod. Butter is used in this, but sometimes olive oil is beaten in too. You can often tell by the slightly green colour.

The drier the potato is before mashing, the better. Much is made of the idea that the best results come from potatoes steamed in their jackets – it prevents them getting waterlogged – before being peeled and mashed. I have done this, but I find the difference not dramatic enough to go through the trauma of peeling steaming-hot potatoes whilst trying to get dinner on the table.

You can make excellent mash from a potato that has been peeled before boiling or steaming, providing you dry it out beforehand by letting the steam leave the potato after draining. The most successful way to do this is to drain the potatoes, leave them in the pan, then cover with a clean tea towel for three or four minutes. The towel will absorb the steam whilst keeping the spuds warm. You can then mash them and beat in the butter.

The mashing varieties

Some floury, some a little waxy, but they all make a good mash. Arran Victory gets my vote as the best choice for producing a fluffy, well-flavoured cloud. Others will have their favourites but the varieties that follow are amongst the most suitable:

Fluffy mash Arran Victory, Avalanche, Dunbar Rover, Kerr's Pink, King Edward, Epicure, Kestrel, Maris Piper, Record, Santé, Snowdrop, Estima, British Queen, Wilja.
Silky mash Accent, Desiree, Edzell Blue, Majestic, Nadine, Picasso, Romano, Maris Peer.

* Cut the potatoes into large pieces before cooking. Small cubes of potato are likely to produce a sloppy mash.
* There is a long-established rule that 'old' potatoes are put into cold water and brought up to the boil, while 'new' potatoes are best dropped directly into boiling water. The theory behind this is that the slow heat involved in bringing the water to the boil allows the inside of the potato to cook at the same time as the outside. I have found this to be true, even though the science of it sounds a bit dodgy. Much depends on the variety of potato and the size to which it is cut.
* Check for doneness with a skewer. As soon as the point will slide in without much pressure, they are ready.
* Once the potatoes are drained, leave them in the hot pan covered with a tea towel to steam for three or four minutes. They will lose moisture this way and produce a fluffier mash.
* Add the butter, and the milk if you are using it, before you start mashing. The extra heat will help the butter melt properly.

A classic fluffy mash for sausages

enough for 4
floury potatoes – 900g
butter – 100g
hot milk – 100ml

Peel the potatoes and boil them in deep, salted water till tender to the point of a knife. Drain them, then return to the pot, cover with a tea towel and let steam for a few minutes. Mash them with the butter, using a potato masher or an electric mixer fitted with the beater paddle.

Now beat in the milk, either with the beater or a wooden spoon. Check the seasoning.

A lovely soft mash with milk and bay

I love buttery, cloud-like mash but sometimes I want something softer. I use a floury-textured winter potato beaten with butter and hot milk to produce a snow-white mash suited to mopping up the juices of winter recipes. The quantity of milk will depend on the level of starch present in the potatoes, so I simply stop adding the warm milk when I have the texture I like.

enough for 4
medium to large floury potatoes – 6
bay leaves – 5
milk – 200ml
butter – 75g

Peel the potatoes and boil them in deep salted water till tender. Put the bay leaves into the milk in a separate pan and bring to the boil. Turn off the heat and set aside. The bay leaves will gently flavour the milk.

Drain the potatoes, then return them to the pan, cover with a tea towel and leave for a few minutes. Tip the potatoes into a food mixer fitted with the beater paddle and beat with the butter and a little black pepper. With the beater on slow, pour in the milk, leaving the bay leaves behind, and continue beating till almost sloppy. Season and serve immediately.

* You can make a deeper-flavoured, more 'earthy' version, by melting the butter and milk together, then whizzing them in a blender with a handful of chopped parsley. The effect is decidedly stronger in flavour, and the mash is pale green in colour.

Mustard and parsley mash

Add a small handful of chopped parsley and 2 tablespoons of grain mustard to 500g buttery mashed potato.

Wasabi mash

Stir 2 teaspoons of ready-made wasabi paste into 500g mashed potato.

A mash with olive oil (and the merest whiff of garlic)

enough for 4
mashing potatoes – 450g
olive oil – 60ml
garlic cloves – 2, squashed flat but not peeled
thyme – a bushy sprig
a thick slice of butter

Peel and cook the potatoes in the usual manner. Warm the olive oil, garlic cloves and thyme sprig in a small pan, then turn off the heat and leave the aromatics to do their work whilst the potatoes cook.

Mash the potatoes as usual, introducing the butter and oil and holding back the garlic and herbs as you go. Grind in a little pepper and serve.

A Parmesan and olive oil mash

enough for 4
mashing potatoes – 450g
olive oil
finely grated Parmesan – a large handful

Peel the potatoes and steam or boil them. When they are tender, drain them, then leave for three or four minutes in the empty pan covered with a tea towel. Mash them, either by hand or using an electric mixer, beating in a couple of tablespoons of olive oil and then the grated Parmesan. The mash should be smooth and slightly glossy.

A soft mash with cream and parsley

The affinity between potatoes and parsley is usually demonstrated by tossing new potatoes in butter and the chopped herb. I like to take it one step further and put the parsley in a soft, almost sloppy purée of potatoes. It excels as a side dish for white fish.

enough for 4
large floury potatoes – 4
parsley – a large bunch
single cream – 150ml
butter – 50g

Peel the potatoes and steam or boil them till tender. As the potatoes approach tenderness, finely chop the parsley and warm the cream in a small pan.

Drain the potatoes, then return them to the pan, cover with a tea towel and leave for a few minutes. Mash the potatoes with the butter, then, when all is light and fluffy, stir in the cream and chopped parsley. Tip the potatoes into a food mixer fitted with the beater paddle and beat with a little black pepper.

Check the seasoning and serve immediately.

The mashed potato cake

Mash, if not made too soft with butter or milk, can be shaped into a patty and fried till crisp. White, floury potatoes give a suitably firm yet tender texture. A mash of waxy potatoes can almost liquefy if you try to fry it. Thyme can be stirred in as you shape your potato cakes, or cooked and hashed greens – cabbage, broccoli, sprouts – or snippets of bacon, a crumbling of black pudding or simply a dusting of ground nutmeg. In so doing, a dollop of mash becomes an entire main course.

I disagree with those who claim you need eggs to hold everything together. A little flour will do the job if you really think your cake will collapse in the pan. Test the mixture by squeezing it in the palm of your hand. If it sticks together, then it won't need the adhesive addition of flour. Leaving it to fry unheeded will also help it keep its shape. When fishcakes and suchlike have fallen apart, it is generally because the cook couldn't resist the opportunity to play.

Famous potato cakes such as bubble and squeak, made with leftover cabbage and mashed potato, were traditionally meant as an accompaniment to Monday's cold cuts from Sunday's roast. The sizzling crust of the reworked mash is a pleasing contrast to the softly pink cold meat.

It is hard to think of anything I haven't tried in a potato cake, from the shredded corned beef of my first student digs to flaked kippers and even smoked salmon. When I was in my twenties, a popular supper involved potato moulded into patties with canned salmon and fried, then later, much later, Arbroath smokies and a sauce of cream and curly parsley. The most successful, to my mind, was some duck confit, pulled off its creaking bones with a fork, then folded into smooth mash, floured lightly and fried in duck fat. Another good one involved a cold sausage, sliced into thick coins.

Much effort is made getting the potato as smooth as silk, but I also like the effect when it is mashed roughly, leaving much of it in uneven lumps. When this is pushed together, thoughtfully seasoned and fried in butter or oil, the texture is more interesting than that of a cake made from a smooth mash, in much the way a crumpet ripped in half by hand toasts more interestingly than one sliced flat with a knife. If that sounds like Zen and the art of the potato cake, then so be it.

A cake of potato and goat's cheese

Goat's cheese – sharp, chalky, a little salty – makes a sound addition to
the blandness of a potato cake. The fun is coming across a lump of melting,
edgy cheese in amongst the quietness of the potato. This is what I eat whilst
picking eagle-style at the carcass of a roast chicken or wallowing in the
luxury of some slices of smoked salmon. It also goes very well with a humble
smoked mackerel.

enough for 2
cooked potato – 400g
goat's cheese – 150g
herbs (thyme, tarragon, parsley) – 4 tablespoons, chopped
plain flour – a tablespoon
cornmeal (polenta) – 6 tablespoons
olive or groundnut oil

Mash the potatoes with a masher or a fork till they are a mixture of sizes
from gravel to pebbles. Cut the goat's cheese up into small pieces and fold
it into the mash with the chopped herbs. Season generously with salt and
black pepper, then stir in the flour.

Divide the mixture into four and pat each one into a rugged patty
roughly the diameter of a digestive biscuit. Empty the cornmeal on to a
plate, then turn the patties in it.

Get a thin layer of oil hot in a shallow, non-stick pan. Lower the patties
into the oil and, without moving them, cook for about four minutes, till
golden and lightly crisp underneath. Turn them quickly and carefully with
a palette knife and cook the other side. Drain briefly on kitchen paper
before serving.

Roast potatoes

Roast potatoes are as much a part of the Sunday roast as the roasting juices or gravy, providing crispness to contrast with the soft tenderness of the meat. Although you could bake them alone, the best flavoured are those cooked around the joint. As they cook, they soak up some of the meat juices, whose natural sugars caramelise around the potato, resulting in a crisp and deeply savoury crust.

You can get a good result by using vegetable oil, butter or lard instead of the roasting juices, but these fats tend to produce a slightly second-rate result, losing out on the heart and soul of the meat. Butter alone, without any meat juices, will produce a burned taste; olive oil should always be a light version. Heavy oils will prevent your tatties from crisping. Dripping or goose or duck fat, on the other hand, can be almost as good as cooking them round the joint itself.

The crispest results will come from potatoes that have been boiled or steamed before you add them to the roasting tin. Roasted from raw, the potato's surface can often harden instead of crisping deliciously.

The single thing that will improve the crust of a 'roastie' is to bruise the edges of the lightly cooked potato before roasting. The bashed edges become frilly and crunchy in the sizzling meat juices.

The roasting varieties

A floury variety produces a roast potato that, cooked correctly, will be crisp on the outside and fluffy within. The actual variety is less critical than the way it is cooked, but the following is a list of suitable candidates:

Accent, Arran Pilot, Arran Victory, Cara, Desiree, Dunbar Standard, Duke of York, Epicure, Golden Wonder, Kestrel, King Edward, Maris Piper, Navan, Osprey, Picasso, Romano, Sharpe's Express.

* The crispest results of all come from using duck fat.
* Summer potatoes usually contain more water than those in winter, which have been in store.
* There is no ideal way to keep roast potatoes warm without them going soft, but the best way is to leave them uncovered in a cooling oven. Failing that, a very loose dome of foil will help, though inevitably at the expense of some of the crispness.
* You can cook new potatoes this way too. Their flesh becomes sweet and fudgy inside but their skin rarely forms a crust.

Classic roast potatoes

Peel the potatoes, cut them into pieces large enough for you to take two bites at each, then bring to the boil in deep, generously salted water. Boil for five minutes or so, then drain and return to the pan. Take the pan in both hands and give it a couple of good shakes. The idea is to fluff the edges of the potatoes so that they become crisp and frilly as they roast.

Tip them around the roasting meat, then turn each one over so that it is coated in the roasting juices. If you are cooking them separately, use a shallow tin containing a little dripping, lard or duck fat (or olive or groundnut oil, if you must), then roast them at 200°C/Gas 6. They will need a good forty-five minutes, maybe a bit longer. Move them once or twice during cooking, so they crisp nicely all round.

If you are cooking the potatoes around the Sunday roast, remove the meat to rest before carving but return the potatoes to the oven. If they look less than crisp and golden, whack the heat up a few notches till they are perfect.

Sea bass with lemon potatoes

Baking a joint of meat or a large fish on top of a layer of potatoes is a reliable way of ensuring they stay moist. The juices from the roast are soaked up by the potatoes, making sure that not a drop of flavour is wasted. Large fish such as sea bass and sea bream can be cooked in this way, as can Cornish mullet. Line-caught, ocean-friendly sea bass is not too difficult to find. I reckon on a 1kg fish being enough for two.

enough for 2

for the fish
sea bass – a whole fish, cleaned but left on the bone
olive oil
a little dried or fresh oregano

for the potatoes
waxy-fleshed potatoes such as Anya or Pink Fir Apple – 500g
olive oil – 4 tablespoons
a large lemon
anchovy fillets – 12
vegetable stock – 250ml

Set the oven at 200°C/Gas 6. Slice each potato three or four times. If you do this lengthways you will end up with long, elegant pieces. Warm a couple of tablespoons of olive oil in a roasting tin over a moderately hot flame, then put the potatoes in and let them colour on both sides. They cook best if you leave them alone for several minutes in between stirring. You want them to be pale gold on both sides. Cut the lemon in half, then into thick segments. Add to the potatoes with the anchovy, and a grinding of black pepper and then pour over the stock.

Lay the fish on top of the potatoes, brush with a little olive oil, then add the herbs and a mild seasoning of salt and black pepper. Bake in the preheated oven until the flesh will slide easily away from the bone in big juicy pieces. This will take a matter of twenty-five to thirty minutes. Serve the fish with the potatoes and spoon over the stock.

Roast new potatoes and salami

Young potatoes of any sort roast sweetly, especially if scrubbed hard so their skin almost disappears and they are allowed to develop a sticky, golden coating in the oven. They need a few minutes in boiling water before they hit the oven if they are not to toughen as they roast.

I match them with robust ingredients – slices of fat-flecked salami or perhaps a spoonful of softly fibrous pork rillettes – as a Saturday lunch.

enough for 4
new potatoes – 16–24, depending on their size
extra virgin olive oil
a bushy sprig of rosemary
salami – 24 slices
black olives – 16

Set the oven to 200°C/Gas 6. Rub the loose skin from the potatoes, then boil them in salted water till tender. Drain and put them into a baking dish or roasting tin. Using the back of a spoon, press down on each potato, crushing it slightly – you just need to break the skin and flesh a little in order to allow the oil to penetrate and the potato to crisp.

Pour a good glug of olive oil on to each smashed potato, then chop the rosemary spikes finely and crumble them over the potatoes. Season and roast for thirty-five to forty minutes, till the potatoes are golden and crisp around the edges.

Divide the salami between four plates, then add the olives, the roast potatoes and a drizzle of olive oil.

Roast potatoes with duck fat and garlic

This is the classic accompaniment to duck confit, though I make it all the time – as a side dish for baked mushrooms or a steak, or sometimes as a main dish in its own right, in which case I make a salad too, perhaps with frisé or French beans.

enough for 4, as an accompaniment
medium potatoes – 4
duck fat – 3 tablespoons
the leaves from a couple of sprigs of thyme
garlic – a single clove, chopped

Peel the potatoes and slice them as thinly as you can. They should be no thicker than a two-pound coin. Melt the duck fat in a shallow, heavy pan – I use a cast-iron skillet – turn off the heat and add the potato slices, neatly or hugger-mugger, seasoning them with salt, black pepper, thyme leaves and a little chopped garlic as you go. Place in the oven and bake at 200°C/Gas 6 for thirty-five to forty minutes, till golden brown.

Fried potatoes

There are two types of fried potato: chips, which are deep-fried, and those that are sautéed in shallow oil or fat. I can think of few things I would rather eat than a chip, hot and salty, dipped into a dish of béarnaise or hollandaise sauce. Yet I rarely make chips at home, partly because we don't eat that much fried food and partly, if I am honest, because I dislike the terror of cooking with deep pans of boiling oil. Whenever I do dig out my deepest pan, half fill it with oil and make a batch of chips, I always fry them twice: first, at a moderate temperature to cook them right through to the middle and then at a higher one to crisp them.

I tend to make sauté potatoes as a way of using up leftover boiled spuds. I often find they fry all the better for having spent the night in the fridge. They dry out overnight and seem to crisp up more reliably.

The frying varieties

I regard pretty much any fried potato as delicious, no matter whether it is waxy or floury, old or new, large or small. Bad chips are better than no chips at all. But just as there are good mashers, there are some potatoes that will fry better than others. I find Golden Wonder the ultimate frying potato for crispness and flavour, and grow it specifically for that. Of the more accessible varieties, it is worth looking at Accent, Cara, Desiree, Kerr's Pink, Kestrel, King Edward, Majestic, Maris Peer, Pentland Javelin, Premier and Winston. Many people, and many chip shops, swear by Maris Piper.

Chips

enough for 2–4
large floury potatoes – 4
dripping, lard or sunflower oil for frying – 2 litres

Peel the potatoes and cut them into long, thick chips, putting them into cold water as you go. The water has the effect of preventing them browning while also washing away some of the starch. Drain and pat dry with a cloth or paper towel. Heat the oil to 150°C in a large, deep pan. Lower the chips into the hot oil – it will bubble up alarmingly – and fry for six or seven minutes, until they are pale and soft. Lift the chips out and leave to drain while you bring the temperature of the oil to 185°C. Lower the chips into the hot oil again and fry for three or four minutes, maybe less, until they are crisp and golden.

Drain on kitchen paper and dust enthusiastically with salt.

A crisp cake of shredded potato

I had heard about Golden Wonder, the rock-hard potato with a deep honey-brown skin that roasts like a dream, but only came across my first a year or so back, at the farmers' market. Hard as ice and crisp white inside, the golden one turns out to hate water and will turn to soup if you attempt to boil it. Give it olive oil, butter, goose or duck fat instead. This is the potato for frying in little cubes with rosemary and salt, and for chips.

If you plant Golden Wonder in April, and are lavish with the water, it will reward you with charming, snow-white flowers flushed with palest lilac and, come September, perhaps the best frying potatoes of all, to be finely shredded and cooked in a flat cake with goose fat and garlic.

enough for 4
Golden Wonder potatoes – 500g
goose fat – about 3 tablespoons
garlic cloves – 4

Peel the potatoes (the skins are tough) and grate them finely. I have done this by hand but it takes just seconds using a food processor fitted with a medium-fine grating blade. You want the strands of potato to be roughly the same thickness as the wool for knitting a pullover.

Melt the goose fat – I sometimes use butter – in a wide, shallow pan and tip in the grated potato. Grind over a little sea salt, then squash the garlic cloves flat and tuck them in amongst the strings of potato. Leave over a low to moderate heat for fifteen to twenty minutes, till the underside is crisp and golden. Loosen the edges with a palette knife as they cook, pushing it further under the cake till it is free enough to slide about.

Lay a heatproof plate on top of the pan, then, holding it firmly in place, turn the whole thing upside down (I find doing this with one positive movement and no dithering tends not to end in tears). Now slide the potato cake back into the pan and cook the other side.

When it is truly golden, crumble over a pinch of sea salt flakes and serve, hot and crisp from the pan.

Potato cake with thyme

Good with lamb.

> *enough for 6*
> medium potatoes (floury are best) – 5
> butter – 90g
> thyme – the leaves from 4 sprigs

Set the oven at 200°C/Gas 6. Peel the potatoes and slice them thinly. They should be so thin that you are almost able to see through them. If you tend to work slowly, put the sliced potatoes into a bowl of cold water to prevent them browning.

Melt the butter, then brush some of it on to the bottom and sides of a loaf tin (or use a round, solid-based tin, if that is what you have). Cover with a piece of greaseproof paper, leaving a little extra overlapping the sides to get hold of when you come to turn out the cake. Cover the bottom of the tin with slices of potato, brush with more butter and season with salt, pepper and a light sprinkling of thyme leaves. Continue layering the potatoes, adding the butter and seasonings every two or three layers, until you have used them all up. Pour any remaining butter over the top. Bake for forty to fifty minutes, till the top is golden and a skewer can be inserted effortlessly into the layers of tender potato. To serve, lift the potato cake out by holding both long sides of the greaseproof paper and pulling upwards. Cut into six pieces. If it falls apart, and well it might, just push the slices back together.

Potatoes with goose fat and thyme

For each person, cut a medium to large potato into large dice. Squash a clove of garlic flat and warm it in a shallow pan with a couple of good tablespoons of goose fat (or oil) and a couple of hearty sprigs of thyme. Introduce the potatoes and let them cook for fifteen to twenty minutes, until they are tender. Turn up the heat so they crisp, dust with salt, then eat as soon as they are cool enough to do so. I sometimes make this just for myself, occasionally scattering the crisp potatoes on to rocket leaves to make me feel virtuous.

Steamed and boiled potatoes

Steaming or boiling a potato is often the most successful way to showcase its flavour. The nutty, lemony or earthy notes are at their most obvious when a vegetable has met nothing but steam or water before we eat it. This alone makes it worth hunting out a really good spud. Local markets are excellent places to track down something more interesting than the average cornershop variety, but nothing beats steaming potatoes we have grown ourselves.

The most important characteristic after flavour is that of holding together during cooking: a potato that doesn't collapse in the steam or break up in the water. Our choice will depend very much on the time of year but also on whether we want a neat, fudgy, little potato to serve whole, perhaps rolled in melted butter and parsley, or a big, fat lump of tatty potato, all floury edges and fluffiness. The sort of spud to mash into your gravy with your fork.

I use as little water as possible and salt it generously, but I prefer to steam them where I can. When they are cooked without water, their flavour seems truer and their flesh stays firmer.

Best for boiling and steaming

For small potatoes, to be served whole Anya, Edzell Blue, Pink Fir Apple, small Maxine and any of the very early varieties such as International Kidney (called Jerseys when grown there), Foremost, Duke of York, Accent and Epicure.
For big, fluffy results to accompany a stew or sloppy braise Arran Victory, Cosmos, Maris Peer, Maris Piper, Estima, King Edward, Nadine, Saxon, Kestrel, Wilja.

Potatoes, crème fraîche and dill

It's the last week of June and the pink-mauve flowers of the Charlotte potatoes have started to fade. The stems are thick like old rhubarb, yet almost transparent in the evening sun. Once the flowers have gone, it's okay to lift them.

The tallest stalk doesn't disappoint. A good dozen potatoes are attached to its fine, creamy-white roots – pale, golden eggs against crumbly black soil. Not just hen's either, there are diminutive spuds the size of quail's eggs and others more like duck's. It is said that they are best left to 'set' for a day before cooking. We don't, and they are rubbed clean with a thumb under running water, then boiled in heavily salted water for fifteen minutes, eighteen for the duck's eggs.

Gently rub the potatoes clean, washing them well under running water. Leave the skin be if it is young and thin. Peel it if not. Put the potatoes into cold water and bring to the boil. Salt generously, then simmer till tender to the point of a knife – a matter of anything from ten to twenty-five minutes, depending on the variety of your potatoes. Drain and return them to the stove, this time over a gentle heat.

Put a large dollop of crème fraîche into the pan and a handful of chopped dill fronds. Cover with a lid until the cream has melted. Fold the potatoes gently over in the melted cream and herbs till they are lightly coated, then eat with gammon or oily fish.

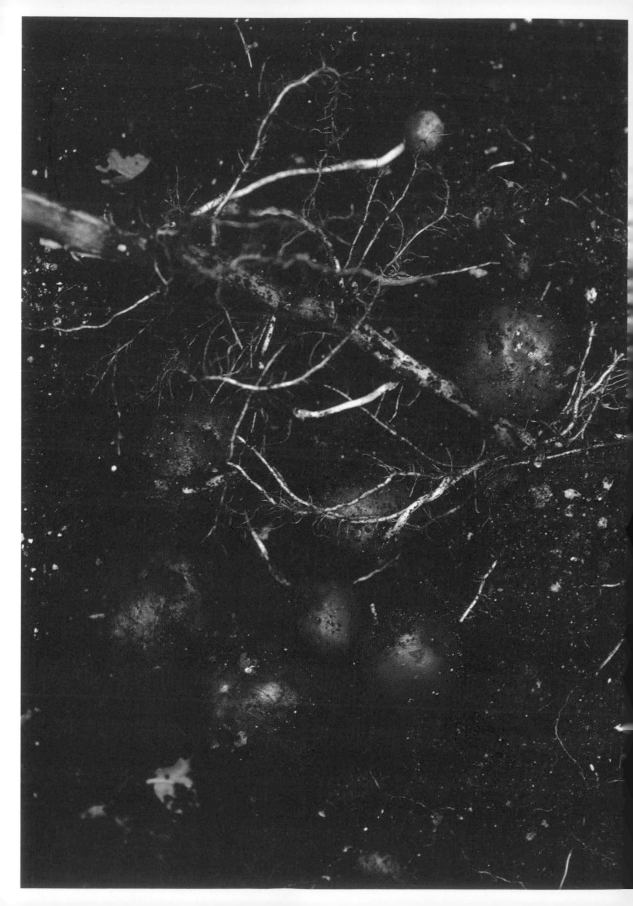

Crushed potatoes with cream and garlic

If you crush a cooked potato with the back of a spoon or fork, its broken edges are receptive to any dressing you wish to trickle over it. Cream and garlic is a rather sumptuous treatment for a virginal new potato, but it works very well.

enough for 4 as a side dish
new potatoes – 500g
new garlic – 3 juicy cloves
double cream – 250ml
thyme – about 8 sprigs

Scrub the potatoes but do not peel them. Boil them in a pan of deep, lightly salted water for fifteen to twenty minutes or so, till tender.

While the potatoes are boiling, peel and lightly crush the garlic cloves. Pour the cream into a small saucepan, add the leaves from the sprigs of thyme, the garlic, a little salt and some black pepper. Let the mixture simmer over a moderate heat until it has reduced by about a third.

Once the potatoes are drained, put them in a shallow dish and crush each one lightly with a fork – you want to break the skin and flatten the potato just enough for its flesh to soak up some of the hot cream. Pour the cream and thyme over the crushed potatoes and eat while hot.

Sorrel with new potatoes

Occasionally in spring I find myself with a bunch or two of sorrel (it is often sold at the farmers' market by the handful). The lemony notes work well with tiny boiled potatoes. Sorrel collapses when it gets hot, loses its colour and almost disappears. But it leaves behind a soft green purée that is very good for tossing freshly boiled Jerseys in.

Cook new potatoes in deep, salted water till tender (you will need about 500g for four). Meanwhile, make a dressing with a little oil and vinegar, then add salt, pepper and the shredded sorrel. As soon as the potatoes are drained, while they are still piping hot, toss them with the sorrel dressing, leaving them to rest for ten minutes before serving.

New season's potatoes with pancetta, walnut oil and sherry vinegar

Steam 400g of new season's waxy or floury potatoes till tender to the point of a knife. Leave the skins on. They will be used uncut, so you need them to be as small as possible.

Put a tablespoon of Dijon mustard in a small bowl with a pinch of sugar and three pinches of sea salt. Whisk in a tablespoon of sherry vinegar then four of walnut oil. Stir in a tablespoon of cold water and a little pepper.

Grill eight thin rashers of pancetta till crisp. Snap them into short pieces. Roughly hash a little parsley.

Tip the warm potatoes into a serving dish, toss gently with the dressing, then fold in the parsley and pancetta.

The perfect baked potato

A baked potato can be a perfect thing, brought rough-skinned from the oven between warm oven mitts, its crust sparkling with salt like a pearlescent frost, its interior the texture of deep snow. I have made many a meal of a single baked potato, huge like a boulder, with ice-cold butter tucked into a craggy slit in its skin. I usually have a beer too and a bowl of salad, whose peppery leaves I stuff into the empty, salt-encrusted skin. It is something to eat alone, a big fat spud all to yourself, a meal of utter simplicity and quiet solace.

When I was a kid, baked potatoes appeared on the table having had their filling removed and whipped up with mashed corned beef or grated cheese, piled back in and baked briefly till the surface was crisp with golden furrows. I rarely go in for that and tend to present them on the table with a packet of butter, a tub of crème fraîche and a bowl of crisp salad, chicory and watercress in a mustardy dressing being a favourite. Supper becomes a delicious assembly job.

In theory, you can rinse your potato, prick it with a fork and stick it in the oven and you will get a perfectly fine result. However, even a baked potato has levels of perfection and there is little point in not at least trying to make each one the best baked potato we have ever eaten.

* Whilst the skin is still damp from washing, a little sea salt can be dusted over the surface. This will help it to crisp.
* A skewer pierced right through the potato and left in position while it is in the oven will help your supper cook more quickly.
* The cooking time will depend on the size of your potato, but even the smallest will take a good fifty minutes at 180°C/Gas 4. For a guaranteed crisp skin, bake them at 200°C/Gas 6.
* To achieve a fluffy interior, the steam must leave the flesh quickly. A good karate chop will suffice, though wrapping a tea towel around the hand first is worth thinking about. Your blow should be hard enough to break the skin but not so hard as to send potato shrapnel all over the kitchen. In time, you can perfect it.

The baking varieties

A variety with a dry, powdery flesh will produce a light, open-textured baked potato – one that is capable of soaking up butter, crème fraîche, salad dressing or whatever lubricant we throw at it without becoming heavy. As a general rule of thumb, any that mash or roast well will usually produce a good, light result when baked.

No single potato will be everyone's preferred 'baker', and some favour a more waxy texture. Many regard Red Duke of York as one of the finest in terms of texture and flavour, but King Edward and Arran Victory have more than a few fans. I find home-grown Kestrel, with its flashes of violet, one of the most enjoyable. Marfona tends to be the one the supermarkets push as the potato for baking but I find it too waxy. Below is a list of suitable candidates:

Arran Pilot, Arran Victory, British Queen, Desiree, Duke of York, Edzell Blue, Epicure, Estima, Foremost, Kestrel, King Edward, Maris Peer, Maris Piper, Nadine, Pentland Javelin, Pentland Squire, Picasso, Romano, Saxon, Swift, Vanessa, Wilja, Winston.

Sea-salt-baked potato, Parmesan greens

The stuffed baked potato, that bastion of comfort eating, given a contemporary treatment.

> *enough for 2*
> large baking potatoes – 2
> butter or olive oil
> green salad leaves – 2 large handfuls
>
> **for the dressing**
> tarragon vinegar – a tablespoon
> Dijon mustard – a teaspoon
> an egg yolk
> olive oil – 100ml
> grated Parmesan – 2 tablespoons
> lemon juice – 2 teaspoons

Set the oven at 200°C/Gas 6. Wet the potatoes, prick them with a fork and roll them in flakes of sea salt, making certain that at least some stick to the skin. Bake them till tender; this can take anything from thirty-five minutes to an hour, depending on your potatoes.

To make the dressing, whisk the vinegar, mustard, egg yolk and olive oil together with a little salt and black pepper, then beat in the grated cheese. Squeeze in the lemon juice, stir and set aside for five minutes.

Serve the salt-baked potatoes, scooping off the top like a boiled egg and stirring in butter or olive oil as you wish. Once the potato flesh has been eaten, toss the salad leaves with the dressing and pile into the vacated potato skins. Eat salad, potato skins and all.

Baked potatoes, leeks and fontina

I say fontina because that is what I had in the kitchen last time I made this – it's a fondue cheese that melts sublimely and doesn't overpower the leeks. But Taleggio, another milky Italian, would be just fine, too.

> *enough for* 2
> baking potatoes – 2, about 350g each
> leeks – 2 or 3
> butter – a thick slice
> fontina – 90–120g, coarsely grated, or Taleggio, cut into thin slices

Scrub the potatoes, prick them with a fork or insert a skewer in them, then while they are still damp, dust them lightly with sea salt. Leave to dry for a few minutes, then bake at 200°C/Gas 6 until the skin is crisp and the inside soft and fluffy – a matter of thirty-five minutes to an hour, depending on the potato variety.

Half an hour or so before you expect the potatoes to be ready, start cooking the leeks (it is worth remembering that baked potatoes are good natured, so a few minutes either way won't hurt). Split the leeks in half, wash them thoroughly, then cut them into finger-thick slices. Melt half the butter in a heavy pan, add the leeks and let them cook slowly over a low heat until they are soft and translucent. This will take longer than you might think, as much as fifteen or twenty minutes to soften them completely. An occasional stir will prevent them browning.

Split the potatoes in half and scoop the flesh into a mixing bowl, then drop in the remaining butter and most of the cheese and beat to a creamy mass with a wooden spoon or electric beater. Taste and season with salt and black pepper. Pile back into the skins, dot the last of the cheese over and return to the oven for a good fifteen minutes, until piping hot.

Baked potatoes, salt cod and parsley

A beautiful marriage of textures, this: creamy salt cod purée and crisp potato skins. As baked potatoes go, this is a lot of work, and much washing up too, but the result is worth the trouble. Salt cod is not easy to track down; Spanish, Italian and Portuguese grocers and major supermarkets are your best bet.

The recipe makes rather too much filling, but it is not worth dealing with a smaller quantity of salt cod. There's no hardship anyway – simply keep the leftover purée in the fridge and eat it the next day with fingers of hot toast.

enough for 2
dried salt cod – 500g
large baking potatoes – 2
milk – 150ml
extra virgin olive oil – 150ml
a large garlic clove
the juice of a lemon
parsley – a small bunch, chopped

Soak the salt cod in cold water for a good twenty-four hours, changing the water regularly.

After scrubbing the potatoes well and pricking them here and there with a fork, put them in to bake at 200°C/Gas 6. Once they have been baking for half an hour or so, drain the fish, put it in a deep pan, cover it with fresh cold water, then bring to the boil. When the water is bubbling, turn off the heat and cover the pan with a lid. Let it sit for fifteen minutes, then drain. Remove and discard the bones and skin. A messy job, and one of the few kitchen jobs for which I will put on a pair of Marigolds. Tip the salt cod into a food processor. Warm the milk (I use the steam nozzle on the coffee machine) and the olive oil separately.

Peel and roughly chop the garlic and add it to the fish. Blitz, pouring in the milk and olive oil in a steady stream, letting the mixture whip to a sloppy cream.

Remove the potatoes from the oven, slit them open and scoop out the flesh with a teaspoon, then tip it into the salt cod. Blitz briefly to mix, then add the lemon juice, the chopped parsley leaves and a few grinds of the pepper mill. Pile the purée into the potato skins and return to the hot oven for fifteen minutes.

Potato salads

There are two schools of thought about the perfect salad potato. Most agree that a waxy potato is best, as it holds its shape during cooking and slices neatly. The waxy texture ensures that the slices remain intact even when soaked with dressing. The other approach is to use a floury King Edward-style potato, boiled till its edges fray, then cut into crumbling slices, dressed with a robust oil and vinegar mixture while warm and tossed with roughly chopped spring onions and parsley. Served with thickly sliced, fat-speckled salami and tiny, piquant cornichons, it provides a salad of hearty rusticity.

Yellow-fleshed potatoes that are waxy to the touch have always been popular in France and Scandinavia but only recently have they become easy to find in the UK. They are recognisable by their soap-like feel, and often by their oval or elongated shape. Rarely larger than a bantam's egg, they are at their most charming when the size of a large pebble.

* It is worth trying to dress the potatoes while they are still hot – they soak up the dressing more effectively.
* The decision about whether to skin potatoes meant for salad is a personal one. I like the rusticity of an unskinned potato salad. But there is also something very elegant about a salad made with skinned new potatoes.
* In this instance, vinegar seems a more suitable acid for a dressing than lemon juice.

Some excellent salad varieties

Amandine, Anya, Belle de Fontenay, Carlingford, Charlotte, International Kidney, Juliette, Lady Christl, Linzer Delikatess, Nicola, Pink Fir Apple, Ratte, Roseval, Royal Kidney.

Linzer, and a perfect potato salad

Long, pale and slim, the Linzer Delikatess is as elegant as a tuber could be. I found this Austrian variety at my usual market on a wet day in early July, and brought them home out of curiosity. The flesh was waxy and yellow, and held together well in salted boiling water. They were tender to the knife in ten minutes. Potatoes that keep their shape well in water tend to hold up when saturated with dressing, making them good for potato salads – in this case, a salad dressed with thick Spanish oil, mustard and dill and tossed with chunks of peeled cucumber. We ate it with a fat, golden-skinned mackerel, smoked that morning by the fishmonger.

A salad of potatoes, mustard and cucumber

At first rich, then intensely warm and piquant, this is a perfectly balanced salad for accompanying fish or maybe a grilled steak. It is just the job with freshly dressed crab or smoked trout or eel. The potatoes should be warm when you dress them, and eaten within twenty minutes or so, giving them time to soak up the flavours but not dry out. If you are dressing the salad in advance, I suggest you make a double quantity of dressing.

enough for 4
half a cucumber
new potatoes – 500–750g

for the dressing
caster sugar – a good pinch (but no more)
white wine or cider vinegar – a tablespoon
Dijon mustard – a generous tablespoon
olive oil – 4 tablespoons
juniper berries – 6, lightly crushed
dill – 2 tablespoons, chopped

Peel the cucumber, halve it down its length and remove the seeds with a teaspoon – they will only make the salad wet. Slice the cucumber into chunks about 2cm in width. Sprinkle lightly with salt and leave in a colander in the sink for about half an hour.

Put a pan of water on to boil. Scrub the potatoes, thumbing off any flaky skin as you go. Salt the water, add the potatoes and let them boil for about fifteen minutes, until they are tender to the point of a knife. Drain them and briefly set aside.

Whilst the potatoes are boiling, make the dressing. Put the sugar and vinegar in a small mixing bowl and stir till the sugar has dissolved. Add some black pepper. Mix in the mustard, then gently whisk in the olive oil. Stir in the juniper berries, the cucumber and the chopped dill and set aside.

Slice the warm potatoes, letting them fall into the dressing, then fold them together gently. Leave for no more than twenty minutes, then serve.

A salad of potatoes, herring and crème fraîche

A sweet-sharp salad with a creamy dressing. Avoid the temptation to over-mix the salad, as the beetroot is inclined to send everything a very unfetching shade of marshmallow pink.

enough for 4 as a light main course
waxy potatoes – 300g
small cooked beetroot – 4
pickled herring fillets – 6
medium gherkins – 4
spring onions – 4
dill – a small bunch
rocket leaves – 200g

for the dressing
red wine vinegar – a tablespoon
olive oil – a tablespoon
smooth Dijon mustard – a teaspoon
crème fraîche – 100ml
yoghurt – 100g

Scrub the potatoes and bring them to the boil in deep salted water. Let them simmer for fifteen minutes or so, until they are tender to the point of a knife.

Peel the beetroot, cut them into thick wedges and put them in a mixing bowl. Remove the little wooden sticks that inevitably come with soused herrings and cut each fillet into six chunks, then add to the beetroot but do not mix. Thickly slice the gherkins and add them to the beetroot and herring. Chop the spring onions and the dill and add to the bowl. Rinse the rocket and check it over, removing any thick stalks or wilted leaves. Keep separate from the rest of the ingredients.

Drain the potatoes, then peel off their skins as soon as they are cool enough to hold. Don't let them get cold, though; you need to dress them while they are still warm. Cut each potato in half if they are very small, quarters if not, and add them to the mixing bowl.

Mix the vinegar and olive oil in a small bowl or jar with a fork and season with salt and black pepper and the mustard. Beat in the crème fraîche and yoghurt. Gently fold the dressing into the rest of the ingredients in the bowl, stirring only lightly to avoid the beetroot sending everything pink. Divide the rocket between four plates and pile the potato salad on top.

Roast potato salad with rosemary and garlic

The idea of a potato salad usually involves slippery potatoes of the purest ivory, but an interesting take entails a much rougher texture brought about by roasting them before dressing.

enough for 4 as a side dish
new potatoes – 24
garlic – a head
olive oil
rosemary or thyme– a few sprigs

for the dressing
red wine vinegar – 2 tablespoons
smooth Dijon mustard – 2 tablespoons
olive oil – 5 tablespoons

Scrub the potatoes thoroughly, then put them in an ovenproof dish or roasting tin. Break the garlic into cloves, but don't peel them. Add them to the potatoes. Drizzle over a little olive oil, then scatter with flakes of sea salt and the leaves from the rosemary or thyme sprigs. Bake at 200°C/Gas 6 for three-quarters of an hour to an hour, till they are puffed and golden and their insides are fluffy.

Pour the vinegar into a small jar with a lid and add the mustard, olive oil and some salt and pepper. Shake it hard to give a thick dressing. You can use a little whisk if you prefer. When the potatoes come from the oven, press down hard on each one with the back of a spoon so that they crack open slightly, then pour over the mustard dressing. As you eat, press the soft garlic from its skin.

Gratins and baked dishes

I rather like the fact that cooks disagree about things. If we didn't, then cooking would be a much less interesting subject and in risk of atrophy. The traditional potato for a gratin, or dauphinois, is a yellow-fleshed, waxy variety that holds its shape, and yet I made my gratins with a floury potato for many years simply because I liked the fact that they collapsed into the creamy sauce. Boulangère likewise – I very much like the effect you get when potatoes collapse into meat stock.

Gratin dauphinois

enough for 6
waxy potatoes – about 1kg
garlic – 2 large, juicy cloves
butter – just enough to butter the baking dish thickly
double cream – enough to cover the potatoes, about 600ml

Set the oven at 160°C/Gas 3. Peel the potatoes and cut them into slices about the thickness of a pound coin. Cut the cloves of garlic in half and rub them round the inside of an earthenware or enamelled cast-iron dish. Smear the dish generously with butter. Lay the potato slices in the dish, orderly or hugger-mugger as the mood takes you, seasoning with salt and black pepper as you go.

Pour over the cream and slide the dish into the oven. Bake for an hour to an hour and half, until the potatoes are virtually melting into the cream.

Some good things to put in your gratin

Smoked bacon Grill it first, then chop roughly and scatter between the layers.
Smoked mackerel For which it is worth looking at my book *Real Food*.
Porcini Soak just a few dried mushrooms in water till soft, then tuck them in between the potatoes.
Cheese Grated Gruyère crumpled over the top before baking will give a deliciously savoury crust. Whether you think this already rich recipe needs more fat is another matter.
Anchovies Wiped of their salt or oil, anchovy fillets can be slipped in between the layers, Swedish style. The effect is more savoury than fishy, and utterly delectable.

A potato supper

There is much comfort, warmth, solace and satiety in a bowl of starch, especially in cold weather. This one has the benefit of stock too, providing either a simple supper or an accompaniment to a roast.

small, waxy potatoes – about 5 per person
a little groundnut or light olive oil
a little butter for greasing the dish and a few knobs on top
bacon or pancetta – about 2 thin rashers per person
sage leaves – 1 per person
stock – a good chicken one, but Marigold bouillon will do

Set the oven at 180°C/Gas 4. If the fine, pale skin doesn't bother you, there is no need to peel the potatoes but you should give them a good rub with your thumb (I must say, I invariably peel mine, or at least scrape them well, but others think I am being pernickety). Whatever, you need to slice them no thicker than a pound coin. Warm enough oil to cover the bottom of a frying pan, then fry the sliced potatoes in it just long enough to colour them lightly on both sides. Lift them out on to kitchen paper.

Generously butter a shallow baking dish or roasting tin. Cut the bacon into pieces about the size of a postage stamp. Layer the potatoes in the buttered dish, scattering the bacon, sage and a grinding of salt and black pepper over them as you go. Dot the surface with a few little knobs of butter, then pour over enough stock to cover. Bake for about an hour, until the potatoes are soft enough to crush between your fingers.

Potatoes with dill and chicken stock

I am constantly on the lookout for potato dishes that will flatter a piece of meat or fish such as grilled mackerel, flash-fried lamb's liver or some thick bacon rashers. This is such a dish.

enough for 4 as a side dish
large baking potatoes – 2
dill leaves – a generous handful, roughly chopped
a large knob of butter
hot chicken or vegetable stock to cover – about 500ml

Set the oven at 200°C/Gas 6. Scrub the potatoes, peeling them only if you particularly wish to, then slice them thinly. Put them into a bowl and toss with salt, black pepper and the dill.

Lightly butter a shallow baking dish. Layer the potatoes and their seasonings in the dish, then pour in enough stock to cover; the liquid should be just lapping at the top of the potatoes.

Bake for about fifty minutes, till the potato slices are truly tender and crusty on top.

A thin cake of potatoes and Parmesan

Potatoes cut thinly are not only good deep fried but can be blissful when cooked with stock or butter till they are sodden and meltingly soft. I wanted a sliced potato dish that had the simplicity of *pommes à la boulangère* but something of the richness of its creamier cousin, *pommes à la dauphinoise*. This is what I have come up with: thinly sliced potatoes layered with garlic, butter and grated Parmesan. Savoury, melting and, yes, rich, they are a near-perfect accompaniment for cold roast lamb or beef.

enough for 4
waxy potatoes – 900g–1kg
butter – 125g
garlic – 2 cloves
Parmesan – 30g, finely grated

Peel the potatoes, then slice them thinly. I do this by hand but if you have a mandolin you can do it in a matter of seconds. The rounds should be so thin that you can almost see through them.

Melt the butter in a small pan. Peel the garlic, then crush it or, if you prefer, chop it finely. Smooth a little of the melted butter over the base of a shallow baking dish or a cast-iron frying pan and cover it with some of the potato slices, overlapping them slightly. Pour on a little more butter, then season with salt, garlic, black pepper and a good dusting of Parmesan. Cover that with a further layer of potatoes, more seasoning, garlic and Parmesan, then continue layering until you have used all the potatoes. Finish with butter and a light dusting of Parmesan.

Bake in the oven at 220°C/Gas 7, pressing the cake down very firmly once or twice with a large fish slice. After forty-five to fifty minutes, you should have a deep golden potato cake sizzling around its edges. Remove from the oven and leave it to calm down for a few minutes before serving.

A winter dish of potatoes, onions and melted cheese

enough for 4, with greens on the side
baking potatoes – 1kg
a large onion
olive oil
Gruyère or other firm cheese – 150g, cut into small pieces
grated Parmesan – a small handful
greens, such as kale, spinach or dark green cabbage – 4 large handfuls

Bring a large pan of water to the boil whilst you peel the potatoes and cut them as you would for boiling. Salt the water, add the potatoes and let them simmer for fifteen to twenty minutes, till just tender enough to take the point of a knife.

As the potatoes are cooking, peel the onion, cut it in half and then into thick slices. Warm a little olive oil in a deep casserole over a moderate heat, add the onion and let it soften and colour lightly, stirring from time to time so that it does not brown. Set the oven at 180°C/Gas 4.

When the potatoes are tender, drain them, then cut through each one (I do this whilst they are still in the pan) so that they are roughly bite-sized. Tip them into the onion pan – if they crumble a bit, that is all to the good – then toss them with the Gruyère. Grind over some salt and black pepper, then scatter with the grated Parmesan.

Bake for about thirty-five to forty minutes, until the cheese is melted and the potatoes and onion are golden. You can steam or boil the greens whilst this is happening, a few minutes before you expect the potatoes to be ready.

Herbed potato cake

This is my version of the Spanish omelette, being lighter, crisper and more studded with herbs than the norm. The point here is that you can mix the herbs to suit your taste. Tarragon and mint are a must for me, but any of the more unusual herbs is worth using too: chopped sorrel leaves, salad burnet, lovage or any of the lesser-known basils. Because the herbs are only lightly cooked in this recipe, their flavour will stay true.

> *enough for 6*
> waxy potatoes – 800g
> spring onions – 6
> eggs – 3
> plain flour – a scant tablespoon
> chopped parsley, mint, tarragon – 10g each
> olive oil

Grate the potatoes into a bowl, peeling them first if you wish. Finely slice the spring onions into rounds and add them to the potatoes. Break the eggs and beat them lightly, then tip them in with the flour, chopped herbs and a good seasoning of salt and pepper.

Warm a little olive oil in a 24cm non-stick frying pan. Add the potato mixture and spread it out so that it covers the bottom of the pan. Let it cook over a moderate heat for ten to fifteen minutes, until the underside is golden brown and the potato is tender. Transfer the pan to a hot overhead grill and leave to brown. Cut into six wedges and serve.

Bubbles, squeaks and rumbledethumps

Colcannon, rumbledethumps, *pyttipanna*, *biksemad*, *roupa velha* and *stampot* – the local names used throughout Europe intrigue and delight but they all describe the same thing, a stir-up of potatoes and greens. In some cases, the two components are served freshly mixed; in others they are fried or baked to acquire a crust. Either way, this is good food at its most frugal. The ingredients may be cooked fresh or taken from yesterday's leftovers. *Roupa velha* is Portuguese for 'old clothes'.

* Irish colcannon is made from mashed potatoes and chopped, boiled kale. It is served unfried, in all its green and white purity.
* Rumbledethumps is a Scottish dish made with fried onions, cabbage and mashed potatoes. After mixing, it is baked until golden.
* Bubble and squeak is generally shaped in rounds and fried in a pan, or left as one large cake, which looks splendid but is difficult to turn in the pan. Either way, the name comes from the sound it makes as it fries in the pan.

Cheese bubble and squeak

A new take on the original, which makes matters a little more substantial. Two of these cheese and potato cakes are ample for a main course with maybe a spinach or chicory salad to follow.

> *makes 4, enough for 2*
> greens (purple spouting, Chinese broccoli, Savoy cabbage etc) – 200g
> cooked potato – 200g, roughly mashed
> goat's cheese – 100g
> nutmeg
> plain flour – a tablespoon, plus extra for coating
> a little olive oil

Wash the greens thoroughly, then cook in deep salted water till bright green and tender. Drain carefully and roughly chop, discarding any tough stalks.

Mix the mashed potato with the greens, then cut up the goat's cheese into small pieces and add to the potatoes and greens. Season generously with salt, black pepper and, if you wish, a very little nutmeg. Stir in the flour.

Divide the mixture into four and shape each one into a rough patty (they will be roughly the size of a thick digestive biscuit). Put the patties on a floured plate, turning them once in the flour.

Get a thin layer of oil hot in a shallow, non-stick pan. Lower the patties into the oil and cook for about four minutes on each side, till golden and lightly crisp. Drain briefly on kitchen paper and serve.

Pumpkin and
other winter squash

Even as I write, in the slate-grey light of a
December afternoon, there is a pumpkin in
the garden, shining orange bright amongst the
blackened leaves and tangled stems. A bowl of
soup waiting to happen.

Winter squash are the hard-rinded, golden-
fleshed siblings of the more delicate green and
yellow summer varieties. They can be exotically
shaped like Aladdin's turban or as homely as
a cottage loaf. I call them sugar pumpkins, on
account of the intense sweetness of their flesh,
and revel in their somewhat sinister overtones.
A fat, round pumpkin is used both as a candlelit ghoul at All Hallows and
as a fairytale stagecoach to whisk Cinderella to the ball. American and
French cooks have long appreciated them; in Britain the pumpkin still has
a stronger association with ghosts and goblins than it does with soup.

As summer slips into autumn, the pumpkin's skin, like that of all the
winter squash, starts to harden. It will keep the sweet flesh in sound enough
condition till early spring – though whether it ends up as risotto or a
doorstop will depend on whether you can still get a knife through it. They
are a fruit really, but one that we use in soups, stews, curries and as a filling
for ravioli.

I would grow a pumpkin even if it weren't edible. Few things are
more beautiful when morning fog swirls round the allotments on a damp
November dawn. But the real point of winter squash is the sweetness of its
flesh – only corn on the cob comes anywhere close. Their frugality should
not be underestimated. You can get a soup-stew of haricot beans, late
tomatoes and cheese out of one for a cheap and filling supper. Half a small
one will make enough simple soup for four. A thick wedge is enough per
person as a side vegetable. I tuck chunks of mine under roast beef so the
sugary flesh picks up the deeply savoury goo that collects under the meat.
Together they make a tantalising forkful.

Everything from the enchanting, miniature Munchkin to the massive

Atlantic Giant can be good to eat, though the flesh of some varieties can be more fibrous or watery than others. The blue-skinned pumpkins such as Crown Prince have the firmest flesh, which doesn't break up when steamed or roasted; the richest flavoured are often the deepest orange. Any will make a satisfying, velvet-textured soup if added to softened onions, sweet spices and a modicum of ripe chilli.

To be honest, we didn't eat the first one. My best friend and I just hollowed out the interior with our hands and a bent kitchen spoon, gouged glaring eyes and cut jagged teeth deep into its skin, then left the flesh in a plastic bag to rot. I must have been about ten. I am not sure we even knew the innards were edible. My family, slaves to the frozen pea, had never heard of pumpkin pie or soup. The giant squash, so enormous that two of us could barely lift it on to the garden wall, was there purely to add witchery to our Halloween revelry. Tired of roasting chestnuts, Dad put a glowing night-light in its belly, sending spooky shadows long into the night. A week later he took a spade to it, now a scene of appalling melancholy, and threw it on the compost heap with his prize dahlia tops that had been unexpectedly caught in the frost.

The plump, orange-skinned fruits are the ones most favoured for Halloween lanterns, with skin firm enough to hold up against the heat of a candle. Rouge Vif d'Etamps and Mammoth are suitable subjects, as is Ghost Rider. Jack O'Lantern is, appropriately enough, the most reliable of all, having a tough, shiny, orange skin that flickers spookily in the candlelight.

The winter squash is now as much a part of my cold-weather cooking as dried beans, fat apples, sweet onions and cheap, bony cuts of meat. It is difficult to think of anything that is capable of bringing quite so much warmth, jollity and good humour to the table on a frost-sparkling night. From September through to the last feeble weeks of February, squashes come at you in succession. Gold, pale blue or deep green fruits, adding weight and cheer to your organic box, are at first a welcoming sight in a shopping bag of winter beige and brown. But just as one leaves the kitchen as a deep orange soup, a pebbledashed crumble or a cloud of buttery mash, another appears. Abundance turns to guilt. A single pumpkin in the vegetable rack will make you smile. Three of them and you feel they are laughing at you.

A pumpkin in the garden

The trailing vines of a pumpkin plant – hollow, fleshy, often spikily hairy – need a bit of space, so I encourage them up a climbing frame with pieces of twine loosely tied round their tendrils. With the exception of the heaviest varieties, it's a good way in for those with limited growing space.

The flowers, like squawking yellow birds at dawn, barely see the day through before they collapse. Male and female blossoms appear on the same plant, the female often discernible by the almost invisible immature fruit lurking behind the flower. Occasionally you need to get the paintbrush out and do a little pollinating yourself if they don't seem to be getting it on. It is a tender moment in the garden, taking pollen from one enormous open bloom to the next with the point of a soft brush.

As well as regular watering (every day at the height of summer), they like extra food in the form of liquid fertiliser. I do mine once every three weeks, as soon as the first fruits have set in late June to late September. You can almost hear them whispering thank you.

To encourage the plants to put their energy into ripening rather than climbing further along the garden path, I pick out the growing tips once enough fruit have set. A large terracotta tile under each fruit will keep its skin clean and reflect the sun's warmth back to it.

I wait till the skin is hard before harvesting, then if they are to be kept for winter, I 'cure' them in a sunny place for ten days or so. A window ledge indoors will do when the weather has turned wet, which it often has by then. Leaving a section of stalk attached to each fruit seems to help it keep. Makes them easier to carry, too. Store them in a cool place, well away from any chance of frost.

Picking a pumpkin or winter squash with a good length of stalk, letting it dry for a few days in the late autumn sun and keeping it dry should ensure that it will last you through the winter. Those that aren't dried in this way tend to shrivel rather than keep. I have sometimes kept them so long that they have been known to require an occasional dusting. It's wise to store one in the vegetable rack; they are said to sweeten with age, like us. Until spring, that is, when the dense, flame-coloured flesh seems to dry and the seeds and fibres coarsen. Even then they can be used for a soup.

A pumpkin diary

May 5 Planted the warty Marina di Chioggia, the flattened, vivid orange Rouge Vif d'Etamps and the smoky-blue Crown Prince, whose flesh is dense and the colour of carrot soup. At the last minute I tuck in some Connecticut field pumpkin seeds too; they are apparently good for roasting. The seeds, possibly the largest you can plant next to broad beans, are soaked overnight, then go into small pots of light, peat-free compost in the cold frame. A windowsill will do. Planting this late, long after any fear of frost, means they germinate quickly. Earlier won't hurt if you can offer enough protection, but I have always found that late starters catch up. Like peas, they hate cold, wet soil.

The shoots usually appear within a fortnight or so, sometimes less, and need a small, thin stake almost as soon as the relatively large first leaves open. I generally plant two to a small pot. Their root systems separate easily enough with a gentle tug on transfer to the garden.

June 8 The Connecticut field pumpkin has six good leaves, is about 20cm high, and ready to go out into the garden. I have had much success previously taking the young plants outside during the day for a week or two to harden them off. But they must come in at night. An early start is needed if they are to ripen fully by autumn. The pale yellow sap in the stems is nectar to a snail, so the young plants get a deep copper ring round them and a wide scattering of coffee grounds to irritate any approaching gastropod.

Mid July The Rouge Vif d'Etamps are getting away, snaking out of their terracotta pot, their crisp, hairy stems dotted every few centimetres with tight, gracefully pointed buds and curling tendrils.

Late July Each morning there is a new, canary-yellow flower singing its heart out. No signs of them setting fruit yet. The leaves have the diameter of dinner plates, and the thick, juicy stems drink as much water as I remember to give them.

August 18 Sometimes, if you stop peering hopefully on a daily basis, things happen of their own accord. I find the same principle works with the bathroom scales. Today I find several miniature fruits hiding under the larger leaves.

Late October The fruits are colouring nicely. The Connecticut squashes are full and round and the Vif d'Etamps has reached the end of the path; its skin is the colour of a setting sun. The Marina di Chioggia, whose dark green, knobbly shell I was so looking forward to stroking, was lost to two young fox cubs, whose early-morning wrestling broke its tender stem.

November 14 The first frost last night turned the plants' leaves to slop, their stems a tangle of slime. I bring the fruits in, one to hack into pieces and turn into a glowing roast with butter and caramelised garlic; the others to sit in the scullery for a week or so till they are ready for winter storage.

Varieties

Crown Prince A pale, steel-blue or grey skin, thick as they come, hides perhaps the most prized pumpkin flesh of all – firm, intense and the deep saffron-orange of a Thai monk's robe. A Crown Prince can last all winter in fine condition, and when you do finally decide to break through its hide and cook its deeply coloured meat, you will find the close-textured flesh holds its shape like no other. To me, this is the perfect squash: a thing of quiet beauty whose flesh refuses to collapse into the sauce of a stew or coconut-rich laksa. The Crown Prince is well named.

Butternut The squash *du jour*. The butternut is neat, shapely and easy to carry home; its flesh is firm, not too sweet and sports a thin skin that poses less of a danger to the cook and their knife than the larger varieties. Roasted with butter and herbs or blitzed to a grainy soup, the skin is edible. The real trump card here is the neat crater that appears once you have dug out the seeds and fibres; a hollow to hold just the right amount of melted mozzarella and pecorino; tomato and chilli sauce; brown basmati and toasted pine kernels.

Ironbark Blue-black, heavily gnarled skin that is a challenge to break into. The tight, deep-ochre flesh keeps well. Giorgio Locatelli and the folks at Moro are fans.

Acorn Squash The black-green ribs and furrows hide a soft lemon or canary-yellow flesh that is less sweet than it might be. The flesh can be described as watery or delicate, depending on your generosity of spirit, but kept till late January it will have firmed up and its sweetness will be more intense. A good one to roast – it takes barely forty minutes – maybe with a rice-based stuffing spiked with fat toasted cashews and thyme.

Onion Squash The onion variety has an unusual earthy quality and makes a firm, proudly standing mash. The colour deepens with age, though this is not one of the best keeping varieties. It has a tendency to develop soft spots in storage. It is generally small enough to bring home without putting your back out.

Rouge Vif d'Etamps It is difficult to think of anything that brings a bigger sense of fun into the garden. A squashed, vermilion globe whose tendrils wind themselves through the beans and over the low box hedges in a desperate attempt to get into the kitchen. I plant two of these each year and pick them around Halloween. They start life as two little leaves unfurling in the late spring sunshine and end up as soup for twenty or more.

Other varieties to consider: Marina di Chioggia for its haunting appearance, like that of a giant toad; Turk's Turban for its startling colours; Mammoth, which does what it says on the packet, and Buttercup, sweet, small and suitable for baking whole.

A pumpkin in the kitchen

The French have an ancient soup-stew whose frugality ensures it falls under the modern label of 'peasant cooking'. They toast thick slices of bread, layer them with fried onions, garlic and marjoram, blanched and skinned tomatoes and thin slices of pumpkin. The dish is then topped up with water and olive oil and baked in a low oven for an hour or two. The lid is lifted for the last half hour to allow the soup to form a crust. They call it a *garbure catalane*, with a nod to its Spanish origins. I make a more robust version with chicken stock, softened onions, toasted sourdough bread and both Gruyère and Parmesan cheeses. Sometimes I use Leicester and grated Berkswell cheese instead, to add a British fingerprint.

In the Rhône you might come across a *pain de courge*, a glowing egg-yolk-yellow bread that is eaten toasted, like brioche. The Sicilians candy the biggest pumpkins in translucent slices to add to the pretty ricotta and marzipan dessert, *cassata*. Mantua, which carries the fruit as its city emblem, uses it as a stuffing for tortelli, sometimes mixed with the mustard pickle of the region. In Lombardy they may add a few crushed amaretti, endorsing the pumpkin's affinity for the almond. I buy these apricot-coloured pillows from a local Italian deli, where they advise a heavy dusting of Parmesan to balance the marshmallow sweetness. In Emilia-Romagna, there is a habit of stirring a purée of the flesh into the dough for gnocchi (*di zucca*), which they boil and toss in melted butter before passing round the grated Parmesan.

Popular in Southeast Asia for coconut-laced broths and in America for a famous sweet, cinnamon-scented pie, for me pumpkins are nevertheless inseparable from the French countryside (where they also make a gratin of them with cream and crumbs), with abandoned farmhouses and decaying winter *potagers*, where a row of pumpkins firming up for winter storage is a familiar enough sight in the autumn. They also form, with beans and corn, the Holy Trinity of American country cooking, but their name, rather endearingly I feel, is from the French, *pompon*.

Putting the knife in – a word of caution

Sometimes the skin is so hard you feel the need for an axe. These old fruits are not called 'ironbarks' for nothing. I cannot over-emphasise the need for great care when breaking open your giant purchase, particularly if it has a smooth skin that might give it a tendency to slide. Put the creature down on the work surface, cut a thin slice from the base so it will stand firm, then peel by cutting downwards towards the board. You can trim up any missed bits later. Slice in half and scoop out the seeds and fibres with a spoon or your fingers. You can toast the seeds if you feel the need for something to crunch between your teeth. You'll need some salt and a cold beer to go with them. Cut the deep orange meat into slices, chunks, dice or whatever your recipe demands. Not that mine ever demand anything. They merely suggest.

The density and colour of a squash's flesh dictates how your supper will turn out. Pale, easy-to-cut squash makes a sloppy mash and sometimes a weak soup. Dense, brightly coloured flesh will produce a mash with backbone and a stew or curry whose principal ingredient hasn't melted into a slush – albeit a beautiful one. The harder your pumpkin is to cut, the sweeter and firmer its flesh will be and the more body and bite your supper will have. I don't despise the pale flesh of the acorn squash, but bake it instead, the heat of the oven concentrating its sometimes timid flavour.

Seasoning your pumpkin

If the traditional pairings are sweet, docile spices, the modern ones are hotter and more lively. The pumpkin is forever linked with fireworks: the bright reds and yellows of the spiky cactus dahlias with which it shares a patch in the garden; the soggy, blackened rocket you find next to it the day after Bonfire Night; the shock of the ripe chillies and lemongrass you can add to a pumpkin curry or a noodle-flecked soup for an autumn supper. How I look at it now is that the velvety sweetness of its flesh demands something upfront – the fireworks – to shake off the sugary notes: grated lemon or orange zest, shreds of crisp, almost burned streaky bacon, toasted bread soaked with garlic butter, a loose tangle of frizzled ginger, chillies and more chillies. As you stir the big pan of soup on your hob, it is worth considering which you might use to add bite to its smooth, candied tone.

Citrus Lemon, lime and especially orange will highlight the pumpkin's fruitiness. I add juice to soup or a roast and zest, dried peel or lemongrass to a South Asian-style curry.

Bacon A few strips, crisp as ice, to a bowl of soup; larger pieces to a warm salad of baked butternut and parsley; hot back-fat to a squash to be roasted.

Chilli Dried, crushed chipotles will lend a smoky layer to a thick soup; fresh orange and red, finely diced, should make a golden stew sing in the mouth.

Sweet spices Cinnamon and cloves for a pie; nutmeg for a gratin with cream and cheese.

Tomatoes Blend a handful into a soup to lift it from its sweet sleepiness; toss a few Gardener's Delight into a pumpkin bake so that they blacken in the heat.

Cheese Parmesan or Spenwood for stirring into soup; mozzarella and pecorino for melting in the hollow of a halved butternut.

Ginger Ground for a soup; grated in a curry; matchsticks to toss with a roast; deep-fried shreds on a plate of soup.

Rosemary For adding to the breadcrumbs of a crumble crust.

Sage For frying to a crisp and scattering over soup, or for lending its dusky notes to melted butter to pour over tortellini.

Almonds A handful, toasted, in a brown rice stuffing; a few added to the filling of a pasta cushion; a dash, no more, of Amaretto liqueur over a mound of mash.

And...

* The sweetness of the pumpkin and winter squash family works best with something very savoury. I often marry slow-cooked sausages, whose skins have turned sticky, with sweet and fluffy pumpkin mash.
* Once a pumpkin has been cut, its storage time is substantially reduced. Rather than covering a wedge of it with clingfilm, which encourages it to sweat, I store it in the fridge unwrapped, then just shave a wafer-thin slice off its edge and discard it each time I use it.
* I have never been convinced about winter squash with fish in the same way that I have about the delights of summer squash and courgettes. The extra sweetness is difficult to match with anything piscine. That said, prawns can work well enough with pumpkin in an Asian-style soup, as will scallops if you cook them on a hot grill so that a golden crust forms on the outside, then eat them with pumpkin purée.
* A pumpkin that sounds hollow when tapped will keep better than one where there is no sound at all.
* The really large members of the winter squash family can be intimidating. It is probably a good idea for new cooks to start with one of the smaller 'onion' squash, which have much of the colour and flavour of the big boys but are a jolly sight easier to handle.

A simple baked pumpkin

Make a sloppy herb paste by mashing four large cloves of garlic with two tablespoons of chopped thyme and four of olive oil. Season with salt and black pepper. Cut a kilo of peeled pumpkin into small dice, tip into a baking tin and toss with the herb mixture. Bake at 200°C/Gas 6 for an hour or till the pumpkin is crisp outside and soft within.

It is worth mentioning that you can cook a whole pumpkin in the microwave in a matter of minutes.

A pumpkin pangrattato with rosemary and orange

Marrying textures and tastes to one another is one of the most satisfying pleasures of cooking: the soft with the crisp, the steamily hot with the icily cold, the spicy with the mint cool. I somehow had a feeling that crisp crumbs might work well with the soft, collapsing flesh of a squash. They do, but are more interesting when the crumbs are not packed on top like a crumble but lightly scattered over and between the pieces of squash.

enough for 4 as an accompaniment, 2 as a principal dish
pumpkin or butternut squash – 1kg
garlic – 3 cloves
olive oil – 5 tablespoons, plus a tad more
a mild red chilli
finely chopped rosemary leaves – a tablespoon
the zest of half an orange
roughly chopped parsley leaves – a handful
fresh white breadcrumbs – 4 handfuls
butter – a thick slice (about 40g)

Set the oven at 180°C/Gas 4. Peel the squash, discarding the seeds and fibres, and cut the flesh into large, bite-sized pieces. Put the squash into a steamer basket or metal colander and steam over boiling water for fifteen to twenty minutes, till tender to the point of a knife.

Peel and finely chop the garlic and put it into a shallow pan with the 5 tablespoons of olive oil over a moderate heat. Thinly slice the chilli and add it to the pan with the rosemary and grated orange zest. The smell will be lightly aromatic. Tip in the parsley and breadcrumbs and stir briefly whilst they colour lightly. They should be no darker than a pale biscuit colour.

Put the pumpkin in a shallow baking dish or roasting tin, salt and pepper it, then add the butter in small knobs. Tip the breadcrumbs over and drizzle lightly with olive oil. Bake for thirty-five to forty minutes, till the crumbs are deep gold and the pumpkin is meltingly tender.

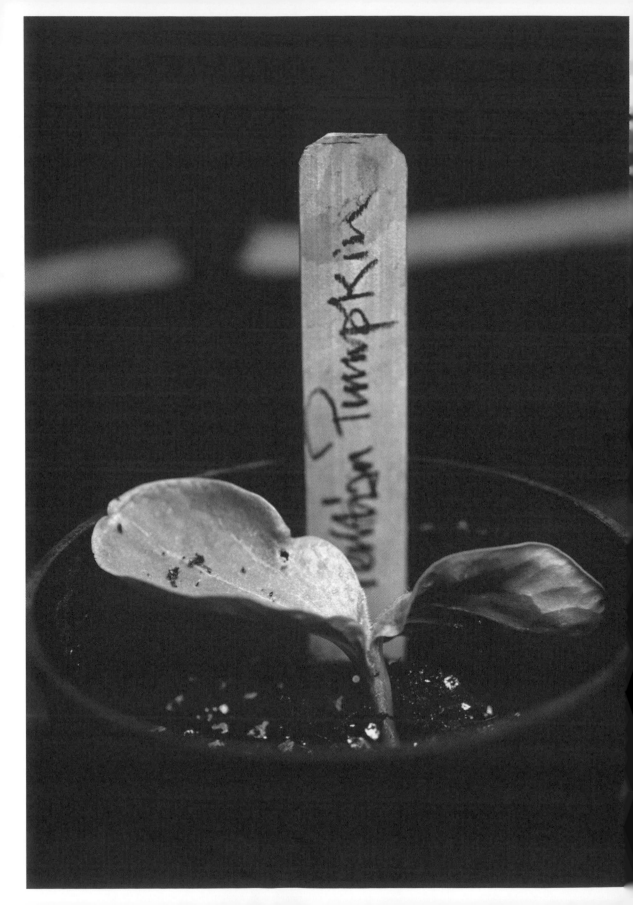

Sausage and a pumpkin mash

An hour after leaving Dijon, I was lost. A tangle of lanes, endless vineyards and a low mist left me confused and desperately looking for a farm at which to ask for directions.

It wasn't the most poetic of farmyards, but there was dry mud and clean straw underfoot and tight bales of hay on which were perched a hundred or more fat, round pumpkins soaking up the late-afternoon sun like a group of ladies in a Beryl Cook painting. I whistled and called without reply; not even a dog barked. As I waited, the pumpkins seemed to be watching me, growing faintly malevolent in the fading golden light. I felt like a lost child in a haunting fairy tale. Whether it was the watching fruits or the deserted farm that spooked me, I got back in the car and left as fast as I could. Thirty years on, I think of them in an altogether friendlier light, but they are still what I want at Halloween and on Guy Fawkes' Night. I came up with this modern take on the classic sausage and mash a year or two ago in an attempt to pacify a herd of boisterous and hungry kids that descended on me one October. It worked.

> *enough for 4*
> pork sausages – 8 plump ones
> seedy mustard – 2 tablespoons
> smooth Dijon mustard – a tablespoon
> runny honey – 3 heaped tablespoons
> lemon juice – 2 tablespoons
>
> **for the mash**
> butternut, pumpkin or other winter squash – 1kg
> a knob of butter (you really don't need much)

Set the oven at 200°C/Gas 6. Put the sausages in a baking tin large enough to take them in a single layer. If they overlap, they won't cook properly. In a bowl mix the mustards, honey and lemon juice and stir well. Pour them over the sausages and toss gently. Bake for twenty-five to thirty minutes, rolling the sausages over in the honey and mustard mixture once or twice, so that they eventually take on a sticky, glossy coat.

For the mash: peel the squash, cut it in half lengthways and pull out the fibres. Cut the flesh into thick pieces and pile into a metal colander or steamer basket. Steam, covered, for about twenty minutes till tender.

Remove the squash from the heat, tip into the bowl of a food mixer fitted with a beater attachment and mash with the butter and a little black pepper till thoroughly smooth. It is probably worth remembering that children generally hate lumps in food.

Divide the mash between four plates and pop the sausages on top.

A pan-cooked pumpkin with duck fat and garlic

January 2007. It is not especially cold, but has been raining non-stop for two days. Even the short dash from bus to front door leaves me soaked through and in need of some sort of carbohydrate and fat. Butter and beef dripping seem suddenly more appropriate than olive oil. Even more so the little bowl of duck fat I saved from last Sunday's roast. Perhaps it was the week before. No matter, it keeps for months. It is said that people used to rub this snow-white fat on their chest to ward off a cold. I prefer to take my duck dripping internally, and set about a simple layered potato dish with thyme and garlic. The addition of the pumpkin was a spur-of-the-moment thing. It works well, adding a sweet nuttiness to the recipe. I like it on its own too, with a sharp and vinegary green salad at its side. It is also a good side dish for meat of some sort and wonderful with cuts from yesterday's roast, just the thing for a cold roast chicken or duck leg.

enough for 4 as an accompaniment
potatoes – 4 medium-sized, floury or waxy
pumpkin – 600g
duck fat – 3 lightly heaped tablespoons
a few sprigs of thyme or rosemary
a single clove of garlic, chopped

Peel the potatoes and pumpkin and slice them no thicker than a two-pound coin. Melt the duck fat in a shallow, non-stick pan (I choose a cast-iron one, so well used it barely needs oiling), add the potato and pumpkin slices, neatly or hugger-mugger, seasoning them with salt, black pepper, thyme or rosemary leaves and a little chopped garlic as you go. Turn the heat to low and cover the pan with a lid. Let the slices cook for about twenty-five to thirty minutes. As they start to soften, press them down with a spatula so they form a sort of cake that will be golden on the bottom, with slices of potato that are soft right through. I check them for tenderness by inserting a skewer right down through the centre. If it goes in effortlessly, then they are done. Serve straight from the pan.

A warm pumpkin scone for a winter's afternoon

A warm scone is an object of extraordinary comfort, but even more so when it has potato in it. The farl, a slim scone of flour, butter and mashed potato, is rarely seen nowadays and somehow all the more of a treat when it is. I have taken the idea and run with it, mashing steamed pumpkin into the hand-worked crumbs of flour and butter to make a bread that glows orange when you break it. Soft, warm and floury, this is more than welcome for a Sunday breakfast in winter or a tea round the kitchen table.

Cooked initially in a frying pan and then finished in the oven, I love this with grilled Orkney bacon and slices of Cheddar sharp enough to make my lips smart – a fine contrast for the sweet, floury 'scone' and its squishy centre.

enough for 4
peeled and seeded pumpkin – 300g
plain flour – 140g
bicarbonate of soda – half a teaspoon
salt – half a teaspoon
butter – 70g
an egg, beaten
warm milk – 90ml
thyme leaves – 2 teaspoons
a little oil or butter

Cut the pumpkin into large chunks and steam until tender enough to mash. Set the oven to 200°C/Gas 6.

Mix the flour, bicarbonate of soda and salt in a large bowl. Cut the butter into small chunks and rub it in with your fingertips. You could do this in a food processor, but it hardly seems worth the washing up.

Crush the pumpkin with a potato masher, then beat in the egg, followed by the milk and thyme leaves. Scoop this into the flour mixture and mix well. Season with black pepper.

Warm a heavy, non-stick frying pan with a metal handle over a low to moderate heat. Melt a little oil or butter in it, then pile in the dough and smooth it flat. Leave to cook over a low heat till the underside is pale gold.

Lightly oil a dinner plate. Loosen the underside of the scone with the help of a palette knife. Put the plate over the top of the pan, then, holding the plate in place, tip the pan so that the scone falls on to the plate. Slide the scone back into the frying pan and cook the other side for four or five minutes. Put the pan in the oven for seven minutes or until the scone is lightly set in the middle.

Turn the scone out of the pan and slice into thick wedges. Serve warm, with cheese or some grilled bacon.

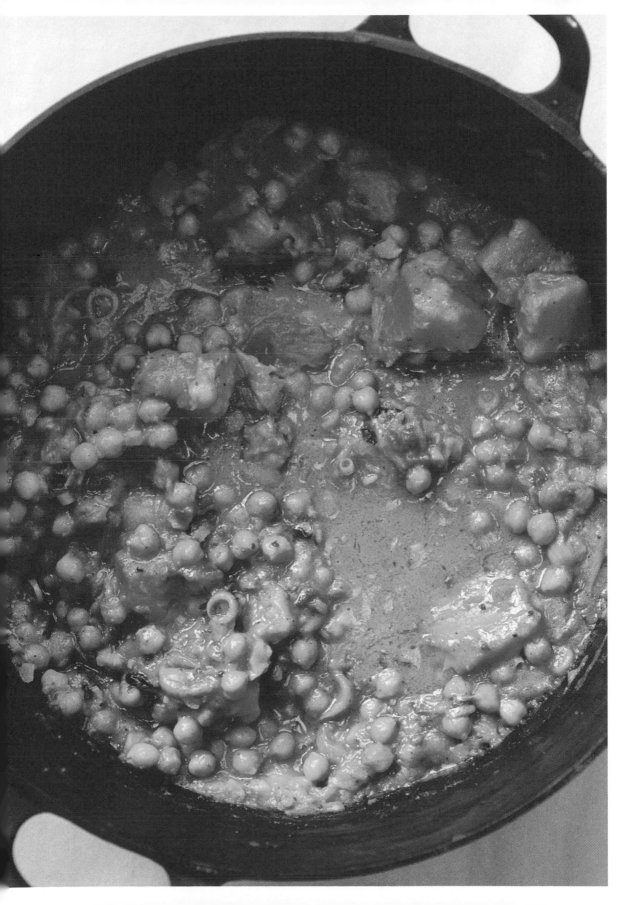

Chickpeas with pumpkin, lemongrass and coriander

Sweet squashes marry well with the earthy flavour of beans and lentils. This is apparent in the dhal and pumpkin soup in *The Kitchen Diaries* and here in a more complex main dish that offers waves of chilli heat with mild citrus and the dusty 'old as time itself' taste of ground turmeric.

Dried (which is the only way most of us know them) chickpeas are the stars of the world's bean dishes, used to fill bellies everywhere from India to Egypt. Their character – knobbly, chewy and virtually indestructible in the pot – makes them invaluable in slow-cooked dishes where you need to retain some texture.

Fresh chickpeas are bright emerald green and have an invigorating citrus note to them that is completely missing in the dried version. I saw some for the first time this year. I have long wanted to put lemongrass with chickpeas, partly to lift their spirits but also to return some of their lemony freshness to them (I use more lemon juice in my hummus than most as well). This recipe, which just happens to be suitable for vegans, does just that. Like many of those slow, bean-based dishes, it often tastes better the next day, when all the ingredients have had a chance to get acquainted.

enough for 4–6
dried chickpeas – 200g, soaked in mineral water for several hours
onions – 2 medium
groundnut oil – 2 tablespoons (plus a little more later)
garlic – 4 cloves
ginger – a thumb-sized piece
lemongrass – 3 large stalks
ground coriander – 2 teaspoons
ground turmeric – 2 teaspoons
green cardamoms – 6
hot red chillies – 2
pumpkin – 500g, peeled and seeded (about 1kg unprepared weight)
vegetable stock – 250ml
coconut milk – 400ml
yellow mustard seeds – a tablespoon
coriander leaves – a handful

to serve
cooked basmati rice for 4–6
limes – 2, halved

Drain the chickpeas and bring them to the boil in deep, unsalted water. Let them simmer for forty to fifty minutes, till tender.

Peel the onions and chop them quite finely. Pour the oil into a deep casserole and add the onions, letting them cook over a moderate heat till soft and translucent. Meanwhile, peel the garlic and the ginger, remove any tough leaves from the lemongrass, then make all into a rough paste in a food processor. Stir into the softened onions and continue to cook. Add the ground coriander and turmeric, then lightly crush the seeds of the green cardamoms and seed and finely chop the fresh chillies before stirring them in. Keep the heat fairly low and on no account allow the ingredients to brown.

Chop the pumpkin into large chunks, though no larger than you would like to put in your mouth, then add to the pan, along with the drained cooked chickpeas and the stock. Bring to the boil, then turn down to a simmer and continue to cook at a gentle bubble till the pumpkin is tender. Stop as soon as the flesh is yielding to the point of a knife; you don't want it to collapse.

Stir in the coconut milk and continue to simmer. Put a splash of oil into a non-stick pan and tip in the yellow mustard seeds. As soon as they start to pop, add them to the pumpkin together with the coriander leaves. Serve with the rice and the lime halves, ready to squeeze over at the last minute.

A fry-up of pumpkin and apple to accompany a meaty supper

The fry-up has always appealed to me, in particular the bits that stay put at the bottom of the pan, the crusty scrapings that brown rather too much. I call them 'the pan-stickings'.

One of potato and duck fat is a deep-winter supper of immense pleasure; another of herb-speckled sausage meat and courgette. This is robust cooking, crisp-edged and flecked black and gold. It is not for those days when you want something genteel or elegant. This is the sort of supper to pile on a plate and eat with a cold beer.

The latest of my fry-ups is extraordinary in that two generally sweet ingredients come together to produce a deeply savoury result. The key here is not to move the ingredients around the pan too much, leaving them to take on a sticky crust whilst allowing them to soften to a point where you can squash them with little or no pressure. The caraway seeds, which people tend to either love or hate, are entirely optional.

serves 4 as a side dish
a little butter
fatty bacon, such as streaky – 80g
a medium onion
pumpkin flesh – 650g
apples, a dessert variety – 400g
a lemon
caraway seeds – a pinch

Melt a slice of butter in a shallow pan, cut the bacon into short strips and let them colour lightly in the butter. Peel and roughly chop the onion, add to the pan and allow to cook with the bacon until translucent but not browned. Cut the pumpkin flesh into manageable pieces and add to the pan, turning from time to time till golden in patches and almost tender.

Core and roughly chop the apples, but don't peel them. Stir them into the pan and leave to putter gently till they are on the verge of collapse. Avoid stirring too much, which is likely to mash the softening pumpkin. Finely grate the zest from the lemon and add it to the pan with the juice, the caraway seeds and a little salt.

You should end up with a pan of highly fragrant, tender pumpkin, onion and apple on the verge of collapse. Serve alongside something meaty or, as I usually have it, as a main dish in its own right.

A new pumpkin laksa for a cold night

The first time I included pumpkin in a coconut-scented laksa was for a Bonfire Night supper in 2004 (see *The Kitchen Diaries*). The soup had to be sensational to make up for our distinct lack of fireworks (I think we wrote our names in the air with sparklers). Rich, sweet-sour, mouth-tinglingly hot and yet curiously soothing, it had everything you need in a soup for a frosty night.

There is much pleasure to be had in the constant tweaking of a recipe to change not its essential character but its details. And so it has been with this soup. I have since gone on to remove the tomatoes or add some shredded greens as the mood and the state of the larder take me. Such improvisations, many made at the last minute, need to be done with care: you don't want too many flavours going on. Vietnamese soups such as this are traditionally ingredient rich but should never taste confused. By the same token, to simplify it too much would be to lose the soup's generosity and complexity and therefore its point.

The laksa appears complicated at first but in practice it is far from it. Once you understand the basics, the recipe falls into place and becomes something you can fiddle with to suit your own taste. The basic spice paste needs heat (ginger, garlic, tiny bird's eye chillies); the liquid needs body and sweetness (coconut milk, rich stock); the finish needs sourness and freshness (lime juice, mint, coriander). The necessary saltiness comes from nam pla and tamari rather than salt itself. These notes in place, you can feel free to include noodles, tomatoes, greens, sweet vegetables or meat as you wish. What matters is balance.

enough for 4
pumpkin, unskinned – 350g
coriander and mint leaves, to finish

for the spice paste
red bird's eye chillies – 3–4
garlic – 2 cloves
ginger – a thumb-sized lump
lemongrass – 2 plump stalks
coriander roots – 5 or 6
coriander leaves – a handful
sesame oil – 2 tablespoons

for the soup
chicken or vegetable stock – 600ml
coconut milk – 400ml
nam pla (Thai fish sauce) – 2 tablespoons
tamari – 1–2 tablespoons, to taste
the juice of a lime
dried noodles – 100g, cooked as it says on the packet, then drained

Peel and seed the pumpkin and cut the flesh into large chunks. Cook in a steamer or in a metal colander balanced over a pan of boiling water until tender. Remove from the heat.

For the spice paste, remove the stalks from the chillies, peel the garlic, peel and roughly chop the ginger and lemongrass. Put them all into a food processor with the coriander roots and leaves and the sesame oil and blitz till you have a rough paste.

Get a large, deep pan hot and add the spice paste. Fry for a minute, then stir in the stock and coconut milk and bring to the boil. Allow to simmer for seven to ten minutes, then stir in the nam pla, tamari, lime juice, pumpkin and the cooked and drained noodles. Simmer briefly, add the coriander and mint leaves over the top and serve in deep bowls.

Salad leaves

In deepest summer, when all is quiet and, ideally, a heavy shower has just taken the edge off the heat, I like to put a single, perfect lettuce on the table together with a knife and a bottle of olive oil. You cut the crisp heart of the lettuce, still wet from the cold tap, into four and eat it as it is, with maybe just a little of the oil to gather in the folds of the leaves.

If the lettuce has long, crisp leaves I will sometimes use mayonnaise instead, thinned with a little cream or hot water until you can trickle it slowly over the ice-crisp ribs. It may not be a lettuce in its purest sense. It may be a vast chicory such as Castelfranco, all pink and cream like a cabbage rose, or a mop-head of green and white frisée, in which case I will use nothing but a squeeze of lemon juice.

There is something peaceful, almost sleep inducing, about a lettuce. The Latin name, *Lactuca*, is a reminder of the milky sap that appears from its stalk as you slice it. It was believed to control lust. I can see what they mean. Even at its crispest, a lettuce is gentle, calm, almost timid. The soporific effects are due to lactucin and lactucopicrin, which in small doses act as a sedative. Large amounts are said to have the opposite result, and lettuce was used as a sexual stimulant by the Egyptians. So, easy does it with the Little Gem.

We tend to take most salad leaves for granted, rarely affording them the respect they deserve. Flavour isn't really the point here. Texture and composition are almost more fundamental to what we are likely to call a good lettuce. Most of all, it must be fresh, almost more so than any other vegetable. When they are newly picked, with the dew still sitting in the waves and dimples of their leaves, you see these greens in a new light, a vegetable of the utmost tender, fragile beauty.

Lettuce loves cool weather, as somehow you might expect from its languid character, and will bolt if left growing in the sun. By bolt, I mean go to seed rather than run off. They prefer to grow in early or late summer rather than August, and in a slightly shaded place. Mine survive well enough under the medlar tree, the light filtered by the loose canopy of leaves. Sorrel grows here too, alongside coriander, French parsley, Reine de Glace lettuce and young green oakleaf.

I adore salad in all its forms, from the huge cups of iceberg to the red-tinged batavias and cheeky Tom Thumbs. Salad leaves are probably at their most romantic when the leaves are in the form of a full-blown rose, but the firmer varieties, with their longer, straighter leaves and snappable stems, are often the most useful. Anything with a rib crisp enough to scoop up hummus gets my vote. They take a dressing more happily than the very soft-fleshed varieties, which are inclined to become sodden once they meet the vinaigrette. Even a spoonful of dressing can dissolve some of the soft outer leaves of a young butterhead.

I feel slightly uncomfortable without a lettuce in the fridge, in much the same way I do without a lemon or a lump of craggy-edged Parmesan. I wouldn't feel much of a cook without the wherewithal to make salad.

The selection of salad leaves available to us in the shops has never been greater, and they go way beyond the simple green lettuce so dear to our hearts, with leaves of every shape, texture and nuance you could imagine (I made a stunning salad from tiny pak choi and watercress leaves the other day). The point of sowing seed at home is not so much the joy of picking your own fat-hearted lettuce (though that can be a proud moment) but having the wherewithal to snip immature leaves as and when you need them.

The perennially useful, pleasingly brittle iceberg and the reliable Webb's Wonder have been joined by all the salad leaves we could ever have dreamed of. Red, slightly bitter ones for eating with cheese; long, thin rabbit ears for dressing with Caesar sauce; great waves large enough to hold a chilli-spiked meatball; and mottled leaves to bring intrigue to a green salad. There are leaves the size of pancakes and others no bigger than a teaspoon. Some are sold still growing for us to keep alive on the window ledge.

Immature leaves, barely the size of a Chinese soup spoon, and micro-leaves as small as emeralds are the leaves *du jour*. I like them, they add charm and curiosity to a bowl of lettuce, but I find it hard to beat the quiet majesty of a simple, hearted lettuce. Micro-leaves pack a punch. Sunflower, pumpkin, radish and sunflower seeds all produce shoots within a week or so of planting and leaves shortly after. They are cheap and straightforward to grow at home. I sprout them in a traditional salad sprouter but they will work on a thick layer of damp cotton wool or kitchen roll too. No matter that they are small; their flavours come in waves of spice and earth, as if to make up for their diminutive stature.

Salad leaves in the garden

I have more success with salad leaves than any other seeds. They germinate in days and grow happily in shallow compost. The difficulties arise once they are large enough to plant out in the garden, where they find themselves at the mercy of all that creeps and crawls in the veg patch.

Lettuce seeds germinate quickly, sometimes in less than a week, and can be grown on a windowsill if necessary. Depending on variety and size, they can be ready to pick in six weeks. Hearted lettuces will often take another month, depending on the weather.

As you might expect from such fragile shoots, lettuce can be capricious. A general rule is to keep it away from fierce heat, which makes it send up seed heads, and sow in spring, late summer and early autumn. It tends to arrive in packets containing hundreds or even thousands of seeds, and needs sowing with a careful hand to avoid clumps. The thinnings, barely the size of your little finger, can be eaten as a particularly tender salad ingredient.

I sow mine in fine compost in a shallow seed tray, water them well and leave in a cool, slightly shaded place to sprout. A covering of a plastic cloche or even the shade of a tree will help keep the worst of the sun off them. Within a week or two, they are up and form a mass of closely packed green leaves, the best of which can then be removed with a dibber or pencil and planted into larger pots or outside in a prepared bed. Only plant them straight outside if you have some slug and snail protection. Lettuce likes fine, free-draining soil without too many lumps. A sandy loam is ideal.

It is best not to over-water the seedlings, as it can result in mildew, particularly with the softer-leaved varieties. I rarely water mine more than two or three times a week. As they start to heart up, most varieties can get very thirsty – a lettuce is about 90 per cent water – so it is worth increasing it to once a day. Too much rain is a problem for anything with very fragile leaves. Not only can it make the smaller leaves soggy (I have just lost a whole tray of unprotected seedlings during a day of torrential rain) but it encourages the slugs and snails to come out to play.

You can use virtually any container for growing a few young leaves. I find wooden seed trays lined with newspaper and filled with compost work very well, as do window boxes. The deep dimensions of the latter allow a more substantial root system, and therefore larger leaves. To be honest, anything will do, even old cans and polystyrene boxes.

Picking

There are two ways to approach picking your lettuces: either harvest the whole head in one swoop or carefully cut the outside leaves, leaving the smaller ones in place for later. New leaves will emerge within a week or two. This cut-and-come again method works well with a mixture of leaves all sown in one box. I use a deep, wooden tray lined with plastic and filled with seed and cutting compost. My choice of leaves varies according to the time of year, but in early summer, as I write, it contains ruby chard, frisée, rocket and oakleaf lettuces. Each leaf is harvested individually, cut just above the growing point. New leaves sprout to replace them within a few days.

Lettuce – the four characters

I think of lettuce as having four distinct leaf types: blousy and soft; crisp; long; and the loose, jagged ones. It is not a correct classification in either a horticultural or a culinary sense, but it helps me compose a more interesting salad and that is what matters.

Each type of leaf has its own virtues. Sometimes I want a simple plate of soft, buttery leaves; other times something crisp and icy. Mostly, I like a little of each, so I don't fall asleep half way through my salad.

Soft leaves – the Peter Rabbit lettuces
Soft, tender butterhead lettuce is often maligned. With their tight, upward-facing leaves in a rosette formation, these are the lettuces of summers past.

Those that fit this description, such as red-blushed Quattro Stagioni, the aptly named Tom Thumb and the milky-sapped Buttercrunch indeed have a sleepy quality. In the garden, I find their low-lying leaves are more attractive to slugs than the upright, crisper varieties. It is as if they are rolling out a carpet in welcome.

The leaves become waxier towards the heart and their softness seems somehow perfect for cold salmon on a blisteringly hot summer's day. They need a light dressing, so as not to make the fragile leaves 'melt'. You can doze off in the shade afterwards. Squeeze them tenderly when you are shopping, to check for a decent heart.

Quattro Stagioni (Marvel of the Four Seasons) Softish, bronze-tinted leaves with good flavour.
Buttercrunch Quick to grow, softly crunchy leaves with a pale, tender heart.
May Queen Lovely old-fashioned variety. Large, soft leaves with a hint of pink around the edges. Resembles an old cabbage rose.
Tom Thumb Small, as you might expect, but with good flavour and fast

growth. Good for small gardens, as they take up half the space
of a big lettuce.

Also look out for the compact butterhead, Fortune, the soft, heavily
blistered leaves of Kagraner Sommer, and Parella, with its ability to cope
with cold weather.

Crisp leaves – adding crunch to the salad bowl
Crisphead lettuces, such as Reine de Glace, Webb's Wonderful and the
icebergs, have a firm heart and a clear, sweet, brightness to their leaves.
The heart is often white, and some have delightfully unruly edges. In the
garden they are mildly frost tolerant. In the kitchen they will take a punchy
dressing, or one thick with lemon and extra virgin oil. A recently picked
one will keep for a week in the fridge, wrapped in newspaper or in a sealed
plastic bag.

Reine de Glace Possibly my favourite lettuce. Crisp but somewhat spiky
leaves, good lettuce flavour, a little unobtrusive bitterness. Easy to grow.
Webb's Wonderful Big, traditional salad lettuce with a pale, crisp heart.
Amorina Pink, frilly leaves, for late-spring planting. A little short on
flavour to my mind.
Bijou Glossy, blistered leaves the colour of dried blood. A very beautiful
lettuce with a hint of bitterness. Cut and come again.
Salardin Pretty, frilled-edged lettuce with crisp, bright leaves. Stands
well in the garden without bolting.
Ice Queen Crisp, wavy, pointed leaves and a tight head. Good
summer lettuce.

Also look out for the tight-hearted early Great Lakes, the waxy, quick-
growing Ice King, and Lakeland, a variety that works well in our climate,
producing more heart than outer leaves.

Long leaves – lettuce of the seven moons
Romaine, or as we know it more bluntly, Cos, has been known as Roman
lettuce since the fourteenth century, when the Popes moved from Rome to
Avignon, bringing this long-leaved, tight-hearted lettuce with them. The
crunch is exhilarating, even eaten without dressing. It will take anything you
care to throw at it, even the rich egg-yolk-and-olive-oil Caesar dressing, for
which it is the only acceptable leaf. Little Gem, as useful as it is ubiquitous,
is a stunted version of Cos.

Lobjoits Sweet, long leaves and will heart up well if you water it well.
Little Gem Sweet, pale lettuce with a firm, pointed heart. Barely bigger
than a head of chicory.

Freckles Thin, pale green leaves with maroon mottling.
Chartwell Crunchy, sweet and with an exceptional flavour.
Balloon Large, red-brown leaves.
Pandero The red-leaved Little Gem.

Also keep an eye open for the magically named Lattuga delle Sette Lune, with its long, tightly packed leaves and faint ruby blotches. I have had much success with this beautiful Roman lettuce.

Loose leaves – canary tongues and oak leaves
Loosehead lettuces often have oakleaf-shaped leaves and a soft texture like silk underwear. They can liven up an everyday affair. I considered them overrated till I planted the canary-tongued Lingua di Canarino, which has the typically notched leaves but a little more crispness than its red-tinged cousins. The hand-sized outer leaves of the larger oakleaf varieties can be a little dull. Inside they are crisp and rather pretty. A few in a mixed leaf salad are interesting but I find they bore in quantity. The point is not to pick them as a whole head – although you can – but to pick the outer leaves a few at a time.

Lollo Biondi Low on flavour but some find the pale, frilly leaves pretty in a salad. Doesn't form a heart.
Lollo Rosso Ditto, but with even less enthusiasm.
Grenoble French alpine lettuce with wavy, pink-tinged leaves. Can be frost tolerant, so worth a late autumn planting.
Rubens Red A crisp, emerald green and burgundy leaf that will also heart.
Salad Bowl A green oakleaf type with a mild flavour. Don't over-water. A red version is available.

Also look out for Ashbrook, a crunchy, long-leaved variety, Batavia Blonde, which doesn't turn bitter in the heat and is good for summer growing, the very frilly Bergamo, the vigorous Black Seeded Simpson, and New Red Fire, with a compact habit and lots of intense, burgundy-red leaves.

Other good leaves

Good King Henry Wide, pointed leaves like a shield and a flavour similar to spinach. A perennial that will withstand some shade.
Orache Growing up to two metres in height, these decorative annuals are mild, soft leaved and rather beautiful. The red version is a delightful addition to the salad patch.
Sorrel My clump of sorrel grows under a tree, and the occasional lemony leaf in a spinach salad is both surprising and refreshing. It comes back

year after year if you can get it established. Pick the outer leaves first. The shield-shaped buckler variety will grow happily in a pot for years. At least, mine has.

Mizuna Feathery, spiky, almost fern-like leaves that add bulk and visual interest to a bowl of salad. Sow right through the summer, picking the leaves when they are the length of your middle finger.

Corn Salad It is almost impossible to kill this little plant. I pick the curiously soft and crunchy leaf by the whole rosette rather than individually, dropping them into a mixture of larger, stronger leaves. Possibly the mildest-tasting leaf of all.

Purslane Rounded, succulent leaves with a very mild flavour and crunchy texture.

Claytonia The prettiest leaf, almost triangular in shape, with a delicate flowering shoot coming from its centre. Mild, refreshing and exceptionally delicate. It needs a light, sandy soil, and can be sown in summer for early spring picking and even in winter with some cloche protection.

Landcress A good little plant this, providing dark, glossy, watercress-like leaves all winter. Almost impossible to kill, it gets very hot to the tongue in summer. Find it a moist corner in rich soil and its rounded leaves will see you through the coldest and most barren of months.

Rocket Throw in a few young rocket leaves and in one stroke you will have added exhilarating bitterness, mild heat and interesting texture. While a bowl of lone rocket leaves is sometimes hard going – they can be spiky in the mouth – a few tucked amongst softer, more rounded leaves bring a little excitement.

A lettuce diary

May A cold, wet day in late May and I plant an assortment of lettuce seed in shallow wooden trays: Reine de Glace, a jagged-edged, crisphead variety that grows no matter how cold the weather is, and the ancient Lingua di Canarino, a loose-headed lettuce with bright green, heavily notched leaves like long, tender oak leaves. Neither variety bolts in hot weather.

June Lettuces dislike their roots being disturbed. Ideally you plant where they are to grow, but snails see off very young seedlings in my garden, so I transplant them when they are 3cm high, holding them by the leaf rather than the fragile root. They sulk for a week, then, after a good rain, they settle and send up new leaves. Each lettuce is surrounded by a copper ring and some environmentally acceptable slug pellets.

July The loosehead varieties in the garden are sending up long plumes of acid-green leaves with wavy edges. The crisp hearts are in good leaf but have yet to plump up. My loathing of frills of any sort extends to lettuce. Lollo Rosso particularly offends. There is no escaping it this month, when it appears at every turn, even showing its face in my organic box. I feel I am being persecuted.

July 27 My ideal lettuce, the salad of a summer's afternoon dream, is a hearted variety, the stems crisp and full of sap, the leaves firm enough to stand on their backs like an open shell. Reine de Glace fits like a glove. The leaves are almost the size of the outer leaves of an iceberg but have a playful movement to them, like a surfer's wave. If you had to design the perfect mixture of softness and crunch, this would be it. They will stand up to a certain amount of heat, so I sow as late as July. This is the lettuce for that high-summer cold chicken salad, with white-tipped radishes, spanking-fresh spring onions, cucumber, watercress and real salad cream.

August Traditionally a difficult time for any fragile leaf. The canary-tongued varieties are magnificent – tall, crisp leaved and very beautifully formed. They are eating well, and strong enough of stature to take a dressing made of lemon juice, tarragon and cream. They will see me through till the frosts.

And…

* Raised beds or plastic cloches are the most appropriate way of growing lettuce in the garden; box-lined hedges, which double as snail hotels, the least.
* If you grow under cloches, make sure your seedlings are well ventilated. Lettuces hate to swelter.
* Slugs and snails are the enemy. Do everything you can to discourage them except resorting to slug pellets without environmentally sound credentials.
* Some varieties can be grown outdoors even in winter; check on the packet before planting.
* Both the seed and the plants like warm soil rather than hot.
* You can sow indoors from as early as January.
* An old fruit crate, lined with plastic and filled with seed compost, can be filled with several different varieties for picking throughout the summer.
* Pick single leaves regularly to encourage new growth, or leave the plant to form a large head.

Salad in the kitchen

Making salad is a daily ritual in our house. I can take all the time in the world over washing the leaves in ice-cold water – I use a large pottery bowl with a jade-green glaze, which flatters the leaves even as you wash them (why shouldn't washing vegetables be a pleasure?). Each leaf is unfolded tenderly, thoughtfully, and inspected for hidden aphids. Finding a slug in my salad is a horror I can live without. The leaves crisp slightly if the water is cold enough. It perks them up just as it would us.

I loathe kitchen clutter and unused gadgets, yet I wouldn't want to live without my salad spinner. Its centrifugal force dries the leaves without bruising them and that, to me, is essential. If I have to do without, then I put a piece of white, dimpled kitchen roll in the drained leaves and toss them gently. It soaks up an amazing amount of water. If you don't spin your lettuce, you will get soggy leaves and a diluted dressing.

You can cook with lettuce, watercress and chicory but not with rocket (though it makes a good pesto) or with the very fragile mustard and cress. Lettuce braised with broad beans and olive oil is a light, soothing summer vegetable dish, and lettuce soup is a possibility, but I wouldn't get fancier than that.

A word about watercress

Watercress makes a famous soup and is exceptional as a flavouring for mayonnaise to serve with cold salmon – though to this cook it is never better than when seen in a fat, thick-stalked sprig, its leaves still glistening with water, tucked into a chicken salad or under a rare steak.

Watercress is the filling for my favourite sandwich. Thick white bread so fresh it is barely cool, unsalted butter so cold it makes holes in the bread, then watercress leaves and their thick stalks, the faintest snow of sea salt. You could add bacon if the fancy takes you, or cold chicken, or some thin slices of posh ham, or smoked salmon or eel, or layers of snow-white goat's cheese, but I wouldn't. For me, a cool, lush green watercress sandwich eaten on a baking hot summer's afternoon, ranks higher than anything.

Due to its heat and slight spicy quality, this leaf is best added in small amounts to other, sweeter leaves. Yet a simple watercress salad with a mustardy dressing and a knife-sharp hit of red wine vinegar is just the thing for a supper of cold duck. A few slices of blood orange would be welcome too.

Putting a salad together

If there was a recipe that stood for everything I believe about good eating, it would be the quiet understatement that is a single variety of salad leaf in a simple bowl. Each leaf should be perfect, the dressing light and barely present, the whole effect one of generous simplicity.

More than baking bread or making a cake, rolling pastry or basting the roast, I am at my happiest in the kitchen when I am putting a salad together. Whether it is a single variety of leaf lightly dressed, or a more complex arrangement of leaves that flatter one another, the making of a salad is where kitchen craft crosses over into art.

There is much pleasure to be had in a bowl of leaves, herbs and even flowers whose constituents have been chosen with great care. In early spring there might be a mixture of rocket, sorrel and trevise; in summer an inspired collection of everything you can find; then later, as the evenings shorten, a darker mix of burgundy and dense green leaves.

I make a salad specifically to fit the season. In spring, a mixture of the growing tips, bright and mild, a testament to rising sap; in summer an offering of full-blown lettuce, soft, tranquil and pale; in winter a bowl of dark and sultry notes with a sting of bitterness from a member of the chicory family. This isn't always as deliberate as it sounds. Just buying or picking the leaves in season will often dictate the nature of your salad.

Salad leaves need to be rinsed. I do this in a large bowl of very cold water, unfurling and rinsing each leaf as I go. They are dried in a spinner, then piled into the salad bowl on top of the puddle of dressing. I then gently toss the salad with my hands, lightly coating each leaf with dressing.

I enjoy choosing which leaves to put in. Sometimes I am after a balance of soft, sweet, bitter and crisp. Another day I might be looking for something especially gentle or hot. Matching certain leaves to what they are to accompany allows a certain amount of poetic licence: bitter leaves with a pork chop; sweet leaves with cold poached fish; a bowl of exclusively mustardy leaves to go with cold, rose-coloured beef. Then there is the day when you just get it wrong – too many earthy flavours together, a plethora of bitter leaves, a mild mixture that leaves you wanting. Even the mistakes can be interesting.

Leaves and their character

The flavour of salad leaves varies according to the age of the leaf and the time of year. Cold weather has a sweetening effect on bitter leaves; the more mature the leaf, the more pronounced its attributes will be.

Cool, mild, sweet These are what I use as a base on which to build. Bitter, hot or spiky leaves stand out against a backdrop of any of the following: Little Gem, butterhead varieties, purslane, nabana, Chinese cabbage, mizuna, pak choi, tatsoi, texel, spinach, endive, corn salad (mâche), pea shoots.
Crisp Long, thin leaves tend to be crisper than fat, round ones. This includes the Cos family, iceberg and fully mature Buttercrunch (a cross between soft butterhead and iceberg).
Bitter The chicories, including radicchio and endive (the endives are generally sweeter), rocket and dandelion. The heart leaves, tucked away in

the middle of the plant, tend to be milder than the outer leaves.
The bitterness is more pronounced in hot weather and in older leaves.
Spiky A few jagged-edged leaves make an exciting contrast to the softer
ones. More than a few is hard going and can tickle the throat. Choose from
mizuna, rocket, frisée and young dandelion.
Brightly coloured The red leaves are good either as the occasional leaf in
a mixture of cool greens or as a dominant theme. Their flavours tend to be
more pungent than the green. Try amaranth, red perilla, beet leaves, red
oakleaf, small ruby and rainbow chard leaves, radicchio, and the red and
freckled lettuces.
Hot and spicy A few hot-to-the-tongue leaves to add to a bulk quantity
of milder leaves: watercress, basil, mint (although generally cooling as a
flavouring, the raw leaf is hot to the tongue, like a Polo mint), kale, mibuna,
radish leaves, rocket, cress. Nasturtium leaves have a light, peppery quality.
Mustard flavour A small number of mustard-flavoured leaves can work
well in a salad destined to accompany pork or perhaps mackerel. You only
need a few. Choose from kailaan, green-in-snow, giant red mustard, cress.
They are all exceptionally easy to grow.
Earthy Kohlrabi, beetroot and chard leaves.
Citrus Sorrel, purslane, buckler-leaf sorrel for adding freshness and
exuberance.

Dressing your salad

A dressing is about balance and harmony, both of the ingredients within
it and that of the dressing and the leaves. That said, it shouldn't be assumed
that we must make a dressing at all. A good aromatic vinegar such as
balsamic or sherry is often all you need, or a trickle of olive oil or a squeeze
of lemon. Rocket leaves, spiky, peppery and vital, often get nothing more
than salt and lemon at my table.

I rarely measure the ingredients for a salad dressing. In fact, whenever
I do it never seems quite right. Ardent recipe followers will be devastated but
good dressing is very much a case of intuition rather than doing what we are
told. Sometimes the recipe is obvious, such as a sweeter dressing for bitter
leaves. Other times you can just go as your appetite takes you.

The salt should be dissolved first in the vinegar or lemon juice. I find
this mellows the acidity of the liquid. I then beat the oil in with a fork or
a 'doll's-house' whisk I keep especially for the job. It is pleasing when the
dressing emulsifies, as it coats the leaves more evenly, but I don't worry if
it doesn't.

A mild Dijon mustard is worth adding for a thicker result, and in
particular for a mild, leafy salad to accompany cold meats. It is also a good
one to use with spinach.

A simple dressing for mild leaves

Dissolve a pinch of sea salt in the juice of half a lemon. Beat in 100ml olive oil, then a little black pepper.

A classic dressing

Proportions vary, according to the exact qualities of the individual ingredients and to our personal taste, but it is generally accepted that a classic salad dressing will be about four parts fruity olive oil to one of red wine vinegar. A small shallot, finely chopped, is acceptable and should be added to the vinegar twenty minutes before the dressing is made, to give it time to mellow. Some like garlic in the recipe too, though not me. Well, occasionally in early summer, when the new, pink-flushed cloves appear.

Put a pinch of salt in a small bowl, then pour over the vinegar. Dissolve the salt by stirring, then whisk in the olive oil and a little black pepper.

A mustardy dressing

You really don't need much mustard, and it should be the mild Dijon variety if it isn't to overpower the leaves. A half teaspoon is enough, beaten into the vinegar of the classic dressing above just before the oil.

A lemon dressing for summer

Mix together a pinch of sea salt, a teaspoon of Dijon mustard and the juice of half a lemon. Beat in 200ml olive oil and a teaspoon of grated lemon zest. Leave for a few minutes for the ingredients to get to know one another.

A walnut oil dressing

The bitter endives particularly appreciate the creamy, nutty notes of walnut oil. Rather than using entirely walnut oil, which runs the risk of cloying, I use it half and half with either sunflower or a light, unpushy olive oil such as those from France.

Put a tablespoon of Dijon mustard in a small bowl with a pinch of sugar and three pinches of sea salt. Whisk in 2 tablespoons of lemon juice, then 3 of light olive oil and 3 of walnut oil. Stir in a tablespoon of cold water and a little pepper. Some toasted walnut halves, scattered amongst the leaves like mushrooms in the autumn grass, would be appropriate and delicious.

A creamy dressing

Dijon mustard – 2 teaspoons
tarragon vinegar – 2 teaspoons
mild olive oil – 3–4 tablespoons
double or whipping cream – 2–3 tablespoons
flat-leafed parsley leaves – a handful

Mix the mustard, vinegar and olive oil with a small whisk, then stir in the cream. Roughly chop the parsley leaves and add them. Season with salt and black pepper. Pour the dressing on to the salad and toss gently.

A salad of lettuce, peas and ham

enough for 4
cooked ham – 250g
shelled fresh peas – 180g
white bread – 75g
a little oil
a large, soft-leaved lettuce
Berkswell or other deep-flavoured, hard farmhouse cheese – 150g
the creamy dressing, above

Shred the ham into large bite-sized pieces. You could use a knife for this if you wish, but I prefer the rough texture of pieces torn by hand. Cook the peas briefly in deep, lightly salted water, then drain.

Tear the bread into small pieces, discarding the crusts as you go. Fry in a shallow layer of oil in a non-stick pan. As soon as they are nicely golden, remove to kitchen paper to drain. Salt them lightly.

Whilst the bread is cooking, wash the lettuce, separate the leaves, tear them into manageable pieces and put them in a serving bowl.

Take shavings of the cheese with a vegetable peeler and toss them into the lettuce leaves with the peas, golden bread and shredded ham. Pour the dressing on to the salad and toss gently.

Cooking with salad leaves

There are odd occasions when you might want to put some heat under your salad leaves. Here are a few of them.

A soup of lettuce and peas

A good soup for a spring day, bright green and not too filling.

enough for 6
a large, round lettuce, about 400g
butter – a thick slice
shallots – 2
shelled peas – 500g
chicken or vegetable stock, or water – a litre
mint – 3 bushy sprigs

Separate the lettuce leaves and wash them thoroughly. Even the smallest amount of grit will ruin the soup. Melt the butter in a deep saucepan over a low to moderate heat. Peel the shallots, slice them thinly, then let them soften in the butter. When they are tender but have yet to colour, chop the lettuce up a bit and stir it into the butter. As soon as it has wilted, tip in the peas, stock and mint leaves and bring to the boil. Turn the heat down, season with salt and black pepper and leave to simmer for seven to ten minutes.

Remove the pan from the heat and blend the soup in a liquidiser till smooth. Check the seasoning and serve hot.

A dish of lettuce for deepest summer

I ate this rather soothing way with lettuce twice last week, once for lunch, accompanied by a piece of salmon, the second time for supper, with nothing but a hunk of soft farmhouse bread, the sort with a dusting of white flour on top. Light, juicy and clean tasting.

enough for 2 as a light meal, 4 as a side dish
medium lettuces – 2
butter – a thick slice
unsmoked bacon – 75g, diced
small leeks – 2
shelled peas or broad beans – 250g
vegetable stock – 250ml

Pull away and discard any tatty leaves from the lettuces, then cut each lettuce into quarters. Wash under cold running water to remove any trapped grit or aphids.

Melt the butter in a heavy-based pan to which you have a lid. Add the diced bacon and leave it to stew in the butter for five minutes or so over a moderate heat. Meanwhile trim and wash the leeks and cut them into short pieces. Add them to the pan and continue cooking, stirring now and again, till they have started to soften.

Tip in the peas or broad beans, lettuce and stock, add a seasoning of salt and black pepper and bring to the boil. Turn it down as soon as it starts to bubble furiously, then cover with a tightly fitting lid. Leave to simmer for twenty minutes, by which time the lettuce will have sunk to four silky mounds and the liquor will have almost vanished.

Lift out the lettuce, leeks, peas and bacon with a draining spoon and place on a serving dish. If there is more than a ladleful of liquid in the pan, turn up the heat and boil furiously to reduce it a little. Check the seasoning and pour it over the lettuce.

Spinach

Green, soothing, yet somehow vibrant, creamed spinach is something I could eat at every meal. I appreciate its calming, 'there, there' quality with slices of warm ham, a pepper-crusted steak, a piece of grilled fish. Forget forks; the best way to get creamed spinach from plate to mouth is with a crisp and salty chip.

At the Saturday market, where I shop for stalks of broccoli no thicker than my little finger and beetroot pulled from the ground the morning before, there is often a wicker crate of spinach. Large leaves by today's standards, with stems thick enough to crunch, this is spinach that is as appropriate in a salad as it is in a soup, its large stems and leaves pert enough to stand up in your hand like a bunch of flowers.

When spinach is truly fresh, it squeaks as you rummage around in the pile, like the sound of wet Wellingtons on a rubber floor. I use this to gauge its freshness. Older leaves tend to relax, even flop, and don't talk to us as we pick them up. They are fine for soup. Sound, freshly picked leaves almost beg you to take them home.

There are two spinaches that really interest me: the coarse-leaved, easy-to-grow 'perpetual' variety, which is botanically related to beetroot and Swiss chard, and the softer, tricky, 'true' spinach, *Spinacia oleracea*. Both are excellent in the kitchen, though true spinach is regarded as having the more refined flavour. True spinach is the one for salads, and can be picked very young; perpetual needs marginally longer cooking and is generally too tough for a salad.

Spinach is thought to have first been domesticated in Nepal, coming to Britain via Persia and Spain around the eleventh century. Many of the classic spinach recipes we use tend to be Indian or Italian, the latter influence coming, like so many other foods, from Catherine de Medici (could that woman eat or what?) and leaving us with such delights as eggs Florentine and all those intricate, layered bakes with cheese on top that are to this day labelled after her native city of Florence. *A la Florentine* always suggests something baked on a bed of the green stuff.

I have had a bumpy ride with this leaf, refusing to eat it until I was at least in double figures. My sister-in-law won me over by shrieking, 'Ooooh, spinach!' on spotting a crate at the greengrocer's. Her excitement (I had never seen anyone get excited over a vegetable before) was contagious and we took it straight home before the leaves had time to wilt. The speed at which the leaves arrived, in a generous emerald curl on the plate, was a revelation. A turning point too, if I think about it. Never before had I experienced a vegetable so tender, so green, so full of life.

Spinach in the garden

Both 'true' spinach and the tougher 'perpetual' spinach need cool, moist conditions and a chance of partial shade if they are to perform well. Perpetual is less fussy but both like plenty of moisture at their roots and prefer the soil to have been well manured before sowing. A dressing of pelleted chicken manure will go down well.

Most people sow the seed directly, as the seedlings are particularly fragile and difficult to transplant. The seeds will not germinate if the weather is too hot, so sow from mid spring and again in early autumn, to keep you going through till the frosts. I sow generously, as the slugs are bound to get more than a few, and they are easier than carrots to thin out. In my experience the perpetual variety can be slow to germinate. Give it a good three or four weeks.

Plants need to be about 18cm apart, in rows with 30cm between them. Mine are often a bit closer than that, due to lack of space. Plants too closely packed in can suffer from mildew. I have had most success using a plastic cloche at the early stages of growth, to protect them from slimy predators and gambolling fox cubs. Space permitting, you can make consecutive plantings during spring and autumn.

Whereas some of the food we grow will carry on regardless of the weather, spinach does like a lot of water. Failure to provide enough moisture will result in the plants running to seed. Of course, the more we water, the more we attract the attention of snails, who find little more to their taste than a freshly watered spinach leaf.

I have little room for spinach. I grow it more as an exercise to see how it behaves. Dominant is a reliable variety, bred for its true spinach flavour and disease resistance, and it has fared well enough on the cool, lightly shaded side of the garden. It's a magnet for greedy slugs, and the capacity for an entire row to shrink to a spoonful in the pan has ruled it out as a regular crop for me. There just isn't the space here.

I plant the spiky seeds straight into a bed on the cool side of the vegetable patch in early April, protect the seedlings as much as I can under cloches and scatter organic slug pellets around the edges. Friends with more space than I have plant perpetual spinach in September, leaving the young plants to over-winter. They pick in early spring, but often complain that the results are not as good as their spring-planted crop. Although perpetual spinach is relatively hardy (after a decade of gardening, I am still surprised when any delicate leaves make it through the frost), anyone hoping to pick spinach in the depths of winter should probably try the coarser-leaved chard family.

Varieties

Spinach is ready for picking about twelve weeks after sowing.

Bordeaux Soft, rather small leaves with purple-red stems. A very tender variety.
Medania Smooth leaves, resistant to mildew, slow to bolt. A good one for mid-season planting.
Giant Noble Enormous thick leaves, but tender nonetheless.
Bloomsdale Crumply, fleshy leaves with good flavour.
Dominant Soft, crinkly leaves with excellent flavour. Sarah Raven's favourite variety.
Perpetual Related to Swiss chard. Tough, lightly crinkled leaves that rarely bolt. Cut and come again.

Spinach in the kitchen

I select spinach as much by feel as by eye. The smoother, waxier leaves are more appropriate for cooking than they are in a salad. Rub them gently between your thumb and forefinger; if they are pale and waxy with wide, smooth stems, then they are best in the pot. These coarser leaves tend to hold their volume a little better during cooking than the softer-leaved varieties.

Choosing spinach leaves for salad is easy. They will have a perkiness to them and an irresistible vitality. Their root ends tend to lose their pinkness as they age. It is never worth making a salad with anything but the freshest leaves. Even the smallest blemish will be exaggerated once it is in the bowl.

I dress and toss my salad as late as possible before eating. I sometimes put a puddle of dressing in the base of the bowl, the washed and dried leaves on top, and only toss the two as I eat. Spinach dressed too early has a habit of blackening.

You can make a salad with cooked spinach, too. I wilt the wet leaves in a shallow, tightly lidded pan, squeeze them almost dry, then toss with either lemon oil or a yoghurt dressing. You can spend too much time untangling a mass of wilted and squeezed spinach, and a loose lump of leaves works well enough.

I am not sure you really 'cook' spinach. It is more a case of showing it the pan. No other leaf eaten as a vegetable becomes tender so quickly – a matter of seconds rather than minutes.

The leaves need little or no water in the pan. They will often cook in the moisture that clings to the folds in the leaves after washing. I generally take them straight from sink to pan, dripping water along the counter as I go. Covered with a lid, that is all the liquid they need in which to steam, though they are less likely to stick to the pan if you pour in a film of water first. I find a pair of kitchen tongs invaluable here, for turning the spinach once, maybe twice, during cooking, each time replacing the lid so that the leaves soften in their own steam.

The only time the leaves get a long cooking is when they are being used as an integral layer in a baked dish – say, between chicken and sauce or between minced beef and pasta in a florentine – or when they are simmered with potatoes in a stove-top Indian *saag aloo*. Although any cooking time longer than a few minutes is normally the death knell for fragile leaves, the cooked spinach survives by being protected by the layers of sauce, and can often emerge a startlingly bright green.

Spinach disappears in the pan. You stuff a green mountain of squeaking leaves into the pot, tucking in stray stalks as you squash down the lid, then four minutes later you lift out a squidgy bundle the size of your fist, maybe smaller. You press the water from it and your green mountain has shrunk to the size of a blackbird's egg. And that is what happens to it in the hands of gentle, watchful cooks. Heaven knows what someone who habitually overcooks their greens is left with.

The general advice is to keep it well away from large quantities of water. But you know what? If you dip your bunch of greens into a pasta pan of deep, angrily boiling water, hold it under with a draining spoon for thirty seconds, then hoick it out, there is less shrinkage, the colour remains more vibrant and the leaves cook more evenly. They relax in seconds rather than minutes (heat-soluble vitamins disappear just as quickly in steam as they do in water). The choice is up to us. When cooking spinach, it's the seconds that count, rather than the method.

Many people experience the famous 'furry-teeth' effect when they have eaten up their spinach. This reaction – the effect of oxalic acid on your teeth – can be lessened by tossing your freshly cooked leaves in melted butter or cream. Curiously, oil doesn't seem to have the same effect. Another way to reduce the feeling is to squeeze a shot of lemon juice over the leaves. People make a bit of a fuss about it but it is honestly not something that particularly bothers me.

Washing spinach

Grit tucks itself into every curl and fold of the spinach plant, particularly at the point where the stalk meets the root. Even the smallest speck can ruin a bowl of soup or a salad. Anyone who has had the teeth-jarring experience of crunching on a piece of grit will probably agree with me that it is worth taking almost obsessive care over washing spinach.

I have never found rinsing the leaves under running water particularly successful and tend to go with the dunking method instead. Washing your leaves in a sink or two of water can use more water than rinsing them under a running tap, so I fill my most capacious bowl and then tip the used water on to the garden.

To clean your leaves thoroughly, fill the sink or a very large bowl with cold water. The icier the water, the crisper the leaves will be. Tip in the spinach and gently swish the bunches around by their roots in the water. Leave for ten minutes, during which time the trapped grit will gradually sink to the bottom.

Depending on how muddy your spinach is, you may need to repeat the process. Check each leaf individually – a very Zen moment – and gently shake them dry. Any destined for a salad will appreciate a ride in the salad spinner.

I am not a fan of the bagged, ready-rinsed salad leaf in general, and even less so of spinach. These round-ended leaves seem to have little going for them in terms of flavour or texture, and are less 'spinachy' than the pointed, crinkly varieties. They also have a curious ability to collapse into a dead faint as soon as you tip them out of their bag.

Seasoning your spinach

Nutmeg The warm, musky notes of nutmeg are an essential part of creamed spinach, working with both the leaves and the cream.
Orange The refreshing quality of sweet oranges, and especially the dark-fleshed 'blood' variety (often cringingly called 'ruby' by the more prissy supermarkets), is a good foil for the mineral notes of the leaves.
Lemon Any bright-tasting citrus fruit will cut the earthier notes of spinach leaves and lift the true flavour a notch or two. Lemon oil (made with olive oil and fresh lemon juice), lemon zest and juice and that of the lime all fit the bill, as does lemongrass.
Cream In soup, creamed vegetables and a dressing for wilted spinach.
Eggs Omelettes, soufflés, the classic *oeufs Florentine* and eggs Benedict all show the two as a marriage made in heaven.
Anchovies The salty little fillets have an extraordinary affinity with spinach. Use them in moderate amounts as a salad ingredient, or in a dressing.

Bacon and pancetta Spinach and bacon salad is a classic, but the two can also meet up in a soup.

Parmesan Include in a dressing for the leaves or as a seasoning for any hot dish. Use to form a crust for a spinach gratin or soufflé.

Pine nuts Waxy, pointed nuts (the round-ended ones are considered inferior by aficionados) marry more successfully with this leaf than any other nuts (though walnuts can be good, too). When they are toasted, their warm, oily quality adds a welcome crunch to a spinach salad. I sometimes scatter them over a mound of the cooked leaves, too.

Mushrooms Spinach and mushroom salad and soup are famous but the best of all to my mind is when spinach and mushrooms are used as a stuffing for pancakes.

Garlic Some vegetables take to the whiff of garlic more happily than others. Courgettes, tomatoes and aubergines love rubbing shoulders with a clove or two; less so French beans, broad beans and beetroot. Spinach cannot get enough of the stuff.

Yoghurt A blissful partnership.

And...

* The size of the leaf is no indication of its quality. Large leaves can be just as tender as those the length of your thumb.
* Washed leaves will keep in good condition for a couple of days in a sealed plastic bag in the lower section of the fridge. Pack them in whilst they are damp, but don't let water accumulate at the bottom of the bag or they will turn slimy.
* I often don't bother with salt when steaming spinach, but it can be added at the same time as you dress the cooked leaves with their melted butter, pan juices or oil.
* Butter is the preferred cooking medium, softening the 'furry-teeth' effect and muting the leaves' more strident mineral notes.
* Walnut and hazelnut oils make a more interesting dressing than olive for these leaves. Even more so if you involve lemon juice instead of vinegar.

Squeaking spinach, sizzling bacon

It's the first week of June, a grey sky threatening rain. I have bought true spinach home, the leaves pointed like the iron head of a prehistoric arrow. Tight little sprigs that stand up proud if you hold them at their pink base and crisp, water-rich stems that crunch when you break them.

It takes four washes to get the Herefordshire mud off them, plunging them over and over in deep water, each spent bowl of water poured over the garden. I have also bought some Ginger Pig long-back bacon, the rashers so long they have to be doubled over in the pan.

No oil, just the hot fat from the frying pan and a splash of sherry vinegar poured over at the last minute. I put the leaves in a dish, then a splash of vinegar, the roughly cut hot bacon and the spitting fat. No salt or pepper, but a few cooked broad beans instead. Just everything tossed immediately whilst the fat is still hot and the spinach cold. Not so much a recipe as an assembly – crisp, juicy stalks crunch under the teeth with the hot, salty, fatty bacon.

Such a simple salad works because the sweet bacon mellows the clean acidity of the spinach and the sherry vinegar unites the two. The vinegar turns the two ingredients into a salad, like someone introducing two friends they know will get on.

I could have included capers, or seeded grapes or even some sliced avocado, or hand-torn croûtons cooked in the bacon fat. But I didn't.

Spinach, orange and feta

A favourite salad of mine is one where the spinach leaves are matched with oranges and feta. Lush, salty, refreshing, I use it to lift the spirits.

For each person, wash a good double handful of small, perfect spinach leaves. Peel and thickly slice a large orange, preferably a 'blood' variety, catching as much of the juice as you can. Make a dressing with some of the juice, olive and walnut oil in equal amounts and a little black pepper, but no salt. Toss the leaves and orange slices in the dressing, then crumble over the feta cheese, keeping the pieces quite large. Add a few sprouted seeds perhaps, or some torn bread, toasted.

Classic creamed spinach

The white sauce way. Yes, it's a fag to make white sauce, but what you end up with here is creamed spinach of extraordinary solace and luxury.

> *enough for 4*
> milk – 300ml
> a small onion, peeled
> a bay leaf
> black peppercorns – 6
> spinach – 1kg
> butter – 50g
> plain flour – 50g
> double cream – 4 tablespoons
> nutmeg

Put the milk in a saucepan with the onion, bay leaf and black peppercorns. Bring to the boil, then turn down to a low heat and leave for ten minutes for the aromatics to do their stuff.

Discard the very toughest spinach stalks, then cook the leaves in a lidded pan with a film of water in the bottom. They should be tender in just a minute or two, maybe less. Drain and cool under cold running water, squeeze thoroughly but gently to remove most of the water, then chop finely.

Melt the butter in a heavy-based non-stick saucepan, stir in the flour and leave to cook for a couple of minutes, stirring so that it doesn't burn. Whisk in the warm milk; you don't need the aromatics, they have done their work. When the sauce starts to thicken, turn the heat to a low simmer and let it bubble gently for a good fifteen minutes. An occasional stir, taking care to get right in the corners, will prevent it burning.

Stir in the cream and chopped spinach, then finish with salt, pepper and a fine grating of nutmeg.

A contemporary take on creamed spinach

Making creamed spinach without the traditional backbone of white sauce produces a quicker, greener and slightly fresher-tasting result. It makes up in speed and greenness what it loses in nannying quality.

enough for 4
spinach – 1kg
butter – 30g
crème fraîche – 3 heaped tablespoons
nutmeg

Wash the spinach, pile it into a saucepan while it is still wet, cover with a lid and steam for a minute or two until it has relaxed. It will need to be turned in the pan a couple of times. Remove, drain, squeeze as much as you can to remove the water, then put into a food processor with the butter and blitz till smooth. Now stir in the crème fraîche, some salt and pepper and a little nutmeg.

A quick, hot spinach side dish

enough for 4 as a side dish
ginger – a thumb-sized piece
garlic – a single, plump clove
chillies – 2 small, hot red or green
vegetable oil – a glug or two
spinach – 450g
garam masala – a scant teaspoon
lemon juice – a squeeze

Peel the ginger, slice it and reduce it to a sludge, either by chopping very, very finely or mincing it in a small processor or grinder. Peel the garlic and mince or chop finely. Chop the chillies.

Get a wok or frying pan hot, pour in the oil and when it shimmers add the minced ginger and garlic. Move the mixture quickly round the pan so it doesn't burn, then add the chopped chillies and the spinach, torn into large pieces (small leaves can be left whole).

Stir the spinach around the hot pan, letting it soften and collapse. There will be some liquid but it should almost evaporate as you continue; if it doesn't, turn up the heat. Sprinkle in the garam masala, toss briefly, then add a little salt and freshen with a squeeze of lemon.

Salmon, steamed spinach and a lemon salad

There is no fish I can think of that doesn't work with spinach. But where creamed spinach seems perfectly fine with a steak of halibut or haddock, the richer, oily fish such as salmon are more appropriately matched to the leaves in a simpler state.

A mouthful of lemon salad, at once breathtakingly sharp, is more than at home on the same fork as a piece of salmon or a bunch of meltingly soft spinach. Bring all three together and you have a dish of extraordinary vitality.

enough for 2
salmon – two 225–250g pieces
olive oil
spinach – 500g

for the salad
lemons – 2
caster sugar – 2 teaspoons
olive oil – 2 tablespoons
flat-leaf parsley – a small bunch
capers – a heaped tablespoon

Brush the salmon on both sides with olive oil, then season with salt. Get a non-stick frying pan hot. Place the fish skin-side down in the pan and leave over a moderate heat for four or five minutes, until the skin has crisped. Turn, cover with a lid and leave for a further five minutes or so, until the fish is lightly cooked through to the centre.

Meanwhile, make the salad by cutting away the skin and white pith from the lemons with a sharp knife and slicing the lemons thinly. Put them into a mixing bowl with the sugar, olive oil and a good handful of parsley leaves, left whole. Add the capers and toss the salad gently. Leave for a few minutes, during which time the sharpness of the lemon will mellow a little.

Wash the spinach thoroughly, then steam in a lidded pan for a minute or two, till tender. Drain.

Put the lemon salad and the spinach on warm plates and slide on the salmon.

A chicken, spinach and pasta pie

A huge pie, lighter and (slightly) less trouble than a lasagne, this is as satisfying as winter food gets. Even with top-notch chicken and double cream, it is hardly an expensive supper, and it feeds four generously (some of us went back for seconds).

> *enough for 4*
> spaghetti – 350g
> mushrooms – 300g
> olive oil – 3 tablespoons
> butter – a thick slice
> cooked chicken – 500g (boned weight)
> white wine – 2 glasses
> double cream – 450ml
> spinach – 200g
> Parmesan – 190g, grated

Cook the spaghetti in deep, generously salted boiling water. Drain and set aside (a little olive oil will stop it sticking together). Set the oven at 180°C/Gas 4.

Cut the mushrooms into quarters. Warm the oil and butter in a deep pan and add the mushrooms, letting them colour nicely here and there. Add the cooked chicken, cut into large pieces, and then pour in the wine. Bring to the boil, scraping away at the sticky remains on the bottom of the pan; they will add much flavour to the sauce. Pour the cream into the pan, bring back to the boil and turn off the heat.

Wash the spinach and put it, still wet from rinsing, into a pan with a tight-fitting lid. Let it cook for a minute or two in its own steam, then drain, squeeze to remove excess water and chop roughly.

Fold the cooked spaghetti, mushroom and chicken sauce and spinach together, then stir in two-thirds of the grated Parmesan and some salt and black pepper and tip into a large baking dish. Scatter the remaining cheese on top and bake for thirty-five minutes, till crisp and golden.

An Indian-inspired dish of spinach and potatoes

The classic Indian spinach dish *saag aloo*, where spinach and potatoes are added to spiced and softened onions, is often cooked a while longer than I would like it to be. Authentically, the spinach goes in before the potatoes, so that it makes an impromptu sauce. Delicious. But I sometimes make it less than classically, keeping the spinach almost whole and adding it last, so that it comes to the table singing brightly, more as an ingredient than a 'sauce'.

enough for 4 as a side dish, 2 as a main dish,
perhaps with warm Indian breads
potatoes – 500g
a large onion
vegetable oil or melted butter – 2 tablespoons
garlic – 2 fat cloves
a small green chilli
ginger – a 2cm lump
black mustard seeds – half a teaspoon
turmeric – half a teaspoon
spinach – 450g
the juice of half a lemon, probably less

Scrub the potatoes, cut them into large pieces, then either boil in deep, salted water or steam till tender. Drain and set aside.

Peel and finely slice the onion. Warm the vegetable oil or butter in a large pan, then add the onion and cook till soft and just starting to colour. Finely chop the garlic, chilli and ginger and stir them in with the mustard seeds and turmeric. Continue cooking briefly, stirring the onion and spices regularly so they do not burn.

Add the cooked and drained potatoes and a wineglass of water. Bring to the boil and simmer for four or five minutes, until any 'crustings' of onion and spices stuck on the pan have dissolved into the liquid. Turn up the heat so that the liquid bubbles almost to nothing and the potatoes are starting to take on some of the colour and flavour of the spices, then add the spinach – thoroughly washed and trimmed of its toughest stalks. Season generously with salt and a little ground black pepper.

Once the spinach has wilted and is bright green, check the seasoning, squeeze over a little lemon juice and eat.

Spinach and mushroom gratin

The cream sauce of a vegetable gratin is something I like to eat with brown basmati rice, but barley, couscous or quinoa would be just as suitable.

enough for 2 as a main dish with rice
chestnut mushrooms – 400g
butter – a thick slice
olive oil
white wine – a small glass
double cream – 300ml (a 284ml carton will do)
spinach – 400g
Parmesan – 150g, grated

Halve or quarter the mushrooms, depending on their size. Warm the butter and 2 tablespoons of oil in a deep pan and add the mushrooms, letting them colour nicely here and there (expect to add more oil if they drink it all). Pour in the wine and bring to the boil. Continue to boil for a couple of minutes.

Pour the cream into the pan and let it come back to the boil, then simmer for two minutes. Turn off the heat. Wash the spinach and put it, still wet from rinsing, into a pan with a tight-fitting lid. Let the spinach cook for a minute or two in its own steam, then drain it and squeeze to remove excess water.

Fold together the mushrooms, drained spinach, salt and black pepper and 140g of the grated Parmesan. Tip into a shallow baking dish. Scatter the remaining cheese on top and bake at 180°C/Gas 4 for thirty-five minutes, till the top is crisp and golden.

A filling, carb-rich supper for a winter's evening

Early February, icy-cold day. I find great spinach in the shops but little to go with it. I grab a bag of those factory-made vacuum-packed gnocchi that always make me feel as if I have just eaten a duvet. With cream, blue cheese and spinach, they have a rib-sticking quality that would keep out Arctic cold, let alone a bit of urban chill. Sometimes I just need food like this.

enough for 2
vacuum-packed gnocchi – 500g
spinach leaves – 200g
creamy Gorgonzola – 250g
double cream – 200ml
a little Parmesan or pecorino

Set the oven at 200°C/Gas 6. Bring a deep pan of water to the boil and salt it generously. Drop the gnocchi into the water and leave until they float to the surface – a matter of a few minutes. Drain and set aside.

Meanwhile, wash the spinach and remove the stalks. With the leaves still dripping wet, put them into a thick-based pan set over a moderate heat and cover with a lid. The leaves will cook in their own steam in a matter of seconds. They are ready when they are completely wilted and bright emerald green. Remove them from the pan and let them cool briefly before wringing them dry. Now tear them up a little and put them, in lumps if that is how they are, into a gratin dish or shallow baking dish. It should be large enough for the gnocchi to fit snugly in one layer. Cut the Gorgonzola into pieces and tuck in amongst the spinach, then scatter over the gnocchi.

Season with salt and black pepper, pour the cream over the lot – it won't quite cover everything, just sort of lap at the edges – then grate over a little Parmesan or pecorino, just enough so that you can see it. Bake until golden and bubbling – about thirty to thirty-five minutes. Serve piping hot.

Spinach, melted cheese and lightly burned toast

Crisp toast, lightly burned at the edges, with a cargo of melting cheese is to my mind the ultimate snack. Spike it with mustard and I am probably at my happiest, but I do play around with the genre too: a layer of apple or homemade chutney under the cheese; a few bitter leaves of chicory or hot watercress on the side; a few capers, maybe.

Sometimes I take the recipe up a notch to give something that is more of a meal than a snack. Like when I trap a layer of cooked spinach between bread and cheese, or just mix the two together and give them a crust of toasted Parmesan. I could add that this is also a sound way of using bits of cheese that have accumulated in the fridge.

enough for 4
spinach – 250g
flat muffins – 4, or a short baguette or other toasting bread
crème fraîche – 5 tablespoons
smooth French mustard – a teaspoon
Taleggio or fontina – 100g
a little nutmeg
grated Parmesan

Wash the spinach leaves in plenty of cold running water and remove any coarse stems. Put them, the water still clinging to their leaves, into a thick-bottomed pan with a lid. Let the spinach steam for a minute or two, then remove it as soon as it is limp but still jewel-bright. Cool it quickly under running water, squeeze the moisture from it with your hands and set aside.

Toast the bread on both sides. If you are using muffins, split them by hand (to get a rough rather than knife-smooth surface) and toast them till pale gold.

Mix the drained spinach with the crème fraîche and mustard. Slice the cheese thinly and add it to the spinach with a good grinding of salt and black pepper. Grate over a very little nutmeg. I use no more than a mere three or four rubs across the fine teeth of the grater.

Pile the spinach on to the toasted bread, thickly to keep it juicy as it toasts, then dust it with grated Parmesan. Toast, on a baking sheet or grill pan, till the surface of the spinach and cheese starts to bubble, the Parmesan turning pale gold. Eat straight away.

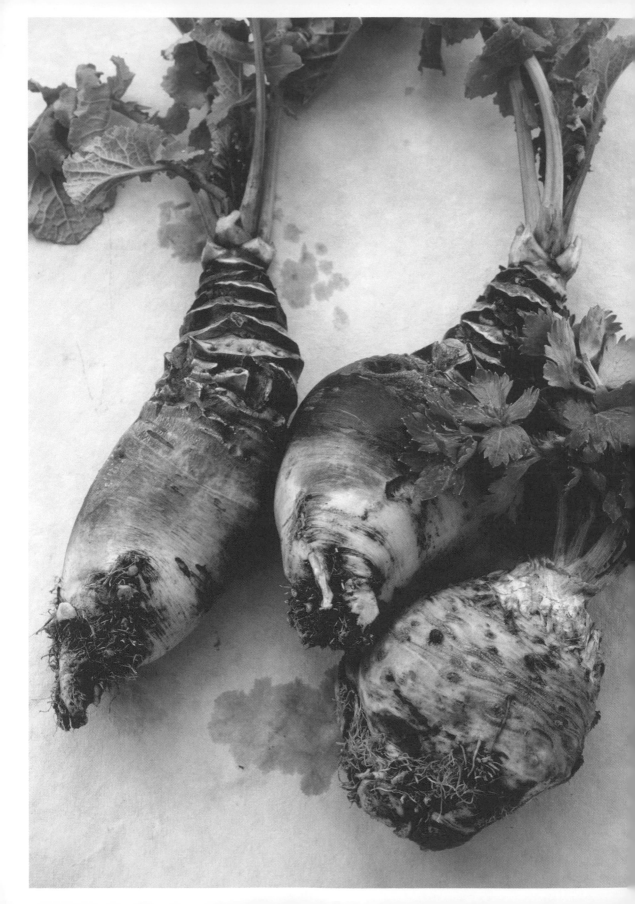

Swede

A creamy amber flushed with viridian, violet and the flat maroon of dried blood, the swede possesses a subtle and unusual beauty. What the Swedish call *kålrot* will make an incandescent mash, introduce a firm footing for a stew and flatter both game and beef. Yet rarely is it treated with much respect.

Autumn is the swede's moment of glory, when the roots are sweet, moist and barely bigger than a clenched fist. A vegetable for when there is a fire in the grate and frost flowers on the windows. The fact that this is not a root at all, but the swollen stem base of a member of the cabbage family, means much to botanists and pedants but is of frankly little interest to the cook. To us in the hot seat, the swede is firmly part of our useful family of 'root vegetables'.

Where some vegetables lose a little of their colour on cooking, the swede deepens to a translucent orange yellow. In boiling water or steam, the rock-hard flesh softens to a loose, shimmering purée the colour of a winter sunset. Enriched with butter and speckled with pepper, it shines brightly against a plate of dark, herby faggots or thin strips of super-soft lamb's liver. Strange, then, that so many seem to end their days shrivelling in a vegetable rack.

Swede sponges up good flavours. It will suck up the burgundy juices of a beef stew or the spice of a lamb hotpot. I often cook mine in chicken stock before mashing, sometimes putting thyme and bay into the pot too, giving the golden purée a faintly savoury edge.

My introduction to what the Americans call rutabaga – literally red bag – came in my early twenties. I had escaped from a testosterone-fuelled kitchen in Yorkshire to the more tender charms of the bed and breakfast trade in Cornwall. I learned to make pasties like the Cornish, with crumbling pastry and a juicy filling of beef, potato, much pepper and golden cubes of swede. The marriage sprouted legs, and I included them in a winter pot of lamb shanks, with vivid parsley, given a freshness with salty-sour preserved lemons from the Middle East. It was in St Ives that I also learned a fondness for mashed swedes (butter, pepper, a splash of gravy) with roast lamb to which you have added garlic and thyme in heroic quantities.

There is much confusion between swedes and turnips – the fact that swede is also known as the Swedish turnip doesn't exactly help. In Scotland the swede is most often known by the name turnip. When they talk of the delicious bashed 'neeps', it is mashed swede that arrives on your plate. But the differences are plain. Swedes are generally harvested when about the size of a grapefruit (a turnip bigger than a tennis ball is rarely worth eating). A swede has several roots coming off its swollen stem (a turnip has just one). The swede is creamy gold in colour (though there is the odd white one) and they are always sold singly, rather than in a bunch like turnips.

But just as we think we have it sorted, nature confounds us by producing a variety of golden turnips.

A swede in the garden

It is said that the swede grows more happily in a field than in a garden. My own space is small, and every inch of bare soil precious. Growing swedes, when they come with such reliability in the organic vegetable box, seems a poor use of valuable resources. Those with more space than I have might like to plant a short row to keep themselves – and their friends – supplied throughout the winter months.

I'm not sure there is a considerable difference in varieties of swede in a culinary sense, but it is worth remembering that there are both yellow (preferred by the British and the Norwegians) and white (preferred by the Swedish). Allotment friends recommend Ruby for its sweetness and Magres for its resistance to mildew.

The ground rules are the same as for cabbages: full sun, plus moisture-retentive, well-manured soil. A recipe that most of us can probably put to better use. Keen growers will sow the seed thinly in May, then thin the seedlings to 30cm or so apart. To prevent their roots splitting, they should be watered regularly when the plants are young.

Swedes sown in May and June will be ready from October onwards. They will probably start to get woody towards early spring, but then who wants to eat even the most buttery mashed swede when the sun is shining? Harvest as you need them from November, leaving them in the ground till the spring. Good luck with extracting a round swede from frozen ground.

A swede in the kitchen

A sloppy, amber mash of swede will have a cooling effect when eaten alongside a plate of robustly spiced faggots and their liverish gravy, a pie or stew with the almost rank flavours of pigeon or hare, or a supper of dark venison sausages. I will take it with pork, too, and in a beef stew, its liquor unthickened, where the vegetables can shine like beacons amongst the general beefiness. Salty bacon, in rashers or as a boiled joint, likes a pool of golden roots, too.

Swede is at its most welcome in our house on a Saturday afternoon in deepest winter, the light fading, the trees standing bare. Then, as we think about making a supper that will warm and fulfil, the fat 'roots' become an essential part of the backbone of vegetables that steadies a stew. I use slightly less swede than carrot, celery and onion, so that its flavour doesn't dominate – one handful to two of each of the others. The pot goes in the oven at about the time we are toasting crumpets, and will come out, a soul-enriching broth of lamb, golden roots and collapsed potatoes, in time for supper.

I adore snow. I adore the quiet solace of stew. If the two come together, it creates a feeling of intense wellbeing and 'all's-right'.

Seasoning your swede

The swede's Christmas card list is not long:
Butter In any shape or form. When mashing, it is almost impossible to beat in too much.
Bacon The saltiness of smoked bacon or baked ham is good with the watery quality of mashed swede.
Dill One of the few herbs really worth including.
Parsley The pairing of the root and this herb just seems right. They somehow belong together.
Lamb In a rich casserole.
Game As a mashed accompaniment to any game bird, the coolness of the swede is a useful balance for the bosky flavour of the meat.

And...

* The fact that the swede is actually a member of the cabbage family (this is *Brassica napus*) becomes of interest once we are looking for things to cook it with. So bacon, pork, apples and the like go rather well.
* When swede is used alone, I have never managed to find a fish with which this root will work.
* Leaving them in the ground is probably the best way of keeping your swedes in good condition.
* If you like this vegetable, then join an organic box scheme. It is a safe bet that there will be one or two in each delivery in winter.

How to make the perfect mashed swede

Rinse the swede of its mud, then peel it. Cut the pale flesh into large chunks and pile into a steamer basket or metal colander. Place over a pan of boiling water and steam for twelve to fifteen minutes, then tip into a bowl and crush with a potato masher. Fold in a slice of butter, some salt and black pepper, then beat hard with a wooden spoon.

A mash of roasted swedes (very good with roast beef)

Roasting intensifies the sweetness of the swede. Peel and cut your roots into cubes, put them in a roasting tin with a thick slice of butter and some salt and black pepper, then cover with a piece of greaseproof paper. Roast for twenty minutes or until the swede has softened but not browned.

Remove from the oven and mash with a potato masher, incorporating more butter and black pepper as you need it.

Another good way with swede

A recipe to tempt the 'swedophobic'.

Peel and cube 500g swede. Melt 50g butter in a deep saucepan with 200ml water and a teaspoon of sugar. Drop the cubes into the pan with a couple of bay leaves and cover with a lid, shaking or turning them over from time to time. They will catch on the bottom of the pan if you don't. Test for tenderness after twenty minutes. They should emerge sweet, softly toothsome and as translucent as a glowing candle. Use as a side dish.

A three-root mash

I'm not suggesting we should inflict anything on our family or friends that they won't eat, but there are worse ways of getting rid of an unwanted swede than in this three-root mash. Works well with pretty much anything, even fish.

enough for 4
swede – about 750g
carrots – 300g
potatoes – 300g
butter – about 40g
nutmeg

Peel the swede, carrots and potatoes, chop them into large, similar-sized pieces and bring them to the boil in lightly salted water. Turn down the heat as they reach the boil and let them simmer enthusiastically for about twenty-five minutes, till all are tender. One may be ready slightly before the others but it really doesn't matter here.

Drain, then crush with a potato masher. Introduce the butter and beat with a wooden spoon till fluffy. If you use an electric beater, then go easy, taking care not to overmix and turn the mash 'gluey'. Season with black pepper and a brief grating of nutmeg.

Swede 'braised' with onion and stock

Even the smallest pinch of sugar will take any possible bitterness out of a swede. The method that follows, of cooking the chopped vegetable with a small amount of butter and stock so that it takes on a deep, earthy richness, is one I use for carrots and turnips too. A very fine side order for roast chicken or something altogether more gamey.

enough for 4 as an accompaniment
a large swede
a smallish onion, roughly chopped
a small clove of garlic, crushed
butter – a walnut-sized lump
sugar – the merest pinch
enough chicken or vegetable stock or water to cover

Peel the swede and cut it into large, fairly even chunks. Put it into a saucepan with the onion, garlic, butter and sugar. Pour in enough stock or water just to cover the swede and bring to the boil. Turn the heat down a little. Place a piece of greaseproof paper or cooking parchment over the top and then cover with a lid. Leave to simmer for twenty minutes or so, then lift the lid and boil vigorously till the liquid has almost evaporated. You should end up with butter-soft swede on the point of collapse.

A good pasty recipe

There have been many highly original versions of the straightforward miner's lunch (if you couldn't come up to the surface for lunch, you took a warm pasty down with you, holding the thickly crimped edge with your grubby hands, then leaving it behind to appease the spirits of the mine) but I have rarely enjoyed one as much as those I have eaten in Cornwall.

My pasty is (categorically) not a Cornish pasty. I precook my filling, you see, which Cornish cooks would never do. I cook the meat and vegetables before wrapping them in the pastry crust purely because it results in a pasty whose filling is especially tender and giving. I also use a proportion of butter in the pastry too. The similarity between my pasty and a Cornish one is purely in the ingredients: beef, potato, onion and swede.

Chaucer was partial to a pasty – they appear in *The Canterbury Tales*, and in several of Shakespeare's plays, including *The Merry Wives of Windsor*, *All's Well That Ends Well* and *Titus Andronicus*. We shall gloss over the small point that Titus uses Chiron and Demetrius's bodies rather than the more traditional beef skirt.

I do suggest you let the finished parcels rest for half an hour before baking, if you get the chance.

makes 6

for the pastry
lard – 110g
butter – 115g
strong white flour – 450g
an egg, beaten with a little milk, for brushing

for the filling
swede – 200g
potatoes – about 400g
onions – 2
butter – a thick slice
beef skirt – 450g

Freeze the blocks of lard and butter for a good hour, making them easier to grate.

Peel the swede and potatoes, cut into 2cm pieces and bring to the boil in deep, lightly salted water. Simmer for ten to fifteen minutes, till almost tender, then drain. Peel and roughly chop the onions, then let them soften in the butter in a shallow pan.

Grate the frozen lard and butter into the flour. This is most easily done if you keep the fats in their paper, dipping the cut edge into the flour every now and again to stop it sticking on the grater. Add a good half teaspoon of salt. Stir the fat into the flour along with enough cold water to make a firm but tender dough. I find about five or six tablespoons usually does it. Roll the dough into a ball and leave to rest in the fridge, wrapped in greaseproof paper, for twenty minutes or so.

Meanwhile, cut the beef into small pieces, then, once the onions are soft, remove and add the beef to the hot pan. Let it colour nicely on all sides, then remove and mix with the onions. Add a splash of water – or stock, if there is some around – to the pan, scrape at any stickings with a spatula, then pour this liquid over the meat. Add the drained swede and potato. Season generously (my feeling is that the mixture should be really quite peppery). Set the oven at 200°C/Gas 6.

Divide the pastry into six. Roll each lump into a disc about 18cm in diameter, using a small plate as a template. Brush the edges with beaten egg and milk, then put a pile of the filling on each disc. Fold the dough over to make a semi-circle, pressing hard to seal the edges. Crimp as you wish (a fork, a twist of the finger and thumb, a nice bit of plaiting, as you fancy), then transfer to a baking sheet lined with baking parchment. Brush all over with beaten egg and milk. Cut a couple of steam holes in the top of each pasty to prevent them splitting. Bake for fifteen minutes, then lower the heat to 180°C/Gas 4 and bake for forty-five minutes or so, till golden.

A swede and cheese pasty

Modern pasty recipes, especially those in the more touristy enclaves of our furthest southern county, stretch the recipe almost as far as Titus, swapping beef for pork, the swede for apple, even daring to crimp the finished turnover on the top instead of at the side.

I make one without meat, in which I use goat's cheese and thyme along with the usual starchy filling of potato and swede. It is filling, yet somehow soft and gentle, too.

makes 6
the pastry recipe above

for the filling
leeks – 2
butter – a thick slice
swede – 200g
potatoes – 400g
the leaves of a bushy sprig of thyme, chopped
goat's cheese – 250g

Cut the leeks in half lengthways, then into thin slices. Leave to soften in the butter in a small saucepan over a moderate heat. Placing a layer of greaseproof paper over the top, then covering with a lid will encourage them to steam a little and stop them colouring too quickly.

Peel the swede and the potatoes, dice them and boil in salted water for ten minutes. Drain.

When the leeks are soft, mix them with the swede and potatoes and season generously with black pepper and chopped thyme. Crumble in the goat's cheese. Set the oven at 200°C/Gas 6.

Divide the pastry into six. Roll each piece into a disc about 18cm in diameter (I find a plate useful here). Brush the edges with beaten egg and milk, then put a pile of the filling on each disc. Fold the dough over to make a semi-circle, sealing and crimping the edges tightly. Transfer to a baking sheet lined with baking parchment. Brush the pasties with beaten egg and milk, then pierce the crust a couple of times to make steam holes. Bake for fifteen minutes, then lower the heat to 180°C/Gas 4 and bake for forty-five minutes or so, till golden.

A baked cake of swede and potato

Swede's ability to sponge up liquid is shown to good effect when it is baked with butter and vegetable stock. When it is teamed up with potato and seasoned with garlic and a spot of mustard, it is as near to a main course as I feel you can safely get with this particular root.

enough for 4
potatoes – 500g
swede – 500g
garlic – 4 cloves
butter – 85g
Dijon mustard – 2 heaped teaspoons
thyme leaves – a teaspoon
vegetable stock – 6 tablespoons

Peel the potatoes, then cut them into very fine slices. A sharp knife is fine but if you have a mandolin (the vegetable slicer, that is, not the lute-like stringed instrument), use that. Whatever, your slices should be almost thin enough to see through. Do the same with the swede, keeping the slices in cold water to prevent them browning.

Set the oven to 190°C/Gas 5. Peel and thinly slice the garlic. Over a moderate heat, melt the butter in a flameproof dish or sauté pan about 25cm in diameter. When it starts to bubble, turn down the heat and add the garlic. It needs to soften slightly without colouring – a matter of five minutes or so. Take the pan off the heat and stir in the mustard. Tip about two-thirds of the mustard and butter out of the pan and into a jug.

Drain the potato and swede slices and pat them dry with kitchen paper or a clean tea towel. Put a third of the vegetables into the pan, layering them neatly or just chucking them in as the mood takes you, then drizzle them with some of the mustard butter in the jug. Season with the thyme leaves, pepper and salt. Be quite generous with the salt. Repeat this twice, so that all the slices of vegetable are layered with the thyme and the mustard and garlic butter. Now pour the stock over the top.

Cover with a circle of greaseproof paper or kitchen foil, pressing it down well on top of the cake. Bake for about an hour and ten minutes, until tender to the point of a knife. Remove the foil, turn the heat up to 220°C/Gas 7 and bake for a further ten minutes, until the top has coloured and crisped a little.

A slow roast of roots and herbs for when there is frost on the ground

Peel and chop up an assortment of swede, parsnip, pumpkin or butternut squash, beetroot and celeriac. A squeeze of lemon on the celeriac will stop it browning. Bring a large pan of water to the boil, tip in all the vegetables except the beetroot and let them simmer for ten minutes. They should just take the point of a knife. Drain.

Warm plenty of butter (60g to 2kg of vegetables) in a roasting tin with a good glug of olive oil to stop it burning. Tip in the drained vegetables and the beetroot, turn them in the butter, then scatter with thyme leaves and a few whole, squashed garlic cloves. Roast in a hot oven (180°C/Gas 4) for forty-five minutes to an hour, till the vegetables are soft inside, crisp and golden without. The initial boiling (you could steam them if you prefer) prevents them getting a hard outer skin as they roast.

Baked swede to accompany a meat dish

There are certain unfashionable meals I want to slap a preservation order on lest they disappear altogether. Faggots and gravy is one such recipe (lardy cake is another). Pease pudding would be many people's chosen accompaniment; others probably a pile of minted fresh peas. To my mind, the faggot needs a cooling sidekick to soften the blow of the liver and onions. A mash of swede is good, but also this rather more subtle approach.

enough for 4
a large swede – about 650g, peeled weight
butter – 40g
onions – 2 medium, thinly sliced
a large sprig of rosemary
chicken or vegetable stock to cover

Set the oven at 200°C/Gas 6. Cut the swede into slices about as thick as a pound coin. It is easier and safer to do this by first cutting a slice from one side to give a flat base as you cut.

Generously grease a baking dish or roasting tin with some of the butter. Lay the slices of swede and onion in the dish, seasoning them with salt and black pepper and strewing over the rosemary leaves as you go. Ladle over the stock so that it just about covers the vegetables – a matter of five or so ladlefuls – then dot on the rest of the butter.

Bake for an hour or so, turning the vegetables in the stock from time to time, until they are tender enough to crush between your fingers. Serve as a side dish, with some of the juices spooned over.

A dish of lamb shanks with preserved lemon and swede

It's late March and green leaves as sharp as a dart are opening on the hornbeams that shield this garden from the most bone chilling of the winter winds. The mornings are still crisp. You can see your breath. Stew weather. Unlike carrots, swede becomes translucent when it cooks, making a casserole the glowing heart of the home.

enough for 4
onions – 2 large
olive oil – 3 tablespoons
lamb shanks – 4
plain flour – 2 tablespoons
garlic – 3 cloves, thinly sliced
light stock (water will do) – 750ml
white vermouth or white wine – 100ml
a large swede
the juice of half a lemon
preserved lemons – 2
parsley – 4 bushy sprigs

Set the oven at 160°C/Gas 3. Peel the onions and slice them into thick segments. Warm the olive oil in a deep casserole and season the lamb shanks. Lightly brown the lamb all over in the hot oil, then lift it out and add the onions to the pan. Let them soften and turn a pale gold, then stir in the flour. Add the garlic, stock and vermouth or white wine and bring to the boil. Peel the swede and cut it into fat chunks about the size of a marshmallow. As soon as the liquid starts to boil, add the swede, pushing the pieces under the gravy, then stir in the lemon juice, pushing the spent lemon shell amongst the swede, plus a seasoning of salt and pepper. Return the lamb shanks to the pan. Cover with greaseproof paper and then a lid and place in the oven for two hours, turning the shanks from time to time.

After an hour and a half's cooking, cut the preserved lemons in half and scrape out the pith. Chop the skin fairly finely. Remove the lamb from the oven, lift the lid and push the chopped lemon down into the gravy. Cover once more and return to the oven for thirty minutes, until the lamb is easy to pull away from the bone and the swede tender to the point of a knife.

Remove the leaves from the parsley sprigs, chop roughly and stir into the gravy. Leave, covered, for a few minutes to settle down, then check the seasoning and serve.

Tomatoes

We expect a lot of the tomato. *Lycopersicon esculentum* is not native to this country. We do not have the ideal climate: too much rain, not enough scorching sun. They are fragile and do not travel well. Neither do we produce the olives and anchovies that seem so much a part of the fruit's soul. Even our basil, the tomato's inseparable seasoning, lacks the pepperiness of that grown in the Mediterranean. Yet for some reason, we expect to have the perfect tomato in our kitchen every day of the year. We import them thousands of miles, chill them and then moan about their shortcomings. Surely we are expecting too much of a fruit that started out as a weed in South America.

The problem is the colour. Red is the colour of richness, ripeness and sensuality. It is the colour of the erotic. Scarlet is for anger and ecstasy, the colour of love and lust (not for nothing is it the colour of a Valentine's rose and a whore's light bulb). Red signals a welcome and a warning. It is synonymous with Christmas and war. It is the colour of blood. It is the colour that probably has the greatest effect on our emotions. No wonder we expect so much of the tomato.

When a fruit is grown for flavour rather than its ability to travel without blemish, when it is given enough searing sun and not overfed and watered, it can add up to an intense experience. The way they are designed to burst in the mouth, to squirt their seeds and juice, to be both sharp and sweet at the same time, is what makes a lacklustre tomato all the more frustrating.

Those I pick from my vegetable plot, their faces distorted with furrows and folds, often taste richer than the ones I buy from the shops. They respond to the wind and the brutal sun more favourably than those cosseted in the greenhouse. When people say tomatoes taste better in Italy, Spain or France it is often because they have been grown outside. A tomato's character is enhanced by a rough life, a certain negligence, a gasping thirst and the occasional drenching downpour. Pamper a tomato, overfeed it, overwater it and you will get a Paris Hilton of a tomato. The rougher time it has, the more ugly its appearance, the more interesting it generally is.

I find the scent of a ripe tomato, especially that of its stem, faintly erotic. I always feel I have been 'had' if there is no deep green, herbal smell to its stalk. I feel a fool for letting myself be seduced into buying. And yet that herbal scent is actually no guarantee of a richly flavoured fruit, as anyone who has splashed out for tomatoes on the vine can testify. The plant and its smell can fool us.

Each time I pass them on my way up the garden, I rub their leaves and instantly sniff my fingers. It's a tender thing, and deeply appetising in its intensity. As the months wear on, the habit becomes compulsive and I will occasionally break from my writing just to go out into the garden and stroke a leaf. By September it has become almost a perversion.

I devour them in the hand, eat them raw with olive oil, salt and basil, grill them with oregano and garlic-rubbed bread, bake them with goat's cheese, and occasionally simmer them as a sauce or soup. I marry them to the herbs of Southeast Asia and the dark spices of India. I simmer them lovingly into a purée, slice them into a sandwich, tuck them around the Sunday roast. It's a feast, a greedy, glorious feast.

But come the first frosts, I shut the door on the tomato. I have learned to live without them for the winter months. Occasionally I pick a few up, normally attached to their vine, hoping for just a shadow of that warm, peppery, herbal hit. Sometimes it is there, the ghost of a summer tomato you have grown for yourself. But more often than not I am disappointed and feel a fool.

A tomato in the garden

I have one precise memory, still as clean and sharp as a pin, of my father standing in his tobacco-scented greenhouse on a Sunday afternoon in late summer, pinching out the tops of his tomato plants with his finger and thumb – his way of encouraging them to direct their energies towards the swelling fruits. The smell of the discarded branches that filled the greenhouse, warm, green and deeply aromatic, is possibly the best excuse I know for growing a tomato plant indoors. The scent is trapped in the humid glasshouse and you are engulfed by the very essence of deepest summer.

My father grew Moneymaker, the high-cropping, oh-so-perfectly-round fruit popular in the 1970s, which being under glass matured too quickly to develop the character of a fruit grown in the open air. The first I raised myself, balanced precariously on the stone windowsill of my first-floor flat, were the marble-sized Gardener's Delight, impervious to disease and almost impossible to kill. They were so refreshing in their sweet-sharpness that I picked as I watered. They never made it as far as the salad bowl.

Open to the rough slap of baking sun, rain and the high winds that can hit this garden even in July, the fruit I plant now – Marmande, Costoluto Fiorentino, Green Zebra and Sungold – brings along a certain expectation. I tend to be more attached to things I have grown myself than anything picked up at the shops. I develop a fondness for them, a certain wonder. My enjoyment may be heightened simply because I have had a hand in their upbringing (I am assuming one tends to like one's own offspring more than other people's).

The skin is a little thicker in outdoor-grown fruit but the flavour, like that of a free-range animal or bird left to cope with the elements, seems to have been cranked up a notch. If the sun has been relentless in July and August, the initial snap of sharpness will be backed up by a deep, mellow sweetness that requires neither salt nor pepper.

A tomato diary

Mid April The plug plants from The Walled Garden have arrived by post, each stem barely the length of my little finger, with six long leaves attached, and ready to be potted on. I use an organic tomato compost, almost black and freckled with grit, which I buy mail order. The delicate plantlets go into tall plastic pots, one into each, and then into the cold frame. Before that I simply grew them on the windowsill, the pots tightly packed into a roasting tray lined with newspaper, where they fared just as well, if grew a little lankier than they do now. Anyone could do it.

May 4 I start to open the cold frame to the air during the day to give the plants a peek at what is to come.

Late May The plants have gone out into the garden, a good arm's length apart, each one supported by a thick bamboo pole to tie them to. They can grow to the height of a teenager. Snails love them, despite their hairy stems, so they are ringed with copper and labelled to make sure I don't forget which is which. For the last four years I have grown Marmande, partly for its gnarled beauty and its flesh that forms in furrows and folds to make an interesting shape on the plate. It is the tomato of the French street market, large enough to stuff and bake.

The most reliable is the large, heavily ribbed Costoluto Fiorentino, a classic variety from Florence. In my London garden, it is rarely ready until late August and will continue until the first frosts. The skins are usually tougher than those I have bought at grocer's shops in Italy, but the dense flesh slices as neatly as a raw steak, holding its seeds and glowing jelly. It is perfect for the classic tomato and mozzarella salad with olive oil and a handful of torn basil.

Late June The plants scattered around the garden appear to be biding their time. They look healthy enough but seem to be standing still, as if unsure what to make of all the rain. Other years have seen them in fruit by now.

Mid July After sulking for weeks, all four varieties seem to have grown a good 20cm overnight. There are young fruits on the Marmande, already showing their characteristic ribs and nobbles. The leaves are covered in fine, white hairs, and just brushing past them emits waves of herbal fragrance on the morning air. I nip off the small shoots that grow at the axes between the stem and the horizontal branches. Left on, they sap the energy that the plant could put into producing fruit.

Late August Each morning I wake to find another Tigerella or Sungold has ripened. I like them best when they are still firm and slightly acidic. The larger fruit ripen slowly, the occasional one being removed if the clusters are too tightly packed. The bottom of the plant is browning but the upper leaves still produce their star-like flowers. Each fruit is treated like a precious egg, picked carefully and brought proudly into the kitchen. One or two of the plants have a bit of blight from the constant rain. I remove any brown, squishy fruit as soon as I spot them, and snip out any branches that are brown and soft. But the blight is almost inevitable towards the end of a wet season. Tragically, it can attack indoor-grown tomatoes too.

Late autumn In a good year, I am picking till the first frosts, by which time many plants will be thin, brown skeletons. At this point I pull the whole plant from the ground, shake off the soil, then hang it upside down indoors. Any stragglers will usually ripen.

Varieties

There are hundreds of varieties of tomato, from plums barely bigger than an almond to beefsteaks the size of a clenched fist. Some are red, pink, orange, yellow, purple, black and even striped; some have thick skins, making them suitable for baking, others so thin they won't travel and need to be grown at home. Flavours vary from sharp and refreshingly sweet to the positively dull.

While some varieties thrive outside in our mixed climate, others need nurturing under glass. The following are those that have done well for me outside, have survived the occasional period of neglect and produced fruit to make this cook's heart sing.

Sungold If you grow only one tomato, let this be the one. Sweet-sharp, small, golden fruit with masses of flavour. I grow it every year and it never fails to delight, even outdoors.

Gardener's Delight Another cherry, but this time red. Probably the easiest to grow, it will never let you down.

Yellow Pear A seventeenth-century variety with a mild flavour and much sugar. Vigorous and tough.

Green Zebra Amber and green stripes, with crisp flesh and sharp, refreshing seeds. Gorgeous in a salad.

Costoluto Fiorentino A large, ridged fruit that is happy outdoors. Rich flavour, almost herbal after a good amount of sunshine.

Marmande A good cooking tomato this, and more than happy in our climate if we get a reasonable summer. Softly ridged, its thick skin means it is suitable for stuffing.

Auriga A large(ish) orange-fleshed variety that does well outside and looks very good in a salad with purple basil.

Brandywine A knobbly, dark red and green variety with a spicy tomato flavour.

Black Krim Dark and interesting-looking fruit with a very fine flavour.

Orange Santa Plum shaped but much smaller than Roma or San Marzano. A nicely sharp, rather cute addition to the garden.

A tomato in the kitchen

The tomato plays less of a part in our traditional cooking than it does in the cuisines of Italy and Spain. You could trawl through old cookery books and rarely come across a recipe that involved a cooked tomato. If we cook with them at all, it is mostly in recipes from other European countries – pizza, pasta sauces, slow casseroles and soups. When we do, it is more often with the canned variety than with those fresh off the vine.

Cooking with fresh tomatoes can be a revelation to those who have been led along the canned tomato route. Cheap and convenient they undoubtedly are (and I would hate to be without a tin or two), but canned tomatoes lack the sweet-sharp quality of a fresh one. They have a monotonous reliability that lacks spirit and vigour. I guess we like them because they always taste the same.

I have long used fresh tomatoes in curries to add a note of sweet acidity – and in braised oxtail and slow lamb stews. I add them to chicken sautés to simmer down to an impromptu sauce and bake them with bony cuts of lamb or with courgettes or aubergines. Slow cooked, they add a sharp richness to any dish.

It is rare, though, that cooked tomatoes are served as themselves. Occasionally they turn up stuffed with rice, onions and sultanas, in the Middle Eastern style or, as the Italians do, with rice, nutmeg and Parmesan. Halved, grilled and flecked with black pepper, they are part of the Great British Breakfast, the one that almost no one has any more. But the tomato is usually very much a member of the chorus rather than a star in its own right.

A cooked tom can be wonderful – a piquant, juice-filled orb of smoky, lip-puckering flavours. I roast mine with just a glug of olive oil and a few thyme leaves, until the skins char and split. I make an instant tomato sauce by crushing grilled or roast fruits with a fork and stirring in a little olive oil and torn basil. I tuck whole cherry tomatoes around the roast to break down into a rich sauce with the roasting juices.

A handful of mixed fruits in various sizes or shades, baked till they surrender their juices, makes a smart contrast to a ball of milkily soft buffalo mozzarella. Sliced, the little pear and cherry varieties add punch to a pizza and can be tossed with linguine and basil. Their uses to the cook are almost endless.

Seasoning your tomatoes

Basil One of the most famous marriages of ingredients. Basil's warm, peppery notes have a profound effect on tomatoes, even more so when cool, milky mozzarella comes along to play.

Oregano The pizza herb. The musty notes work better in tomato sauces than in salads.

Salt Coarse, for teasing the sweetness out.

Cheese An age-old pairing. Any cheese, any tomato, it just works.

Anchovies The salty little fillets have an affinity with sweet, juicy tomatoes.

Olives In part, it is the saltiness of olives that makes them perfect for tomatoes, but they are linked in so many recipes that it is hard not to imagine them together. They form an ancient Mediterranean double act.

Thyme Tuck the odd sprig between the fruit as they bake.

And...

* Early-ripening tomatoes are often best for growing outside. Cherry varieties are particularly reliable.
* Growbags are an excellent way to grow tomatoes for those with no garden. Tomato roots will happily grow horizontally if they cannot grow straight down.
* The key to a healthy plant is good ventilation. Try not to overcrowd them, and allow space for them to get plenty of air around them.
* A sunny spot is vital. They will take any amount of direct sunshine once they start fruiting.
* Blight is the biggest problem. It thrives in wet, humid summers. At the first sign of it, remove any infected leaves. It may not stop it, but it will slow down the spread.
* Feed plants with a good proprietary liquid feed about every two weeks once the first fruit appears.
* The change from orange to red signifies the sweetening of the flesh within. If you like your tomatoes tart, pick them before they become deep crimson.
* Tomatoes hate fridges. Keep them in a cool room if you can. The cold affects both their flavour and their texture.
* To peel tomatoes, nick a small cross in the pointed end, dunk into boiling water for thirty seconds, then peel off the skin where it has started to split.
* Use the seeds and jelly from hollowed-out stuffed tomatoes in the stockpot.
* Ignore recipes that tell you to peel a tomato for salad. The skin would have to be very thick before this would be necessary.
* Bake tomatoes in a very hot oven. A cool one will make them watery.

A tomato for its own sake

You have found your tomato, sweetly ripe yet with a bite to it. It may still have the green shoulders of youth, or a few yellow freckles near its stalk. The seeded jelly inside will shine as you slice. As you have already resisted the temptation to eat it whole, you might like to slice it thinly, but no thinner than two one-pound coins on top of one another. You lay the slices, overlapping, on a plate and trickle olive oil over them, so that it falls in rivulets over the fruit. Fruity, peppery, green or grassy, the choice is yours. A little salt, barely noticeable, but no pepper this time. Just your tomato, oil and a flick of sea salt.

A salad of bread and tomatoes

I have yet to have a panzanella that excites me. The name is so tempting, as is the sight of ripe tomatoes tossed with bread, herbs and olive oil, but I have never found one that wasn't disappointing. At their best lacklustre, at their worst slimy. One day I will find the glowing, basil-scented classic that so many people rave over.

My own version of this bread and tomato salad involves tossing pieces of garlic-rubbed toast with chopped red and orange tomatoes at the last minute, so that at least some of the bread stays crisp amongst the green oil and scarlet fruit. I chop up a mixture of tomatoes – red, orange, green, cherry and pear shaped, even the odd beefsteak if it's very ripe – then tip them and their juices into a bowl. I don't skin or seed, only twist out the herb-scented stalks, sniffing each one as I go.

I toast thin slices of sourdough loaf on the grill, till the centres are crisp and the outsides are black here and there. Pour olive oil – very green and fruity – over the tomatoes, toss in some torn basil leaves and just a little wine vinegar. A clove of garlic, peeled and sliced as thin as tissue. Then a scattering of salt, and a twist of the pepper mill. I remove the toast from the grill, rub it with a cut clove of garlic and tear it into pieces. The tomatoes and their juices are tipped into a deep dish, the toast tucked in, and then tossed, gently, briefly, before eating.

And with anchovies and basil

Slice your tomatoes in half and then into thick wedges. Toss them with olive oil and some torn basil leaves, then tuck in a few rinsed anchovy fillets. Pass round with a loaf for everyone to tear off as much as they need. The trick of this salad is to leave it for half an hour so that the anchovies and basil have time to season the juice.

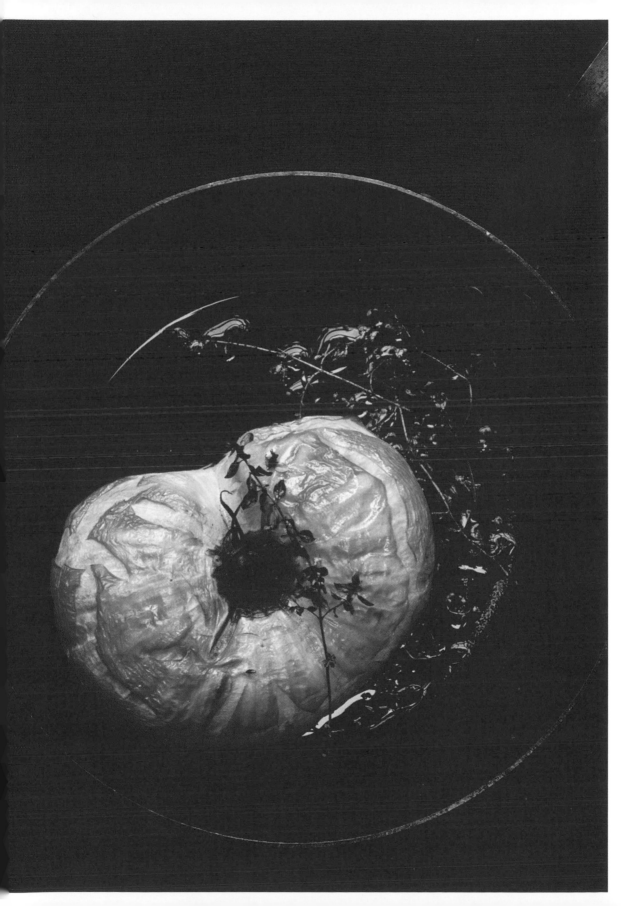

Roast cherry tomatoes

Put your tomatoes in a shallow roasting tin and trickle olive oil over them. Grind over a little black pepper and add a few drops of balsamic vinegar. Toss them around in the dressing, then roast at 200°C/Gas 6 for about thirty minutes, until they are soft and oozing juices. Leave them to cool in their dish, so as not to waste a drop of their juice.

Baked tomatoes with cheese and thyme

The first time I made this, I discovered a wealth of delights: the way the tomato holds the little cheese like an eggcup holds an egg; the point at which the juice of the tomato and the melted cheese meet; and the subtle difference in smell and flavour depending on which cheese you use.

Two of these tomatoes are lunch for me if there is something else on the table – a couscous salad, perhaps, or some bread and salami. Others may want more.

> *enough for 2*
> large, ripe tomatoes – 4
> olive oil
> thyme – 4 or 5 bushy sprigs
> 2 small, fresh goat's cheeses or other small cheeses

Set the oven at 180°C/Gas 4. Cut a thick slice from the top of each tomato. Using a teaspoon, scoop out enough of the seeds and flesh to make room for half a goat's cheese (don't add the cheese yet). Put them snugly in a baking dish, salt and pepper the inside and add a teaspoon or so of olive oil to each one. Pull the leaves from the thyme and sprinkle them inside the tomatoes. Bake the tomatoes for twenty-five minutes or until they are soft and lightly coloured. Slice the cheeses in half if they are small, or in large pieces if they are larger than the diameter of the hollow. Whatever, just make the cheese fit into the tomatoes. Spoon a little oil from each tomato over the cheese, or add fresh oil if it has escaped, then return to the oven for ten minutes, until the cheese has melted.

A salad of roast tomatoes

A tomato's flavour intensifies in the heat of the oven. All its sweet-sharpness comes to the fore. I eat these warm, sprinkled with a little herb vinegar, sometimes sandwiched inside a crisp and chewy baguette.

enough for 4 as a side dish
medium tomatoes – 12
olive oil
thyme – 6 bushy sprigs
red wine vinegar

Wipe the tomatoes and slice them in half across the middle. Put them cut-side up in an ovenproof dish. Shake over a generous amount of good, though not expensive, olive oil and season with salt, coarsely ground black pepper and the leaves from the thyme sprigs. Roast at 200°C/Gas 6 for about forty minutes, depending on the ripeness of your tomatoes, till they are puffed and tender. A few black edges will only add to their flavour.

As the tomatoes come from the oven, shake a little of the vinegar over them, then serve warm with crusty bread.

Slow-roast tomatoes with thyme and mozzarella

Late summer, the sun high, the vegetable patch is filled with slow-moving bees and tiny, piercing-blue butterflies. The day stands still, baking in the sunshine. The cats lie silently on the dusty stone terrace, too hot to move. It is the day for a lunch of melting softness. I wander into the kitchen on bare feet to roast tomatoes and break open a milky, silky buffalo mozzarella.

enough for 4
small to medium tomatoes – 16
olive oil
thyme leaves
buffalo mozzarella – 2 balls
basil – a small bunch

Set the oven at 160°C/Gas 3. Remove the stalks from the tomatoes and put the fruit into a small baking dish. They should fit snugly. Drizzle with olive oil and season with salt and black pepper. Pull the thyme leaves from their stalks and toss with the tomatoes and seasonings. Bake until they are truly soft and collapsing – a good hour or more. Pull the mozzarella in half. Put a half on each plate and season it with olive oil and torn basil leaves. Serve the roast tomatoes alongside.

Yellow tomatoes, grilled peppers

Grill a couple of red peppers till the skins blacken, then peel them. I find the easiest way to do this is to put the still-hot peppers in a bowl and cover with clingfilm for ten minutes. This will help loosen their skins.

Once they are peeled, you will be left with soft, scarlet flesh, which should be sliced into thick strips, then tossed with quartered yellow tomatoes, olive oil, salt and roughly torn basil leaves. You could add oregano, too, or coriander if that is what is around. Leave the salad for a good twenty minutes before serving.

Parmesan tomatoes

A good savoury little number this, fantastic with all manner of roasts and grills but equally worth making as a side dish for cool, almost liquid mozzarella or a bowl of basmati rice flecked with torn herbs.

> *enough for 4 as a side dish*
> tomatoes – 450g
> olive oil – 3 tablespoons
> basil – a small bunch
> Parmesan – 40g, grated

Set the oven at 200°C/Gas 6. Cut the tomatoes in half and put them into a bowl. Pour over the oil, then add a good grinding of black pepper and a little salt. Tear the basil leaves and add them with the grated Parmesan. Toss the ingredients gently together, then tip them into a baking dish and bake for twenty-five to thirty minutes, until the tomatoes are soft and the Parmesan is slightly crisp.

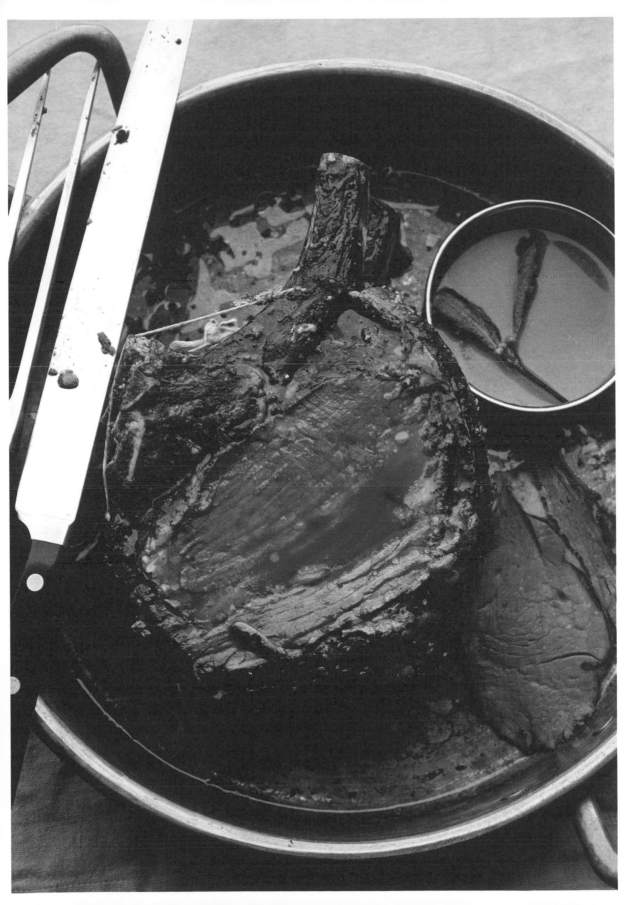

Roast beef with tomato gravy

Beef and tomatoes have enjoyed a long history together. Whether it's tomato ketchup on your burger or tomato purée in your beef casserole, the two have an established friendship.

Winter tomatoes – why do we buy them? – can add a surprising depth to gravy if they are roasted alongside the Sunday beef. I chuck them in with the onions and bay leaves that provide the background music for the gravy. The tomatoes sharpen up in the searing heat, their skin catches and burns, and they add a certain piquancy to the sweet onion and caked-on roasting juices. The winter tomato has at last found a point.

You may well want some roast potatoes to go with this. I usually boil them first for ten minutes, then drain and add to the roasting tin.

> *enough for 6*
> onions – 4
> beef rib on the bone – 2kg
> a little oil or beef dripping
> garlic – 6 cloves
> tomatoes – 2
> bay leaves – 3

> **for the gravy**
> plain flour – 2 tablespoons
> Madeira – a wine glass
> stock – 600ml
> smooth Dijon mustard – a tablespoon
> grain mustard – a tablespoon or more to taste

Set the oven at 220°C/Gas 7. Peel the onions and boil them in unsalted water for fifteen minutes, then drain them. Smear the beef all over with oil or beef dripping, sea salt and freshly ground pepper. Lay it in a roasting tin with the boiled onions, the whole, unpeeled garlic cloves, the tomatoes and the bay leaves. Roast for twenty minutes. Turn the heat down to 180°C/Gas 4 and continue roasting for a further ten minutes per 500g. When the beef is done, remove from its tin, then set it aside somewhere warm, lightly covered with foil to keep it warm while it rests and while you make the tomato gravy. (If you are roasting potatoes to accompany this, now is the time to take them out, put them in another dish and continue roasting till crisp and golden.)

Squash the onions, tomatoes and garlic in the tin with the back of a wooden spoon. Dust the flour on top and place the tin and its contents over a moderate heat, stirring almost constantly, until the flour browns a little. Pour in the Madeira and let it bubble a while, then add the stock and the mustards, stirring and scraping at the stuck-on roasting juices. Season, then leave to simmer, with the occasional stir, for ten to fifteen minutes (any longer and the gravy will lose much of its character). Check the seasoning and push through a coarse sieve into a warm jug – it really must be warm. Serve with the beef.

Seared beef, tomato salad

Most Asian shops carry Japanese nanami togarashi seasoning. It is a mixture of ground chilli, orange peel, spices and sesame seeds. For this beef salad, it is simply a question of rolling the beef in the seasoning and searing it quickly in a heavy pan. The beef is barely cooked and is eaten thinly sliced, like carpaccio. There will be some left over for tomorrow. I cannot think of a better accompaniment for it than a simple tomato salad.

enough for 4 as a light main dish
fillet of beef – 500g
olive oil
togarashi – 3 teaspoons

for the tomato salad
large, ripe tomatoes – 6
olive oil – 75ml
red wine vinegar – 2 tablespoons
sugar – a pinch
coriander leaves – a handful

Roll the fillet of beef in a little olive oil, then dust with the Japanese seasoning. Warm a couple of tablespoons of olive oil in a shallow pan and, once it starts to sizzle, brown the beef on all sides. Set aside to cool, then refrigerate for two hours.

Slice the tomatoes thinly and lay them on a serving plate. Make the dressing by mixing the olive oil, red wine vinegar and a good pinch of sugar together, then stirring in the coriander. Spoon the dressing over the tomatoes.

Remove the beef from the fridge and slice very, very thinly. It should be as thin as you can get it. Lay the slices on plates and serve with the tomato salad.

Baked tomatoes with chillies and coconut

How a dish smells is important. It whets the appetite, brings us to the table and opens up a host of pleasures. With coconut, cardamom and coriander, this simple dish of baked tomatoes is heady and aromatic. It curdles a bit, but no matter. You will need some rice or bread to go with it.

enough for 4
garlic – 2 cloves
a hot red chilli or two
ginger – a thumb-sized piece
olive or groundnut oil – 3 tablespoons
chilli flakes – half a teaspoon
ground coriander – a teaspoon
ground turmeric – a teaspoon
cumin seeds – half a teaspoon
green cardamoms – 6
moderately large tomatoes – 12
creamed coconut – 50g (some brands come in handy 50g sachets)
coriander leaves – a handful

Peel and thinly slice the garlic. Halve the chillies and discard their seeds, then chop finely. Peel the ginger and slice it finely. It should be thin enough to see through. Warm the oil in a deep frying pan, then add the garlic, chilli and ginger, letting them soften but not colour over a moderate heat.

Stir in the chilli flakes, ground coriander, turmeric and cumin seeds, then pop the cardamoms out of their husks, crush the seeds lightly and stir them in. Once the spices have warmed through, chop four of the tomatoes, stir them into the spices and pour in 300ml water. Bring to the boil, then slice each of the remaining tomatoes horizontally in half and lay them cutside down in the sauce. Leave to cook for seven or eight minutes, until they are starting to soften. Turn each tomato over and continue to cook for a few minutes, till they are thoroughly tender.

Introduce the creamed coconut to the pan in small pieces, letting it dissolve into the sauce. A helpful stir with a teaspoon will work wonders here. From this point on, the sauce shouldn't boil, just simmer very gently till it is thick and the tomatoes are soft.

Once the tomatoes are tender to the point of collapse, they are ready. Scatter them with coriander leaves and eat with a little rice or bread to mop them up.

A soup of tomatoes and crab

There is a small but distinguished group of seafood and tomato dishes, from the Provençal soups with their croûtes and brick-red rouille to Portuguese soup-stews reeking of garlic.

With those dishes as a starting point, I spent some time working on a soup of tomato and crab. After making several versions that were too thick and rich, I took the step of bringing chilli and lemongrass into the proceedings to add a breath of freshness and vitality. This is a bright-tasting soup that sings with the sweet heat of chilli and crustacean.

To add enough substance to treat it as a main dish (when this recipe will serve 3–4), I introduce a last-minute addition of bean shoots or maybe some shredded, very lightly cooked mangetout.

enough for 4–6
small spring onions – 5
lemongrass – 3 stalks
olive oil – 2 tablespoons
a hot red chilli
medium tomatoes – 4
chicken stock – a litre
the juice of a small orange, or half a large one
mixed white and brown crabmeat – 500g
nam pla (Thai fish sauce) – a tablespoon
a lime, large and ripe
coriander – a small bunch

Slice the spring onions thinly, peel the outer leaves from the lemongrass and cut the tender inner leaves into paper-fine slices. Warm the olive oil in a large, thick-bottomed saucepan over a moderate heat, stir in the spring onions and lemongrass and let them soften without colouring. Seed and finely chop the chilli, then add it to the pan.

Chop the tomatoes. You can peel and seed them if you wish but I really can't see the point. Stir them into the onions and leave to soften for a few minutes before pouring in the chicken stock and orange juice. Stir in the crabmeat, nam pla and a little salt, bring to the boil, then turn down the heat immediately and leave to simmer for four or five minutes, stirring from time to time.

Squeeze in the lime juice. Roughly chop a good handful of coriander leaves and stir them in. Check the seasoning and serve piping hot.

A tomato salad with warm basil dressing

This colourful, big-flavoured tomato salad is something you could eat alongside rose-pink cold roast beef, but it could easily make a more substantial candidate for a main course with the addition of a few croûtons or some slices of olive-oil-drenched toast. The colours are important here if the salad is to look lively – I usually use a mixture of tomatoes, including little pear-drop ones and yellow cherry tomatoes. I think it is worth adding that this is also good with coriander instead of basil.

enough for 4 as a side salad
small shallots – 3
olive oil – 100ml
garlic – 2 cloves
flat-leaf parsley – 6 bushy sprigs
the juice of half a lemon
red wine vinegar – a tablespoon
anchovy fillets – 8
medium to large basil leaves – 20
small tomatoes – 25–30

Peel the shallots, chop them finely and warm them in a shallow pan with the olive oil. Peel and finely slice the garlic and add it to the softening shallots. Remove the parsley leaves from their stalks and chop them roughly. Stir them into the shallots with the lemon juice and red wine vinegar.

Rinse, dry and roughly chop the anchovies, tear up the basil leaves and add both to the dressing. Taste and add a little black pepper if you think it needs it.

Cut the tomatoes in halves or quarters, depending on their size, dropping them into a mixing bowl as you go. Pour over the warm dressing (you should never get basil too hot), toss gently and serve.

Turnips

I came rather late to the turnip. I had wriggled out of school dinners by living so close that I could walk home every day to eat. But once I had been moved to a school whose journey home through the country lanes took an hour or more, there was no choice but to queue up for stew and sponge. If the most eagerly swallowed dish was rhubarb crumble, with its soft, pebbledash crust, the most difficult was turnip. It arrived at the table white and sour, a watery pulp as a side dish to leathery liver. A plate of hate. Yet it was served up with love and a smile, and lapped up by the rest of the local farming community. It just wasn't my thing.

Then I read, in a cookery book borrowed from the travelling library that pulled up once a month, that a woman called Elizabeth David cooked turnips with butter and caster sugar till 'the sauce turns brown and slightly sticky' and served them as an accompaniment to duck casseroled with bacon and celery. Mrs David pointed out that during their brief youth they cost 'nearly as much as a hothouse peach'. The mysterious woman with her foreign tastes got my curiosity up, though I am not sure I did anything about it.

Thirty years later, the arrival of the organic box scheme in my neck of the woods brings lettuce so fresh its milky sap still sits on the cut stem, tomatoes whose stalks smell of warm spice, and carrots complete with their feathery tops. It also brings turnips. For months, I would lovingly place the new arrivals in the vegetable rack, sliding out last week's wizened bunch and sneaking them guiltily into the compost: 'This week I will use you. I promise.'

The turnip can be white, ivory, red or golden. It can come with its shoulders brushed with lavender, moss green or the hue of a wine stain. For a brief point in its life, it is small enough to hold in a bunch, like a posy. It can be cooked in butter and sherry, mashed with cream and butter or given a glossy coat with sugar.

In the late 1800s, there were as many as fifty varieties listed, and the old names still intrigue: Long White Vertus, Vetch's Red Globe, Golden Ball or Orange Jelly, and Red-top Norfolk. Some have long, rat-like tails. In 1857 a seedsman said of Golden Ball, 'A Cheshire variety of a handsome round form with a small top. The skin is pale orange, the flesh yellow and juicy, sweet and tender. When boiled, it almost acquires the consistency of jelly.' Who could resist such a description? Perhaps he should have mentioned that the flowers smell of honey.

The Romans knew the turnip, though hardly worshipped it, and part of its problems may stem from the fact that it has always been used as animal fodder. It has taken me most of my life to appreciate the turnip. To be charmed by its smooth skin, to be amused by the cheerful golden variety I get at the market and to be happy to include it in my slow weekend cooking. There will always be a place in my kitchen for the turnip.

A turnip in the garden

Listen. I have never grown a turnip. I buy them from the farmers' market or the greengrocer when they are no bigger than a hen's egg. The ground space in an urban garden is precious and I find it wasteful not to use my few spare feet for growing something that is expensive or difficult to buy. And yet, if I had more room I would grow a row or two of turnips. Just to taste, and let others taste, how good the freshly harvested ones can be, with their thin skins and flesh that cooks in minutes.

The seed needs to go in where the vegetables are to grow – like carrots, they dislike being transplanted. Sow early and late, but not in high summer. They will need to end up a hand's width apart, so thin the seedlings as they get older. Friends tell me their turnips like a lot of water. You can do little with the green tops at this stage, bar chucking them in with green salad, but as they get towards eight or ten weeks old we can eat the green tops too, steamed for a minute or so. Unlike the swede, the turnip won't stay in the ground over winter. They need to be pulled before the frosts.

Varieties

Orange Jelly Also known as Golden Ball, a yellow-fleshed variety that I rate above all others for its tender flesh and mild flavour.
Snowball Old variety, crisp and white. Good for grating raw.
Market Express Ready in six weeks or less. The one to grow if you want a sweet bunch of creamy white turnips only slightly bigger than a radish.
Purple-topped Milan Crisp, mauve-shouldered white variety, popular for the last hundred years.

A turnip in the kitchen

The older turnip appreciates a slowly ticking clock. Brought to tenderness in a stew deep with broth; simmered in chicken stock and mashed with a fork; baked slowly under a lid with sugar and sherry, the more mature turnip needs time if it is to get our interest.

Young specimens, barely bigger than a golf ball, can be cooked in half the time. These young turnips often have skins so thin they don't need peeling. They can be grated and tossed into a dressing or steamed and dressed with herb butter.

Whilst I draw the line at saying every kitchen needs a turnip, I would suggest they are underused. Young and old alike are worth steaming, mashing and buttering. They respond to a generous hand with the seasoning, and nothing good will come from being a tightwad with the butter.

As a vegetable with which to start a stew, the turnip provides a balance to the sweetness of the carrot, which alone justifies its place in the kitchen.

Seasoning your turnips

Orange Add grated zest or juice to the dressing of a raw turnip salad.
Sugar As valid a seasoning as salt and pepper for this vegetable.
Sherry Pour a little into a pan of butter-fried baby turnips.
Game Venison, mallard, pheasant and pigeon will all benefit from a side dish of buttered roots.
Dill One of the few herbs that have any worthwhile effect here.
Bacon Add boiled and drained baby turnips to bacon that you have sautéed till golden.
Vinegar Sarah Raven has a lovely way with very young turnips, sweating them for five minutes in butter, then adding a little sugar and white wine vinegar before simmering them for a further ten. Very good with ham.

And...

* As a member of the cabbage family, the turnip likes a cool patch in the garden.
* You can store freshly dug turnips in the fridge if they are very small, in a box or sack in a cool place if they are larger than an orange. The larger ones will keep better than the small.
* Turnip greens make for good eating. Chop the washed leaves and thinner stalks, then cook in a very little water, as you might spinach. Toss with olive oil, or melted butter and the merest squeeze of lemon juice.

Golden turnips with butter and sherry

First week of December 2007, cold and raining. The Fern Verrow stall at the market has a tray of golden turnips, the colour of lavender honey and the size of Christmas baubles. I decided then and there to bake them in thick chunks with chicken stock and dill. I'm not sure where the dill idea comes from, other than the fact that it works with other root vegetables such as carrots, potatoes and beetroot.

Once I get them home, it strikes me, perhaps rather later in life than it should, that a turnip might be better cooked without liquid. I cut each round root into six from stalk to tip, put them in a heavy-bottomed pan with a thick slice of butter, a pinch of fudge-coloured organic sugar, black pepper, a splash of sherry and some snipped dill. They sit over a low flame, covered with a puttering lid, till soft enough to crush between finger and thumb.

We eat them with a tray of faggots and gravy from the butcher. It could have been sausages. Sweet, earthy, warmly honeyed – I like the idea that something as mundane as a turnip could end up being unforgettable.

A little dish of sweet turnips

Drop tiny turnips into lightly salted boiling water and cook for ten minutes or so, till tender. Drain. Melt a thick slice of butter in a shallow pan and tip in the turnips and a spoonful of sugar. Leave over a moderate heat, shaking the pan from time to time, until the little orbs are glossy and sweet. The contrast between the sweet outer shell and slightly bitter turnip is astonishing with roast game birds.

Rabbit with bacon and turnips

Whereas most meats give us a choice of cooking on the bone or not, wild rabbit is one that really needs its bones if it is not to be dry. It is not the meatiest of choices, so you need to be generous with quantities here. Rabbit bones are small, and it's important to watch out for the more fiddly ones. The turnips in this provide all the carbs you need to soak up the sauce. It just needs some purple sprouting broccoli on the side.

enough for 3
wild rabbit (legs and saddle pieces) – 600g
plain flour
butter – 40g
groundnut oil
pancetta, in the piece – 200g
small shallots – 6
turnips – 4 small to medium ones
dry Marsala – 100ml
chicken or vegetable stock – 900ml
a little parsley
double cream – 4 tablespoons

Season the rabbit and dust it lightly with a little flour. Melt the butter in a little oil in a shallow pan over a moderate heat. Lightly brown the rabbit on all sides, then remove from the pan.

Whilst the rabbit is browning, cut the pancetta into thick strips or cubes, then peel and chop the shallots. Once the rabbit is out, introduce the bacon and shallots to the pan and cook over a fairly low heat until the shallots are soft but not coloured. Cut the turnips into thick wedges and add them to the pan, together with 2 tablespoons of flour. Continue cooking briefly, then pour in the Marsala and stock. Bring to the boil, stirring gently.

Return the rabbit legs to the pan, but retain the saddle for the moment. Lower the heat, cover with a lid and leave to simmer for an hour and ten minutes, adding the saddle halfway through, till the meat is tender enough to slip from the bones with relative ease.

Roughly chop the parsley and stir into the pan with the cream. Check the seasoning and serve.

A sweet and sticky casserole of duck with turnips and orange

As turnips do so well with orange, it is only a small step to use them with marmalade. Duck has this affinity too, so the three can come together successfully in a darkly sweet and rich casserole. Like duck à l'orange but sweeter and more suitable for a freezing winter's day.

The orange flavours here, from both fruit and bitter marmalade, should not dominate. The final flavour can be tweaked to your taste at the end with lemon juice or, better still, a bitter Seville orange.

Rice, pure and white, would be my first choice of accompaniment. If you start this dish the day before, you will have a better chance of removing most of the fat that floats to the surface.

enough for 3
groundnut or vegetable oil
a large duck, cut into 6
smoked bacon – 250g
onions – 2 medium to large
turnips – 4 smallish
ginger – a 3cm lump (about 50g)
light stock (or water at a push) – 1 litre
the juice of 2 large, sweet oranges
bay leaves – 3
a stick of cinnamon
star anise – 2
marmalade – 2–3 tablespoons
the juice of a lemon or a Seville orange
rice, couscous, cracked wheat or quinoa, to serve

Warm a very little oil in a deep, heavy-based casserole and lightly brown the duck in it, two or three pieces at a time. Drain them and set aside on kitchen paper. Cut the bacon into thick strips and add to the pan, letting them crisp lightly in the fat. Remove them and add to the duck. Meanwhile, peel and roughly chop the onions.

Pour off all but 2 tablespoons of the fat from the pan, then add the onions and cook over a moderate to low heat, stirring occasionally. As the onions cook, peel the turnips, cut them into thick wedges and add them to the pan. Cut the ginger into fine matchsticks, then add that too.

Once the onions have well and truly softened and are starting to turn pale gold, add the stock, orange juice, bay leaves, cinnamon stick, star anise, a generous grinding of salt and some black pepper. Bring almost to the boil. Return the duck pieces and bacon to the pan, turn down to a slow simmer and leave for forty-five minutes to come slowly to tenderness.

Check the duck. It should be soft, but far from falling from its bones. Put the pan to one side and let it cool (if possible, you should leave it overnight). Scoop off as much fat as you can and discard. There will be quite a bit of this, and some is integral to the richness of the stew, so don't be too thorough about it. Just remove the excess.

Bring the pan back up to simmering point. Stir in the marmalade, then correct the seasoning with salt, pepper and the juice of the lemon (or Seville orange, if you have one). The flavours should be warm, sweetly spiced and with the homeliest hint of marmalade.

A few other good things

This book is principally the story of my own vegetable patch and my own kitchen. One or two favourite vegetables such as salsify, cardoons and sweetcorn are missing for the simple reason that I have never grown them and tend to leave them to the experts. In this short chapter of bits and pieces are some things that, for one or reason or another, have evaded me and my trowel and some, like radishes and cucumber, that only needed a few lines.

Globe artichokes

Handsome, huge and utterly delectable as they are, this garden has consistently failed to please the globe artichoke, both the egg-sized purple Romanesco and the fuller-figured Green Globe.

Artichokes generally grow well in this climate, sometimes prolifically, their jagged, silver-green leaves forming majestic clumps. I have tried them in four out of six beds in my garden and even, in desperation, in large pots, but to no avail. This year, too late for full inclusion in this book, it looks as though I may have succeeded, with the current incumbents looking hale and hearty, happy in their place in (would you believe?) the rose bed.

Globe artichokes, with their sharp, sometimes prickly-edged 'petals', are actually the plant's flower buds and will, if left, open up into showy mauve thistle heads. When picked young, their heads small and tight, they can be boiled and eaten in their entirety (they are splendid fried in batter at this point). A little later on, the globes can be boiled and presented whole, the petals plucked from the head and sucked clean of their flesh.

The real treasure – the soft, mild-flavoured heart that makes up the base of the flower – lies hidden. This is found by removing all the petals and the inedible, hairy 'choke' within. A soft, grey-green in colour, this tender heart is there for eating with vinaigrette or a buttery hollandaise sauce, or if exceptionally large, stuffed with breadcrumbs, lemon and herbs.

I am disappointed not to be able to offer you a fuller account of this luxurious and highly prized vegetable. But every gardener, like every cook, meets their match. Mine, inexplicably, appears to be the artichoke.

Cucumber

Those with small gardens may have to forgo this one. The succulent, hairy-stemmed plants work best growing up a frame of twigs. Make it a strong one, as cucumbers can be heavy in quantity. A freshly cut cuke is a thing of joy and the flavour is often surprisingly intense. In many respects, they work best in a greenhouse, but they will grow happily outside during a hot summer. Find a sunny spot sheltered from the wind. If I had one foot of extra space I would grow a cane frame of cucumbers. They ask nothing from us save a strong support, lots of water and a mid-season feed with a drop of tomato fertiliser or liquid seaweed. They will reward us with small, firm fruits with an exceptional flavour.

Yes, I love this fruit thinly sliced with a crisp lettuce and chicken salad, grated and stirred into yoghurt with fresh mint to cool down a spicy little meat patty, and even cooked slowly in butter to accompany a piece of white fish. But the best use I have come across is as a sandwich filling, held between two thick slices of the freshest white bread.

Try this: peel a medium cucumber, removing only the tough, outer part of the skin, leaving the outside still bright green. Slice thickly down its length and then cut each slice into small dice. Put in a colander in the sink, scatter salt over and leave for thirty minutes or so.

Put six heaped tablespoons of mayonnaise into a mixing bowl and add half a teaspoon of smooth, mild mustard and a grinding of black pepper. Discard the roots and the toughest of the green shoots from a couple of spring onions, then slice the rest into fine rings. Add to the mayonnaise with a teaspoon of capers and the roughly chopped leaves from a bushy sprig of mint. Pat the cucumber dry and stir it into the mayonnaise, adding a dribble of tarragon vinegar to brighten the flavours. Use as a dressing for smoked fish or as a sandwich filling.

Radishes

I grow the French Breakfast radish because of its sweet heat and pretty white tips but it is less successful than the all-red varieties – the ones that look like clowns' noses. There is no formal row of this member of the mustard family in my veg patch, just a few seeds sprinkled hugger-mugger between the other plants. They grow like Topsy in warm, light soil on the sunny side of the garden, and I have often eaten them within four weeks of planting. My first are sown even before the daffodils have finished flowering, the last in early September.

Radishes are ready to pick when you see their shoulders nudging through the surface of the soil. They are best eaten young and crisp, with cold, pale butter and a little saucer of sea salt flakes in which to dip them.

Ignore any suggestions of cooking them; the writer is clearly deluded.

Try them sliced and dropped into yoghurt with white wine vinegar, fresh mint or dill and some salt. They need no pepper. They are in their element in a light lemon juice and olive oil dressing with masses of coriander and mint leaves. A bright, knife-sharp salad for a sizzling-hot summer's day.

Spring onions

Rarely is my fridge without a bunch of these elegant, mildly flavoured alliums. Whilst they are at their best perched in snow-white and green stripes atop a curl of crisp lettuce in an 'English' salad, I also find them endlessly useful in the kitchen.

The white part is what we really want, but I add the coarser-textured green end to a stir-fry at the same time as the garlic. My enthusiasm for this immature onion has much to do with its ease of preparation – it needs no peeling. I have only grown this usually pain-free crop twice and have had less luck than I expected. They are generally easy – especially the gorgeous North Holland Blood Red and White Lisbon varieties – in a sunny, well-drained corner. You can sow the seed at any time from March to August. The plumper ones are good grilled and dressed with a splash of dark, mellow balsamic vinegar, or chopped and stirred into mashed potato.

Fennel

Once in a blue moon, I crave the hard white flesh and clean bite of a fennel bulb. It is usually on a needle-cold day, when the sky is grey-white and I want something with a steely crispness to go in a winter salad.

Fennel is hardly the most versatile of vegetables, and aniseed at this intensity is not to everyone's taste. I appreciate it in paper-thin slices, so fine you can see through them. In a green salad to accompany smoked salmon or poached haddock, it really shines in small amounts. Overused, even slightly, and it will dominate an entire dish and ruin your wine.

Growing in a garden or laid out on a trestle table at the market, the plants are astonishingly beautiful, with their fat white bulbs and mane of feathery leaves. In autumn, their smell is enticing. You can tuck thin wedges of fennel into a fish's belly as it bakes, or under the bones of a roasting rabbit.

Fennel is very fine on a crisp October day, each bulb cut in half lengthways and left to cook slowly in butter in a tightly covered heavy pan. A low heat and a splash of water will keep it from scorching and lessen its pushy character; a careful eye will ensure it emerges sweet and tender, its edges lightly caramelised, its scent like that of warm aniseed cookies. A lovely thing to eat with some thin slices of pork and their roasting juices.

A note on the type

Claude Garamond (c. 1480–1561) cut type for the Parisian scholar-printer Robert Estienne in the first part of the sixteenth century, basing it on the type cut by Francesco Griffo for Venetian printer Aldus Manutius in 1495. Garamond refined his typeface in later versions, adding his own concepts as he developed his skills as a punchcutter.

Adobe Garamond, the type used in *Tender*, was designed by Robert Slimbach in 1989. The roman weights were based on the true Garamond, and the italics on those of punchcutter Robert Granjon. This font has been expanded to include small caps, titling caps, expert fonts, and swash caps, which were typical in the fifteenth and sixteenth centuries.

From **Tender** | Volume II

When I dug up my lawn to grow my own vegetables and herbs I planted fruit too. A handful of small trees – plum, apple and pear – some raspberry, blackberry and currant bushes and even strawberries in pots suddenly joined my patch of potatoes, beans and peas. These fruits became the backbone of my home baking, the stars in my cakes and pastries and even inspired the odd pot of jam. More than this, I started to use them in new ways too, from a weekday supper of pork chops with cider and apples to a Chinese Sunday roast with spiced plum sauce. The hot family puddings and fruit ices we had always loved so much suddenly took on a delicious new significance.